THE CHANGING FACES
OF FEDERALISM

MANCHESTER
1824

Manchester University Press

EUROPE IN CHANGE

SERIES EDITORS: THOMAS CHRISTIANSEN AND EMIL KIRCHNER

Sergio Ortino, Mitja Žagar and Vojtech Mastny

THE CHANGING FACES OF FEDERALISM

Institutional reconfiguration in Europe from East to West

MANCHESTER UNIVERSITY PRESS
Manchester and New York

distributed exclusively in the USA by Palgrave

Published by Manchester University Press
Oxford Road, Manchester M13 9NR, UK
and Room 400, 175 Fifth Avenue, New York, NY 10010, USA
www.manchesteruniversitypress.co.uk

Distributed exclusively in the USA by
Palgrave, 175 Fifth Avenue, New York,
NY 10010, USA

Distributed exclusively in Canada by
UBC Press, University of British Columbia, 2029 West Mall,
Vancouver, BC, Canada V6T 1Z2

British Library Cataloguing-in-Publication Data
A catalogue record for this book is available from the British Library

Library of Congress Cataloging-in-Publication Data applied for

ISBN 0 7190 6996 3 *hardback*
EAN 978 0 7190 6996 3

First published 2005

14 13 12 11 10 09 08 07 06 05   10 9 8 7 6 5 4 3 2 1

Typeset in Minion
by Servis Filmsetting Limited, Manchester
Printed in Great Britain
by CPI, Bath

Contents

Contributors

András Bozóki is Professor of Political Science at the Central European University in Budapest, Hungary.

Bruno de Witte is Professor of European Law at the European University Institute, Florence, Italy

Orsolya Farkas is Researcher at the European Academy of Bolzano/Bozen, Italy

Anna Gamper is Professor of Constitutional and Administrative Law at the University of Innsbruck, Austria.

Kristian Gerner is Professor of History at the Department of History, Lund University, Sweden.

Vojtech Mastny is Senior Fellow at the National Security Archive and Senior Scholar at the Woodrow Wilson International School for Scholars in Washington, DC, USA.

David M. O'Brien is Leone Reaves and George W. Spicer Professor of Government and Foreign Affairs at the University of Virginia in Charottesville, USA.

Sergio Ortino is Professor of Economic Law at the University of Florence and Professor of Constitutional Law at the European Academy in Bolzano/Bozen, Italy.

Francesco Palermo is Professor of Comparative Constitutional Law at the University of Verona, Italy, Adjunct Professor of International and Comparative Law at the Vermont Law School, USA and Senior Researcher at the European Academy in Bolzano/Bozen, Italy.

Peter Pernthaler is Professor of Constitutional and Administrative Law at the University of Innsbruck, Austria.

Giovanni Poggeschi is Senior Researcher at the European Academy in Bolzano/Bozen, Italy.

Peter H. Russell is Professor of Political Science at the University of Toronto, Canada.

Gabriel N. Toggenburg is Researcher at the European Academy of Bolzano/Bozen, Italy.

Jens Woelk is Researcher of Comparative Constitutional Law at the University of Trento, Italy and Senior Researcher at the European Academy of Bolzano/Bozen, Italy.

Mitja Žagar is Senior Research Fellow and Director of the Institute for Ethnic Studies and Associate Professor of Comparative Government and Ethnic Studies at the Faculty of Social Sciences of the University of Ljubljana, Slovenia.

SERGIO ORTINO, VOJTECH MASTNY AND MITJA ŽAGAR

Introduction

This book is the outcome of the project 'The Applicability of the Federative Model in the Relations between States in Postcommunist Europe'. This project was established as one of the Pan-European Research Groups of the Council for European Studies in New York in 1994. It was designed to bring together scholars from North America, and Western and Eastern Europe to jointly study different aspects of federalism at both national and supranational levels within the interstate setting of post-Cold War Europe. Drawing on expertise from different disciplines, including political science, sociology, history, and constitutional and international law, the project has been directed by Vojtech Mastny and Sergio Ortino.

The project envisaged a series of three meetings with the final goal of producing an authoritative volume on the past, present and future of federalism in Europe. After identifying the principal avenues of inquiry and agreeing on the structure of the volume, the participants in the group prepared drafts of their respective contributions, which were discussed by the group as a whole at its successive meetings and subsequently revised to reach the final form. The contributions included case studies on federalism in different countries, analysis and interpretation of historical experiences with federalism, discussion of theoretical issues, and presentation of federative models potentially applicable at the national and international levels.

The first meeting of the group was held in March 1995 at the Johns Hopkins University School of Advanced International Studies in Bologna, Italy. The second meeting was held in May 1996 at the Open Media Research Institute (OMRI) in Prague, Czech Republic. The third meeting took place in August 1997 at the European Academy in Bolzano, Italy, which also provided financial support. At this meeting, the group appointed Sergio Ortino and Mitja Žagar as co-editors of the book, and Vojtech Mastny as a co-director of the project agreed to assist the editors.

Taking into account the evolution of the project over a period of time during which some of the perspectives on federalism had changed, the group altered the original title of the project to better reflect the broader scope of the volume after additional contributors had been brought in. The new title is that of this book.

The group agreed on the desirability of presenting the almost completed manuscript of the book prior to its publication to a selected wider audience of scholars, journalists and public officials from different parts of Europe and North America. The Institute for Advanced Studies in the Humanities (Kulturwissenschaftliches Institut) in Essen, Germany, provided the forum for this discussion in June 1998. The meeting in Essen, which resulted in revisions of the manuscript, was co-sponsored by the European Academy of Bolzano. However, this was not the final version of the manuscript.

While the manuscript produced after the Essen meeting was in the hands of Gary Bruce for language and copy editing, the process of enlargement of the European Union made an incredible acceleration. The so-called EU eastern enlargement included eight former – Central European and Baltic – communist countries along with Malta and Cyprus. New developments required additional revisions of the manuscript. After the setting up of the European convention the editors decided to ask the authors for the last time to update and revise their con-tributions for the publication, thereby completing the project and process that had started ten years previously. In this process some additional authors joined the team – some of them replacing original contributors who were no longer able or willing to participate.

Initially, the project began with a focus on Central Europe (Middle Europe, *Mitteleuropa*) – the group of countries situated between the European Union and former Soviet Union. The aim was to consider how these countries might associate with one another while they were waiting – as many clearly were – for their eventual inclusion into the European Union. It quickly became clear, however, that Central Europe as a free-standing association of its own had no future and that an inquiry into federal possibilities for this region had to pay attention to the wider European experience with federalism – both to the east and to the west. Hence the geographic range of the present volume is much broader than Central Europe. It includes the Russian Federation, and Eastern, Central and Western Europe. Special attention is paid to the European Union and federalism in the context of the future developments in Europe. This is reflected also in the structure of this book.

Peter H. Russell provides the theoretical introduction to the volume. He presents the fundamental concepts that frame the discussion on federalism in Europe. The chapter examines the actual and possible role of federalism, its prospects and limitations, in the reuniting of Europe after the end of the Cold War and the fall of communism. This chapter is followed by Vojtech Mastny's contribution on historical federal experiences in Central and Eastern Europe – focusing on economic and federal relations among the countries. Case studies begin in the East with David O'Brien's study of Tatarstan and Chechnya in the Russian Federation. They then move geographically westward to the countries of Eastern and Central Europe (Baltic and Central European countries) with contributions by Kristian Gerner and András Bozóki , and a chapter by Mitja Žagar on the collapse of the Yugoslav federation. The book reaches Western Europe with chapters on federalism in Austria by Peter Pernthaler and Anna Gamper, on the federal experience of Germany by Jens Woelk, on proposals for federal reforms in Italy by Francesco Palermo, on federal developments in Spain and Belgium by Bruno De Witte, and a chapter on federalizing activities in the UK and France by Giovanni Poggeschi. Orsolya Farkas and Gabriel von Toggenburg analyse the federal dimensions of the EU itself and its projected expansion eastward in their chapter. The book concludes with Sergio Ortino's contribution on 'functional federalism'.

The common denominator of all the chapters is their focus on the federal relationships – past, present and future – within and among the peoples and states of Europe. There is a common expectation that the future of Europe is and ought to be profoundly federal. In this context it is, of course, equally clear that federalism is a complex and multi-faceted concept and that the possible federal developments of Europe will be long and complex processes.

This book would not have been possible without a grant from the Council for European Studies in New York and the generous assistance of the European Academy of Bolzano and the Institute for Advanced Studies in the Humanities in Essen. The contributing authors and editors owe special gratitude to them. The editors would like to thank also all contributing authors for their excellent cooperation. The authors and editors would like to thank Gary Bruce and Savio de Sousa, who as copy editors did an excellent job revising the manuscript for language and style. The editors would also like to thank the publishers, Manchester University Press, for their decision to publish the book, their reviewers for valuable comments, and their editors for their support and assistance in publishing this book.

PETER H. RUSSELL

1

The future of Europe in an era of federalism

The project that gave rise to this book began with a focus on Middle Europe – the group of countries situated between the European Union (EU) and former Soviet Union. The aim was to consider how these countries might associate with one another while they were waiting – as many clearly were – for their eventual absorption into the European Union. But it quickly became clear that Middle Europe as a free-standing association of its own had no future and that therefore an inquiry into federal possibilities for this region had to pay attention to the wider experience with federalism both to the east and the west. Hence the geographic range of the present volume is much broader than Middle Europe. It begins with Vojtech Mastny's discussion in chapter 2 of historical federal relations among the countries of Eastern and Central Europe, then moves from Eastern to Central Europe with the studies by David O'Brien on Tatarstan and Chechnya in the Russian federation; by Kristian Gerner on the Baltic states, Poland and Hungary; by András Bozóki on Central Europe; and by Mitja Žagar on the collapse of the Yugoslav federation. It reaches Western Europe with chapters on the federal experience of Austria by Peter Pernthaler and Anna Gamper on Germany by Jens Woelk, on Italy by Francesco Palermo, on Spain and Belgium by Bruno De Witte, a chapter on federalizing activities in the UK and France by Giovanni Poggeschi, and a chapter by Orsolya Farkas and Gabriel Toggenburg analysing the EU itself and its projected expansion eastward.

The book concludes, appropriately, with Sergio Ortino's discussion of 'functional federalism'. The common denominator of all the studies in this book is the federal relationships – past, present and future – within and among the peoples and states of Europe. There is a common expectation that the future of Europe is and ought to be profoundly federal. But, of course, it is equally clear that federalism is a complex and multi-faceted concept. Ortino's chapter considers the range of federal possibilities and prescribes the kind of federalism he believes should be Europe's destiny. I too will begin this introductory chapter with a discussion of federalism and its salience for our times.

An era of federalism

The present era, in world historical terms, might well be described as the moment of federalism. It is the moment in the evolution of political man when the limitations of the nation-state are broadly recognized and the main option for overcoming those limitations in a non-imperial, democratic manner is seen to be federal arrangements that combine self-rule and shared rule. In an overview of federal developments around the world today, Ronald Watts puts it this way: 'We appear to be in the midst of a paradigm shift which is taking us from a world of sovereign nation-states to a world of diminished state sovereignty and increased linkages of a constitutionally federal character.'[1]

The societal forces generating this moment of federalism are captured well in Marshall McLuhan's concept of the 'global village'. The analyses of many of the contributions to this voluIntrome are framed by a recognition of the forces pulling the nation-state in opposite directions, both stretching it and loosening it. To deal effectively with the economic challenge and technological opportunities of globalization, nation-states have incentives to pool their sovereignty in supranational organizations. At the same time, ethnic and territorial communities that were never dissolved into the political community of the nation-state, and regions freshly animated by the principle of subsidiarity, are demanding more autonomy within the state. Thus the federalizing movement flows in two directions: upwards and outwards as states combine for certain functional purposes in larger, transnational configurations, and downwards and inwards as sources of national diversity within the state are not just tolerated but honoured and, in varying measures, afforded opportunities for self-rule.

Corresponding to these two federalizing forces are two paths towards the establishment of federal arrangements. One is the path of aggregation, whereby independent states combine together retaining much of their autonomy but pooling their sovereignty for certain purposes in common, central agencies of governance. The other is the path of devolution, whereby a unitary state devolves political authority to sub-units of the country and these sub-units come to enjoy a significant measure of autonomy.[2] It is abundantly evident from the discussion of European politics in this volume that the forces of the global village can stimulate action along both of these paths simultaneously. Chapters 9, 10 and 11, on Italy, Belgium and Spain, and Britain and France, show how integration in Western Europe – the aggregating path – has made the devolutionary path more attractive and accessible in a number of the European Union's member states. In Central and Eastern Europe, the coming apart of federal structures – devolution in the extreme – now generates interest in aggregation and integration.

In understanding the sense in which the contemporary era might be seen as the era of federalism it is important to recognize that 'federalism' is being treated here as a process, not as a specific form of government. In this sense all of the contributors to this volume are responsive to the admonition of Carl Friedrich, one of the great scholars of federalism, that 'theorists have been slow to learn that federalism is a process rather than a static pattern'.[3] Federalism is a political tendency – supported by societal forces and ideology – to move governmental organization towards federal structures. Seen in this light, federalism is always a matter of more or less not either–or.

Even if in this way we distinguish federalism from federation, the question still remains – what is this federal destination towards which the process of federalism inclines political communities? Not all of the authors take the same position on this question. In chapter 3, David O'Brien, reflecting on the ebb and flow of power between centre and periphery in Russia's federal arrangements, questions the usefulness of the classic distinction between confederations and federations. At the other end of the book, Sergio Ortino takes a stricter view of what constitutes a 'federative' state. For Ortino, the essential feature of a federative political order is that its constituent founding units retain their sovereignty. The constituent states may agree to limit their sovereignty in certain fields of policy in favour of a central government only so long as they reassert their sovereignty in the decision-making of the institutions at the centre. By this standard, the European Union remains safely on the list of federative political orders while the United States, Germany and Austria fail to qualify. Other authors seem more inclined to follow Toggenburg in Farkas–Toggenburg (chapter 12), who sees both federal and confederal elements in the existing structure of the EU as well as in the new constitution – the 'strange dog' – now being contemplated.[4]

While admitting there is no more futile task among academics than attempting to legislate how concepts of political analysis are to be used, still there must be some boundaries to what can be considered a federal arrangement or tendency. The federal concept will be drained of all meaning if it is used to refer to any form of interstate cooperation or intrastate devolution. András Bozóki gives an account in chapter 5 of various forms of regional and trans-border cooperation taking place among the states of 'the new Central Europe'. But Bozóki rightly warns us against confusing the concepts of decentralization, regionalism and regional cooperation with federalism. Though any of these might eventually lead to a federal outcome, such an outcome cannot be assumed to automatically result from any and all such governmental arrangements that deviate from the independent and unitary nation-state. Similarly, Palermo and Poggeschi in chapters 9 and 11 show us that the devolution currently under way in Italy, as well as in the UK and France, is still a step removed from a genuine federal system.

The phrase – or slogan – that is a good starting point to mark out the essential features of a federal condition is Daniel Elazar's 'self-rule plus shared rule'.[5] This phrase points to the conditions that are essential at each end of a federal union. At the sub-units' end there must be a genuine form of autonomy such that each has freedom to express some of its distinctive character in legislation and administration, and the capacity to do so does not depend entirely on the convenience or good-will of a central authority. At the union end there must be some institutionalization of common purpose which, while not impossible to dismantle, is intended to be permanent and engages, somehow, directly with the citizens of the member states. Some might add that the common purpose – the competences – of the centre must embrace more than a very narrowly circumscribed set of functions or interests.

Such a conception delineates only the bare structural requirements of a federal union. Beneath these structural features are more fundamental political conditions. The presence or absence of these features of political culture will be more telling as to whether a genuine federal condition is in place or is imminent than are institutional arrangements that might exist, formally, on paper. One condition is that federalism achieves its ends through a constitutional order. A constitutional order requires more than having the rules of the federal union formally set out in a constitution. It also requires a capacity for practising constitutionalism. Constitutionalism is a condition of societies whereby those who govern are effectively constrained, be it by the force of public opinion or judicial review or both, by the terms of the constitution.[6] Watts' book on federalism in the 1990s lists twenty-three contemporary federations.[7] However, if the practice of constitutionalism is factored in as a requirement, then we might question the inclusion on this list of countries such as Nigeria and Pakistan, or of two of the seven European federations listed – the Russian federation and what remains of the federal republic of Yugoslavia.

If a federal union exists as a constitutional order, it is not held together by force. Its unity must depend on the freely given consent of its constituent units to come or remain together for certain purposes and to go their own way in other matters. As Michael Burgess puts it, 'Federations, then, to be genuine, cannot be the result of force or coercion imposed from above and sustained by the threat of military force.'[8] Mitja Žagar's account of the collapse of the Yugoslav federation (chapter 6) shows how federal arrangements among these Balkan states could not survive the removal of an authoritarian party. While a Russian federation may have nominally survived the collapse of one-party communist rule, the chaotic relationships of two of its fragments (described in chapter 3 by David O'Brien) demonstrate that the Russian federation today is still struggling to function as a constitutional order. The freedom of Russia's regions and republics, though often considerable, results more from the weakness and incompetence of the centre than from the operation of an agreed upon set of constitutional rules and principles.

The fact that the European Union has not been formed by a constitution in the way federal states have been has not excluded the possibility of its becoming a constitutional order. In chapter 12 Farkas and Toggenburg trace the evolution of the EU's constitutional order through a collection of highly technical and inaccessible international treaties to something resembling the constitution of a state. This process has been led by the bold jurisprudence of the European court of justice,[9] whose decisions have fashioned the constitutionalism which is the legal prerequisite of a functioning constitutional order – a set of rules and principles that effectively constrain how the EU's governors govern. The EU now seems poised to take the logical next step and transform its constitution from a ramshackle collection of treaties into a single, reasonably short and accessible constitutional text. Although in chapter 13 Sergio Ortino refers to such a constitutional treaty as 'formal procedural contamination',[10] Farkas and Toggenburg tell us that two-thirds of the EU's citizens support the idea of a European constitution, though they concede that overall awareness of what is involved in this transformation remains low. Moreover, it remains to be seen whether the new constitution will secure the approval of all twenty-five governments of an about-to-be-expanded EU let alone popular approval when put to the test of direct democracy in the member states that ratify by referendum. The one thing about which we can be sure is that if this new twenty-one language constitution for Europe is adopted, it will provide the foundation of a constitutional order different from any the world has known up to now.

Of course the element of a constitutional order that is missing from the EU is its popular, affective side. Those cumbersome complex treaties – from Rome to Nice – do not live as a constitution in the political consciousness of the European Union's citizens. The transition to a constitution that at least looks and reads like a constitution, plus popular referenda in many member states (if successful), may begin to give the EU's constitutionalism a more democratic base. Popular identification with the constitution is the very element that looms so large when one thinks of the American constitution, authored by 'we the people' of the United States. Indeed, from the perspective of federalism, the United States is problematic in the opposite sense from the EU; it has become such a powerful union of individual citizens that it is in danger of ceasing to be a union of states. Many factors have contributed to this process, including the tainting of the cause of states' rights with slavery, a civil war, the centralizing effects of the new deal and of the supreme court's jurisprudence which followed, and then, perhaps above all, the emergence of the USA after World War II as the world's most powerful superpower. The result is a political community in which the citizen's allegiance and identity attaches, overwhelmingly, to the nation as a whole rather than to its federal sub-units.

A genuine federal union is a peculiar kind of political association – it is an association of associations. This is how Johannes Althusius, the first European theorist of federalism, understood the concept. As Friedrich explains, Althusius, in asserting the federal principle against the centralizing idea of sovereignty as formulated by Bodin, interpreted all political life as a layered series of contractual associations so that 'The village was for him a union of families . . . the town a union of guilds; the province a union of towns and villages; the kingdom a union of such provinces; and the empire a union of such states and free cities.'[11] In a federal state, or what Althusius called 'a complete confederation', 'its inhabitants, are fully and integrally coopted and admitted into the right and communion of the realm by a communicating of its fundamental laws and right of sovereignty'.[12] But if the Althusian federal principle is to be maintained, these same inhabitants must maintain their political association with the communities that form the federal state. Thus, a federal political union requires a delicate balance of dual loyalties and attachments to the union as a whole and to its constituent units – a balance which in fact is always tending to tilt one way or the other both in the minds and hearts of its individual citizens as well as in the distribution of power in the political life of the federal polity.

If, as this volume suggests, the European Union is destined to grow into a 'United States of Europe', the distribution of political sentiment and power within it will bear little resemblance to that in the United States of America. For the foreseeable future it will function much more as a union of states than a union of citizens, and in that sense fall short of being a fully fledged federation – or, in Althusius' terminology, a complete confederation. Sergio Ortino need not fear that in the foreseeable future the EU will cease to be what he calls a federative state and become a sovereign federation.

In ways that were probably unforeseen by its architects the EU functions well as a preserver and even an enhancer of federations within its borders. After first appearing to have a relentless centralizing effect on federalism within its member states, at least since Maastricht recently it has been animated by the spirit of subsidiarity and a bias towards respecting local particularisms and initiatives. This has led to the establishment of a European committee of regions and, more significantly for its truly federal members, arrangements through which the governments of member states of federations can participate in EU policy-making in their areas of competence. Chapter 10 by de Witte contains an analysis of the ways in which these arrangements have accommodated the federal structures of its two federal states, Belgium and Spain, where deep-seated cultural divisions have provided a strong societal base for federalism. As Woelk's chapter (chapter 8) on the German federal system brings out in more detail, it is the German federation, based on a desire to protect local autonomy rather than on ethnic diversity, that has spear-headed the establishment of these EU arrangements. The right of Italian regions and of Scotland to participate in EU governance in Brussels, as Palermo and Poggeschi show in chapters 9 and 11, is one of the more clearly federal aspects of devolution in Italy and Great Britain.

Not only has the EU enabled federal states to integrate in a political union in a way that does not undermine their own internal federalism, but it has also enveloped member states in a an outer political framework secure enough to make federalizing trends within its unitary states less frightening and less contested than they might otherwise have been. This was the case with Belgium, the one federation to be born within the sheltering womb of the European community. Italy and the United Kingdom appear to be moving along the same path. And yet, de Witte is probably right when, reflecting on the Belgian and Spanish experience, he speculates that the EU has had a restraining effect on separatist aspirations. On the other hand, the earlier chapters on Central and Eastern Europe and on Russia suggest that if the regionalization fostered by the EU is applied to the much more ethnically divided and less secure Eastern European states it could pose a serious challenge to their boundaries and identities.

The nation-state and the problem of sovereignty

It is a mistake to see the nation-state as a casualty of the federalizing process. Nation-states are the key actors in establishing and maintaining transnational political bodies such as the European Union. The European community was put together by nation-states of Western Europe that had enjoyed reasonable periods of national independence. Participation in the EU does not pose a serious threat to their national identity. But the experience of being at the centre of two World Wars has given the peoples and governments of these nation-states tremendous motivation to work at the organization of their continent in a manner that can contain the excesses of nationalism.

The nation-states of Central and Eastern Europe, on the other hand, have only briefly, and for the most part only recently, enjoyed the status of being independent nation-states. The chapters in this book that focus on these countries show how ill prepared they are for the transition to being member states of a quasi-federal political union such as the EU. As Vojtech Mastny (chapter 2) concludes, 'The peoples of East Central Europe have not been adequately conditioned by their history to readily embrace the habits and attitudes of international federalism.'[13] From Mastny's account of the region's historical experience of federalism we learn how little chance federalism had earlier in the twentieth century when it came up against the prevailing but unfulfilled nationalism of the region. Then under communism, state structures that were federal in form rather than accommodating nationalism suppressed it. Kristian Gerner's chapter (chapter 4) on the Baltic states, Poland and Hungary helps us appreciate that these states have needed a breathing space to pull themselves together and learn to function as internally coherent, reasonably confident and tolerant nation-states before entering the European Union. Only states that are able to function reasonably well as democratic nation-states will be able to participate effectively in the EU.

For *homo sapiens* the nation-state like the city will endure as one of its major forms of political community. What is at issue are the sovereign claims of the nation-state. It is the nation-state's claim to being the highest possible source of legal authority, its claim to being a universal, all-purpose government and its claim to the citizen's undivided allegiance and focus of identity that are challenged in this federalizing age. When Althusius published his *Politics* at the beginning of the seventeenth century it was not the nation-state that he challenged but Bodin's idea of sovereignty. Though Bodin's idea prevailed in Europe for nearly four centuries, Althusius' time has come. The European Union has paved the way in creating a legal framework that can function as a higher law binding on the courts and legislatures of its sovereign member states. Sergio Ortino's concluding chapter, drawing on much of the contemporary 'beyond sovereignty' literature,[14] analyses the global–local interplay of forces at the end of the twentieth century that are fatal to the nation-state's pretensions to be a universal government or to monopolize the social, economic and political space of its citizens.

The concept of sovereignty does not work well in these federalizing times. It survives more as an ideology than as a useful tool of juridical or political analysis. Theoretical formulae exist for accommodating sovereignty to federalism. Within a federation sovereignty can be spoken of as divided between the two levels of government. Indeed, dual sovereignty has been a defining feature of the classical conception of federal government in political science and constitutional law.[15] In the supranational governmental orders created and maintained by sovereign nation-states there is talk of pooling sovereignties. But the concept of sovereignty rests uneasily in these formulations. Sovereignty, as Bertrand de Jouvenal taught, is an absolutist concept – those who claim it aspire to a power that is supreme and entire.[16] It is a zero-sum kind of concept – you either have it all or not at all. Dividing or pooling sovereignty is like having a little more or less virginity.

In Poggeschi's discussion of Scottish 'devolution' (chapter 11) we can see what an ideological bar sovereignty is to the development of a federal Britain. The indivisible sovereignty of parliament still has a strong lock on the British – or more precisely, the English – constitutional mind. It is true that a significant number of former British colonies became federal states. But the federal design of these states grew primarily out of local political conditions and leadership rather than a predilection among Britain's imperial statesmen for federalism. A century ago, when the British Empire was being transformed into the Commonwealth there was a Commonwealth federation movement. However, it planted no political roots in Britain or its colonies. The Commonwealth with its membership of independent sovereign states is for the English a scary model of shared rule for the United Kingdom.

In Italy sovereignty, according to the constitution, 'belongs to the people',[17] so an indivisible sovereign parliament poses no barrier to federalism. Attractive as this formula is in a democratic age, it tends to beg the federal question. If the Italian people exercise their sovereignty simply through the will of the majority, then what about the regions and the wills of their majorities? Palermo's account of the constitutional reforms adopted in Italy in 1999 and 2001 (chapter 9) shows how close Italy's regional system has come, in a functional sense, to being a federal system. Application of the principle of subsidiarity has meant that many functions of government are passed from the centre to regions and municipalities, but the regions and their peoples are not yet recognized as the constituent units of the federation – sharing its sovereign powers – in the same sense as Spain's autonomous regions, Belgium's regions and communities or

Germany's *Länder* are. In federations whose people are sovereign in a constitutional sense it takes more than a simple majority voting in a referendum to amend the constitution: in Australia and Switzerland majorities in a majority of cantons or states are also required. In a political community that is truly federal popular sovereignty is a complex and problematic ideal. Modern Canada in seeking to democratize its constitutional process has come close to breaking itself up through disagreement over the weight to be given to the sovereign claims of its constituent provinces and constituent peoples – the Quebecois and the Aboriginal nations – in expressing popular sovereignty.[18]

Conflicting sovereign claims have bedevilled efforts to renovate the Russian federation. David O'Brien's chapter (chapter 3) on the contrasting experiences of Tatarstan and Chechnya provides a valuable lesson about the style of politics best suited for a federal political life. Tatarstan, unlike Chechyna, has been able to establish through peaceful negotiations an arrangement which gives it the autonomy it sought – more than any other Russian republic enjoyed at the time – and yet remain part of the Russian federation. The key to this outcome, O'Brien tells us, was that the leaders in Moscow and Kazan (the Tatarstan capital) 'deliberately side-stepped the thorny issue of sovereignty'.[19] Contradictions between claims to sovereignty in the Russian and Tatarstan constitutions were allowed to stand. Federal arrangements are not apt to survive for long contests between political leaders fighting under competing banners of sovereignty. In successful federal regimes, what Friedrich refers to as a 'federal spirit' develops. This is 'a highly pragmatic kind of political conduct, which avoids all insistence upon "agreement on fundamentals" and similar forms of doctrinaire rigidity'.[20] In Mitja Žagar's account of the collapse of the Yugoslav federation (chapter 6), it is the absence of such a 'federal spirit' more than flaws in institutional structures that seems most telling in the failures of its ethnic leaders to refashion a federal order after the fall of communism.

The problem of sovereignty for the aggregating federalism of the European Union is the antithesis of the sovereignty challenge faced by devolving states: the absence of any meaningful sovereignty at the centre. The EU's member states do not see themselves as sharing a divided sovereignty with the Union's governmental instruments. Sergio Ortino's federative ideal remains the governing concept: the only sovereignty the EU's members regard as fundamental is that which belongs to themselves as nation-states, bits of which are loaned or pooled to create the EU's powers. Functionally, so far as accomplishing the internal objectives of EU policy is concerned, the absence of a clear and independent share of sovereignty at the centre does not seem to have been a major problem up to now. Though the compliance of member states with EU directives and regulations is less thorough than it would be if the commission had the enforcement capacity of a federal state, still the level of compliance is impressive and improving.[21] Under the proposed European constitution, as under its present structure, treaty or constitutional changes require the unanimous approval of all member states. This is the key to the member states' retention of their national sovereignty. But,

as we learn from chapter 12 by Farkas and Toggenburg, the straight-jacket resulting from the unanimity requirement will be the strongest incentive for modifying it. The 2003 intergovernmental conference expressed the wish for a more
flexible rule for constitutional revision to avoid '*total paralysis of the Union*'.[22] A
further mark of the members' retention of sovereignty under the proposed new
constitution, as Ortino acknowledges, is each member's right of voluntary withdrawal from the Union.

It is in foreign policy – especially the political and security side of foreign
policy – that the absence of a real share of sovereignty at the centre gives rise to
a major functional weakness. This is evident in the EU's failure to intervene
effectively in the major security problem on its own European doorstep in the
Balkans. The treaty of Amsterdam may have written peacekeeping and peace-
making into the Western European Union's (WEU's) mandate,[23] and the creation of a union minister for foreign affairs may strengthen this element of the
EU. But NATO is likely to remain Western Europe's main source of collective
security for quite some time. And, as both the Bosnian and Kosovo crises have
shown, NATO depends for its political leadership and military effectiveness on
the United States – a very sovereign federal state. Provision in the draft European
constitution for a 'union minister of foreign affairs' to be elected, like the EU
president, by the European council, would be a major step towards remedying
this deficiency.

The arena of international politics in this federalizing age continues to be
dominated by nation-states. The strongest players in this arena are those states
– be they unitary or federal – whose central governments can effectively assert
sovereign powers. There is, indeed, a danger that states which through internal
devolution or external aggregation have gone a long way down the federalizing
path will in this period of transition be somewhat at the mercy of the strong
sovereign dinosaurs that continue to stalk the world scene. Superpower status is
not compatible with a genuine federal condition of dual sovereignty, let alone
the even weaker EU federative model. Europeans may dream of their own union
providing the basis for a superpower capable of balancing the power of the USA,
the one superpower now operating on our planet. But for such a dream to
become a reality, they will need to support and identify with a European Union
that has a much stronger, more coherent and more confident government in its
capital than operates there now.

Europe the epicentre of federalism

Though the federalizing tendency is a worldwide phenomenon, it surely has its
epicentre in Europe. Western Europe with Austria, Belgium, Spain, Germany
and Switzerland organized and operating constitutionally as federal states has
more of the world's federal democracies than any other region or continent.
With Italy, the United Kingdom, Denmark (with respect to Greenland and the

Faroe Islands) and possibly France heading in a federalist direction, it may soon have even more. Europeans have also learned from federalism failures as well as successes. Mastny's contribution to this volume (chapter 2) makes us aware of the extent to which Central and Eastern Europe are littered with the remains of abandoned, failed or false attempts at federal political arrangements. These include the Polish–Lithuanian state, the Austro-Hungarian dual monarchy, the modern Czechoslovak and Yugoslav federations, and the federal camouflage of communist Russia's imperialism. Mitja Žagar reminds us in chapter 6 that two of the successor states of the Yugoslav federation, the federal republic of Yugoslavia (Serbia and Montenegro) and Bosnia-Herzegovina, are, at least in form, federations.

Europe's centrality to the federalizing process goes well beyond its experience with federal states. European thought and practice are now exploring forms of political association that transcend the classic federal state. There is historic logic in this. Just as it was Europe that invented the modern nation-state which became the hegemonic unit of politics in the modern era, it is European thinkers and leaders, the latter day apostles of Althusius, who are designing forms of political integration that lead beyond the nation-state, and defy analysis in terms of Bodin's idea of sovereignty. As a great scholar of federalism, Daniel Elazar, put it: 'Today, at the outset of the postmodern epoch, the Europeans have concluded they must go beyond the state system. To do so, they have revived the very confederal option that they rejected at the outset of the modern age, in new postmodern terms.'[24] Elazar saw this movement writ large, of course, in Western Europe in the achievement of the European Union. As for the Central–East part of Europe, there he could see only 'some kind of looser, shadowy affair in the middle'.

The chapters in this volume that deal with the middle of Europe agree that these countries between the European Union and the former USSR do not have a future together as a confederal bloc or region. Chapter 5 by András Bozóki shows that relations between the states of the 'new Central Europe' since the fall of communism and the break-up of the Czechoslovak and Yugoslav federations have been more competitive than cooperative. More recently there has been a considerable amount of bilateral cooperation between states in the region but nothing that has a real federalizing potential. Through the 1990s it became increasingly clear that 'the manifest destiny' of the states that make up Middle Europe is to become part of the European Union and NATO.

Pressure on these states to meet the European Union's standards of comity and civility provides the strongest incentive for interstate cooperation in the region. The most powerful motive Czechoslovakia, Hungary and Poland had for signing the Visegrád Agreement in 1991 was recognition that the appearance of a relatively high level of cooperation was necessary to assure Western Europe that they could behave as 'civilized', 'normal' European countries. Similarly, Bozóki points out how cooperation among three members of the Visegrád group, Poland, Hungary and the Czech Republic, was revitalized after the 1997 decision to admit them to NATO. But, as he also points out, this kind of regional cooperation among countries in Middle Europe was not taken so far that it could be used by Western Europe as an excuse to keep them out of the EU. These states have no desire to remain permanently as a weak and vulnerable *cordon sanitaire*. The economic and security objectives that were the immediate rationale for federative integration in Western Europe point the countries of Central and Eastern Europe not to each other but to Western Europe. The main lines of trade and commerce for the countries of Middle Europe lie along an east–west trajectory – as spokes of the Western European economy, especially Germany's. Any moves towards economic union in the region would be more likely to divert trade than to increase it. A survey of Central Europe by *The Economist* did not uncover any grounds for closer economic collocation in the region. On the contrary, *The Economist* asserted that 'Central Europeans simply do not want to be regarded as a block any more . . . Membership of Comecon and of the Warsaw Pact . . . has made them sick of working in political harness'.[25] Similarly the pursuit of collective security which is a major objective of all countries in the region leads towards integration with the West rather than with one another. Protection from the threat of a revival of Russian nationalism which all of these countries urgently seek, they now expect to find through the eastern expansion of NATO.

It is a broader kind of security, security of their newly established liberal democratic systems, that provides the deepest incentive for Middle Europe to integrate with Western Europe in a manner that goes well beyond membership in a military alliance. Across Europe there is an awareness of how participation in the European Union strengthened the democratic foundations of Germany, Greece, Italy, Portugal and Spain – countries that were emerging from long periods of authoritarian and fascist rule. It is reasonable for peoples who are emerging from a long period of communist dictatorship to look upon membership in the EU as an insurance policy for the liberal democracies they have so recently established.

Another dimension of the political security to be achieved through European integration is the containment of nationalism. In the past this region of Middle Europe has been an arena of virulent ethnic-based nationalism. The Soviet Empire and the Cold War froze but did not kill the roots of this nationalism – as is so evident in the nationalist conflict unleashed by the unravelling of the Yugoslav federation. Dissolution of the Czechoslovak and Yugoslav federations has accentuated a tendency to establish ethnically homogeneous nation-states. This tendency threatens cultural and linguistic minorities in the region, the largest of which are the Germans and Hungarians in neighbouring states of these countries, and the Russians in the Baltic states. The denial of cultural minority rights can lead to regional insecurity through either the migration of oppressed minorities or aggression by their 'mother countries' to protect those whom they identify as 'their people'. Joining a multinational political community such as the EU with member states as ethnically diverse as Belgium and Spain is a good way to learn how to contain the forces of ethnic nationalism.[26]

The European federalizing process discussed in this book – most specifically in chapters 4 and 12 – can be portrayed as completing the Westernization of Europe. Gerner (chapter 4) draws the historical parallels between the Christianization of Europe in the Middle Ages and the eastward expansion of the European Union. The West's expansion is no longer fuelled by Christian ardour but by a kind of secular religion – belief in the virtues of liberal democracy and welfare capitalism. The countries of Middle Europe at the head of the queue for eastern expansion – the Czech Republic, Hungary, Poland, Slovakia and Slovenia, and the Baltic states, Estonia, Latvia and Lithuania – are the countries that have moved the fastest and furthest towards practising the political economy of the West. There is a concern that, excluding for a long time the countries given a lower place in the queue, namely Bulgaria, Romania and Turkey, could jeopardize the possibility of overcoming the historic bifurcation of European civilization.

A new federal order faces old federal problems

The contributors to this volume are in broad agreement that the 'manifest destiny' of the countries of Central and Eastern Europe is to become part of the European Union. Indeed the book reflects an image of all of Europe from the Arctic to the Mediterranean and from the Atlantic to the borders of the former USSR belonging to an emerging 'Euro-polity'. It is in this sense that Europe is seen to be in a federalizing process.

But towards what kind of federal order is this Europe-wide process of federalism headed?

The thinking reflected in this book appears to rule out the two classic types of federal order: a confederation and a federal state. The existing fifteen-member Union already has too binding a constitutional order and too much independent strength at the centre to be considered a confederation. Though Europeans feared that enlargement east and south might dilute and diversify the bonds of membership, the drafters of the constitution of Europe boldly seek to move in the opposite direction. These constitutional engineers are gambling that they can deepen the Union as they widen it. Even if this *beau risque* succeeds no one foresees the twenty-five member Union soon becoming a true federal state. The lack of a Europe-wide political space deep and meaningful enough to provide the affective, popular base for a central government that can claim its own independent share of sovereign power, rules out, for the foreseeable future, a European federation of classic dimensions.

Thus the one thing that seems reasonably certain about the emerging federal European order is that it will have a structure and politics that do not fit the classic federal categories. Not only is the EU in its internal structure likely to continue to function as a 'strange dog', but the associations that the Union and its members have with other European structures add to the complexity. The 'emerging Euro-polity' is not based on a single organizational structure but on an array of regional organizations, with partially overlapping memberships and a wide range of functional mandates including security (e.g. the WEU and NATO), trade (e.g. the European economic area) and human rights (e.g. the council of Europe). Complicating the picture is the fact that not only will the European Union be the most important organization in this Eurocracy but the influence of its norms and policies will extend well beyond its official membership. The countries that are negotiating their entry into the EU and those just behind them are all under pressure to conform to European Union standards of democratic government, human rights and economic liberalism. As the EU's boundaries expand to the east and south, other states on its frontier, possibly including members of the Community of Independent States, will join the ranks of these EU want-to-be's.

Though the emerging federal configuration of Europe does not fit the structural categories of classical federal thought, it is encountering the classical political challenges of federalism. One of these is symmetry v. asymmetry. A number of the contributors to this book comment on how essential asymmetric arrangements are for accommodating differences of commitment, capacity and culture. A major theme in Mitja Žagar's analysis of the collapse of the Yugoslav federation (chapter 6) is its failure to provide sufficient asymmetry in its structures and operations. Two of the EU's federal members, Belgium and Spain, have been able to accommodate deep diversities only by not insisting on equality of status and form for their constituent members. Its other two federal members, Austria and Germany, have given different weights, based on population, to the voting rights of their constituent members in the federal councils of their national legislatures, and Austria has accorded special protection for the Slovenian and Croatian minorities in several of its states. The European Union itself is riddled with asymmetry: the varying strength and procedures of its different pillars; the opting out provisions for Britain and Denmark needed to gain their adherence to Maastricht; the voluntary and involuntary exclusions from its monetary union and its accord on border security; and the differential strength of constituent states, *de jure* and *de facto*, in its central bodies – to mention only the most obvious. Provision in the draft constitution allowing 'enhanced cooperation' for groups of eight or more member states would increase the opportunities for asymmetry. And then the larger emerging Euro-polity itself with its layers of cross-cutting associations is the very soul of asymmetry.

Asymmetry is the norm rather than the exception among federal polities.[27] Indeed, it is difficult to think of a federal system which is perfectly symmetrical both in design and operation. The world has not known a federation in which all of the constituent units are equal both formally in law as well as in actual power and influence. But if some asymmetry is an inescapable feature of the federal condition it is also the source of some of the most difficult issues confronted by the citizens and states of a federal polity. These issues often raise what are in effect important questions of political justice. Should member states that have greater autonomy locally have less power at the centre? Should states that do not accept all of the mutual obligations of a federal union be eligible for all of the benefits that flow from that union? Which ethnic, linguistic or cultural minorities merit constitutional recognition and protection, and which do not? How far should equality of power for individual citizens of the federal community give way to equality of power for each of its constituent units regardless of size? What is the obligation of wealthier member states to transfer wealth to poorer members or regions of the federal community? The last two questions will become more pressing as the European Union takes in new members nearly all of whom are smaller and significantly poorer than the average among the existing fifteen members. And beyond these questions of justice within the EU will be the justice of excluding European states on the outside who are subject to its sway.

The differential treatment of the members of a federal polity that are introduced to accommodate differences in their resources, needs and aspirations can give rise to jealousies and resentments that may threaten the survival of federal communities. Canada is a text-book example. Quebec as Canada's one province with a French majority has accumulated a number of incidents of special status by way of power at the centre and autonomy at the provincial level but still not enough to satisfy a majority of its citizens. Efforts to obtain for Quebec a special status that is larger and clearer have mobilized stiff opposition from other parts of the federation which resent Quebec's special treatment, all the more so when they have to help pay for it. When attempts to deal with the resulting conflict are transferred from the quiet diplomacy of elite accommodation into the increasingly democratic forum of constitutional politics, the pragmatic art of compromise so essential to federal survival gives way to the appeals of populist leaders who refuse to rise above principle. There are very real limits to how far the emerging Euro-polity can be developed *à la carte*. A federalizing Europe will have to work hard at finding the limits of the asymmetry it can safely digest.

The other classic federal challenge Europe confronts is the quality of democracy that its interacting layers of governance will afford. Federal arrangements carry with them the promise of a democratic bonus – the ideal of retaining as much governance accountable to local electorates as is consonant with achieving the objectives of the wider community. The European Union, with its commitment to applying the principle of subsidiarity to its three levels of government: regions, nation-states and supranational institutions, partakes of this promise. It may, however, be a very empty promise if the parameters of what can be decided and controlled locally are set primarily at the highest and most remote transnational level. For, of course, it is at that level that a federalizing Europe encounters not a democratic bonus but a democratic deficit.

This infamous democratic deficit of the EU arises not so much from its central institutions being the most distant and least inaccessible to citizens, as from its failure as yet to establish a popular political space. Citizens of a democratic federal community must simultaneously occupy several political spaces where they can encounter the issues and engage with the personalities of their different levels of government. Once the unit of government moves beyond the very local level, such spaces are constructed primarily by the mass media. In Europe, such a political space at the EU level or beyond is still very under-developed. One reason for its under-development is Europe's growing addiction to one of the great curses of federalism – intergovernmentalism. In modern federal communities where few areas of public policy can be contained within neat, water-tight jurisdictional compartments, there is a natural tendency to coordinate overlapping interests and responsibilities through intergovernmental negotiations. In chapter 5 András Bozóki speaks of the EU becoming a 'multi-level bargaining system'.[28] Negotiations of this kind may, euphemistically, be referred to as facilitating 'cooperative federalism', but because they tend to be highly technical and carried out by executive branch officials behind closed doors they add considerably to the democratic deficit.

Concern about the possibility that a federal Europe may be a depoliticized Europe is unlikely to deflect Europe from the federalizing path set out in this volume. For many Europeans – perhaps for most – a diminishment in the intensity of their political life, for the time being, is a price worth paying for the advantages of containing the political excesses of nationalism and securing the democratic gains resulting from the fall of communism. And, as Bozóki observes, a devaluation of politics goes along with the 'market-regulatory regime' which the European Union has fostered. But such conditions are not likely to prevail for long. Already there are indications of deep-seated social discontent arising from the limits of market-dominated economics and of a serious nationalist backlash on the fringes of European politics. Responding to the first and resisting the second may provide the context for a democratic political community at the European level. It should not be beyond the European political genius that democratized Bodin's sovereign nation-state to democratize Althusius' non-sovereign federal community.

Notes

1 R. Watts, *Comparing Federal Systems in the 1990s* (Kingston: Queen's University Institute of Intergovernmental Relations, 1996), p. 4.
2 For a discussion of the two modes of establishing federal arrangements, see R. Watts, 'Contemporary views on federalism', in B. de Villiers, *Evaluating Federal Systems* (Dordrecht: Martinus Nijhoff, 1994), pp. 1–29.
3 C. Friedrich, *Trends of Federalism in Theory and Practice* (New York: Praeger, 1968), p. 12.
4 See pp. 262, 264.
5 D. Elazar, *Exploring Federalism* (Tuscaloosa: University of Alabama Press, 1987), p. 12.
6 See P. Russell, 'Constitutions and constitutionalism', in Adam and Jessica Kuper (eds), *The Social Science Encyclopaedia* (London: Routledge & Kegan Paul, 1985), pp. 157–8.
7 Watts, *Comparing Federal Systems in the 1990s*.
8 M. Burgess, 'Federalism and federations: a reappraisal', in M. Burgess and A.-G. Gagnon

(eds), *Comparative Federalism and Federation* (London: Harvester Wheatsheaf, 1993), p. 6.

9   G. F. Mancini, 'The making of a constitution for Europe', *Common Market Law Review*, 26 (1989), 595.

10   See p. 288.

11   C. J. Friedrich, 'Preface', in F. S. Carney (ed.), *The Politics of Johannes Althusius* (London: Eyre & Spottiswoode, 1965), pp. 9–10.

12   *Ibid.*, p. 84.

13   See p. 42.

14   See, in particular, D. Elkins, *Beyond Sovereignty* (Toronto: University of Toronto Press, 1995).

15   See K. C. Wheare, *Federal Government* (Oxford: Oxford University Press, 1946).

16   B. de Jouvenal, *Sovereignty: An Inquiry Into the Political Good* (Chicago: University of Chicago Press, 1963).

17   Art. 1, c. 2 of the Italian constitution.

18   See P. Russell, *Constitutional Odyssey: Can Canadians Become A Sovereign People?* (Toronto: University of Toronto Press, 1993).

19   See p. 55.

20   See Friedrich, *Trends of Federalism*, p. 39.

21   M. Cappelletti, Monica Seccombe and Joseph Weiler, *Integration Through Law: Volume 1 – Methods, Tools and Institutions* (Berlin: de Gruyter, 1986).

22   See CONV 850/03, Official Journal, C 169 (18 July 2003).

23   *Amsterdam, 17 June 1997, A New Treaty for Europe: Citizen's Guide* (Luxembourg: Office for Official Publications of the European Communities, 1997), p. 11.

24   D. Elazar, *Federalism in the New Europe* (Melbourne: 7th Wolfsohn Memorial Lecture, Australia, 1994).

25   'Survey', *The Economist* (18 November 1998), p. 6.

26   For a full discussion of this point, see J. Tully, *Strange Multiplicity: Constitutionalism In an Age of Diversity* (Cambridge: Cambridge University Press, 1995).

27   For a discussion of various kinds of asymmetry in different federations, see de Villiers (ed.), *Evaluating Federal Systems*, chapters 4, 5 and 6.

28   See p. 101.

VOJTECH MASTNY

2

The historical experience of federalism in Eastern and Central Europe

The admission of the formerly communist countries of East Central Europe into the European Union has cast the historical experience of the peoples of the area with federalism into a new and potentially disturbing light. How well has that experience prepared them for membership in the twentieth century's most successful confederation and the likely centrepiece of the emerging post-Cold War international order on the continent? In particular, how have the fate and impact of federalist ideas and institutions in the region influenced the candidates' readiness to enter an interstate structure which requires from its members a substantial surrender of sovereignty? And how has their historical experience shaped their aptitude to the kind of international cooperation that is essential to keep the EU functioning?

In assessing the record of federalism in East Central Europe, too narrow a definition of the term ought to be resisted. The primary subject of this inquiry is interstate federalism, which is distinguished from the intrastate variety by both its motives and its thrust; rather than curb the excesses of centralism and state power, interstate federalism aims to contain nationalism and prevent international anarchy. Yet the overwhelming majority of the historical antecedents have been federations as vehicles for the assertion of group rights within states rather than for the preservation of peace between states. Downgrading the importance of the former in favour of the latter would result in a badly distorted picture.

Intentionally or not, the distinction between the two types of union – federation (*Bundesstaat*) and confederation (*Staatenbund*) – has often been blurred. Since groupings of both kinds have frequently influenced each other, drawing too sharp a line between them can indeed be misleading. The European Union, too, influences the internal affairs of its member states in countless ways, despite their sovereignty. It claims the right, for example, to protect minorities by ensuring the passage of appropriate national legislation of a federalist nature or providing for autonomy for the minorities in question. Although autonomy differs from federation, the two are so closely interrelated that striving for autonomy cannot be left out of the discussion, particularly not in view of their contentious history in as ethnically heterogeneous an area as East Central Europe. Thus, the scope of inquiry is much larger than suggested by a narrow definition of federalism; at issue is the proper selection of what is relevant to the subject.

Before the age of nationalism: the German Empire and the Polish Commonwealth

Invoking historical antecedents is risky as often those invoked are historical curiosities with scant relevance to modern times.[1] Such is the case, for example, of the 1335 Visegrád agreement, chosen to bestow the blessing of history on the 1991 decision of the heads of state of Poland, Czechoslovakia and Hungary to link their countries by regular consultation and cooperation in matters of common interest. The original agreement was an obscure dynastic deal which, as was customary at the time, ignored the people while proving the monarchs' inability to collaborate for any length of time.[2] No sooner was it concluded than it fell apart – as did, too, its latter-day namesake after but a few years.

Similarly, the sixteenth-century plan of the Czech king George of Podiebrad for a league of Europe's Christian monarchs against their common Ottoman enemy, sometimes depicted as something of a precursor of a united Europe, was, if anything, the opposite. An attempt by the ruler of a heretical country to break its international isolation, the plan elicited little support, thus highlighting Europe's division rather than its unity.[3] Nor did the religious thrust of the proposed alliance prevent the split between Catholics and Protestants from climaxing a century later in what was up to that point the continent's most devastating war.

The two federal models antedating the age of nationalism that are most germane to the theme of East Central Europe's integration into a wider Europe have retrospectively commanded little admiration: the Holy Roman Empire, with its successor the Germanic confederation, and the Polish Commonwealth. Not only did these models prove remarkably durable – the former lasted a thousand years, the latter three centuries – but they also left behind constructive legacies that have tended to be overshadowed by their familiar deficiencies.

The medieval German Empire anticipated the latter-day united Europe in its constitutional arrangements of often bewildering complexity which, by applying the principle of dual allegiance, were designed to allow independent entities to prosper by submitting to the authority of the emperor while preserving their separate identity. The status of the Czech principality and later kingdom of Bohemia was a case in point which left an indelible mark on the Czech–German relationship for centuries to come.[4]

Of the non-Germanic peoples of East Central Europe who formed states in the Middle Ages, the Czechs shared most extensively in the development of the Holy Roman Empire. For most of the period, the Czech ruler was a privileged vassal of the emperor, eventually becoming one of the seven imperial electors and, in the fourteenth century in the persons of Charles IV and his two sons, even the emperor himself. Charles made Prague his capital city and one of Europe's premier cultural centres at the time, before the Hussite revolution and its aftermath rendered the constitutional connection with Germany tenuous. Even then, the Empire remained for the Czechs, more than for other Slavs, the gateway to Western Europe.

During the Empire's long existence, but especially once its decline began, the complexity of its problems challenged the minds of some of the leading theoreticians of federalism, such as Johannes Althusius and Johann Stephan Pütter. Yet much of the voluminous writing about German federalism remained excessively preoccupied with its legal dimensions at the very time when, following the religious division that split the venerable structure apart, its preservation became mainly a question of the political will of its constituent parts, whose full sovereignty was recognized in the 1648 Peace of Westphalia. Looking beyond an Empire whose days had already been numbered, the philosopher Immanuel Kant grasped the central contribution federalism could make to the maintenance of peace and order among nations. 'The law of nations', he insisted, 'shall be founded on a federation of free states.'[5]

The 'Holy Roman Empire of the German Nation' sought to define the place among nations of Europe's largest but most fragmented territorial unit. The plans for its federalist reform and the evolution since the early nineteenth century of the Germanic confederation as its successor have usually been viewed within the context of the movement for German unity, and rightly so. Federalist traditions antedating the unification remained an important part of German political and legal heritage, traditions which were not extinguished by the authoritarian and totalitarian rulers who successively governed the unified country. After World War II, those traditions provided a receptive base for the absorption of federalist concepts of the Anglo-American variety in western Germany, triumphing in the eminently successful synthesis implemented in the Federal Republic of Germany.

The other historical federal model, that of the Polish Commonwealth, resulted from the transformation of a conventional dynastic union between the kingdom of Poland and the grand duchy of Lithuania. After the conclusion in 1569 of the treaty of Lublin, the union evolved into a confederation which preserved the identity of its constituent units while maintaining common features. Besides the figurehead king, these included compatible laws, common diet and common foreign policy.

The arrangement was attractive and potentially beneficial to neighbours. In 1658 the minority of westernized Cossacks attempted to bring the Ukraine into the Commonwealth as its third constituent member but did not succeed.[6] Afterwards, their rivals turned to Russia, leading to the annexation of the

Ukraine to Russia. Most Ukrainians came to regard this as a historical misfor-
tune, which took more than three hundred years to be undone.

Except for the union between England and Scotland, the Polish–Lithuanian
aristocratic republic was unparalleled in contemporary Europe. Similar to Great
Britain, its constitution was made possible by the weakness of the royal power;
however, unlike in Great Britain, the nobility constituted a significant segment
of the population by the standards of the time – about 10 per cent, or a million
people. Within this large group, political discourse was rife, much attention
being paid to such subjects of impeccable modernity as safeguards against the
abuse of state power, preservation of minority rights and power-sharing.[7]

The hallmark of the Polish–Lithuanian state was the length to which it went
in its attempts to protect individual and group rights within the confederation.
Ultimately, its inability to find the right balance brought about its downfall.
During the three centuries it lasted, however, the Commonwealth went further
than any other contemporary state in addressing the practical problems of federalism, until the North American colonies took the lead and created the United
States as a new model. The unique American circumstances, however, meant
that the model could not be easily imitated. East Central Europeans became cap-
tivated by American democracy, freedom and prosperity, not federalism; *The
Federalist Papers* did not become required reading for even their educated elite.

Although Poland ceased to exist as a state in 1795, it continued to maintain
a political discourse richer than any European nation east of Germany. The
problem of how to reconcile nationalism with federalism preoccupied the political elite in their quest for the restoration of an independent Poland in a congen-
ial Europe.[8] After the failure of the uprising of 1830, the leading figure of the
Great Emigration, Adam Czartoryski, developed while in exile in Paris proposals for the organization of the continent in order to protect the smaller nations
and ensure their vital contribution to common European good.[9] He dissemi-
nated his thoughts through his extensive international contacts.

In envisaging confederations based on nationalism, Czartoryski echoed the
ideas of one of the fathers of Italian unity, Giuseppe Mazzini, about the necessary fulfilment of national aspirations as a precondition for the voluntary association of the peoples of the continent – ideas which anticipated the process
through which European unity would evolve in the following century.[10]
Czartoryski influenced the 1844 *Načertanije* by Serbian foreign minister Ilija
Garašanin, which proposed the establishment of a Slav federation with Serbia as
its core, marking the controversial debut of Balkan federalism and indicating
both its promise and its main problem.[11]

The multinational monarchies: unattractive models

Long after the medieval affiliation of the Czechs with the Holy Roman Empire
had ended, the issue of their participation in a new federal state dominated by

Germans was revived in 1848 by the Frankfurt constituent assembly seeking to replace the Austrian-dominated Germanic confederation by something more desirable and modern. The project was a liberal and nationalist undertaking, and participation in it was rejected on both grounds by the conservative Czech leader František Palacký.[12] His reply to the Frankfurt parliament showed how much Kant's postulate of a federalism of free states had been superseded by a yearning for states, federal or otherwise, whose primary purpose would be the satisfaction of national aspirations.[13] According to Palacký, federalism applied only to internal, not international law. In his view, its purpose was not a union of states but rather the devolution to nationalities of all the power that was not essential for a state to maintain its unity.[14]

Palacký elaborated on these ideas at the Kremsier constitutional convention, where representatives of different nationalities of the Austrian Habsburg monarchy sought to respond to their Frankfurt counterparts by reorganizing the monarchy in a manner which accommodated both the old local privileges of its territorial units and the new national aspirations of its diverse peoples.[15] Trying to reconcile historic political units with the desire for national unity and self-government was at the heart of federalism in East Central Europe during the nineteenth century and much of the twentieth. The constitution drafted at Kremsier may have been the most promising attempt to transform the Austrian Empire into a federation acceptable to its different nationalities, yet neither this constitution, nor any of the numerous later schemes aimed at achieving that goal, were ever implemented.

Instead, the Austro-Hungarian compromise of 1867 was designed to satisfy only one of the discontented nationalities – the Magyars. Consisting of only two, very unequal members, the resulting dual monarchy was a dubious federation, which made the establishment of a genuine one that much more difficult.[16] Since sovereignty remained vested in the emperor, the dual monarchy was not a confederation either, regardless of the common institutions established to handle the monarchy's foreign affairs, defence and finances. There was a gross imbalance between the ethnically more diverse and more tolerant Austrian part and the historic kingdom of Hungary, where the preponderant ruling nationality could afford more easily to assert its privileges without the corresponding responsibilities at the expense of the weaker ethnic groups.

In a subsidiary compromise the following year, the Magyars granted some privileges to the Croats, but not to any other group, successfully resisting any reform of the dual monarchy that would give status to any of its other nationalities, notably the Czechs, equal to that of the Magyars.[17] While the Austrian government extended a measure of autonomy to the Poles in Galicia, the Magyars blocked anything similar that would benefit the southern Slavs or Romanians, an approach comparable to the Austrian handling of their Italian minority. As the frustrations of these irredentist groups strained Austria–Hungary's relations with its neighbouring states – Serbia, Romania, Italy – its flawed federalism became a prescription for international instability. It helped precipitate the tragic sequence of events which led to the outbreak of World War I.

A response to the defeat of Austria by Prussia in the war of 1866, the quasi-federal reorganization of the Habsburg monarchy was an unhappy byproduct of the process of German unification, which excluded East Central Europe. It was a constitutional arrangement difficult to imitate and unworthy of imitation. Nevertheless, two later imitations were acts of desperation undertaken under duress, and fared accordingly. One was the 'second' republic of Czecho-Slovakia, formed in 1938 after the catastrophic Munich agreement to appease the Slovaks, that lasted five months; the other was the 1939 *Sporazum*, by which the Serb-dominated Yugoslavian government tried to accommodate the independence-minded Croats, that disintegrated under the German attack the following year.[18] If the bygone monarchy merits the nostalgia that it later generated among the latter-day descendants of its peoples, this could possibly be justified only by its comparison with the dismal regimes that followed it rather than by any compelling merits of its constitutional setup.

In contrast, the restricted but real federal system of the second German Reich, designed to reassure Prussia by giving it greater weight than all the other constituent units combined, did represent a model that was later followed, if only by disreputable regimes. It was successfully borrowed by Stalin in making the Soviet Union a vehicle of Russian dominance; but not so successfully by Slobodan Milošević in trying to achieve the same for Serbia in post-Tito Yugoslavia. Unlike these two dictatorships, however, pre-World War I Germany was, despite all its deficiencies, a state based on the rule of law, which allowed federalism to function within clearly set limits, thus ensuring its vital continuity.[19]

By allowing, however imperfectly, for the articulation of the particular interests of its component parts, both Central European monarchies differed from Russia, whose autocratic system precluded even a hint of federalism.[20] The mutually satisfactory position of Finland within the otherwise overbearing tsarist state entailed autonomy, not a federal relationship. Nor did the similarly oppressive Ottoman Empire allow for the rise of such relationships in the Balkans. The politics of the newly independent states that emerged from its shambles were too rudimentary to nurture the kind of subtlety necessary to develop a commitment to federalism. Hence, the agents of the French and Piedmontese governments, who in 1850 approached the Hungarian revolutionaries as well as the Romanian prince Alexander Cuza with the proposal of a Danubian confederation, were bound to be disappointed.[21]

Late nineteenth- and early twentieth-century imperialism, with its propensity for social darwinism and jingoism, was not hospitable to the progress of federalism – a fruit of tolerance and readiness to compromise. Besides free-traders, whose campaign against tariff barriers and for common markets sometimes had a federalist thrust which the ascendant protectionism had not, the main proponents of federal solutions to contemporary political and social problems were the social democrats. The 1879 proposal by French economist G. de Molinari for a sweeping mid-European customs union comprising countries from France through to Austria–Hungary, inspired by the success of the Prussian *Zollverein* as the harbinger of German unification, foreshadowed the pattern by which a hundred years later European unity would grow from the common market.[22] Social democrats, drawing on the federalist thrust of early French socialism, were responsible for some of the most imaginative plans for the restructuring of Austria–Hungary. These included Karl Renner's design for a federal state based on the principle of personality rather than territorial division. One hundred years later, this design would be relevant for a brief time in the discussion of the possible reorganization of postcommunist multiethnic states, notably the former Soviet Union and Yugoslavia.[23]

Apart from the 'Austromarxists', marxism did not lean unequivocally towards federalism. Friedrich Engels did favour the restoration of the Polish state as a federation of Poles, Lithuanians, Belorussians and Ukrainians,[24] but Rosa Luxemburg and other radical Polish socialists regarded any restitution of the multiethnic Poland as economically, and hence politically, retrogressive.[25] In tsarist Russia, the lone advocates of a federal solution to its nationality problems were the anarchist-oriented social revolutionaries rather than the social democrats,[26] whose faction, led by the Bolsheviks, rejected such a solution as incompatible with the concept of a dictatorship of the proletariat, which they hoped to exercise through a centralistic revolutionary party. Their leader, Lenin, in his vitriolic pamphlet *On the Slogan of the United States of Europe*, lambasted the idea as a capitalist ploy.[27]

World War I brought an upsurge of federalist thinking, though not before the senselessness of the slaughter and its catastrophic disruption of international order became evident, and even then only among a thoughtful minority. In 1915, *Mitteleuropa* by chastened German nationalist Friedrich Naumann, became an instant bestseller – and was immediately attacked by both Slav nationalists and their German counterparts, albeit for different reasons.[28] The former decried it as a manifesto of the German *Drang nach Osten*, the latter as a prospectus for a sellout to the Slavs.[29] Naumann's problem – and his claim to fame – was in coming much too early in prophesying the primacy of a democratic, tolerant and generous Germany in a prosperous Central Europe of like-minded nations exercising their self-determination in mutual economic integration and political cooperation.

Rather than on any federal institutional structure, Naumann proposed to rely on an interstate network of boards and committees (awkwardly referred to as *Oberstaat*) supervising common projects in a manner which would allow the representatives of different nations to gradually acquire the habits of cooperation. Prescient as he was of the road that Germany's eastern neighbours would eventually take to a united Europe, Naumann remained a prisoner of his narrowly Central European outlook. Not only did this German patriot expect the region's happiness to grow out of victory in the war by his country and Austria–Hungary – whose political systems he wanted to be liberalized but otherwise preserved – but he also envisaged high tariff walls that would protect the German-dominated economic zone from the rest of Europe. As a passionate advocate of mutual understanding and partnership between Germans and other Central Europeans, he nonetheless stood out as a man with an inspiring vision of the future at a time when the horizon of his critics was still limited by prejudices inherited from the past.

From World War I to World War II: reluctant federalists

Founded in the year after the publication of Naumann's book and dedicated to the rejection of his liberal concept of postwar Europe, the journal *New Europe* edited by the leader of the Czech exiles Thomas G. Masaryk and his Scottish supporter R. W. Seton-Watson, promoted an obstructionist alternative that was both retrogressive and short-sighted: a vindictive international order perpetuating a division between the victors and the vanquished. Although a convinced democrat, Masaryk had ambivalent feelings towards liberalism. He associated liberalism with the centralistic nationalism of Austrian Germans, while federalism reminded him of the efforts to salvage Austria–Hungary, the state he sought to destroy.[30]

In October 1918, Masaryk, with other East Central European exiles, initiated in Philadelphia the democratic Mid-European Union with the intention 'to replace the German plan of Mittel-Europa with a positive plan of organization of the many small nations located between the Germans and the Russians'.[31] Within weeks, however, the project fell victim to mutual bickering. The future Czechoslovak president understood that a successful federation presupposed the freely exercised will of its constituents, but did not actively promote it.[32] Later, he showed benevolent interest in the plans of the Austrian proponent of 'pan-European' federalism, Richard von Coudenhove-Kalergi, but did not regard them any less utopian than did most of his contemporaries.[33]

The only federal entity that emerged in post-World War I East Central Europe was, besides Weimar Germany, the diminished Austria – now ethnically the most homogeneous of the dual monarchy's successor states. Its system of self-governing *Länder* was primarily designed to foster the country's cohesion by ensuring a balance between the oversized working-class metropolis of Vienna and the rural provinces, some of which would have preferred to have gone separate ways; Vorarlberg, for example, wanted to join the neighbouring Swiss federation. The system served its limited goal fairly well, although all decisions of any importance were made at the national level.[34]

In contrast to Austria, the ethnically most diverse heirs of the defunct monarchy – Czechoslovakia and Yugoslavia – opted for variants of centralism. Their politicians' occasional talk of applying in their countries the Swiss cantonal system – a product of centuries of organic development in a relatively isolated part of Europe – was either wishful thinking or simply pulling the wool over the eyes of their public. The Czech-dominated Prague government soon abandoned the faint federalist impulse underlying the wartime Pittsburgh agreement between Masaryk and the representatives of Slovak Americans, which had expressed the intent to give Slovakia an unspecified form of autonomy. The unfulfilled agreement thus became a rallying cry of Slovak nationalists.[35] In never seriously considering either federation or autonomy as ways towards a solution of its perhaps insoluble structural problems, Czechoslovakia was the true heir of the old Austria, whose fate it would eventually share by disappearing from the map.

The representatives of the Serbs, Croats and Slovenes who in 1918 launched their national council in Zagreb agreed on the creation of a common state, but not on its constitution.[36] They never spelled out clearly the terms of the future relationship of their very different peoples, who had never lived in a common state before and inhabited an ethnically mixed territory. It remained undecided whether the ensuing 'Kingdom of the Serbs, Croats and Slovenes' was a union of three sovereign entities or an extension of the Serbian state. In any case, the dominant Serbs were not prevented from enforcing a centralistic system of government, in turn encouraging the disillusioned Croats to entertain federative schemes of doubtful viability.

The most prominent of Croat politicians, the erratic leader of the Peasant Party Stjepan Radić, flirted with the communist international, endorsing its call for a Balkan federation.[37] This was Moscow's scheme to undermine the integrity of the anti-Soviet Balkan states by agitating their many minorities while invoking proletarian internationalism as the answer to their needs. When Radić was shot and killed in the Yugoslavian parliament, King Alexander's first impulse was to offer the Croats complete separation from the state rather than to contemplate further how a federal solution might be applied to save its unity. Upon reflection, however, he introduced a still more centralistic system, thus perpetuating Croat disaffection.

Restoration of the old Polish Commonwealth in a new form figured prominently in Poland's political discussion after the achievement of its independence in 1918, although of the two main parties only Marshal Józef Piłsudski's Polish socialist party, not the conservative national democracy, wanted to federate with other peoples. Again, however, no serious effort was undertaken to decide what such a union should look like. When in 1919 Piłsudski seized by force the Lithuanian capital of Vilno, he remained notably silent about any federation. Since his advocacy of it never matured into any theory, much less a programme, his claim to fame as a 'European federalist' is specious.[38]

The prevailing nationalism in East Central Europe's post-World War I successor states dimmed the prospects of federative arrangements among them. As Czechoslovak foreign minister Edvard Beneš pertinently, though not regretfully, observed, the Danubian peoples had an 'instinctive aversion' to such arrangements because of their experiences with Austria–Hungary – the former oppressors.[39] Hence, the 'little entente' of Czechoslovakia, Romania and Yugoslavia, for which Beneš was a chief architect, had been designed as no more than a loose confederation lest it infringe on the jealously guarded sovereignty of its member states, thus making it a poor instrument of their common policy in the event of a crisis.[40]

The little entente originated as an attempt at an alliance against a common but secondary enemy – the revisionist Hungary – by states which each had different great powers as their primary adversary: for Czechoslovakia, this adversary was Germany, for Yugoslavia Italy, and for Romania the Soviet Union. With the unimportant exception of the short Czechoslovak–Romanian border, however, their territories were not contiguous, making effective defence planning all but impossible. Economically, the members of the grouping were competitors, and little effort was made to regulate their competition. They proved reluctant to proceed towards creating common institutions and to collaborating on any but the least contentious matters. Not surprisingly, the little entente had never been seriously tested before it crumbled in the harsh international climate of the 1930s.

Eastern Europe's most lasting, if phony, federation was formed after World War I by the world's self-proclaimed outlaw state, Soviet Russia. Although the Russian Bolsheviks had ruled out a federal reorganization of the tsarist Empire, their chief strategist, Lenin, genuinely abhorred what he condemned as 'Great Russian chauvinism'. His declarations about the new kind of relations that ought to be established after the Empire's downfall between its diverse peoples invoked the kind of 'federalism' contemplated by the French revolutionaries at the end of the eighteenth century. They understood federalism as a brotherly association of the liberated people but did not pay much attention to its institutional expression. The Bolsheviks avoided a clarification of what else their federalism might mean; once they came to power, however, they made it sufficiently clear that it did not mean any substantive devolution of power.[41]

Lenin underwent a change of heart after exasperating negotiations with the Georgian communists about the manner of associating their land with Soviet Russia, in effect endorsing the concept of Stalin, the party's supposed expert on nationality questions.[42] Stalin regarded federalism as little more than window dressing that could help divert nationalism in a harmless direction, thus making the country safe for centralism. Whatever the differences between these two accomplished practitioners of power politics, neither Lenin nor Stalin attempted to disguise his belief that a federal system was merely a 'transitional form to the complete unity of the toilers of the various nations'.[43]

This was the frame of mind from which originated in 1922 the Soviet Union, officially called the Union of Soviet Socialist Republics, with its heartland designated as the 'Russian Socialist Federated Soviet Republic'. What was founded as an allegedly transitory form came to endure as a convenient framework for the exercise of Stalin's tyranny, once the Bolsheviks abandoned their early illusions about the spread of their revolution abroad and embraced his concept of 'socialism in one country'.

The more the revolutionary regime degenerated into personal despotism, the more it paid lip service to federalism. Stalin enhanced federalism's trappings in the Soviet constitution of 1936, the year his terror reached its climax, even proclaiming the constituent republics' right to separation.[44] In practice, the system allowed the despot to better avail himself of willing executioners of his policies from among non-Russian party ranks of these nominal republics, thus tainting them with complicity in his crimes and making the coalescence of nationalist opposition that much more difficult. Little did he suspect that in the fullness of time the hapless republics, whose status and boundaries he manipulated with utter cynicism, would provide the framework along which the Soviet Union would split and finally disintegrate into real states.

Like the communists, the fascists opposed federalism because of their totalitarian ambitions. Unlike the communists, they at least did not pretend otherwise. After the Nazi seizure of power in Germany, Hitler made the liquidation of the residual self-government in Germany's historic provinces one of his first priorities.[45] During World War II, the Nazi propaganda of the 'New Order' appealed to European unity without any trace of federalism, extolling in nebulous terms the future benefits that the racially proper inhabitants of the continent would presumably enjoy under German tutelage.[46]

Accordingly, federalism became one of the mainsprings of the movement of European unity promoted by the wartime resistance movements in the Western countries under German occupation. The disunity of the continent nations that the fascist aggressors had been able to exploit to their advantage, and the failure of the league of nations to stop them, helped to make interstate rather than intrastate federalism the top priority for the first time, particularly in contemplating the postwar order. The leading minds of the French resistance considered European integration on a federalist basis as a way towards the resolution of the German question, thus removing once and for all Franco-German enmity as a threat to peace.[47] According to the Catholic philosopher Jacques Maritain, a federated Germany was necessary for a federated Europe.[48]

Further east, however, the federalist impulse was much less evident. If in France and elsewhere in Western Europe World War II did not generate the same overriding desire for revenge as World War I had done, that was not typically the case in Eastern Europe. There, enemy repression was more brutal and the war often provided the different peoples a welcome opportunity to settle their accounts against one another. Consequently, a readiness for future reconciliation with present enemies was notably absent.

Documents from the Polish underground were exceptional in Eastern Europe in their advocacy of an international federation on a democratic basis. They still presupposed, however, the summary expulsion of Germans from Polish territory as a precondition for any future reconciliation. While the question of which countries were to form the federation remained undecided, the most open-minded spokesmen for the Polish resistance at least indicated a desire to overcome mutual animosities in a supranational union. With a wary eye on the Soviet Union, they saw a particular need for safeguards against centralism disguised as federalism.[49]

East Central European federalist projects, such as there were, originated mainly among the exiles in London rather than in the occupied homelands. The 1942 proposal by Slovak politician Miroslav Hodža, formerly a prime minister of Czechoslovakia, came close to the vision of a collaborative and democratic Central Europe that Naumann had hoped could thrive under German auspices.[50] For Hodža, however, Central Europe was a Danubian Europe without a dominant great power, excluding such potential troublemakers as Germany and Poland, although he did desire keeping the door open to the latter, as well as to Greece.

A design for the union of Czechoslovakia, Austria, Hungary, Romania and Yugoslavia, Hodža's plan surpassed previous East Central European federalist schemes after World War I by being well thought out, unambiguous and specific. It envisaged a rather tight federation, complete with a common president, chancellor and parliament, whose inhabitants would retain their national citizenship but who would also automatically hold federal citizenship. Written after Hodža had given up political ambitions of his own following his expulsion from the Czechoslovak government-in-exile, his proposal was remarkably even-handed and free from nationalist rancor. As such, it never found a wider resonance and, unlike Naumann's book, did not even generate a controversy. Ignored rather than debated, its fate augured ill for the future of federalism in Eastern Europe once the Nazi 'New Order' had gone.

The onset of the Cold War: parting of the ways

The project initially promoted most actively by the London exiles was that of a Polish–Czechoslovak confederation.[51] Conceived by the Poles as a means of combining forces to resist the expected Soviet ascendancy in the region, it was embraced in 1940 by Czechoslovak president Beneš mainly for another reason: to help bolster his government's still precarious international standing by associating his government with the seemingly more secure Polish one. He never contemplated more than a loose association – a customs union with additional cooperation in foreign and trade policies but without common institutions of any substance. Neither partner ever seriously grappled with the two countries' severe disparities in territory, population, economy and foreign policy priorities.

After the initial declaration of intent, the Poles pressed for a specific understanding. In 1942 a second agreement was signed providing for the establishment of several commissions to deal with various aspects of the proposed union. By that time, however, Beneš' commitment to the project, known to be resented by the now allied Soviet Union, had been superseded by his quest for a special relationship with Moscow, in which close ties to the London Poles were a liability. As a result, the confederation died of neglect before it was even born. Nor did the less advanced project of the exiled Yugoslav and Greek governments for a future union of their homelands fare any better, as the communists, ascendant in both countries' resistance movements, propagated their alternative version of federalism.

The federalism of the Yugoslav communists under Tito, who managed to transform the idea into a reality in the Balkans for the first time, was a powerful force. Propelled by their marxist internationalism, their admiration for the Soviet model and their nascent imperialism, it was a daring attempt to overcome the region's endemic ethnic fragmentation by sheer revolutionary will. In 1942 Tito's associate Milovan Djilas went so far as to temporarily proclaim a Soviet union republic in the communist-controlled part of his native Montenegro – the land whose eighteenth-century prince had made a similar gesture by declaring its allegiance to the distant Russian tsar.[52] In a more practical way, the communists strove to restore Yugoslavia as a truly federal state and possibly add to it further countries as constituent units.

The Yugoslav communists followed the Soviet model by making their federation a cloak for centralistic rule by their party and by arbitrarily drawing the boundaries of six republics, which included two ostensibly autonomous provinces.[53] The scheme differed from the Soviet pattern by not serving to perpetuate the predominance of the largest nationality – the Serbs – thus keeping the door open to possible devolution of power and the eventual transformation of the state into a more authentic, albeit still communist, federation of several centralized units instead of one. Such a system, to be sure, was no prescription for democratic self-government.

Yugoslav federalism crossed the borderline between intrastate and interstate federalism once Tito and his associates began to actively indulge their ambition to include Albania, Bulgaria, Greece, and perhaps other countries, in a large Balkan union of communist states dominated by Belgrade. Albania was in effect included after its communist party, organized and controlled by Yugoslav emissaries, gained the upper hand in the resistance movement, thus making the country's formal annexation simply a question of time. The future of Greece, depending upon the ability of the communists to prevail over the royal government supported by the British, was not so clear.

The critical component in the construction of this edifice was Bulgaria – a German ally bound to lose the war and come under Soviet control. In anticipation of this outcome, the Yugoslav and Bulgarian communists had been negotiating since 1943 an association of their countries. Although they were unable to agree on whether Bulgaria should join as an equal partner with Yugoslavia as a whole – as preferred by the chief Bulgarian negotiator Traicho Kostov – or be reduced to the status of one of Greater Yugoslavia's constituent republics – as Tito would have liked it – the two parties nevertheless broadly concurred in their views about the desirability of a union. However, when their emissaries approached Stalin in January 1945 to solicit his blessing, they found that Stalin was against the idea. Instead, the cautious Soviet dictator made them put the project on hold, pending the clarification of the objections raised against it by his British allies.

As the progress of the war opened up the prospect of a vast expansion of Soviet power and influence in Europe, Stalin had his own problems about how, if at all, he should try to reconcile imperialism with federalism. Contrary to the desires of his zealous Yugoslav disciples and the fears of anticommunists everywhere, he ruled out further expansion of the Soviet Union through forced annexation of sovereign states as constituent units – the method he had applied in 1940 to Estonia, Latvia and Lithuania, and the area of Finland he had made into the Karelo-Finnish Soviet republic.

Stalin did entertain towards the end of the war the expansion of the formal rights and privileges of the already existing Soviet republics, particularly those that had been afflicted by an upsurge of anti-Soviet nationalism during the German occupation, such as Ukraine and Belorussia. In the end, little changed besides the creation of their make-believe foreign and defence ministries, ostensibly in appreciation of the special burden they had borne in fighting the enemy. The charade helped Stalin's successful bid for the admission of the two republics to full membership in the United Nations as if they were real states.

At the same time, Stalin signalled in no uncertain terms his disapproval of any federalist arrangements west of Soviet borders that might enable the smaller European nations to better stand up to him. This concerned not only the stillborn Polish–Czechoslovak confederation but also British encouragement of a regional association in Western Europe, consisting of the low countries and possibly France.[54] In contrast to Churchill's vision of a United States of Europe, the Soviet planners of the postwar order, working in the Moscow foreign ministry under the direction of the former foreign commissar Maxim Litvinov and the former ambassador to London Ivan Maiskii, envisioned a future Europe of sovereign national or multinational states, overshadowed by the Soviet Union as the only remaining great power on the continent.[55]

Both the Soviet Union and its Western sympathizers opposed international federalism as both unrealistic and undesirable. Rudolf Schlesinger, an Austrian political scientist exiled in Britain and the author of still the most useful, if unbalanced, 1945 study of East Central Europe's federalist experiences, shared the Soviet view that only national or multinational states would have a place in Europe's international system in the foreseeable future. He argued that any creation of supranational federal entities was fraught with the danger of another war, allegedly because of their tendency to develop into hostile blocs.[56] He correctly anticipated the Cold War, though not its real causes.

In Western Europe, the trend towards international federalism was an effect rather than a cause of the evolving Cold War, having been largely limited to that area less by Western design than by Eastern default even before the Cold War began. The delimitation reflected the different outlooks of the noncommunist resistance movements in the two parts of the continent. Whereas in the West those movements tended to be patriotic *and* European, in Eastern Europe they were more narrowly nationalist and parochial without the same concern for postwar international reconciliation and accommodation. They left the promotion of the region's only important federalist project in the hands of the Balkan communists.

Stalin's reluctance in 1945 to support the Balkan integration project proposed by his Yugoslav disciples was suggestive of his uncertainty about how, if at all, East Central Europe could be organized to suit Soviet interests. As East–West tension mounted, however, he warmed to the idea. Less inclined to heed Western sensibilities about the integration project, by 1947 he no longer discouraged Tito and his Bulgarian partner, Georgi Dimitrov, from taking further steps towards its realization. At their meeting at Bled in July, the two reached a basic understanding about forming a union between their countries, although Stalin subsequently intervened to make them delay any further steps until the peace treaty with Bulgaria came into effect two months later. Once it did he took no action to prevent them from making public statements favouring a possible expansion of the prospective federation or confederation by including in it Albania, Romania, even Hungary and – most importantly – Greece.[57]

By this time the movement for Western European unity, encouraged not only by Britain but increasingly also by the United States, was gaining momentum. Although nothing as advanced as the Tito–Dimitrov project had yet developed in the West, unlike that project driven by party oligarchs, the support for European integration ran deeper, extended wider and grew more organically. It had been encouraged by the adoption in July 1947 of the Marshall plan, which made its Western European recipients work more closely in pooling their resources, expressing their needs and sharing the American assistance under the auspices of a transnational authority supervised by the United States. All this helped them to gradually acquire the habits and experiences necessary for the successful building of international structures and institutions on a voluntary basis.[58]

The exclusion of the people under Soviet domination from the same kind of formative experience marked a critical divergence in the development of the two parts of divided Europe. Stalin's intervention was decisive in preventing the participation in the Marshall plan of those countries within his sphere of influence that had been interested in participating, particularly Czechoslovakia and Poland. Even before his intervention, however, their interest had been mainly in receiving American economic aid rather than taking part in the international collaboration that was to complement it. The Czechoslovak government, though not yet controlled by the communists, had always made it clear that it would accept the plan only if its special relationship with Moscow would not suffer as a result.[59] In this sense, the Soviet bloc had been in the making even before Stalin acted to formalize it.

In view of these circumstances, the European federalists, who gathered at three major congresses between mid-August and mid-December 1947, simply recognized the reality of the situation when they excluded the pro-Soviet states of East Central Europe from their deliberations.[60] They rightly judged that their own plans would have been undermined, and therefore placed their hopes in the prospective integration of that part of Europe which escaped Soviet domination.

For the same reason, Moscow's satellites were not invited to join the meeting at which the council of Europe was founded in 1949.[61]

There was a connection between the progress of Western European unity accelerated by the Marshall plan and the fate of the Balkan federation. In January 1948, shortly after British foreign secretary Ernest Bevin had made a public plea for advancing not only Western Europe's economic integration but also its political and military integration, to counter the progressing sovietization of Eastern Europe, Stalin abruptly reversed himself by forcing his Yugoslav and Bulgarian followers to shelve the unification project he had previously abetted.[62] At first he toyed with the idea of preserving it as a means of controlling Yugoslavia through Bulgaria, but then decided to enforce the safer option of unifying all his Eastern European dependencies by imposing upon them the Soviet system without any federalist pretences.

In 1948 George F. Kennan, one of the architects of the Marshall plan, feared that the creation of a Western military alliance, which was established the following year in the form of NATO, would prevent 'the development of real federal structures in Europe which would aim to embrace all free European countries, and which would be a political force in its own right'.[63] His concern was misplaced, for the structures continued to develop along different lines, particularly once in 1950 the Schuman plan for the European coal and steel community set the pattern for economic integration under the authority of new transnational institutions. Their particular federalism subsequently became accepted as part and parcel of the international order by millions of Western Europeans.[64]

The communist experience: the legacy of dictatorship

The Soviet response to the rapid progress of Western economic integration after the Marshall plan was the establishment, but not actual utilization, of the council for mutual economic assistance, or Comecon, in January 1949. As long as Stalin was alive, the organization remained little more than an empty shell as the Soviet Union continued to exploit its Eastern European dependencies without any pretence of partnership. Unlike Western Europeans, the citizens of Eastern Europe therefore had good reasons to regard the kind of economic integration they were experiencing as tantamount to plunder.

Stalin mistrusted internal federalism within the part of Europe he controlled as well. In occupied Germany, he opposed the establishment of a federal system of government – ostensibly because of its high cost and inefficiency but in reality because of its being conducive to self-government. Hence the model applied in West Germany was not implemented in East Germany. The only federal experiments in East Central Europe after World War II took place in Czechoslovakia and Tito's Yugoslavia, the latter of which after 1948 remained outside the Soviet bloc. They differed substantially from each other.

At issue in Czechoslovakia was not the establishment of a true federal system but rather its avoidance, by appeasing and sidetracking Slovak demands for autonomy. Slovak communists had initially been ardent advocates of the federal system but after the free elections of 1946, which exposed their limited local base of support, they became supporters of Prague centralism. After the communist party took power in Czechoslovakia in 1948, Slovakia's special status was officially considered neither federal nor autonomous; it was in fact a Soviet-style façade for party centralism. The Bratislava 'board of commissioners', as the term aptly suggested, functioned not as an autonomous executive but as an agency of the central government for the local implementation of matters of secondary importance, while the separate Bratislava parliament was of the same rubber-stamp variety as the national assembly in Prague.[65]

The transformation of Czechoslovakia into a nominally federal state after 1968 was the only apparent concession to the reform movement of that year, in which Slovak demands for self-government had played a secondary role and could be subsequently manipulated as a substitute for the country's democratization.[66] Its Czech and Slovak parts each received separate legislative as well as executive bodies, in addition to which parallel agencies were maintained at the 'federal' level of government as well. No similar reorganization took place within the communist party, whose 'leading role' in the state was enshrined in its constitution, thus ensuring continued centralism.[67] The only significant difference from the previous practice was the increased proportion of Slovaks in the bloated bureaucracy of the intensely unpopular central government, which made future accommodation between two peoples themselves not inclined to accommodation, in a single state more difficult than it would have been otherwise.

Nor was Yugoslav federalism, though a paragon of power-sharing compared with the Soviet case, a system of good government. Instead, it provided a framework for manoeuvring by corrupt party cliques from the different constituent republics in which the communist monopoly of power kept the rest of the population from effectively participating in their self-government.[68] Worse, by creating the wrong impression of such participation, the system poorly prepared the people for demanding genuine federalism. Hence, when the moment of truth came, each ethnic group resorted to crude nationalism, asserting its interests against one another and each without respect for the other, in the end burying the promise of multiethnic federalism amid the orgy of an inter-ethnic war.[69]

In the Soviet Union, the reforms undertaken after Stalin's death did not include attempts at its transformation from a sham into a genuine federation. The May 1953 central committee resolution (adopted on the initiative of the dictator's former security chief Lavrentii P. Beriia) envisaged nothing more substantial than increased employment in the ethnic republics of cadres belonging to the titular nationality. This was a political, rather than constitutional, measure which was, in any case, rescinded as soon as its proponent fell from power the following month.[70] Later on, Nikita S. Khrushchev continued the Stalinist practice of arbitrarily tinkering with the status of the different territorial units by administrative means: the downgrading of the Karelo-Finnish Soviet republic to an 'autonomous' one and the transfer of the Crimean district from Russia to the Ukraine were cases in point. Under the Brezhnev regime, the potentially troublesome question of the meaning of Soviet federalism was characteristically avoided in official party pronouncements, thus giving rise to a genuine, if inconclusive, debate on the subject among the country's political scholars.[71]

Within the Soviet bloc as a whole, the gradual loosening of the Stalinist system after the despot's death manifested itself in the growing reassertion of the diversity of different states amid attempts at their closer integration from above by less brutal means. Symptomatic of the extreme Soviet sensitivity to any sign of attempted integration from below was the near panic that seized the Kremlin in 1968, when it perceived the rapprochement between Czechoslovakia, Romania and Yugoslavia as another 'little entente' in the making. Following the Soviet intervention in Czechoslovakia, the 'Brezhnev doctrine' heralded accelerated efforts to tighten the Soviet Empire under the guise of a 'socialist commonwealth'.

Since the member states of the presumed commonwealth were formally sovereign but in fact beholden to Moscow and consequently subjected to its will, the key question of federalism – that of transferring and sharing sovereignty – did not arise. The formal transfer of sovereignty from the Soviet Union to the German Democratic Republic as early as 1955, which followed a similar action by the Western allies in regard to the federal republic, merely entailed the termination of most of the responsibilities assumed temporarily by the victorious powers at the end of World War II. The net effect was to bring East Germany's status closer to that of other Soviet dependencies – a process accomplished in 1961 by sealing the country's last open border through the construction of the Berlin Wall.

The Soviet bloc's two transnational organizations – Comecon and the Warsaw pact – were created by Moscow as instruments for controlling and managing its allies rather than as an expression of a common will to define and maintain the terms of their partnership. Like Comecon in 1949, the Warsaw pact in 1955 was originally created in response to advancing Western integration. A primarily political undertaking mainly intended to support Khrushchev's contemporary diplomatic initiatives aimed at altering the European security environment in favour of the Soviets, the alliance continued but remained devoid of military substance for several years after those initiatives had failed to bring the desired results.[72]

Instead, Khrushchev from 1956 onwards proceeded to revitalize Comecon as a framework for closer economic cooperation and division of labour under Soviet supervision. Although the organization established common transnational institutions, it hardly bore any resemblance to the West's European economic community (EEC), evolving concurrently after the conclusion in 1957 of the treaty of Rome. Instead, Comecon was very much what Moscow maintained the EEC to be, namely an extended arm of the dominant superpower designed to exploit the economy of its allies for its own benefit.

The dynamism of the Soviet trading bloc contrasted sharply with that of the

West's common market. Within Comecon, the flow of trade linked its smaller members mainly with the Soviet Union rather than with one another, thus restricting rather than expanding their economic cooperation.[73] Hence it was understandable that, once Romania in 1955 successfully asserted its right to decide its own economic priorities against Moscow's attempt to dictate them, the tendency of the members of Comecon was to break out of its restrictions.

Given the paucity of additional candidates for membership, other than communist states outside of Europe and Moscow's impoverished clients in the Third World, Comecon failed to develop the kind of elaborate procedures for bringing in eager new members that became the hallmark of the EEC. Nor did the similarly elaborate voluntary transfer of decision-making powers from the national governments to Brussels, implemented by its member states ever so carefully over the years, have a parallel in the Soviet-dominated part of the continent. While in the long run the prevailing desire in the communist part of Europe was for the weakening, in Western Europe it was for the strengthening of the respective supranational institutions.

Because of its ideological blinders, the Soviet Union proved conceptually incapable of grasping the true nature of the new kind of international federalism that took roots in the West.[74] Falling back on Lenin's polemic against the United States of Europe – whose creation he had regarded 'either impossible or reactionary' under the capitalist system[75] – Soviet analysts interpreted the economic integration initiated by the Schuman plan as an American ploy for the rearmament of West Germany. There was no difference between the interpretation offered to the public and the one insiders believed among themselves. In the expert opinion commissioned confidentially by the Soviet government from the prestigious economist A. Arutunian in 1951, at issue in the economic integration was 'the preparation of a third World War by creating a western European economic base for the aggressive North Atlantic pact under U.S. hegemony'.[76]

Soviet observers could not bring themselves to believe that European integration could take place voluntarily. They saw even its successes as manifestations of contradictions between competing capitalist monopolies, prophesying its ultimate failure. In 1962, Khrushchev for the first time conceded that the 'imperialist integration in Western Europe' was permanent, professing Soviet readiness for 'peaceful political competition not only between the states with different political systems but also between their economic alliances'.[77] It took Moscow another ten years, however, to recognize the European community as a vigorous international organization in its own right rather than a tired creature of American imperialists. Only in the early 1980s, when Comecon's deficiencies had become too glaring to be ignored, did its members begin to seek formal relations with its thriving Western counterpart; even so, lest they become infected by the contagion, the Soviet Union allowed them to do so only as a group rather than individually. By 1989, Comecon's members had come to see the way to Comecon's salvation in its increased collaboration with and adaptation to the EC. By that time, however, it was too late.[78]

Nor did the Warsaw pact organization have the potential to become the training school for the supranational partnership into which NATO developed during the forty years of the Cold War. Transformed into its military counterpart from a mainly political structure only in the late 1960s, the communist alliance was in effect an extended arm of the Soviet ministry of defence. It trained the officer corps of its member states at Soviet military academies in unswerving obedience to Moscow, imbuing them with a mental rigidity poorly suited to the growth of democratic, much less federalist attitudes. The Warsaw pact was used by the Kremlin as an instrument of repression and regimentation of its Eastern European dependencies; once the will to repress and regiment was lost, it simply melted away, leaving behind warped notions about how the strong and the weak could collaborate in a common institutional setting.

After the Cold War: applying Western models

For want of attractive indigenous alternatives, Western international institutions remained the only credible models available to the peoples of East Central Europe as communist rule and the Soviet Empire were approaching their end. Those institutions, however, had not been developed with the intention of application in an area whose separation from the West was widely expected to last for the foreseeable future, if not forever. The reveries of anticommunist exiles in the early years of the Cold War about how their liberated countries could be united after the demise of communism had faded away without noticeable impact.[79]

Prior to the unexpected end of the Cold War, transnational federalist initiatives intended to include in some ways the communist part of Europe were rare and modest. They included in particular the effort of the Hungarian government to forge a special relationship with neighbouring Austria on the premise that small nations on each side of the ideological divide, because of their geographical location, might have a useful role to play in reducing the rigidity of the two power blocs. The one quasi-federalist scheme that was actually put into effect was the Italian-inspired Alpe-Adria project of 1978.

Exploiting for a good purpose the lingering nostalgia for Habsburg Central Europe, the project brought together some of the old empire's former territories in an ingenious attempt to promote collaboration across the ideological boundaries, bypassing the respective national capitals. The collaboration was limited to such relatively uncontentious agenda as culture, tourism, transportation and environment, and gradually involved the Italian regions of Veneto and Friuli-Venezia Giulia, the Austrian *Länder* of Carinthia, Styria and Upper Austria, the Yugoslav republics of Croatia and Slovenia, two Hungarian provinces, and other regional entities as members or interested observers. As a low-key undertaking, the scheme survived the end of communism and briefly blossomed into the Italian-sponsored Pentagonale and Hexagonale after the addition of

Czechoslovakia and Poland, before falling victim to the Yugoslav war and the Italian corruption crisis.[80]

When the Soviet Empire in East Central Europe collapsed, the majority of its inhabitants, regardless of their enthusiasm for European unity, did not have a clear conception of what this meant. What was clearer in their minds was that the Europe they believed in ended at the former Soviet borders, thus including themselves but not the peoples further east whom they tended to look upon with disdain. While thinking of themselves as belonging to the Western-centred Europe, they did not sufficiently grasp the manner of its integration, with its diverse nations' respect for each other, their willingness to part with significant portions of their sovereignty, their acceptance of unfamiliar concepts for the protection of individual and group rights, and the essential requirement of their constant readiness to compromise, all of which had been so conspicuously missing under communist rule.

The obstacles to federalism in East Central Europe, while aggravated by forty years of communism, had been rooted in a much longer historical experience of its peoples. There had been little in that experience that would make the idea attractive or even interesting. Federal structures of any kind had been exceptional and federalist thinking at best marginal in the part of Europe whose modern history had been so prominently shaped by a quest for self-assertion within national states. The notion of a citizen owing legitimate allegiance to more than one state entity had been alien in that region.

Having reached the eastern part of the continent later than the western part, nationalism proved more durable in the former than in the latter; having encountered more resistance in asserting itself, it intensified. It had been the principal force in the emancipation of its peoples from communist internationalism and Soviet hegemony; even as both began to recede from memory, it continued to provide the all but exclusive source of self-identification which in much of Western Europe had been widely complemented, sometimes superseded, by identification with Europe as a whole. With few exceptions, the successor states of the three defunct federations – the Soviet, the Yugoslav and the Czechoslovak – defined themselves as those of their dominant nationalities rather than of all their citizens regardless of ethnicity. The bloody disintegration of the Yugoslav federation was a dismal reminder of the pitfalls of such a concept. Both the residual 'Yugoslav' federation of Serbia and Montenegro and the newly federated Bosnia-Herzegovina faced severe tests of viability.

In East Central Europe, only Germany and, less importantly, post-1918 Austria could boast a substantive and successful federal tradition. The success of internal federalism in West Germany facilitated its smooth and solid integration into a united Europe, making Germans foremost advocates of Europe's further federalist transformation. Quite apart from Germany's economic power, the vitality of both its internal and international federalism positioned it as a key intermediary for the formerly communist countries aspiring for admission into a united Europe. President François Mitterrand's attempt to claim this role for

France by initiating in 1991 his stillborn European confederation project – itself
a successor of a similar non-starter launched by Paris in 1930[81] – only proved
that his country was not up to the task.

For more than a decade after the disintegration of the Soviet Empire, the
prospects for the growth of federalism in postcommunist Europe remained
uncertain. The promise of the 1992 Maastricht treaty, generally judged as having
tried to accomplish too much too soon, is unlikely to be fulfilled any time soon,
despite progress towards closer integration in such important matters as a
common European currency. Nor did the 2000 Nice summit of the European
Union, which affirmed the intent to expand it by including the formerly communist countries, establish clear guidelines concerning the structure of an
enlarged Union. The progress towards it continued to follow the established
pattern of mainly economic cooperation while integration in foreign policy,
security matters, and social legislation lagged behind because of the prevailing
unwillingness to part with sovereignty in these areas that, rightly or wrongly, had
traditionally been regarded as preserves of a national approach.[82]

Such a development did not augur well for the applicability of the federal
model in the prospective integration of additional members from the formerly
communist part of the continent. The association agreements which the
European Union concluded with them in preparation for their eventual membership were understandably and justifiably modest, seeking to help them gradually acquire the habits and patterns of cooperation already established among
the existing members.

At the dawn of the twenty-first century, the European Union remains
despite its shortcomings the unrivalled beacon for the future organization of the
continent. Yet its 'widening' is not any more likely to move it substantially closer
to a federation than is its 'deepening'. The peoples of East Central Europe have
not been adequately conditioned by their history to readily embrace the habits
and attitudes of international federalism. In preparation for their life in a cooperative rather than confrontational Europe, at issue is more an overcoming than
a fulfilling of their historical legacy. It took Western Europeans forty years and a
perceived Soviet threat to make the European Union what it has become. Now
the threat has receded and in a relatively short time Western Europe has become
an inspiration and an incentive.

Notes

1 Of the two brief surveys of federalism in the history of East Central Europe, the former
   attributes greater importance to the pre-nationalist antecedents than the latter: O.
   Halecki, 'Federalism in the history of East Central Europe', *Polish Review* (Summer
   1960), 5–19; R. Wierer, 'Der Föderalismus bei den kleinen und mittleren slawischen
   Völkern', *Der Donauraum*, 4:1 (1959), 3–16.
2 J. W. Sedlar, *East Central Europe in the Middle Ages, 1000–1500* (Seattle: University of
   Washington Press, 1994), p. 355.

3 O. Odlozilik, *The Hussite King: Bohemia in European Affairs, 1440–1471* (New Brunswick: Rutgers University Press, 1965), pp. 152–60.

4 F. Seibt, *Deutschland und die Tschechen: Geschichte einer Nachbarschaft in der Mitte Europas* (Munich: List, 1974), pp. 41–83.

5 I. Kant, *Perpetual Peace: A Philosophical Essay* (Bristol: Thoemmes Press, 1992), p. 128.

6 W. Konopczyński, *Dzieje Polski nowożytnej* [A History of Modern Poland], Vol. 2 (Warsaw: Gebethner and Wolff, 1936), pp. 35–40.

7 N. Davies, *God's Playground: A History of Poland*, Vol. 1 (New York: Columbia University Press, 1982), pp. 321–72.

8 P. S. Wandycz, 'The Polish precursors of federalism', *Journal of Central European Affairs*, 12 (1952–53), 346–55; S. Kalembka (ed.), *Wielka Emigracja i sprawa Polska a Europa, 1832–1864* [The Great Emigration and the Polish Question in Europe] (Toruń: Uniwerzytet Mikołaja Kopernika, 1980).

9 M. Kukiel, *Czartoryski and European Unity, 1770–1861* (Princeton: Princeton University Press, 1955).

10 V. Mastny, 'Italy and East Central Europe: the legacy of history', in V. Mastny (ed.), *Italy and East Central Europe: Dimensions of the Regional Relationship* (Boulder: Westview Press, 1995), pp. 1–16, at pp. 5–7.

11 L. S. Stavrianos, *Balkan Federation: A History of the Movement towards Balkan Unity in Modern Times* (Northampton, Mass.: Smith College, 1944), pp. 51–2, 63–4.

12 L. B. Namier, *The Revolution of Intellectuals* (New York: Anchor Books, 1964), pp. 91–2.

13 F. Palacký, *Gedenkblätter: Auswahl von Denkschriften, Aufsätzen und Briefen* (Prague: Tempsky, 1874), pp. 148–55.

14 R. Schlesinger, *Federalism in Central and Eastern Europe* (London: Kegan Paul, 1945), p. 171.

15 R. A. Kann, *A History of the Habsburg Empire, 1526–1918* (Berkeley: University of California Press, 1974), pp. 311–13.

16 W. A. Jenks, 'Economics, constitutionalism, administrative and class structure in the monarchy', *Austrian History Yearbook*, 3:1 (1967), 32–61, at pp. 34–5, 49–50.

17 C. Jelavich, 'The Croatian problem in the Habsburg Empire in the nineteenth century', *Austrian History Yearbook*, 3:2 (1967), 83–115, at pp. 99–100.

18 T. Prochazka, *The Second Republic: The Disintegration of Post-Munich Czechoslovakia, October 1938–March 1939* (New York: Columbia University Press, 1981); J. B. Hoptner, *Yugoslavia in Crisis, 1934* (New York: Columbia University Press, 1962), pp. 154–5, 169, 198.

19 E. Deuerlein, *Föderalismus: Die historischen und philosophischen Grundlagen des föderativen Prinzips* (Munich: List, 1972), pp. 116–54.

20 In the four-volume publication by R. G. Abdulatipov, L. F. Boltenkova and I. F. Iarov, *Federalizm v istorii Rossii* [Federalism in the History of Russia] (Moscow: Respublika, 1992–93), the term is stretched so far as to amount to nothing less than the manner in which the heterogeneous Russian state has been governed ever since the Middle Ages.

21 B. Jelavich, *History of the Balkans: Eighteenth and Nineteenth Centuries* (Cambridge: Cambridge University Press, 1983), p. 332.

22 H. C. Meyer, *Mitteleuropa in German Thought and Action 1815–1945* (The Hague: Nijhoff, 1955), pp. 58–66. The applicability of the *Zollverein* model for later European integration is questioned by R. H. Duhmke, 'Der deutsche Zollverein als Modell ökonomischer Integration', in H. Berding (ed.), *Wirtschaftliche und politische Integration in Europa im 19. und 20. Jahrhundert* (Göttingen: Vandenhoeck & Ruprecht, 1984), pp. 71–101.

23 R. Wierer, *Der Föderalismus im Donauraum* (Graz: Böhlau, 1960), pp. 104–11; H. Mommsen, *Die Sozialdemokratie und die Nationalitätenfrage im habsburgischen Vielvölkerstaat* (Vienna: Europa, 1963).

24 N. Rjasanoff, 'Karl Marx und Friedrich Engels über die Polenfrage', *Archiv für die Geschichte des Sozialismus und der Arbeiterbewegung*, 1 (1916), 175–221.

25 J. P. Nettl, *Rosa Luxemburg* (Oxford: Oxford University Press, 1969), pp. 500–19.

26 O. H. Radkey, *The Agrarian Foes of Bolshevism: Promise and Default of the Russian Social Revolutionaries, February to October, 1917* (New York: Columbia University Press, 1958), pp. 37–40.

27 V. I. Lenin, *Collected Works*, Vol. 21 (Moscow: Progress, 1960), pp. 339–43.

28 F. Naumann, *Central Europe* (New York: Knopf, 1917).

29 Meyer, *Mitteleuropa in German Thought and Action*, pp. 194–214.

30 R. Szporluk, *The Political Thought of Thomas G. Masaryk* (New York: Columbia University Press, 1981), pp. 92, 115–16.

31 Memorandum by Masaryk to Woodrow Wilson, 1 November 1918, quoted in Meyer, *Mitteleuropa in German Thought and Action*, p. 340.

32 T. G. Masaryk, *The New Europe: The Slav Standpoint* (Lewisburg: Bucknell University Press, 1972), p. 77.

33 R. Pražák (ed.), *T. G. Masaryk a střední Evropa* [T. G. Masaryk and Central Europe] (Brno: Masarykova univerzita, 1994).

34 Schlesinger, *Federalism in Central and Eastern Europe*, pp. 248–74.

35 C. S. Leff, *National Conflict in Czechoslovakia: The Making and Remaking of a State, 1918–1987* (Princeton: Princeton University Press, 1988), pp. 152–3.

36 B. Jelavich, *History of the Balkans: Twentieth Century* (Cambridge: Cambridge University Press, 1983), pp. 146–57.

37 *Ibid.*, pp. 318–19; J. Rothschild, *East Central Europe between the Two World Wars* (Seattle: University of Washington Press, 1974), pp. 221–2.

38 The claim is promoted in M. K. Dziewanowski, *Joseph Piłsudski: A European Federalist, 1918–1922* (Stanford: Hoover Institution Press, 1969).

39 E. Beneš, speech of 21 March 1934, in J. W. Wheeler-Bennett and Stephen Heald (eds), *Documents on International Affairs, 1934* (London: Oxford University Press, 1935), pp. 274–91, at p. 285.

40 P. S. Wandycz, *The Twilight of French Eastern Alliances, 1926–1936* (Princeton: Princeton University Press, 1988), pp. 89, 129, 174.

41 R. Pipes, *The Formation of the Soviet Union: Communism and Nationalism, 1917–23* (Cambridge, Mass.: Harvard University Press, 1964), pp. 242–7, 280–2.

42 R. Pipes, 'The establishment of the Union of Soviet Socialist Republics', in R. Denber (ed.), *The Soviet Nationality Reader: The Disintegration in Context* (Boulder: Westview Press, 1992), pp. 35–86.

43 V. I. Lenin, *Selected Works*, Vol. 10 (New York: International Publishers, 1938), pp. 233–4.

44 G. Gleason, 'The evolution of the Soviet federal system', in Denber (ed.), *The Soviet Nationality Reader*, pp. 107–20.

45 K. D. Bracher, *The German Dictatorship: The Origins, Structure and Effects of National Socialism* (New York: Praeger, 1970), pp. 202–10.

46 N. Rich, *Hitler's War Aims: The Establishment of the New Order* (New York: Norton, 1974), pp. 326–30.

47 W. Loth, 'Die europäische Integration nach dem zweiten Weltkrieg in französischer Perspektive', in Berding (ed.), *Wirtschaftliche und politische Integration in Europa*, pp. 225–46.

48 J. Maritain, 'De la justice politique', in W. Lipgens (ed.), *Europa-Föderationspläne der Widerstandsbewegungen, 1940–1945* (Munich: Oldenbourg, 1968), pp. 183–5.

49 W. Lipgens (ed.), *Documents on the History of European Integration*, Vol. 1: *Continental Plans for European Union 1939–1945* (Berlin: De Gruyter, 1985), pp. 628–37.

50 M. Hodža, *Federation in Central Europe* (London: Jarrolds, 1942).

51 P. S. Wandycz, *Czechoslovak–Polish Confederation and the Great Powers, 1940–1943* (Bloomington: Indiana University Press, 1956).

52 P. Shoup, 'The Yugoslav Revolution: the first of a new type', in T. T. Hammond and R. Farrell (eds), *The Anatomy of Communist Takeovers* (New Haven: Yale University Press, 1975), pp. 258–9.

53 B. Petranović and M. Zečević (eds), *Jugoslovanski federalizam: Ideje i stvarnost, Tematska zbirka dokumenata* [Yugoslav Federalism: Ideas and Formation, Collection of Documents], Vol. 2 (Belgrade: Prosveta, 1987).

54 K. Larres, 'A search for order: Britain and the origins of a Western European Union, 1944–55', in B. Brivati and H. Jones (eds), *From Reconstruction to Integration: Britain and Europe since 1945* (Leicester: University of Leicester Press, 1993), pp. 71–87, at pp. 73–7.

55 'Zaniatsia Podgotovkoi Budushchego Mira' [Preparations for a Future World], *Vestnik Arkhiva Prezidenta Rossiiskoi Federatsii*, 4 (1955), 114–58.

56 Schlesinger, *Federalism in Central and Eastern Europe*, pp. 519–26.

57 V. Mastny, *The Cold War and Soviet Insecurity: The Stalin Years* (New York: Oxford University Press, 1996), pp. 34–7.

58 D. Reynolds, 'The European response: primacy of politics', *Foreign Affairs*, 76:3 (1997), 171–84.

59 V. Mastny, 'Stalin, Czechoslovakia, and the Marshall Plan: new documentation from Czechoslovak archives', *Bohemia* [Munich], 32 (1991), 139–44.

60 G. Zellentin, *Die Kommunisten und die Einigung Europas* (Frankfurt: Athenäum, 1964), pp. 47–9.

61 M.-T. Bitsch, 'Le rôle de la France dans la naissance du Conseil de l'Europe', in R. Poidevin (ed.), *Histoire des débuts de la construction européenne (mars 1948–mai 1950)* (Brussels: Bruylant, 1986), pp. 165–98.

62 Mastny, *The Cold War and Soviet Insecurity*, pp. 37–9.

63 Draft memorandum by Kennan, 26 September 1948, quoted in P. Winand, 'United States–European relationships, 1957–1963' (Oxford: paper presented at the conference 'Acceleration, deepening and enlarging: the European Economic Community, 1957–1963', 21–24 April 1996), p. 3.

64 W. Loth, 'General introduction', in W. Lipgens and W. Loth (eds), *Documents on the History of European Integration*, Vol. 4: *Transnational Organizations of Political Parties and Pressure Groups in the Struggle for European Union, 1945–1950* (Berlin: De Gruyter, 1991), pp. 1–7.

65 E. Táborský, 'Slovakia under communist rule: "democratic centralism" versus "national autonomy"', *Journal of Central European Affairs*, 14 (1954–55).

66 H. G. Skilling, *Czechoslovakia's Interrupted Revolution* (Princeton: Princeton University Press, 1976), pp. 451–89, 870–7.

67 V. V. Kusin, *From Dubcek to Charter 77: A Study of 'Normalisation' in Czechoslovakia* (Edinburgh: Q Press, 1978), pp. 119–23.

68 D. Rusinow (ed.), *Yugoslavia: A Fractured Federalism* (Washington, DC: Wilson Center Press, 1988).

69 S. P. Ramet, *Nationalism and Federalism in Yugoslavia, 1962–1991* (Bloomington: Indiana University Press, 1992), p. 251.

70 Mastny, *The Cold War and Soviet Insecurity*, pp. 179, 186–7.

71 G. Hodnett, 'The debate over Soviet federalism', *Soviet Studies*, 18 (1966–67), pp. 458–81.

72 V. Mastny, 'The Soviet Union and the origins of the Warsaw Pact in 1955', in N. E. Rosenfeldt, B. Jensen and E. Kulavig (eds), *Mechanisms of Power in the Soviet Union* (New York: St. Martin's Press, 2000), pp. 241–66.

73 M. Kaser, *Comecon: Integration Problems of the Planned Economies* (London: Oxford University Press, 1967), pp. 143–4.

74 V. Zubok, 'The Soviet Union and European integration from Stalin to Gorbachev', *Journal of European Integration History*, 2:1 (1966), 85–98.

75 Lenin, *Collected Works*, p. 340.

76 Quoted in K. Zueva, '"Plan Shumana" i Sovetskii Soiuz' [The Schuman Plan and the Soviet Union], in A. S. Namazova and B. Emerson (eds), *Istoriia evropeiskoi integratsii, 1945–1994* [The History of European Integration] (Moscow: Institut vseobshchei istorii RAN, 1995), pp. 55–65, at p. 58.

77 Quoted in A. Grachev, 'Soviet leadership's view of western European integration (1950–1960s)' (Oxford: paper presented at the conference 'Acceleration, deepening and enlarging: the European Economic Community, 1957–1963', 21–24 March 1996), p. 11.

78 V. Zuev, 'Gorbachevskaia perestroika v otnosheniiakh s ES' [Gorbachev's Perestroika in Relations with the EC], in Namazova and Emerson (eds), *Istoriia evropeiskoi integratsii,* pp. 257–66.

79 E. K. Valkenier, 'Eastern European Federation: a study in the conflicting national aims and plans of the exile groups', *Journal of Central European Affairs*, 14 (1955).

80 S. Romano, 'East Central Europe in post-World War I Italian diplomacy', in Mastny (ed.), *Italy and East Central Europe*, pp. 17–34, at pp. 29–31.

81 Schlesinger, *Federalism in Central and Eastern Europe*, p. 446.

82 M. Welsh, *Europe United? The European Union and the Retreat from Federalism* (New York: St. Martin's Press, 1996); D. Sidjanski, *The Federal Future of Europe: From the European Community to the European Union* (Ann Arbor: University of Michigan Press, 2000); M. Burgess, *Federalism and European Union: The Building of Europe, 1950–2000* (New York: Routledge, 2000).

David M. O'Brien

3

The Russian federation and 'functional federalism': lessons from Tatarstan and Chechnya

'Federalization is the only way to preserve Russia as an integral state.' Those are the words of Sergei Shakhrai, Russian minister for nationalities and regional policy, in 1994 when pressing for the need to work out various forms of integration within Russia, based on treaties recognizing the respective competences of the central government and of the republics and regions. He likened the Russian federation to a 'common house where there is room for all forms of self-organization – republics, regions, [and] autonomies'.[1] However, after almost a decade of devolution, in the early 2000s president Vladimir Putin has struggled to reassert central control, with mixed success and a renewed war in Chechnya.

Federalism in the Russian Federation has undergone, and continues to undergo, a massive intergovernmental transformation. The process of federalization, as Shakhrai observed, is fluid and remains in flux. As such, it provides an illuminating case study of a process of federalization and of the changing face of federalism. The next section of this chapter discusses what Professor Sergio Ortino calls 'functional federalism' within a comparative context. The centrifugal forces confronting the Russian Federation are then briefly reviewed. The next two sections are devoted to the Russian Federation's handling of demands for greater autonomy from Tatarstan and Chechnya, as well as to the Federation's handling of other republics and regions. The basic argument, though, may be stated at the outset. From 1991 to 1993, the central government in Moscow had no clear policy for restructuring intergovernmental relations or for dealing with the increasing threat of break-away republics and regions. The 1993 election, and approval of a new constitution, changed that. President Boris Yeltsin's government finally undertook serious negotiations with Tatarstan and achieved a treaty in 1994 that became a model for negotiating subsequent treaties with other republics and regions. In other words, the 1994 treaty became the basis for a new process of federalization and decentralization within the Russian

Federation. Circumstances developed very differently with Chechnya, resulting in a highly unpopular and costly invasion of that republic. An explanation of the different courses taken with Tatarstan and Chechnya is followed by a discussion of the continuing process of federalization and renewed attempts to strengthen central control and to defend the 'common house' in the on-going reconstruction of the Russian Federation.

The fluidity of 'functional federalism'

Federalism appears to be enjoying a world-wide renaissance, from the movement towards decentralization of social and economic programmes in the United States, to the expansion and further integration of the European Union and, possibly, to the reintegration of the Russian Federation. The renewed interest in federative principles arises from competing forces ostensibly pushing in opposite directions but which, arguably, may prove complementary. On the one hand, international economics pull in the direction of emerging federative and confederative systems that promote regional cooperation and common economic interests. On the other hand, the rising tide of nationalism and ethnic identification appear to push in precisely the opposite direction – towards the recognition of ethnic and regional self-determination on smaller scales. Yet, the latter may actually prove complementary to the international economic forces by reinforcing the push towards federal and confederal organizations. The resurgence of interest in federalism underscores the importance of what Professor Ortino calls 'functional federalism'; that is, a federalism capable of 'redesigning and reshaping' itself 'upwards', 'downwards' and 'outwards'.[2]

Federalism has too often been studied primarily in structural terms. Political scientist William Riker, for example, defined federalism as 'a political organization in which the activities of government are divided between regional governments and a central government in such a way that each kind of government has some activities on which it makes final decisions'.[3] This definition is not very helpful, however, largely because its generality does not take one very far. Arend Lijphart elaborated on the definition of federalism by specifying certain structural characteristics of federal systems.[4] Like Riker's definition of federalism, Lijphart's list of structural features associated with federalism rests on the fundamental distinction that, in a federal system, the central government possesses the power to make policy directly affecting individuals in states or regional units without the formal compliance of the states or regional governments. By contrast, in a confederation, the central government has authority over the regional government but not directly over individuals. Regional governments possess 'sovereignty'. This regional sovereignty was exemplified by the brief experiment with the Articles of Confederation of the United States, for instance. Confederative systems are therefore ultimately dependent on the cooperation of regional governments in order to exercise authority.

Such structural approaches to federalism invite criticism, however.[5] Federalism, as Daniel Elazar and others contend, 'is as much a matter of process as structure'. In Elazar's words:

> Elements of a federal process include a sense of partnership on the part of the parties to the federal compact, manifested through negotiated cooperation on issues and programs and based on a commitment to open bargaining between all parties to an issue in such a way as to strive for consensus or, failing that, an accommodation which protects the fundamental integrity of all partners.[6]

In addition, as Vojtech Mastny observes, there are good grounds for no longer 'drawing a sharp distinction between federation and confederation'. That is both because 'there have been few, if any, pure models of either kind' and because it is 'the process or tendency in either direction that matters'.[7] Indeed, from a comparative perspective, the difference between federative and confederative systems appears one of degree, not of kind, and recent developments increasingly bear this out. In short, federalism and federative principles are fluid, as a comparison of federalism in Canada, Germany, Switzerland and the United States underscores. Although diverse, each of those federal systems bears a 'family resemblance'. So too, the process of federalization is always, more or less, in flux, as illustrated by the historic changes in relations between state and national governments in the United States, among other countries.

Concomitantly, the concept of 'sovereignty' is undergoing a fundamental transformation, due not only to the collapse of the former Soviet Union but also to international treaties and agreements, such as the North American Free Trade Agreement and developments in both Western and Central–Eastern Europe. Because of international economic forces and treaties, 'sovereignty' has become clouded, ambiguous and, put differently, no longer generally considered worth fighting over. That appears to be the lesson from the Western European experience over the last four decades as the European Coal and Steel Community, composed of six countries, grew into the European Economic Community with twelve countries, and in 1995 started the transformative process into the European Union, with a membership of fifteen countries and even greater enlargement to twenty-five countries in 2004.

Although beyond the scope of this chapter, the development of federative structures and organizations in Western Europe would appear to demand the reconsideration of 'sovereignty' and 'subsidiarity' in light of the European Union's drive towards even greater integration of socio-economic regulations.[8] As discussed in the next section, in the 1990s the Russian Federation moved in the opposite direction towards maintaining its territorial integrity while achieving reintegration through a devolution of power from the central government to the republics and regions. Developments in both the European Union and the Russian Federation demonstrate the importance and fluidity of 'functional federalism'.

Centrifugal forces and the Russian Federation

The post-1989 changes in Eastern and Central Europe demonstrated the historical fragility of the existing borders. To put the matter into historical perspective:
'Less than a quarter of [European borders] predate the nineteenth century,
about a quarter had been established around the time of World War I
(1910–1922), and about one-third emerged in the aftermath of World War II.
Well over half of all European borders are twentieth-century creations.'[9] Some
scholars became preoccupied with the fragmentation of Europe – Western,
Central and Eastern – along ethnic and nationalistic lines. Nation-states were
said to be going the way of empires by dividing into regions. Politicians talked
about the inexorable 'parade of sovereignties'.[10]

The disintegration of the former Soviet Union appeared (and still appears)
to threaten the Russian Federation itself. Russia, the largest and dominant
republic in the former Soviet Union, was one of three republics to declare the
demise of the Soviet state on 19 December 1991. On that day, the former Soviet
Union's constituent republics were declared autonomous states and a
Commonwealth of Independent States was created to coordinate economic,
defence and foreign affairs policies for Russia, the Ukraine and Belarus. The
Russian Federation itself now includes 21 autonomous respublikas (ethnically
defined provinces), 49 oblasts (provinces without ethnic identification), 6 krais
(district or county containing smaller ethnic subdivisions, or okrugs), 1 autonomous oblast, 10 autonomous okrugs (ethnic subdivisions of a krai or oblast),
and 2 federal cities (Moscow and St Petersburg).

Moreover, the fragmentation of the Russian Federation appeared to cut
along ethnic and regional lines. The Chechens, the Ingushs, the Tatars and the
Yakuts proclaimed their own sovereignty. Initial attempts to counter ethno-
nationalism and claims of regional autonomy in 1991–93 did not work well. The
fact that Russia includes over a hundred different nationalities compounded the
problems of ethno-nationalism.[11] Russia's problems are also external affairs,
since 25 million Russians live outside Russia, primarily in Kazakhstan, Ukraine,
Moldavia and the Baltic states.

Still, the more serious centrifugal forces facing the Russian Federation arose
not primarily from ethnic nationalism, but instead from regional conflicts due to
the ineffectiveness of the central government. In other words, the major problems
with the potential for the further disintegration of the Russian Federation are
different from those that brought about the collapse of the Soviet Union,
Czechoslovakia and Yugoslavia. In contrast to the former Soviet Union, in which
non-Russian republics constituted about 25 per cent of its territory and about 50
per cent of its population, non-Russians amount to only 18 per cent of the Russian
Federation's population, leaving over 80 per cent ethnic Russian. Only in the
northern Caucasus republics of Dagestan, Chechnya, Chuvashia and Kabardino-
Balkaria, as well as North Ossetia, does the percentage of the titular nationality
constitute more than 50 per cent. Russians are substantially outnumbered only in

Dagestan and Chechnya, where they account, respectively, for only 9.2 and 23 per cent of those republics' populations. Furthermore, even in other republics where ethnic Russians are outnumbered, Russians make up substantial portions of the respective populations. In Tatarstan, for instance, Tatars outnumber Russians by only 48.5 to 43.3 per cent.[12] Thus, as political scientists Reneo Lukic and Allen Lynch argue: 'The danger of Chechnya is not one of an impending *ethnic* disintegration of Russia but rather that, by dramatizing the collapse of effective civil and military institutions within Russia, it may accelerate and thus transform a fragmentation of authority within Russia that is already far advanced.'[13]

In any event, by the mid-1990s the growing centrifugal forces and the ineffectiveness of the central administration gave Yeltsin's government little option but to develop a process of federalization in order to preserve the Russian Federation's territorial integrity, while accommodating the increasingly conflicting interests of the republics and regions.

Toward reintegration: Tatarstan and the Russian Federation

In the words of Tatarstan's vice-president Vasily Likhachev: 'Tatarstan became a kind of a test ground for the evolution of [a] new federalism.'[14] The 1994 Russia–Tatarstan treaty provided, in Likhachev's words, 'a model [for the] state–legal structure of the Russian Federation'. He understood that 'against the background of armed conflicts taking place in the world [most notably in Chechnya]', 'this [treaty] assumes ever greater importance'.[15] The treaty indeed provided a basis for an on-going process of federalization within the Russian Federation.

In 1990, Tatarstan and Chechnya both declared their own sovereignty, but subsequently pursued very different paths. To be sure, both republics were encouraged to do so by Boris Yeltsin who, during his campaign for the presidency against president Mikhail Gorbachev, urged the republics to assert their sovereignty and to support economic and political reforms. The religious factor was also certainly a consideration in the path to greater regional autonomy and a process of federation. Muslims form the majority in both Tatarstan and Chechnya, while they compose only 12 per cent of the Russian Federation's total population. Moreover, in 1993 Muslims held just 14 (3.1 per cent) of the then 450 seats in the Duma, the lower house of parliament, and complained of longstanding discrimination. Tatarstan and Chechnya thus appeared to present serious problems of ethnic rivalries, potentially threatening the integrity of the Russian Federation. This threat was borne out in the case of Chechnya, where its relations with Russia deteriorated into years of fighting. However, Tatarstan's signing of the 1994 treaty with the Russian Federation held out the promise of establishing a 'functional federalism'.

Tatarstan issued a Declaration of State Sovereignty on 30 August 1990, becoming the first republic within Russia to proclaim its sovereignty. Tatarstan's

Declaration appeared tantamount to, but actually fell short of, a declaration of independence. Notably, it omitted any reference to the republic not remaining part of the Russian Federation. In contrast, Chechnya proclaimed both its sovereignty and its independence from the Russian Federation.

Between 1990 and 1992, authorities in Moscow negotiated three treaties, collectively known as the Russian federation treaty of 1992. This treaty, along with the constitution, aimed to preserve the Russian Federation. Unlike Bashkortostan, Yakutia-Sakha and other republics, however, Tatarstan and Chechnya refused to sign the Russian federation treaty. As a result, tensions grew between those two republics and the central government in Moscow. Although some jurists and Kremlin officials argued that the 1992 Federative Treaty 'envisages decentralization of the state and gives legal grounds for removal of tension in many spheres', it did not go far enough towards decentralization for either Tatarstan or Chechnya.

In April 1991, Tatarstan revised its constitution's preamble and other articles to reject the supremacy of Russian law and legislation. Specifically, Article 61 of its constitution states: 'The Republic of Tatarstan is a sovereign state and a subject of international law, associated with the Russian Federation/Russia on the basis of a Treaty on Mutual Delegation of Powers and Objects of Jurisdiction.' Tatarstan, then, appeared to go further the following year by scheduling for March 1992 a referendum asking voters to decide whether they supported 'basing relations with the Russian Federation and other republics and states on treaties between equal partners'.[16]

Tatarstan's 1992 referendum appeared to constitute an early move towards the creation of a confederate system out of the former Soviet Union and its principal successor, the Russian Federation. The 1992 referendum would ostensibly 'cement' Tatarstan's 'special status' as a 'sovereign state and subject of international law associated with the Russian Federation'. That formula had been, in fact, already incorporated into Tatarstan's constitution.

Remarkably, Tatarstan's move towards greater autonomy was initially largely ignored by authorities in Moscow. However, the central government could not ignore Tatarstan's 1992 referendum, nor its refusal to send tax collections to Moscow. Although Tatarstan was not the only state or region within the Russian Federation to do so, it appeared to be at the forefront of a 'parade of sovereignties' threatening to tear the Russian Federation apart. Prior to Tatarstan's March 1992 referendum, a group of Russian deputies in Moscow petitioned the Russian constitutional court to review the referendum's constitutionality. The court promptly held a hearing, which representatives from Tatarstan refused to attend. Within days, it declared Tatarstan's 1990 Declaration of Sovereignty and its proposed 1992 referendum to be in violation of the Russian constitution. Subsequently, the Russian parliament passed a resolution directing Yeltsin to enforce the constitutional court's ruling on Tatarstan's referendum. The parliament also called on Tatarstan to sign the 1992 federation treaty and to enact legislation bringing its constitution into accord with the court's ruling, thereby joining the Russian Federation.

The principal provisions for the Russian constitutional court's ruling are less important than Tatarstan's reaction to the ruling, because the court had warned that Tatarstan's failure to comply with the ruling would present 'a collapse of the constitutional order'.[17] Tatarstan, nonetheless, defied the court and held its referendum, which won overwhelming approval. In retrospect, in the words of constitutional law scholar Herman Schwartz, 'once the forces of nationalism, resentment, and separatism took command in Tatarstan, they [inexorably] would produce defiance of a court decision opposing them. The central authority that the court was trying to assert was the very thing being challenged by Tatarstan in the referendum.'[18]

Circumstances within the Russian Federation grew worse and resulted in the violent end of the parliamentary government on 4 October 1993. President Yeltsin then governed by executive decree, while a constitutional convention he had convened worked on drafting a new constitution. The tensions between Moscow and Kazan, the capital of Tatarstan with a population of over one million, continued to escalate during this period. An initial draft of the convention's proposed constitution alarmed Tatarstan's president Mintimer Shaimiyev and the speaker of Tatarstan's Supreme Soviet, Farid Mukhametshin. They promptly issued a joint statement criticizing the draft for 'minimizing and modifying the very idea of a qualitatively new type of federative relations'. The draft, in their view, 'ignore[d] the legislative initiative of the Tatarstan Republic urging a new concept of federalism in Russia and the formalization in its Fundamental Law of the principle of constitutionally-based treaty relations between the Russian Federation and the Republic of Tatarstan'.[19]

Throughout the autumn and winter of 1993, Tatarstan and Chechnya increasingly demanded greater control over socio-economic policy. Both looked towards establishing treaties with the Russian Federation that would recognize their respective 'sovereignty'. Chechnya, unlike Tatarstan, also continued pressing for recognition of its independent status.

On 25 December 1993, Yeltsin's constitution officially went into effect. The new constitution ostensibly stripped the republics of their 'sovereignty' while strengthening central control, particularly the powers of the president.[20] This aspect of the 1993 Russian constitution drew sharp protests from not only the leaders of Tatarstan and Chechnya. Murtaza Rakhimov, chair of the Bashkortostan Supreme Soviet, summarized the opposition of leaders of several republics: 'The time when the Kremlin could dictate to the peoples of the regions how they should live is past.'[21]

In spite of opposition from Tatarstan, Chechnya and several other republics, Article 5 of the 1993 constitution states that

> the federated structure of the Russian Federation shall be based on its state integrity, the uniform system of state power, delimitation of scopes of authority and powers between the bodies of the state power of the Russian Federation and the bodies of state power of the subjects of the Russian Federation, equality and self-determination of the peoples in the Russian Federation.

The 1993 constitution of the Russian Federation by no means laid to rest the on-going controversies over Tatarstan's and Chechnya's demands for greater autonomy.[22] However, after the people of Tatarstan refused to vote in two all-Russian referenda, Yeltsin ordered in 1994 the negotiation of a bilateral treaty with Tatarstan. Within six weeks, though, to be sure, following three years of on-and-off talks between Moscow officials and leaders in Kazan, the treaty was fully drafted. Finally, on 21 March 1994, the leaders of Russia and Tatarstan signed a treaty, whereas the situation in Chechnya grew worse and Russian troops were eventually sent into Chechnya.

In retrospect, as important as Yeltsin's initiative was Tatarstan's willingness to step back from earlier demands for recognition as a 'sovereign state' and a 'subject of international law'. Moscow adamantly opposed such language from the outset of the negotiations. As Yeltsin explained in 1993, if the republics and regions were recognized as having 'sovereign' status, there would no longer be a Russian Federation but rather a 'confederative structure'. That was completely unacceptable, Yeltsin underscored, because it presupposed the possibility of 'secession from the Federation at any time'.[23] Throughout the crisis period of 1992–93 and the negotiation process during the winter of 1994, leaders in Tatarstan, unlike in Chechnya, rejected any discussion of secession. Significantly, unlike the leadership in Chechnya, Tatarstan's president Shaimiyev consistently spoke cautiously about his republic's quest for greater autonomy and a new federative relationship with Moscow. In April 1992, for instance, when addressing the First Congress of the Tatar Business Community on the government's refusal to sign the Treaty of the Russian Federation, Shaimiyev explained that while 'seeking republican sovereignty, we cannot speak of immediate and complete independence. On the other hand, we cannot sign the [1992 Russian] Federative Treaty as it is. It is the matter of [negotiations to find a] treaty with Russia to find a new formula of Tatarstan status, while preserving the integrity of the Russian Federation.'[24] In short, in spite of the contradictions between the constitutions of Tatarstan and the Russian Federation on the issue of 'sovereignty', there was a basis for developing a process of 'functional federalism'.

Instead of conceding Tatarstan's 'sovereignty', the 1994 treaty recognized that Tatarstan:

> As a state, is united [not associated] with the Russian Federation by the Constitution of the Russian Federation, the Constitution of the Republic of Tatarstan, and by the treaty on the demarcation of areas of responsibility and the mutual delegation of powers between the organs of state power of the Russian Federation and the organs of state power of the Republic of Tatarstan, and participates in international and foreign economic relations.[25]

Article 2 delineates the powers of Tatarstan, including responsibility for the protection of human and civil rights; for taxation and the republic's budget; for social and environmental policies; and, most notably, it outlines Tatarstan's authority to enter into treaties and to establish relationships with other regions and local governments as well as foreign countries, provided they 'do not run counter to the Constitution and the international obligations of the Russian Federation, the Constitution of the Republic of Tatarstan, or this treaty'. Article 3 in turn delineates the powers shared by the Russian Federation and Tatarstan, while Article 4 lists seventeen powers reserved exclusively for the Russian Federation.

The 1994 treaty between the Russian Federation and Tatarstan signified the Russian Federation's move towards decentralization. The treaty acknowledged the competences of the republics or, put differently, the incompetences of the central government's bureaucracies. To be sure, the then president Yeltsin and other Russian leaders continue to talk of the federation and the inviolate 'constitutional principle of our federation's structure'.[26] Indeed, in agreeing to the treaty, Tatarstan accepted the indivisible sovereignty of the Russian Federation. At the same time, however, it achieved recognition of 'the demarcation of areas of responsibility and the mutual delegation of powers between the organs of state power of the Russian Federation and the organs of state power of the Republic of Tatarstan'.[27] Notably, Tatarstan retained control over its natural resources and won acceptance of its right to independently participate in international relations as well as to conduct foreign economic relations. In addition, Tatarstan retains Article 61 of its constitution, proclaiming the republic's 'sovereignty'. The 1994 treaty with the Russian Federation did not call for amending its constitution to conform with that of the Russian Federation. In sum, the contradictions over 'sovereignty' in the two constitutions were allowed to stand. Their resolution would have been an insurmountable barrier to the creation of a 'functional federalism'.

When the treaty was signed, Tatarstan president Mintimer Shaimiyev stressed that 'the treaty was concluded on the basis of two constitutions now in force – those of Russia and Tatarstan, not violating these fundamental laws but being guided by them'. In an interview on 12 February 1994 with *Rossiiskaya Gazeta*, he further described the treaty as a 'document which proclaims the primacy of the human being, and the [new] principles of Tatarstan's relationships with the Russian Federation, foreign states, and international organizations'. The treaty, he emphasized, recognizes 'the right to self-determination, equality, defense of sovereignty and territorial integrity, and the single economic space. Tatarstan exclusively owns and uses its land.'[28]

Tatarstan won more independence from Moscow's central government than any other republic at the time. It was able to do so because leaders in Moscow and Kazan deliberately side-stepped the thorny issue of sovereignty. Instead, they focused on the practical matters of intergovernmental relations and socio-economic policy. As Yeltsin put it, in a rather glib repetition of one of his campaign promises, when travelling to Tatarstan shortly after signing the treaty, Tatarstan 'may take as much sovereignty as [it] can swallow'.[29]

Tatarstan's treaty with the Russian Federation became possible, according to Shakhrai, the Russian minister for nationalities and regional policy, because negotiators concentrated on settling concrete policy disputes. They dropped preoccupations with 'political and national ambitions' as well as abstract concepts such as 'sovereignty'. 'Tatarstan moved towards a compromise by not insisting on the wording giving them some kind of superstatus', in Shakhrai's words, while 'Russia yielded, let's say, the ambitions of the centre to decide everything in Moscow, and will leave the republic a larger sum of tax revenues'.[30]

The issue of sovereignty remains blurred and controversial. Both sides talk at times in terms of their respective sovereignty – the sovereignty of the Russian Federation and that of Tatarstan. On the one hand, Tatarstan's agreeing to hold parliamentary elections for representatives to the Russian parliament 'is the recognition of Russian sovereignty on the territory of the republic of Tatarstan', as Sergei Shakhrai contended.[31] On the other hand, Tatarstan's prime minister Muhammat Sabirov claimed that the treaty did not deprive Tatarstan of sovereignty or the freedom of foreign economic activity, though the republic renewed its commitment to contributing its share of federal taxes.

The treaty between Russia and Tatarstan, nonetheless, was a watershed event. It remains a landmark in the development of federative relationships based on a new regional policy for the reintegration of the Russian Federation. Moscow described the treaty as a 'breakthrough in the promotion of federative relations'.[32] In the words of Sergei Shakhrai, the treaty 'ends a dangerous political crisis and the threat of an interethnic conflict'. Similarly, in the summer of 1994, Sergei Filatov, Yeltsin's chief of staff, optimistically observed that 'Russia is not threatened with a fate similar to that of the broken-up Soviet Union'. Pointing specifically to the bilateral treaty with Tatarstan as a prologue for a new regional policy, Filatov claimed that the treaty strengthened the federation, while at the same time moving the Russian Federation towards 'the establishment of new relations between the centre and the component parts of the federation'.[33]

The alternative path: Chechnya

Following Moscow's and Kazan's agreement on a bilateral treaty, Sergei Shakhrai called for normalizing relations with Chechnya through the negotiation of a similar treaty. In 1993 and 1994, Yeltsin also repeatedly called for treaty negotiations with Chechnya. These meetings, when convened, proved unproductive and Yeltsin maintained an uncompromising stance towards Chechnya's separatist leaders. In the autumn of 1991 he had initially ordered troops into the breakaway republic but withdrew them in the face of opposition in the Russian parliament. Three years later, on 10 December 1994, Yeltsin again ordered Russian armed forces into Chechnya, a move which was unpopular and grew increasingly costly. Thousands of Russian soldiers and several thousand Chechen fighters, as well as over thirty thousand other residents, died in the fighting. Indeed, the Russian Federation's military casualties in Chechnya exceeded the former Soviet Union's losses in its decade-long war with Afghanistan from 1979 to 1989.

A partial peace accord with Chechnya was reached on 30 July 1995, but the fighting continued. Another temporary breakthrough was made on 8 December 1995, when Russia signed an agreement with Chechnya. That agreement recognized Chechnya's 'special status', but it did not extend the same sort of economic autonomy that Tatarstan had received, although the agreement did devolve authority to Chechnya to undertake trade and other foreign relations.

Within two weeks of signing the 1995 treaty agreement between the Russian Federation and Chechnya, elections were held in Chechnya, with Doku Zavgayev winning the presidency. Zavgayev, the former chairman of the Supreme Soviet of Chechneno-Ingushetia, was strongly backed by Yeltsin's government. Zavgayev promised to negotiate further agreements with the Russian Federation and Chechnyan separatists, but almost immediately the latter resumed fighting which continued into 1996.

According to Moscow officials, the use of military force in Chechnya in December 1994 was necessary to preserve the territorial integrity of the Russian Federation, yet Chechnya had declared its sovereignty and independence three years earlier. Hence, the question arises as to why Yeltsin did not press for a negotiated solution with Chechnya, as he did with Tatarstan. Writing in *Foreign Policy*, Michael McFaul argued that the December 1993 parliamentary elections convinced Yeltsin to adopt tougher policies towards Chechnya for three reasons. First, his pro-reform electoral bloc, Russia's choice, fared poorly at the polls. Vladimir Zhirinovsky's liberal democratic party won almost a quarter of the electorate's vote with its appeal to nationalistic sentiments in a law-and-order campaign. Secondly, the outcome of the elections deepened divisions between Yeltsin and his inner circle, on the one hand, and other reformist leaders and organizations, on the other. Thirdly, the 1993 elections in turn had consequences for the drafting of a new constitution. During the preceding two years, Moscow's central government had had confusing and ambiguous relations with the republics, besides facing growing demands for greater autonomy from Tatarstan and Chechnya, among other republics and regions. The 1993 constitution offered a potential solution by clarifying that all republics, oblasts and small states were equal subjects of the federation. It also held out the promise of legal resolutions to the growing number of centre–regional conflicts. 'While bilateral negotiations between Moscow and the other republics continued through 1994', McFaul argued, 'only one republic – Chechnya – held out against recognizing the new constitutional basis for Russia's federal framework. In 1994, therefore, Chechnya's independence became the exception rather than the rule and was a major eyesore for a Russian president seeking to consolidate and strengthen state power.'[34]

McFaul's analysis tells only part of the story. Equally important were Tatarstan's and Chechnya's respective historical conflicts with and ties to Russia, as well as the differences in the leadership of each of those republics. Unlike Tatarstan, Chechnya and other republics in the North Caucasus have warred periodically with Russia for centuries. These North Caucasus republics, as noted earlier, constitute both the most ethnically diverse and the most densely populated region within the Russian Federation. After World War II, the former Soviet Union undertook a massive deportation of Chechnya's population, along with those of Inguish, Karachai to Central Asia, because of resistance to Soviet collectivization.[35] In short, bitterness between Chechnens and Russians is deep seated.[36] In contrast, land-locked Tatarstan remains dependent on Russia for the processing of its oil and gas production. Tatarstan is larger and, arguably, economically more significant than Chechnya for the Russian Federation because it produces approximately 10 per cent of Russia's oil and has some of Russia's largest industrial plants. Chechnya and other North Caucasus republics make up a major agricultural region and, although having low levels of industrial development, have major geopolitical and economic importance due to the oil fields around Grozny and because the only pipeline and railway from the Caspian Sea run through Grozny and Chechnya. As a result, the North Caucasus republics are highly dependent on subsidies from the central government, yet are viewed as geographically strategic because they are at the crossroads between the Caspian and Black Seas and, hence, the bridge for trade between the North and South, as well as the East and West.

The differences in leadership of the republics also contributed to the differing paths taken in relations with Russia. Tatarstan's president Mintimer Shaymiyev was never as militant or as separatist in his demands for greater autonomy and local control over economic and social policy. Shaymiyev remained a pragmatist, firmly committed to working out a process of federalization and decentralization. By doing so, he was able to mollify more extreme Tatar nationalists who, like Chechnya separatists, had called for the republic's complete independence.

In contrast to Tatarstan, when Chechnya proclaimed its sovereignty and independence, Zavgayev was ousted from office by General Dzhokhar Dudayev, who had earlier adopted an anti-Soviet stance as commander of Soviet airforces in Estonia. Dudayev was much less interested in compromise or negotiating with Moscow than Tatarstan's president Shaymiyev. In response, Yeltsin's government made little effort at negotiating. Yeltsin's government and the military were wedded to a strategy of using military force. Indeed, with the Russian constitutional court's ruling that the intervention in Chechnya was 'absolutely constitutional' and the fighting continuing into 1996, Russian leaders grew even more resistant to negotiations with Dudayev's separatists. Still, mounting opposition within Russia increased pressure on Yeltsin to find a solution before the June 1996 elections.[37]

A settlement was reached with the signing of the Khasavyurt Accords on 31 August 1996, followed by the signing of the Chechen–Russian treaty on 12 May 1997. The critical issue of Chechnya's status within the Russian Federation, however, was postponed for five years. Moreover, the underlying constitutional and political conflicts between Chechnya and the Russian Federation remained unresolved.[38] In the autumn of 1999, violence in Chechnya again erupted and has continued. Then, after the international terrorist attacks on the World Trade

Center and the Pentagon on September 11 2001, and later elsewhere, Putin esca-lated the war in Chechnya and defended renewed aggression as part of the global war against terrorism. Yet, the seizure of the Dubrovka theatre in Moscow by Chechen fighters in October 2002 that resulted in a gas attack by Russian secur-ity forces, killing nearly 130 hostages, underscores the persistence of Russia's problems in Chechnya. Whether a 23 March 2003 referendum on a new consti-tution for Chechnya, endorsed by the European Union Commission on Human Rights and which would keep Chechnya under Russian control, marks the resumption of a political resolution to the conflict remains to be determined.[39]

Decentralization and recentralization in the reconstruction of the Russian Federation

After the treaty between Tatarstan and the Russian Federation, the latter entered into similar arrangements with other republics and regions. Russia signed treaties on the 'division of competence spheres and powers' with Kabardino-Balkariya and Bashkorotostan in 1994. The following year it agreed to treaties with Karachaevo-Cherkessiya, North Ossetia, Yakutia-Shakha, Buryatia, Udmurtia and Itkutsk. On the occasion of signing the treaty with Buryatia, Yeltsin reflected on the new course in the federalization of Russia: 'Russian regions must learn to solve most of their problems independently.'[40] In fact, the central government in Moscow had little alternative other than to negotiate such agreements because of its failure to deliver promised funding, supplies and social services.

In addition, in January 1996 Yeltsin's administration entered into agree-ments with a series of oblasts and krais. The regions increasingly resented the Russian Federation's special treaties with the republics and, hence, demanded their own treaties. Likewise, they resented the central government's failure to provide goods and social services. Eduard Rossel, governor of the Urals region of Sverdlovsk who had earlier defeated a Yeltsin candidate in a key election, reached the first of those agreements, after demanding for several years prefe-rential tax terms. Next, Kaliningrad, an important industrial port on the Baltic Sea and a detached enclave of the Federation, located between Poland and Lithuania, secured its deal. They were followed by Orenburg, which borders the Central Asian state of Kazakhstan, and Krasnodar, which is located on the edge of the North Caucasus.

The story of the Russian Federation's treaties with these regions is much the same as that with the republics. Moscow's central government was forced to enter into agreements with these outlying regions in order to preserve the Russian Federation – a federation which had become precarious because of the central government's inability to pay salaries on time and to provide effective law enforcement as well as other goods and social services. The ineffectiveness of the central government was underscored by its inability in 1994–95 to collect more than 50 per cent of the tax revenue required for its budget. On the signing of its treaty, Orenburg's governor, Uladimar Yelagin, for instance, emphasized that the regional legislature could now pass laws, which the Russian parliament had failed to do, controlling the immigration of refugees from Central Asia.

Notably, the treaty signed on 26 June 1995 between Moscow and Yakutia-Shakha surpassed, in terms of the political and economic freedoms recognized, the treaty concluded with Tatarstan. Moreover, Russia faced no ethnic rivalries or divisions in dealing with Yakutia-Shakha. Moscow thus not only conceded Yakutia-Shakha's right to sovereignty as of 1991, but also acknowledged its right to diplomatic representation. More importantly, under the treaty Yakutia-Shakha became the recognized owner of its natural resources. Instead of turning over to Moscow 100 per cent of its profits from mining precious metals, Yakutia-Shakha negotiated ownership of 26 per cent of its diamond output, 30 per cent of its gold output, and slightly smaller percentages of its oil and gas production.

The treaty between the Russian Federation and Tatarstan remains significant in more ways than one. The treaty not only averted armed conflict but, equally importantly, it pointed towards, in the words of Tatarstan's president Shaymiyev, 'a stage of positive cooperation' and 'the path of formation'.[41] That 'path of formation' ran throughout the 1990s towards the further development of a functional and asymmetrical federalism – a federalism at once fluid and in flux.

President Yeltsin's successor, however, embarked on a process of reversing course and reasserting central authority. Shortly after his inauguration in May 2000, president Putin appointed seven envoys to oversee new administrative districts that were superimposed on top of the existing eighty-nine republics and regions. They were charged with bringing local laws into conformity with federal law and the constitution, as well as reasserting central authority. Within a year, it was apparent that they were having only mixed success in dealing with often rebellious leaders of various republics, including Tatarstan and other regions.[42] By the end of 2002, when new federal reforms for local governance were introduced by Putin, there was growing separatist opposition in Tatarstan and other republics in the Volga region. The matter of Tatarstan's 'sovereignty' also remained a matter of continuing and serious dispute.

Thus, the Russian Federation remains in flux, still struggling to reconstruct and defend a 'common house', based on an ad hoc patchwork of bilateral treaties made in the 1990s that devolved power in order to preserve the Federation, but also threatened to become a 'house of cards' without the reimposition of central authority and accountability. Whether Putin's reassertion of central control ultimately strengthens the 'common house' or has the opposite effect of collapsing a 'house of cards' remains to be seen. In sum, as elsewhere in the world,[43] the process of federalization remains fluid, with the ebb and flow of power between the centre and the periphery constantly changing and shifting.

Notes

1 Quoted in L. Yakovelev, 'To build the Russian Federation', *Parker School Journal of East European Law*, 1 (1994), p. 1.

2 S. Ortino, 'The applicability of the federative model in the relations between States in Postcommunist Europe' (Bologna: paper presented at the meeting of the Pan-European Research Planning Group, Johns Hopkins University Center, Italy, March 1995).

3 W. Riker, 'Federalism', in F. Greenstein and N. Polsby (eds), *Handbook of Political Science: Governmental Institutions and Processes*, 5 (Reading, MA: Addison-Wesley, 1975), p. 101.

4 A. Lijphart, 'Non-majoritarian democracy: a comparison of federal and consociational theories', *Publius: The Journal of Federalism*, 15 (1985), 4.

5 See, e.g., J. Steiner and R. Dorff, 'Structure and process in consociationalism and federalism', *Publius: The Journal of Federalism*, 15 (1985), 49; R. Dorff, 'Federalism in eastern Europe: part of the solution or part of the problem?', *Publius: The Journal of Federalism*, 15 (Spring 1994), 99.

6 D. Elazar, 'Federalism and consociational regimes', *Publius: The Journal of Federalism*, 15 (1985), p. 22.

7 V. Mastny, 'The historical experience of federalism in East Central Europe' (Bologna: paper presented at the first meeting of the Pan-European Research Planning Group, Johns Hopkins University Center, Italy, March 1995).

8 See, e.g., P. D. Marquardt, 'Subsidiarity and sovereignty in the European Union', *Fordham International Law Journal*, 18 (1994), 616; T. C. Fischer, ' "Federalism" in the European Community and the United States: a rose by any other name . . .', *Fordham International Law Journal*, 17 (1994), 389.

9 See, e.g., J. Roeder, 'Europe's new frontiers: remapping Europe; political aftermath of the end of the Cold War; after Communism: what?', *Daedalus*, 123 (June 1994), 25; M. Foucher, *Fronts et Frontieres* (Paris: Fayard, 1991), pp. 471–512.

10 T. Judt, 'Nineteen eighty-nine: the end of which European era?' *Daedalus*, 123 (June 1994), 1. See also, A. Kortunov, 'Relations between former Soviet Republics', *Society*, 30 (March 1993), 36.

11 See, e.g., V. Tishkov, 'Ethnicity and power in the Republics of the USSR', *Journal of Nationalities*, 1 (1990), 34; T. Remington, 'Renegotiating Soviet Federationism: Glasnost and regional autonomy', *Publius: The Journal of Federalism*, 19 (1989), 145; R. Wixman, *The Peoples of the USSR: An Ethnographic Handbook* (Armonk: M. E. Sharpe, 1988).

12 See S. Solnick, 'Federal bargaining in Russia', *East European Constitutional Review*, 4 (Autumn 1995), 52–3.

13 R. Lukic and A. Lynch, *Europe From the Balkans to the Urals: The Disintegration of Yugoslavia and the USSR* (New York: Oxford University Press, 1996), p. 392.

14 T. Ivanova, 'Tatarstan celebrates five years of sovereignty', *Tass* (25 August 1995).

15 N. Sorokin, 'Tatarstan can be Eurasian Union Center', *Tass* (9 February 1995).

16 Quoted in H. Schwartz, 'The new East European Constitutional Courts', in A. E. D. Howard (ed.), *Constitution Making in Eastern Europe* (Washington, DC: Woodrow Wilson Center Press, 1993), p. 186.

17 Quoted in *BBC Summary of World Broadcasts*, 'Head of Constitutional Court on Tatar referendum' (20 March 1992).

18 Schwartz, in Howard (ed.), *Constitution Making in Eastern Europe*, pp. 186–7.

19 Quoted in R. Batyrshin, 'Tatarstan leaders withdraw from constitutional conference', *Russian Press Digest* (25 June 1992).

20 See R. Sharlet, 'The prospects for federalism in Russian constitutional politics', *Publius: The Journal of Federalism*, 24 (1994), 115; R. Sharlet, 'Russia's "ethnic" Republics and constitutional politics', *Eurasia Reports*, 3 (1993), 39.

21 Quoted in R. Batyrshin, 'Russian Federation: the provision on republic sovereignty is

stricken from draft constitution', *Current Digest of the Post-Soviet Press*, 45:43 (23 November 1993), p. 6.

22 See J. Knechtle, *Analysis of the Constitution of the Russian Federation* (Washington, DC: ABA/CEELI, 1994); E. Walker, 'Designing center–region relations in the new Russia', *East European Constitutional Review*, 4 (Winter 1995), 54.

23 Quoted in V. Kononenko, 'Boris Yeltsin favors equality of subjects of federation, but is against right to secede from Russia', *Russian Press Digest* (4 November 1993).

24 Quoted in N. Sorokin, 'Tatarstan president calls for treaty with Russia', *Tass* (14 April 1992).

25 Preamble, Treaty between Russian Federation and Tatarstan, *Russian and Commonwealth Business Law Report*, 4 (21 March 1994).

26 B. Yeltsin, 'Yeltsin's message to federal assembly', *BBC Monitoring Service* (20 February 1995).

27 Preamble, Treaty between Russian Federation and Tatarstan.

28 Quoted in N. Sorokin, 'Russian–Tatar Treaty based on constitutions of both sides', *Tass* (16 February 1994).

29 Quoted in R. Batyrshin, 'How much sovereignty has Tatarstan swallowed? Boris Yeltsin has decided to look for himself', *Russian Press Digest* (31 May 1994).

30 Quoted in A. Barnard, 'Shakhrai: Tatar Pact saves federation', *The Moscow Times* (17 February 1994).

31 Quoted in P. Kuznetsov, 'Treaty with Tatarstan eliminates Crisis – Shakhrai', *Tass* (18 February 1994).

32 Quoted in R. Batyrshin, 'Tatarstan "Unites" with Russia', *Russian Press Digest* (16 February 1994).

33 Quoted in T. Zamyatina, 'Russia is not threatened with breakup as the Soviet Union', *Tass* (10 June 1994).

34 M. McFaul, 'Eurasia letter: Russian politics after Chechnya; Civil War', *Foreign Policy*, 99 (22 June 1995), 149.

35 See, S. Arutiunov, 'The cultural roots of ethnic radicalization in the North Caucasus', *The Berkeley Program in Soviet and Post-Soviet Studies, Newletter*, 1 (Winter 1995), p. 8; and A. M. Nekrich, *The Punished Peoples: The Deportation and Fate of Soviet Minorities at the End of the Second World War* (New York: Norton, 1978), pp. 58–60, 97–8.

36 For further discussion see C. Gall and T. de Waal, *Chechnya: Calamity in the Caucasus* (New York: New York University Press, 1998); A. Lieven, *Chechnya: Tombstone of Russian Power* (New Haven: Yale University Press, 1998).

37 See D. Hoffman, 'Yeltsin urged to seek peace in Chechnya', *The Washington Post* (8 February 1996), p. A18.

38 For a further discussion see E. Walker, 'Constitutional obstacles to peace in Chechnya', *East European Constitutional Review* (Winter 1997), p. 55.

39 See, generally, M. Evangelista, *The Chechen Wars: Will Russia Go the Way of the Soviet Union?* (Washington, DC: The Brookings Institution, 2003).

40 Quoted in A. Shtorkh, 'Russia and Buryatia sign treaty on division of power', *Tass* (29 August 1995).

41 M. Shaymiyev, 'Tatarstan's President's speech on occasion of Republic Day', *BBC Summary of World Broadcasts* (9 September 1994).

42 See, e.g., Peter and Susan B. Glass, 'Regions resist Kremlin control', *The Washington Post* A1 (31 May 2001), A1; 'Russia: more of the same', *The Economist* (31 May 2001), p. 48.

43 For further discussion, see D. M. O'Brien, 'Federalism as a metaphor in the constitutional politics of public administration', *Public Administration Review*, 49 (1989), 411–19.

KRISTIAN GERNER

4

The role of the Baltic states, Poland and Hungary in the new Europe

The changing political map of Europe

The Soviet era had come to an end and by 2002 a new idea of Europe was emerging which would see the enlargement of the European Union. The period called 'transition' was relegated to history. It marked the transition of the Baltic and Central European states from the Warsaw pact and the Soviet bloc to NATO and the European Union. Originally, transition was a concept used only to denote that the former communist states were on the track towards establishment of a market economy, democracy – or democratization – and the *Rechtsstaat*. The latter concept with its special connotation to German, was translated into English as 'the legal state' or 'a state of law'. The transition period had lasted from early 1989, when the round table talks between the government and the opposition started in Poland, soon to be followed by a similar process in Hungary, up to late 2002, when the European Union decided to offer the Baltic and Central European states full membership in the Union. This occurred at a time when the EU had appointed a committee under former French president Valery Giscard d'Estaing to design a convention. The ultimate aim is to make the European Union some kind of federation.

The eastern enlargement of the European Union is a good example of the interaction of political goals between certain actors with belief in historical destiny and the same and other relevant actors. Many are spellbound by the concept of 'Europe' and act accordingly. The famous W. I. and Dorothy Swaine Thomas theorem from 1928 (concerning the social psychology of children) is valid for this situation; that is, if men perceive situations as real, they are real in their consequences.[1] The European Union can be viewed as imagination turned into reality.

Seen from the perspective of the people in the Baltic states and Central Europe, the eastern enlargement of the EU represents the third time since World

War I that these states have been invited to join a larger European community. The first project was launched by the victorious allied powers at the Paris Peace Conference in 1919–20 as they decided to heed the wishes of leaders of (ethnic) nations claiming states. The president of the United States, Woodrow Wilson, defended the right to national self-determination for former member nations of the defeated and fallen German, Austrian–Hungarian, Russian and Ottoman Empires. The idea was that as a result of the monitoring of the minority policy of the new states by the League of Nations, in combination with defence agreements with France, these states should be protected against German and Hungarian revisionism and irredentism. The Munich agreement in 1938 and the outbreak of the new World War in 1939 demonstrated that Wilson's project for a new European structure had failed.

The second project concerning the Central European states was Stalin's creation of the Soviet bloc after World War II. There were no safeguards for democracy or any collective rights for ethnic minorities. The Soviet army and the new governments of Central Europe chose the policy of ethnic cleansing instead. More than ten million ethnic Germans were expelled to Germany. Ethnic Poles were 'transferred' from the Soviet Union to Poland.

Thus the eastern enlargement of the European Union is the third attempt to create political stability of Central Europe by way of including the states of this region in a larger community. When the Warsaw pact began to disintegrate in 1989, intellectuals and politicians in Hungary, Poland and Czechoslovakia began to strive for closer cooperation between themselves with the aim of preparing for membership in both NATO and the EU. This effort should be viewed not as a continuation of old politics but rather as a logical and a historical counterpart to, and continuation of, developments in Western Europe that started immediately after World War II. A guiding principle behind the Marshall plan and Robert Schuman's and Jean Monnet's policies in 1947–48 was to bring an end to the civil wars in Europe between French and Germans by promoting economic integration and political and military cooperation.

Because of Stalin's resistance to the acceptance of the Marshall plan in the Soviet bloc, uniting Europe meant excluding the Soviet Union's vassal states. Whereas most of the states on the territory of the ancient West Roman Empire were included in the European Community, those Central European countries that had been christianized in the early Middle Ages, and thus had belonged to the West Christian community of that era, were omitted.

When the Iron Curtain was finally lifted in 1989, all Christian nations of the former Soviet bloc aspired to again become part of 'Europe'. The ideologues of the Estonians, Latvians, Lithuanians, Poles, Czechs, Hungarians, Slovaks, Slovenes and Croats usually refer to themselves as belonging to Northern, Central or East Central Europe and not to Eastern Europe. To the ears of these peoples, the adjective 'eastern' has a derogatory ring.

The clear picture, which suggested a certain homogeneity in a broad and vaguely defined Central Europe, was blurred considerably when, after 1991,

Slovakia and Croatia under their respective leaders, Vladimír Mečiar and Franjo Tudjman, failed to live up to EU standards concerning democratic credentials and fair treatment of national minorities. These incidents made the idea of the integration of the former communist states in the European Union seem more complicated.

The Slovak premier Mečiar's authoritarian manner placed Slovakia in limbo. Originally, the European Commission did not recommend it for negotiations on membership, and on 4 December 1997 the European parliament explicitly declared that Slovakia was 'not yet sufficiently democratic' to be considered for EU membership.[2] However, in contrast to Croatia, which remained outside the circle of prospective new EU members even when Tudjman had died, Slovakia managed to catch up with the other Central European states after Mečiar had been defeated in both the parliamentary and presidential elections in 1998. With Roman Schuster as president and Mikulas Dzurinda as premier of a centre-right cabinet, the country obtained satisfactory democratic credentials to be accepted as a candidate by the EU.

In practice, Western European politicians have defined the orthodox states in the Balkans (Greece excepted) and in the former Soviet Union as not belonging to 'Europe', in spite of their leaders' repeated assertions that they do belong. True to form, the then secretary general of NATO, the former Belgian foreign minister Willy Claes, declared in 1994 that there was a clear difference between Protestant–Catholic and orthodox Europe: 'Only the first may be integrated with Europe without problems. The other Europeans should not nurture great hope.' Notably, orthodox Greece, which was already a member of both NATO and the EU, was omitted from Claes's argument about the orthodox states not being fit for 'Europe'.[3] Greece has an important ideological advantage over the other orthodox states. Because of its ancient history, it is viewed by many Western Europeans as the cradle of their civilization. The French historian Jean Baptiste Duroselle did not succeed in his attempt to create a European historical identity on Celtic foundations, excluding the Greek 'roots'.[4] Moreover, the word 'Greece' has a nice ring of democracy to it, the reference, of course, being the aristocratic democracy in ancient Athens.[5]

The view among politicians and economic actors in Western Europe on the importance and salience of the historical East–West divide is to be found also in mainstream contemporary European historiography. In the introduction to his volume in the very prestigious series 'Building Europe', *State and Nation in European History*, the German historian Hagen Schulze wrote that after the division of the continent between an East and a West Roman Empire around 300 AD, two European civilizations emerged which for almost two thousand years developed in some contact but without any real fusion. The history of the interaction between state and nation had taken place only in the Western cultural sphere of Europe, in a civilization that, in contrast to the Byzantine and Russian–orthodox East, had been characterized by separation of secular and spiritual power and secularization of the spirit. This was captured by concepts such as the

Renaissance and the Enlightenment and, in their wake, national sovereignty and democracy.[6]

The American historian Larry Wolff has demonstrated that the view about the 'barbaric East' which was implied by Schulze is deeply ingrained in Western thinking.[7] The conclusion of these and similar deliberations is that Europe has a core – Western Europe – and a fringe, Central Europe and the Baltic Sea's eastern shore, the destiny of which is to be incorporated with Western Europe. Eastern Europe is beyond Europe. After 1989, politicians in Europe worked on the assumption that Europe was more or less predestined to become united within the old boundaries of Western Christendom. Of course, there were different reasons behind the mostly positive views on the expansion of the EU and NATO. One reason can be labelled pragmatic or utilitarian. It is based upon the assumption that an expansion of the EU would bring material benefits to all involved, to the old member states as well as to new members. On the Eastern side, potential members were interested in joining Western organizations in order to enhance military security and material welfare. It was generally assumed that the climate for foreign investments would improve because of the basic security provided by NATO membership. It was thus viewed as economically profitable, in spite of the higher defence costs that it would entail. On the Western side, members were interested in expanding both the common market and the security zone towards the east. As indicated above, another reason was ideological, based upon the belief that European political unification and unity were a natural outcome of an assumed cultural community.

The process of 'returning to Europe': geopolitics and history

It is important to bear in mind that the question of restructuring the state system in Europe after the end of communism was not placed on the agenda as a result of long deliberations among political leaders in the East and West. Intellectually, the grounds for the idea that the old Habsburg lands and Poland belonged with Western Europe had been prepared primarily through the widely discussed 1983 treatise by the Czech writer living in Paris, Milan Kundera, about Central Europe as a kidnapped West, and a morally and culturally better West at that.[8] However, the restructuring process was set in motion not because of such arguments, but as an unintended consequence of Mikhail Gorbachev's attempt to reform the Soviet Union. His policies of perestroika, glasnost and new thinking released centrifugal forces which he could not master. In 1988, popular fronts for the promotion of perestroika were founded in the three Baltic Soviet republics. By 1989 they had already changed into fronts for the promotion of independence and sovereignty. 1988 was the decisive year because, in addition to the creation of the popular fronts in the three Baltic Soviet republics, János Kádár was unseated as leader of Hungary and replaced by a more liberal leader. In Poland, the first serious contacts regarding negotiations for change were made between the government of Mieczysław Rakowski and the leaders of the still 'suspended' Solidarity movement.

The political processes in the Baltic region and Central Europe after 1989 were formed by a mixture of contingencies and actions. It was a blend of pragmatism and ideology. The first catchword was 'transition'. From the Western point of view, transition implied the construction of democracy, market economy and the legal state (*Rechtsstaat*) in the states of the East. Thus economic and political homogenization of Europe to the west of Russia and to the north of the Balkans was placed on the agenda. Without defining the concept rigidly, one may say that some kind of European federation became a conscious goal, the varieties of which are discussed elsewhere in this book.

The process of bringing Central Europe and the Baltic states into Western Europe was, naturally, future oriented. However, different actors were influenced by perceptions of history; that is, by their interpretation of destiny, of 'self-evident' uniting bonds and dividing lines in Europe. The geographic location of the individual states to the east of the EU and NATO, and the structure of relations between the latter states in the Soviet period, helped to determine the perceived range of political options. Western European politicians and opinion makers also categorized the former socialist states in certain configurations and not as a bloc *en masse*. The Baltic and Central European actors lived up to expectations by referring to themselves in a similar manner and by arranging multilateral meetings. In 1990, the new post-communist governments of Czechoslovakia, Hungary and Poland began to coordinate aspects of their foreign policy in turning from East to West. In the same year, before the dissolution of the Soviet Union, the leaders of the three Baltic republics also established mechanisms for cooperation among themselves. After successfully breaking out of Yugoslavia in June 1991, Slovenia's leaders rejected the notion of belonging in the same company as the other post-Yugoslav states and stressed the historical bonds with Austria, Italy and the Czech lands, or with the mythical 'Central Europe'.

However, in spite of all the names and acronyms concerning cooperation projects such as the Visegrád four, the Hexagonal, CEI (Central European Initiative) and CEFTA (Central European Free Trade Agreement), the countries in the respective groups had, at the time when they were finally accepted as prospective members of the EU, comparatively weak political bonds and little trade between themselves. Certain ethnically motivated animosities, which had been nurtured in the interwar period, were revived after 1989.

Among the candidate states, Poland emerged as a regional great power and as a spearhead of both NATO and the EU in the eastern part of Europe. The geographical location of Poland, its relatively large population of almost forty million, its relative success with economic reform and its ability to cope with internal ideological diversity and political turmoil, made it emerge as the pivotal state in the area. Poland shared with the Czech Republic and Hungary the honour of being invited in early 1997 to start negotiations to join both NATO and the EU, but its population was almost twice as large as that of the other two together, and up to this time its economic growth had been more rapid. The geo-political aspect was, given the other two criteria of a comparatively large popu-lation and a large territory, also very important. Under the new international political conditions, Poland became a frontier state of 'Europe', facing the three eastern Slav states of Russia – Poland has a common border with Russia's Kaliningrad district in former East Prussia – Belarus and Ukraine. The western parts of Belarus and Ukraine, as well as the neighbouring Baltic state Lithuania, were parts of the Polish commonwealth up to the partitions of Poland in 1772, 1792 and 1795. A legacy from this period is that there are Polish minorities in Lithuania, Belarus and Ukraine in spite of the fact that some two million ethnic Poles were expelled from the area in 1945. In fact, these people and their descen-dants in contemporary Poland contribute to keeping the old Eastern territories – Kresy wschodnie – alive in the historical consciousness of Poland.

The Baltic scene

The Baltic states are not a homogeneous entity in terms of history, political tra-ditions, language and religion. They share the experience of having been part of both tsarist Russia and the Soviet Union, but they have never been a unitary political actor nor have they had very much in common in terms of culture. It should hardly have come as a surprise that after re-gaining sovereignty in 1991, economic and political trends would be different in the respective states.

   Although an extensive survey of the history of this region is beyond the scope of this chapter, it is important to draw attention to certain historical facts. Contemporary Lithuania, as has been indicated above, is a remnant of the Polish–Lithuanian commonwealth and is predominantly Catholic. Estonia belonged to Sweden for 150 years, has historical monuments from that time (1561–1710), is Protestant and has a language closely related to Finnish. Latvia was patched together in 1918 from the southern part of Livonia, Latgalia, Semgalia and Courland. Its capital Riga was founded by Germans in 1201 and remained strongly German up to 1918. After 1949, the influx of Russians was greater in Latvia than in either of the two other states, making 'Russian speakers' (a term felt to be derogatory by ethnic Russians) a majority in Riga. With the exception of the Catholic Latgalians, most Latvians are Protestants. Their language is related to Lithuanian, but it is not so close that speakers understand each other.[9]

   An important historical, confessional and political divide in the Baltic area runs between Catholic Lithuania and Protestant Latvia. The historical divide between Latvians and Estonians is less visible, because these peoples had a common history in Livonia, where the University of Tartu served as a breeding ground for nationalists of both peoples in the nineteenth century. They also have a common Lutheran confession, but because Protestant churches are territorial and in this sense national, the common confession is not much of a uniting bond. Besides, religion is not a significant ethnic marker for these peoples, partly because the churches were traditionally linked to the Balt ruling class, the Germans. Moreover, in spite of having been part of the Swedish Empire for ninety years (1621–1710), Latvia's – that is, southern Livonia's – bonds with Sweden were looser than Estonia's. The contemporary states of Estonia and Latvia do not have very much in common with each other or with Lithuania.

The three Baltic peoples do not understand each others' languages. In the late nineteenth century, Russian was introduced as a state language, and Russification was reinforced in Soviet times as a matter of expediency. Today, the attitude towards Russian is rather cool, and the post-1991 generation is therefore being taught English and to a certain extent German. The usefulness of these languages is not primarily to serve as a *lingua franca* between Balts but rather to further their contacts with Western Europe and the United States.

For historical and for contemporary geopolitical reasons, Lithuania belongs with Poland, Belarus and Ukraine, in spite of Lithuanian nationalism being defined with the Poles in the role of the Other. In light of both perceptions of history, and measured in the intensity of economic relations and cultural contacts in the present era, Estonia can be said to be Nordic; that is, to be in the same group as Finland and Sweden. Latvia with its capital Riga was part of the German orbit, and the Russian presence was more in evidence. Latvia turns out to be, in the narrow sense of the word, the only truly – exclusively – Baltic state. It is in the position of being situated next to a Russia with an imperialist political discourse among some politicians in its state Duma, which may be perceived as a menace to Latvia.

With regard to the perceived Russian menace, which many Latvians – and Estonians – believe corresponds to reality, it is worth noting that immediately after NATO's decision to invite the Czech Republic, Hungary and Poland to negotiations, a spokesman for the Russian foreign ministry offered Estonia and Latvia 'security guarantees'. The then Estonian prime minister Mart Siiman observed that his country 'sees international security guarantees in unification with European structures, including NATO', and Latvia's president in the late 1990s, Guntis Ulmanis, declared that 'under no conditions, even on the level of discussion, will we speak about Russian guarantees'.[10] The oblique reference was to the infamous guarantees offered by the Soviet Union after the Molotov–Ribbentrop pact in 1939 and the following annexation of the three Baltic states in 1940.

The issue of the Baltic states and their relations with Western Europe is further complicated by the existence of the Kaliningrad exclave which belongs to the Russian federation. It is part of former German East Prussia but populated almost exclusively by Russian immigrants. It is a rather poor region with a severely neglected civilian infrastructure. It has an important naval base at Baltiisk and is regarded by the Russian regime in Moscow as an inalienable part of the Russian federation.[11] In 1994 Belarus started to move closer to Russia and distanced itself from the other neighbours. Lithuania was sandwiched between

Belarus and the Russian Kaliningrad district, much as Poland divided Germany from East Prussia in the interwar years. From the point of view of military security, this was a rather dangerous situation. However, there was a way out for Lithuania: the Polish connection.

An important political factor in Estonia and Latvia, but not in Lithuania, is the minority question. When the Soviet Union was set on the road to dissolution, the Lithuanian Supreme Soviet ruled that all regular inhabitants of the republic could opt for citizenship, regardless of ancestry. Almost all inhabitants accepted the offer and, upon regaining independence, practically all of Lithuania's inhabitants were also citizens of the state. Lithuania has national minorities but one cannot say that they create serious political problems. According to statistics from 1996, of Lithuania's population of 3.7 million people, 81.3 per cent are ethnic Lithuanians, 8.4 per cent Russians and 7 per cent Poles. The Russians have not posed a political problem, whereas there has been friction between Poles and Lithuanian authorities and government members. However, because successive Polish governments after 1994 have refrained from making an issue of this, minority questions have not destabilized Lithuania or impaired its relations with either Poland or Russia.

In Estonia and Latvia, the minority question has been politically significant both internally and in relations with Russia and the EU. In the process of regaining independence, Estonian and Latvian politicians across the political spectrum unanimously asserted that because independence was regained and not 'received' from Russia, conditions as of June 1940 – that is, before the Soviet occupation in July of that year – should be re-created. This implied both that the boundaries with Russia should be slightly changed back to the prewar line (they had been pushed westward by Stalin) and that only those people who had lived in the respective state in 1940 and their descendants should be entitled to citizenship without having to apply for it and without having to pass rigid examinations. This legal standpoint had significant consequences for ethnic minorities. Most of the immigrants after 1940 were 'Russian speakers' and the two states thus emerged as sovereign states on the European arena with huge ethnic minorities that were disenfranchised. It was difficult to obtain citizenship because of strict regulations regarding knowledge of the local languages, history and customs. For former members of the Soviet state security and military forces, citizenship was out of the question.

In 1996, 64.2 per cent of the Estonian population were ethnic Estonians and 32.9 per cent Russians, Ukrainians and Belarussians. Similarly, 54.8 per cent of the Latvian population were ethnic Latvians, whereas Russians, Ukrainians and Belarussians formed 39.8 per cent. The Russian non-citizens amounted to almost half the population in Latvia's capital Riga and to more than 90 per cent in the Estonian industrial town of Narva on the Russian border. On the other hand, some 100,000 of the Russians in Estonia were citizens of the Russian federation. Politics in Latvia and Estonia have not been characterized by ethnic strife. However, this situation is laden with future instability because, in the long run, the many 'Russian speakers' will acquire citizenship. This will probably make the ethnic factor important in internal policies.[12] In late 1997, the minority question was still a question mark in connection with Estonia's pending negotiations with the EU for membership. However, in December of the same year Estonia's premier Mart Siiman declared that policies would be aimed at integration of the Russians and that legislation would be adjusted to allow for 'alien' children born in the country to receive citizenship at birth.[13] This certainly helped improve Estonia's status as a solid legal state worthy of joining the EU. This assessment was borne out by the EU's decision on enlargement in 2002.

Latvia's president Ulmanis demonstrated that he was well aware of the issue's potential for conflict as he warned in the summer of 1997 that the growing split between Latvians and Russians might lead to 'increasing strains in relations rather than to integration'. He warned against alienating the Russian minority by excluding its members from public office and making it too difficult to obtain Latvian citizenship.[14] However, because Latvia's major political parties were against any softening of the citizenship laws, its policy can be compared to that of Poland against its German minority (whose members were Polish citizens) in the interwar period and labelled *differential*. The state becomes an ethno-democracy.[15] Remarkably, the issue of the Russian minority did not become a hindrance for Latvia in 2002, when the state was included among the prospective members of the EU.

With regard to external orientation, the three Baltic states have increasingly parted ways since 1991. Estonians gravitated towards Finland and Sweden during the late Soviet period. The similarity between the Estonian and Finnish languages made it possible for Estonians to follow Finnish television programmes and thus develop a closer acquaintance with democratic Finland. Some Estonian intellectuals learned the Swedish language, some because of an interest in Estonia's Swedish history, others because they believed that the Finnish-language programmes on Finnish TV were 'finlandized' – that is, pro-Soviet – and less trustworthy than the Swedish-language programmes.[16]

Latvia's economy has to a certain degree remained in the grips of economic actors that have evaded control of the legal authorities. Latvia will also in the foreseeable future have close economic bonds with Russia. Some politicians are looking to Germany, but the latter's response has been lukewarm.[17]

When it dawned upon Lithuanian politicians that Poland was becoming a prospective member of both NATO and the EU, they realized that 'splendid isolation' was a dubious option. Although Lithuania as early as 1994 had declared its interest in joining NATO, this was a premature bid and no one outside the country seemed to take it seriously. It was evident that Lithuania had had little success in trying to develop in isolation. After seventy-five years of conflict with Poland regarding territorial and ethnic questions over Vilnius and the surrounding district – in 1920, Poland conquered Wilno, which was returned to Lithuania by the Soviets in 1940 – the time had finally come for a Polish–Lithuanian detente. Speaking to the Polish *sejm* on 21 February 1997, the speaker of the

Lithuanian *seimas*, the renowned leader of *Sajudis* (the popular front that led Lithuania on the road to independence in 1988–91) Vytautas Landsbergis, proposed the establishment of an interparliamentary commission. He underlined the importance of the traditional links between the two countries and stressed that Lithuania belonged to Central Europe rather than being a 'Baltic state'.[18] Interviewed about his position, Landsbergis stated:

> The Estonians stress certain things, while Lithuanian politicians stress other things, other geopolitical possibilities. Culturally, historically, and geographically, we are a Central European state. At the same time, we are a Baltic-region state. Certain policies, such as our special relations with Poland, reflect this [reality], which is, perhaps, not the case with Estonia, but Estonia has special relations with Finland instead.[19]

Landsbergis's assertions were well founded as far as Lithuania was concerned. However, Estonia's relationship with Finland is not as emotional, being based more upon the fact that the Finnish language in the Soviet period, as noted above, served as a gateway to the West for Estonian intellectuals. One cannot speak of a 'special relationship' in the same sense as between Lithuania and Poland. The multi-faceted historical relations between Lithuania and Poland are more similar to the intimate Swedish–Finnish relationship through the ages. The political impact of Landsbergis's statement came from the fact that it gave vent to the conviction that there is no special common interest among the three Baltic states. It is not far-fetched to assume that Landsbergis's idea of a new Polish–Lithuanian commonwealth grew out of the wish that Lithuania would join NATO and the EU by way of Poland. This seemed to be a safer way to gain alignment with the West than to be one of three 'Baltic' states. By 2002, it had become evident that a choice between Poland and the other Baltic states was not necessary. However, with the new political figuration of an expanding EU emerging in late 2002, it seemed that a common concern regarding Russia's Kaliningrad province would necessarily bring Lithuania into close relations with Poland, Kaliningrad's boundary state on the other side.

The Central European scene

It should also be recognized that as 'reconstruction' of the Central European states began after the demise of the Soviet system, a specific legacy from the period before Soviet domination made itself felt: nationalism and the question of ethnic minorities. Central European nationalisms had been constructed in the nineteenth century and were reinforced in the era of the two World Wars. They were defined with the ethnic minorities and the neighbouring states in the role as hostile and/or untrustworthy Others. The animosities were not eliminated in the Soviet period, only suppressed. In the late 1980s, because many political leaders stressed that the identity of the state was ethnic, historical animosities burst into the open. This implied that national minorities might become a political issue. Those who were ethnically different inside the state were not co-owners and the ethnic brethren in neighbouring states might need protection. Such was the logic.

The new constitutions of Croatia (1990), Romania (1991) and Slovakia (1992) defined these states as those of the Croats, the Romanians and the Slovaks, respectively. Although Croatia's constitution addressed minorities and their rights, this only added to tensions, because the Serbs in particular experienced a loss of status. They had not been used to regarding themselves as a minority within the previous state, communist Yugoslavia. Conversely, Hungary's interim constitution addressed the state's responsibility for the welfare of the Hungarian – Magyar – cultural nation, including Magyars beyond its frontiers. In all the countries, ethnicity interpreted with recourse to historical arguments was at the forefront, thus structuring political discourse. An interesting effect of the somewhat different Hungarian, Slovak and Romanian wording was that Hungary and not Slovakia or Romania emerged as the protector of the culture of the Magyars in the latter two states. It is not a coincidence but a common historical legacy that the structural relationship between the state and 'its' minorities on the other side of the state boundary is similar in the cases of Germany and Hungary. This is the enduring effect of boundary-making in 1919–20 in Versailles and Trianon which created huge German and Magyar minorities in the neighbouring states but left Germany and Hungary with only small national minorities. In the 1990s as well, the minority question was mainly about Germans and Hungarians in the neighbouring states. In the German case, the political role of the *Heimatvertriebene* from Silesia in Poland and the Sudetenland in Czechoslovakia diminished over the postwar decades. However, after 1989 the *Sudetendeutsche Landsmannschaft*, with its centre in Bavaria, where the Sudeten Germans were recognized as the fourth tribe when they settled there after having been expelled in 1945 (the other tribes were the Bavarians, the Franconians and the Swabians), became very active and caused some friction in relations between Germany and the Czech Republic as late as the summer of 2002.

In Czechoslovakia, the main controversy between the two victors in the 1992 parliamentary election, the Czech Republic's Václav Klaus and Slovakia's Vladimír Mečiar, arose over economic policies. When Mečiar, in an attempt to prop up Slovakian heavy industry through demands for subsidization and preservation of the existing structure, threatened Klaus with separation, Klaus accepted the 'offer'. He believed that the Czech lands would be better off and better prepared for joining the EU once they were relieved of the 'burden' of Slovakia. Against the expressed wishes of the majority of its population, Slovakia was forced to become a sovereign state. It is another matter that the process was hailed as a triumph by Mečiar when it was already under way. After Slovakia's separation on 1 January 1993, its relations with Hungary soured. Nationalism and ethnic questions were central factors in this process, as the

Mečiar government defined the national interests of Slovakia as being endangered by the Magyars.

In Slovakia political life under Mečiar's rule was characterized by polarization, the players even questioning one anothers' legitimacy. One may speak of a pattern reminiscent of the Soviet period, with its lack of respect for political minorities, and even of a certain resemblance to the prewar authoritarian regime of Jozef Tiso in the German puppet state Slovakia (1939–44).[20] Mečiar's coalition partner, the Slovak National Party (SNS), praised Tiso. In 1997, the cultural organization Matica Slovenská published a textbook, *The History of Slovakia and Slovaks*, which idealized Tiso and depicted the deportation of Jews to extermination camps as ordinary travels to labour camps. The book was sponsored by the EU PHARE programme – which demanded its money back after learning how it had been used – and distributed by the Slovak ministry of education.[21] As is well known, Tiso headed a clerical-fascist party and assisted the Nazis in their extermination campaign against the Jews.[22]

Poland, which in many respects is a key political actor in the enlargement project of the EU, went through interesting political developments after 1989. The political landscape that emerged after the parliamentary elections in September 1997 was hailed by the prominent journalist Adam Krzeminski as an expression of European normality: Poland was 'the new land of the middle', with a strong social democracy, a strong Christian right and a liberal centre holding a pivotal role in government formation.[23] This outcome can be described as the result of a learning process. Following the first completely free elections in 1991, twenty-nine parties were represented in the parliament. It was impossible to create a stable government. In the 1993 elections, a 5 per cent threshold for parties and an 8 per cent threshold for coalitions were introduced. Only five parties made it into the parliament, making it possible to create a reasonably stable coalition government of social democrats and a remnant from the old socialist state's political set-up, the agrarian PSL. However, 40 per cent of the voters were left without representation in parliament. The political legitimacy of the government therefore was somewhat in doubt. In 1996, Marian Krzaklewski from the labour branch of the Solidarity movement managed to create an election coalition, AWS, which embraced almost all the small Christian and nationalist factions. In the 1997 elections, the AWS emerged as the biggest coalition with 34 per cent of the vote. Together with the liberals, the Union of Freedom, UW, which received 13.4 per cent, the AWS was able to form the new government. Taking into consideration that the AWS was predominantly Catholic and that Poland is regarded as a Catholic bulwark, it is noteworthy that a Protestant from Cieszyn Silesia, Jerzy Buzek, was appointed prime minister, and an ethnic Jew, Bronisław Geremek, became foreign minister. With the liberal Leszek Balcerowic as minister of finance, the picture of Poland as a middle-of-the-road European country was rounded off. This image of Poland as a 'normal' European country was not considerably changed when the social democrats returned to power as a result of the parliamentary elections in 2001, once again forming a coalition government with the PSL. In March 2003, the social demo-crat premier Leszek Miller decided to lead a minority government after becom-ing tired of the obstructive policies of the PSL in the parliament.

The local elections in Poland in June 1994 yielded results that are interest-ing from the perspective of trans-state integration and national disintegration in Central Europe because they pointed to a possible geographic split of the country in terms of views on the state and on the economy. The three main cur-rents, the left, consisting of socialists and peasants (SLD and PSL), the Catholic right and the strongly market-oriented, liberal centre (UW) each acquired roughly one-third of votes cast. However, regional differences were of great sig-nificance.[24] The SLD won a relative majority in Warsaw and took thirty of a total of forty-nine county capitals. Coalitions headed by the UW won in six cities, among them Cracow, Gdańsk, Poznań and Wrocław. In Wrocław the UW alone gained an absolute majority. The PSL was successful in districts with a majority vote in the countryside. The Catholic right was strongest in nine county capitals in eastern Poland and gained an absolute majority in Białystok at the Belarussian border.[25] The victory for the Catholic right in eastern Poland should be inter-preted as an expression of Polish nationalism and Polish identity in the face of the orthodox (and Uniate[26] – the latter is a complicated matter of competition rather than alienation) neighbours in Belarus and Ukraine. These Poles turned their back on the East. However, they did not look to the West either. Rather, they looked inwards. Here political resistance to joining the EU and becoming subject to its agricultural policies was obvious.

It is equally significant that the cities which saw a triumph of political forces in favour of both a market economy and of local self-government are situated in those parts of Poland that before 1918 belonged to Germany. After 1989, Euroregions with a strong German influence were created to the west of these cities on the rivers Oder and Neisse: Pomerania, Pro–Europa–Viadrina, Spree–Neisse–Bober and Neisse–Nysa–Nisa.[27] Even before the June 1994 elec-tions, a Polish scholar expressed the preconditions for economic success: large regions that were administratively and economically 'decentralized'; that is, more autonomous than the counties 'inside' Poland.[28]

Thus, in western Poland voters, local politicians and economic planners revealed an interest in loosening Warsaw's control and turning towards Germany and the European Union. It must be added that regional voting patterns in Poland measured along a liberal–conservative axis show a high correlation with traditions from the partition period, the most backward-looking being agrarian areas in the former Russian and Austrian parts and the most modernist the former German cities in the west and on the Baltic Sea.[29] It has also been argued that the liberal ethos in western Poland can be explained as an effect of the pop-ulation transfers after World War II from the territories lost to the Soviet Union in the east. Social uprooting in combination with location on the frontier fostered individual initiative among the newcomers and laid the foundation for policies based upon trust and not upon family relations in the territories that were acquired from Germany in 1945.[30] We have here a typical case of the problem that behaviour which is seemingly the same, or similar, may have different causes. In this case the implication is that the Polish settlers did not inherit the characteristics of the previous German territories but were conditioned by their own experience and situation. Of course, their behaviour fitted well into the political culture of the remaining indigenous population in western Silesia and Pomerania. In any case, the results of the parliamentary elections in September 1997 confirmed the established east–west pattern. The UW and SLD were strong in the western part of the country, whereas the AWS held the south and the east.[31]

After 1989, Poland increasingly grew into the role of a key state in East Central European politics. At the world economy forum in Davos in February 1997, Poland's president Aleksander Kwaśniewski praised Germany as a champion of European integration; he even hailed the German unification in 1990 as a factor contributing to increased security of Poland. At the same time, Kwaśniwski urged NATO to include Ukraine in its 'security concept for Europe'.[32] Poland emerged as a potential link for Germany, NATO and the EU with Ukraine, a state with almost fifty million inhabitants trying to balance between Russia and 'Europe'.

If we add to developments on Poland's western border the fact of Germany's strong economic influence in the Czech Republic and the existence of border regions here as well, that the western counties of Hungary are economically better off than those east of Budapest, and that Estonia and Slovenia managed to redirect their economies towards the West much more than did their regional neighbours, one might conclude that the westernmost parts of the former socialist bloc were in the process of being functionally incorporated into the EU. This process was being influenced most prominently by Germany, even before the July 1997 recommendation of the European Commission and the invitation from the EU in Luxembourg in December 1997.

Politics and ethnic questions in Central Europe

The reemergence of the ethnic question in political discourse occurred before the dissolution of the Soviet bloc. Hungarian internal politics in the 1980s were influenced by concern for ethnic Hungarians in neighbouring countries, especially Romania, to such a degree that it had implications for Hungarian foreign policy.[33] The change of the political system in 1989–90 was preceded by the communist regime's successful mobilization of the nationalist intelligentsia for a policy that aimed at anchoring Hungary in the Western world without jeopardizing internal stability. The common denominator was a concern for the plight of the Hungarian minorities in Slovakia and Transylvania. In the late 1980s their survival as communities was threatened by the consequences of the Gabčikovo/Bös hydropower station on the Danube just outside Bratislava and of the 'systematization' of villages in the Romanian countryside. The Hungarian government cancelled its participation in the former project and the Hungarian parliament adopted a resolution which condemned the latter.

When Gorbachev's new foreign policy increased the leeway for the vassal states, prominent critics of the regime in Hungary agreed not to try to topple the government if the latter took upon itself the task of helping improve the situation for the Magyar minorities in the neighbouring states of Romania and Slovakia. The Hungarian government's treatment of the Romanian question turned out to be the crucial factor. With the aim of raising international opinion against Romania, Hungary decided to grant political asylum to ethnic Hungarian refugees from Romania. By this act, Hungary committed itself to following the rules of international law. The barbed wire on the border to the democratic neighbour to the west, Austria, was removed. On 20 August 1989, the day of St Stephen, the patron saint of Hungary, Otto von Habsburg, the son of the last Austrian emperor and Hungarian king and a member of the European parliament for Bavaria, obtained permission to arrange a peace picnic on the Austrian–Hungarian border at Ödenburg/Sopron. Tens of thousands of young East Germans on vacation in Hungary learned that the border was open. They poured out from Hungary, thus emigrating from East to West Germany. In East Germany, a collective psychosis developed and resulted in mass emigration. The East German government agreed to let a train with its own citizens travel from Prague through Saxony to West Germany. It thus deprived itself of the last vestiges of political legitimacy.

When the shattered East German regime publicly declared on 9 November 1989 that the border was to be opened, frontier guards in Berlin took it literally. The Berlin Wall came down and with it the East German regime and state. In 1990 Germany was united. Gyula Horn, who was Hungary's foreign minister in 1989 and the real architect of the politics that caused the drama, received a German order as a token of appreciation.

The lesson lies in the fact that Hungary's policy in 1989 was not dictated by any concern for German unity or for the demise of the whole Soviet bloc. The simple truth was that the political elite wished to stay safely and comfortably in the country when the support of Soviet bayonets was withdrawn. They chose to play the nationalist card and were highly successful. It was, therefore, the communist leaders themselves who dismantled communist rule in Hungary and monitored the transition to democracy in 1990. After the elections in 1994, they returned to power in Budapest, as regular social democrats and Europeans. The granting of membership in the European Union made Hungary accept amending and watering down its so-called 'status law', which was adopted in 2001 and had the implication that some Hungarian citizens' rights were extended to Magyars in the neighbouring countries, with the exception of Austria. After 2002, Hungarians could believe in a future 'spiritualization of frontiers'. This was the slogan of the non-revisionist leftist opposition in Hungary in the interwar years. The goal was to minimize the significance of the state boundaries instead of attempting to revise them.

As a consequence of the policies towards Slovakia and Romania, the general election in 1990 was held in an atmosphere of nationalist feelings and brought the nationalist Magyar Democratic Forum to power. József Antáll, the first post-communist government's premier, declared that he felt responsible for fifteen million Hungarians, which meant also those living in the neighbouring states. To the neighbouring states this was not only 'a message to proclaim that the identity of democracy was to be based on the legacy of the pre-communist era', as Bozóki states on p. 91 of this volume, but also a message that the government of Hungary would show a very active interest in the situation of the Hungarian minorities in these states. Successive Hungarian governments insisted on the principle of collective rights for national minorities, whereas the successive Mečiar governments in Slovakia as well as Romania under president Iliescu insisted on the principle of individual – democratic – rights only. Relations with Romania improved markedly after the shift in 1996 to a government under the liberal president Constantinescu, a government which counted representatives of the Hungarian minority. Not much changed after the socialist Ion Iliescu returned as president in 2000. Hungary's relations with Slovakia remained cool, as Mečiar's government refused to heed the solemn declarations about minority rights of the Hungarian–Slovak friendship treaty which was signed under the supervision of the EU in 1995.

As the other Visegrád three moved towards closer relations with NATO and the EU, Slovakia under Mečiar continued to alienate itself from its neighbours, especially Hungary. On 15 November 1995 Slovakia's parliament adopted a language law, which prohibited minorities from using their maternal language in an official capacity. The law was aimed at the huge Hungarian minority, comprising 10 per cent of the population.[34] The adoption of the language law showed that the Hungarian minority was isolated from the Slovak majority. Even those normally critical of the Mečiar government did not support Hungarian demands for autonomy or special collective rights. President Kováć, although a political adversary of Mečiar, ratified the language law on 28 November 1995.[35]

The law on the protection of the republic which the Slovak parliament approved on 27 March 1996 by a vote of 77 to 57, meant an additional curtailing of the rights of minorities, albeit implicitly. The new law allowed the prosecution of individuals who 'spread false information' that could damage Slovakia's interests or who organized public rallies 'with the intention of subverting the country's constitutional system, territorial integrity, or defense capability'. Sharon Fisher noted that critics claimed that 'the vaguely worded legislation allowed for arbitrary interpretation and endangered freedom of expression and assembly'. She also noted concern lest the new law 'remove Slovakia from the list of front-runners for EU membership'. Among the critics of the law were the leaders of the Catholic church and trade unions as well as judges and civic organizations.[36]

It was no coincidence that only a few hours after approving the law on the protection of the republic, the parliament ratified the Slovak–Hungarian treaty on the status of minorities by a vote of 119 to 1 with 19 abstentions. It also adopted 2 accompanying clauses specifying that the treaty could not be interpreted as granting minorities collective rights or the right to autonomy. This was in line with the consistent Slovak resistance to the concept of collective rights. As Sharon Fisher observed, the 'interpretation' clauses were not binding on Hungary. She also noted that the ratification was delayed because of opposition from the SNS. It was not until January 1996 that the SNS agreed to support the treaty and then only on the condition that a law on 'protection of the republic' was also adopted. It was a sign of the tense atmosphere that ethnic Hungarian deputies abstained from the vote. They complained that the parliament had taken several steps to restrict minority rights in spite of the treaty with Hungary.[37] In September 1997 Mečiar, in a political rally in Bratislava, indicated that he supported 'repatriation' of ethnic Hungarians 'who [did] not want to live in Slovakia'.[38] The minority question remained a stumbling block on the road to smooth relations between Hungary and Slovakia until the change of government in Slovakia in 1998.

In 1996–97 the Sudeten German question that had been an obstacle in the development of more cordial Czech–German relations was finally solved. In an agreement which was published in December 1996 and ratified the following year by the respective parliaments, Germany and the Czech Republic exonerated one another for atrocities during the war and in its aftermath. Germany admitted its responsibility for the illegal occupation of Czechoslovakia in 1939–45 and the Czech Republic issued a statement of regret for the 'forced resettlement' of Sudeten Germans in 1945, and for the fact that president Edvard Beneš had pardoned Czechs that had murdered German civilians in the process.[39] Their expulsion, which was cruel and cost many lives, remained an important issue in Czech, Bavarian and Austrian politics.[40]

Historical precedents, ethnic relations, political culture and economic developments imply that the prospects for an independent federative model in the Baltic area and Central Europe are slim. Instead economic factors and political goals suggest that the pattern of the Middle Ages will be repeated, in that the European Union will advance in a piecemeal manner. This actually began to happen in 1997. In our time it is not the Teutonic crusaders, the Hanseatic League or the Holy Roman Empire that will conquer the East, not a new Napoleon Bonaparte or Adolf Hitler, but the European Union. However, in historical terms it is a matter of 'German' expansion. The Union symbolizes the reunification of the empire of Charlemagne: the Carolingian Franks spoke a German language, the predecessor of contemporary Dutch. Aachen is not far from either Brussels or Strasbourg. And it is not very far to Tallinn, Prague, Cracow, Budapest and Ljubljana.

As early as 1991, Poland, Hungary and Czechoslovakia signed association agreements with the EC. In 1994, Poland, Hungary and the Czech Republic were promised to be the next candidates for negotiations with the EU after the EFTA (European Free Trade Association) states. In 1997, the commission of the

European Union decided to put the Eastern enlargement of the EU on the agenda. This answered in the negative the question of whether an independent federalization was feasible in Central Europe or the Baltic area. The idea and reality of an enlarged European Union took precedence. Keeping in mind the pragmatic and ideological mixture of motives mentioned in the introduction to the present chapter, it is possible to conclude that each of the successful bidders stressed the pragmatic discourse and behaved as a singular actor. On the other hand, their endeavour was facilitated not only by Germany's pragmatic motives to let other EU states share the economic burden of developing its *Mark* (open boundary) to the east, but also by the ideology of European unification in Brussels.

As soon as they had arrived on the safe shore by being selected as early Central European members of the EU, the political leaders of the Czech Republic and Hungary began to show great concern for the fate of Slovakia, which at this time (1997) seemed to be left on the sidelines. The Czech foreign minister, Josef Zieliniec, reacted by stressing that his government was interested in seeing Slovakia join both NATO and the EU.[41] At the height of the discussion on who would be invited in the first round to join NATO and the EU, respectively, Hungary's premier Gyula Horn appealed to Poland and the Czech Republic not to ignore Slovakia's efforts to integrate into NATO. Horn called for a 'reactivating' of the Visegrád group, but not as a means of exerting pressure on Slovakia. He added that Budapest wanted Slovakia to meet NATO and EU requirements 'as soon as possible'.[42]

The logic behind the original Visegrád scheme of February 1991 – that is, not to create a Central European federation but to prepare to join NATO and the EU individually – became operative again in July 1997. Developments between the two dates demonstrated that, far from viewing a federation among themselves as useful, Poland, the Czech Republic, Slovakia and Hungary all dismissed the idea. In a similar way, Estonia and Slovenia at this stage – in 1997 – shunned away from their respective Baltic and Balkan neighbours. Their goal remained Europe or nothing. Their strategy met with success, although Estonia would experience the 'return' to a 'Baltic' identity when Latvia and Lithuania were accepted as membership candidates of the EU on an equal footing with Estonia. Slovenia remained the only candidate among the former Yugoslav republics.

In the period 1989–2002 the new dividing line which had become visible in 1989–91 gradually hardened in Central Europe. This left the three Baltic states, Poland, Hungary, the Czech Republic, Slovakia and Slovenia on the 'European' side; whereas Belarus, Ukraine, Russia, and for the time being Bulgaria and Romania, as well as Croatia, Albania, Bosnia-Herzegovina, Macedonia, Serbia and Montenegro were all practically excluded.

A serious problem remains that the emerging new eastern boundaries of the EU divide ethnic groups, such as Magyars and Poles, but also Russians (in the case of Estonia and Latvia).

Concluding remarks

There are different ways of solving minority questions and averting eventual boundary conflicts in Central Europe and the Baltic region.[43] The significance of state boundaries may be diminished to such an extent that communications will continue unhampered in practically all fields. Another, complementary solution is to grant territorial autonomy to national minorities within the established territorial states. The challenge to the EU is to incorporate, by way of some kind of agreements regarding boundary regions – similar to the Euroregions that were established before the EU enlargement on the Oder river – the western part of Ukraine (Belarus seems to be an impossible case for many years to come) and Romania's districts on the Hungarian border. In the latter case, the Carpathian Euroregion may be employed. It was proposed in 1991 and formally established in 1993, when an agreement was signed in Debrecen in Hungary by the Ukrainian, Polish and Hungarian foreign ministers. In addition to six Polish, five Ukrainian and three Hungarian counties, the proposed region also included the central and eastern districts of Slovakia (two-thirds of the state) and seven counties in Romania. However, no Slovak or Romanian representatives were present at the meeting in Debrecen.[44] Without the cooperation of these states, the project will remain dormant.

The position of Poland's president Kwasńiewski as the champion of both Lithuania and Ukraine in their endeavour to get closer to 'Europe' has been noted above. To this should be added the government programme presented on 10 November 1997 by the then new premier Jerzy Buzek in the parliament. Naturally, Buzek expressed his desire for good relations with all neighbours and with all (other) EU states and the United States as well. However, he underlined that 'the relations between Poland and Ukraine evolved better than anyone would have been able to imagine only a few years ago'. He also recalled that Solidarity at its congress in 1980 had sent an appeal to workers in the neighbouring socialist states, and to the subjugated peoples of the Soviet Empire, to emulate the Polish example: 'Today we are neighbors with our historical partners a free Ukraine and a free Lithuania. To support democratic and market reforms in these countries is for us both a moral duty and a political interest.'[45]

Poland, as a new member of NATO and the EU, is striving for peaceful cooperation and good relations with Ukraine and Lithuania, taking up the tradition of the Jagiellonian commonwealth, the *Rzecz Pospolita*, which existed from the fourteenth to the eighteenth century and which the first ruler of the resurrected Polish state in 1918, Józef Piłsudski, attempted in vain to re-create through his Soviet campaign in 1920. Although it was multinational, interwar Poland was an ethno-democracy and, after 1926, an ethno-authoritarian state. In any case, with Poland as a new member, the *Ostpolitik* of the EU (i.e. of Germany) will be complemented by the Polish *polityka wschodnia*. This means that in the long run, Polish federalist traditions may colour the discourse on regionalism and federalist tendencies within the EU as much as Germany's related legacy has done. The mythological heritage of Jagiellonian Poland may become a factor in European politics. This is not the only possible new challenge.

Its membership in NATO and the EU will enhance Hungary's possibilities to lead a more assertive foreign policy vis-à-vis its northern, southern and eastern neighbours. In order to visualize this prospect, it is necessary to place it in a historical and mythological Hungarian framework, that of *Regnum Hungariae*, the Hungarian state which included not only contemporary Hungary but also Croatia, Slovakia, Transylvania, the Banat, Carpathian Ruthenia, Vojvodina, Slavonia and Burgenland up to the river Leitha. All Hungarian politicians, from the communist Béla Kun, to the liberal Mihaly Károlyi, to the conservative Admiral Horthy, refused to accept the 'mutilation' of Hungary in 1919–20. Under German protection, Horthy's Hungary in 1938–41 regained some of the territories lost in the peace of Trianon in 1920. In 1945–47 the Trianon boundaries were resurrected and, in addition, Hungary lost territory on the Danube to Czechoslovakia.

What is topical today, after Hungary has entered NATO and the EU, is that Hungarian leaders twice after Trianon proved their ability to make use of changing conditions to promote their nationalist cause. In 1938–41 the result was that Hungary could re-conquer some of its lost territories. In 1988–89 the result was a civilized and decent but spectacular dissolution of the socialist system. In the former period, Hungary acted under cover of the strongest state in the area, Germany. In the latter period, as has been shown above, Hungary exploited the sudden weakness of the Soviet government and the permanent, but in 1989 especially precarious, lack of legitimacy of the East German government.

As a member of NATO and the EU, Hungary will be at the forefront when it comes to the evaluation of the situation of the Magyar minorities in Romania, Serbia and Ukraine, which are all unstable and weak states. On the south-eastern front of NATO and the EU, Hungary acquires a role similar to Poland's and so to a certain degree does Lithuania on the eastern front. It is enticing to recall the historical fact that Hungary, Poland and Lithuania were the great powers of East and South East Central Europe in the Middle Ages, situated along the fault line between Western and Eastern Christianity recently highlighted by Samuel Huntington in his treatise on the 'clash of civilizations'.[46]

Poland and Hungary have emerged as NATO's and the EU's frontier states in the east. This means that political stability in Europe will depend on how these two states arrange their relations with their neighbours to the east and south. It is noteworthy that Poland has a tradition of federative statehood whereas Hungary traditionally has been a rather centralized and Magyarizing power. I am not insinuating that either Poland or Hungary could be suspected of harbouring expansionist and aggressive goals. On the contrary, they will try to emulate West Germany's successful *Ostpolitik*. They will become main actors in the coming *Osterweiterung* of the federated Europe, of the EU. It is of interest to note that Poland's president Kwasniewski at a conference in Warsaw in the early spring of 2003 on the eastern enlargement of the EU argued that Poland would play a significant role in creating the new *Ostpolitik* of the European Union.

Notes

1 W. I. Thomas with Dorothy Swaine Thomas, *The Child in America: Behavior Problems and Programs* (New York: Alfred A. Knopf, 1928).

2 'European Parliament excludes Slovakia from membership talks', *RFE/RL News Line* (5 December 1997).

3 W. Koydl, ' "Manchmal fühlt man sich in Stich gelassen." Schelju Scheljew: Begriffe wie Kerneuropa führen zu einer neuen Spaltung des Kontinents' *Süddeutsche Zeitung* (28 September 1994).

4 J.-B. Duroselle, *Europe. A History of its Peoples* (London: Viking/Penguin, 1990).

5 See M. N. Todorova, *Imagining the Balkans* (Oxford: Oxford University Press, 1997).

6 H. Schulze, *Staat und Nation in der europäischen Geschichte* (Munich: C. H. Beck, 1994), pp. 16–17. The book was published also by Blackwell, Oxford; Crítica, Barcelona; Laterza, Rome-Bari; and Le Seuil, Paris.

7 L. Wolff, *Inventing Eastern Europe: The Map of Civilization on the Mind of the Enlightenment* (Stanford, CA: Stanford University Press, 1994), p. 371.

8 M. Kundera, 'The tragedy of Central Europe', *The New York Review of Books*, 31:7 (1984), 33–8.

9 See K. Gerner and S. Hedlund, *The Baltic States and the End of the Soviet Empire* (London/New York: Routledge, 1993), chapter 3.

10 'Estonia, Latvia reject Russia's offer of security guarantees', *RFE/RL News Line* (17 July 1997).

11 See e.g. 'Russian official says Kaliningrad is not "Fourth Baltic Republic"', *RFE/RL News Line* (15 December 1997).

12 V. Pettai, 'Political stability through disenfranchisement', *Transition*, 6 (1997), 23.

13 'Estonia seeks integration, not assimilation of Russian speakers'. *RFE/RL News Line* (9 December 1997).

14 'Latvian President warns of growing ethnic tension', *RFE/RL News Line* (11 July 1997).

15 See R. Brubaker, *Nationalism Reframed: Nationhood and the National Question in the New Europe* (Cambridge: Cambridge University Press, 1996), pp. 86–97.

16 Personal information, gathered in Soviet Estonia by the author.

17 C. Leonzi, 'La transition économique dans les Etats baltes, une marche à trois temps vers l'Occident', *Le courrier des pays de l'Est*, 403 (October 1995), 10.

18 See J. Karpinski, 'Poland and Lithuania look towards a common future', *Transition*, 3:6 (1997), 15.

19 V. Landsbergis 'Our problems are Europe's problems', *Transition*, 3:6 (1997), 19.

20 S. J. Cohen, *Politics without a Past: The Absence of History in Postcommunist Nationalism* (Durham/London: Duke University Press, 1999).

21 'Slovakia still keeping money for anti-Semitic textbook', *ÈTK News from Slovakia* (16 October 1997).

22 H. Stehle, 'Ein Nationalstaat von Hitlers Gnaden. Der Preis für eine unabhängige Slowakei: 60 000 tote Juden – Die politische Karriere des Monsignore Jozef Tiso', *Die Zeit* (19 September 1991), pp. 57–8.

23 A. Krzeminski, 'Polen – das neue Land der Mitte', *Die Zeit* (26 September 1997), p. 13.

24 See A. Sabbat-Swidlicka, 'Local elections redress political imbalance in Poland', *RFE/RL Research Report*, 3:27 (1994), 1–8.

25 J. Paradowska, 'Polska gminna – zwrot na prawo? Nikt nie wygrał, wszyscy sie ciesza,' [Provincial Poland – a Turn to the Right? Nobody Won, All Are Happy], *Polityka* (2 July 1994), p. 11.

26 Uniates are Catholics with orthodox rites.

27 See M. Klodzinski and J. Okuniewski (eds), *Multifunktionelle Entwicklung der ländlichen Räume in den Grenzgebieten* (Warsaw: Friedrich-Ebert Stiftung, Verlag SGGW, 1993).

28 Zdzisław Pulecki, 'Współpraca Polski ze zjednoczonymi Niemcami' [Poland's Cooperation with United Germany], in H. Pracowity (ed.), *Polska i jej nowi sasiędzi (1989–1993)* (Poznań and Toruń: Wydanictwo Adam Marszalek, 1994), p. 73.

29 H. Tworzecki, *Parties and Politics in Post-1989 Poland* (Boulder: Westview Press, 1996), pp. 97–100.

30 T. Grabowski, 'Breaking the old Intelligentsia ethos: the roots and fragility of polish Liberalism' (Seattle: paper presented at the National Convention of the American Association for the Advancement of Slavic Studies, 22 November 1997).

31 M. Janicki and W. Władyka, 'Wymiana Luster' [Change of Mirrors], *Polityka*, 40 (4 October 1997), pp. 6–8; T. Zarycki and A. Nowak, 'Hidden dimensions: the stability and structure of regional political cleavages in Poland', *Communist and Post-Communist Studies*, 33 (2000), 331–54; T. Zarycki, 'Politics in the periphery: political cleavages in Poland interpreted in their historical and international context', *Europe-Asia Studies*, 52:5 (2000), pp. 851–73.

32 'Der polnische Präsident lobt Deutschland', *Frankfurter Allgemeine Zeitung* (4 February 1997).

33 See K. Gerner, 'Ethnic rights as human rights: the case of the Baltic states and Hungary', in V. Mastny and J. Zielonka (eds), *Human Rights and Security. Europe on the Eve of a New Era* (Boulder: Westview Press, 1991).

34 B. Kohler, 'Italienische Oper auf slowakisch? Das neue Sprachgesetz sorgt in Pressburg und Budapest für Aufruhr', *Frankfurter Allgemeine Zeitung* (17 November 1995).

35 S. Fisher, 'Ethnic Hungarians back themselves into a corner', *Transition*, 1:24 (1995).

36 S. Fisher 'Slovak Parliament approves law on protection of Republic', *OMRI Daily Digest* (27 March 1996).

37 S. Fisher, 'Slovakia ratifies treaty with Hungary', *OMRI Daily Digest* (27 March 1996).

38 'Hungary criticizes Slovak proposal on minority exchanges', *RFE/RL News Line* (10 September 1997).

39 'Unrecht kann nicht ungeschehen gemacht, es kann allenfalls gemildert werden', *Frankfurter Allgemeine Zeitung* (11 December 1996).

40 See Koning, H., 'Germania Irredenta', *The Atlantic Monthly* (Digital Edition, July 1996), www.theatlantic.com/issues/96jul/germania/germania.htm, accessed 30 January 2003; M. D. Brown and E. Hahn, 'Sudeten dialogues', *Central Europe Review*, 3:16 (2001), www.ce-review.org/01/16/odsun16.html, accessed 30 January 2003.

41 'Czechs want Slovakia to join NATO, EU', *RFE/RL News Line* (11 July 1997).

42 'Polish Premier in Hungary', *RFE/RL News Line* (3 July 1997).

43 Historical examples from the interwar period and general theoretical considerations are analysed in S. Tägil, K. Gerner, G. Henrikson, R. Johansson, I. Oldberg and K. Salomon, *Studying Boundary Conflicts. A Theoretical Framework* (Lund: Esselte Studium, 1977); S. Tägil (ed.), *Regions in Upheaval: Ethnic Conflict and Political Mobilization* (Lund: Esselte Studium, 1984).

44 See Z. Hajdú, 'Emerging conflict or deepening cooperation? – The case of the Hungarian border regions', *Border Regions in Functional Transition* (Berlin: REGIO. Series of the IRS, 1996); A. Duleba, 'Karpatský Euroregión – geneza projektu transhraniè021nej spolupráce' [The Carpathian Euroregion – the Genesis of a Project of Transboundary Cooperation], *Medzinárodné Otázky*, 2:4 (1993), 93–115.

45 'Program Naprawy Państwa. Sejmowe exposé premiera Jerzego Buzka, 10 listopada 1997 [The Programme for Curing the State. Parliamentary Address by Prime Ministery Jerzy Buzek, 10 November 1997], *PAP* (10 November 1997).

46 S. Huntington, *The Clash of Civilizations and the Remaking of World Order* (New York: Simon & Schuster, 1996).

ANDRÁS BOZÓKI

5

The image of Europe: European integration and the new Central Europe

This chapter discusses the changing relations between states in Central Europe after the collapse of communist rule and also their perception of 'Europe'. I offer an overview of the political history of East Central Europe and its subregions (Baltic region, Central European region, South East European region), focusing on the Central European countries before, during and after communist rule. At the end, I discuss some obstacles to integration concerning the internal conditions of these countries, the chance of regional cooperation and some scenarios for the integration of Central Europe to the wider European structures. Special attention is paid to the practice of competition, cooperation and geopolitics as well as to the political uses and chances of federalism and regionalism in forming the new Europe.

Regime change and the image of Europe

One of the symbolic events bringing the 1989 regime changes in East Central Europe into action happened when the Iron Curtain was torn down and East German refugees staying in Hungary could leave for the West. It was generally believed at the time that the ousting of the communist regime would be enough for the West to welcome back the countries 'kept hostage' for decades. The essence of the regime change in those Central European countries was 'to join Europe'. The Hungarians, Czechs, Poles and Slovaks became part of the euphoria notwithstanding the disappointment they had suffered on previous occasions, for example when the West had failed to keep its promise to help the Hungarians in the 1956 revolution.

This feeling of euphoria showed itself first in Hungary and Poland, since these two countries pioneered in changing regimes. The negotiated revolution started almost at the same time in the two countries. In Poland round table discussions were carried on between February and April 1989, which, following a provisional pact between the two elite groups, resulted in a restricted free election in June 1989 with a sweeping victory for Solidarity. The negotiations in Hungary took place between June and September 1989. This two-month shift in time was enough for the Hungarians to avoid what happened in Poland, namely the provisional pact with the communists, and, gaining impetus from the accelerating revolutionary process in the other countries, they succeeded in fighting entirely free elections. In these two countries there were hardly any newly formed parties, which, though with some slight shift in emphasis, did not include in their programmes the idea of joining the institutions of the then European Community. NATO, however, was handled more cautiously as the Soviet troops had not yet left these countries and the Warsaw Treaty Organization (WTO) still existed up until the summer of 1991. First, the idea of 'finlandization' – that is to say, to become neutral – had been popular; later, however, this idea was also relegated to the background having been replaced by a more open policy of westernization.

When George Bush, the US president, visited Poland and Hungary in the summer of 1989 and the process of change had also started in East Germany and Czechoslovakia, the region came into the limelight of the international press. Apparently, it was thought an appropriate moment to exploit so long as Gorbachev was in power in the Soviet Union. The idea was not to miss this 'period of grace' to opt out of the WTO and the council for mutual economic assistance (CMEA), and to make a decision on the withdrawal of the Soviet troops as well as to sign association agreements with the European Community.

From this point of view, the disintegration of the Soviet Union in 1991 slowed down rather than accelerated the rapprochement between Central Europe and the West. The European bank for reconstruction and development (EBRD) was established and the 'Poland Hungary assistance for the reconstruc-tion of the economy' (PHARE) programme was launched in 1989 when the Soviet Union was still one country. The disintegration of the Soviet Empire, however, obviously quenched the feeling of 'Euro-enthusiasm' in the West since the enemy had disappeared. It was not so urgent for the Western countries to sustain their previously rapid process of rapprochement. The issue now became more complex. It was not simply the question that some East Central European countries had to be 'transposed' to the Western camp but new definitions had to be given to the most important Western organizations (NATO, the European Union). The Cold War consensus came to an end at a time when there were no practical concepts to define the 'post-Cold War' identity.

East Central Europe from buffer zone to sovietized belt: a historical overview

In many aspects the histories of East Central European countries do not have much in common. The Baltic states, Poland and Prussia have their own history.

The Central European countries, which used to belong first to the Habsburg Empire and then to the Austro-Hungarian Monarchy, have their separate history and so have those Southern European countries which were under Turkish rule for hundreds of years.

Countries belonging to East Central Europe are those that lie to the east of the previously existing Iron Curtain but to the west of Russia (and most of Ukraine). Relying on the analysis of Jeno Szűcs, there is a historical basis for separating Western Europe and Eastern Europe as well as a third historical region between the two, namely East Central Europe ('Europe in-between'). According to Szűcs, the historical chronology is as follows:

> The first expansion of the Barbarian peoples, having engulfed the western heritage of Rome, led to the birth of the notion of the 'West' (500–800); the first great eastward and northward expansion of the West (1000–1300) then enlarged the bounds of *Europe Occidens* (to include Northern and East Central Europe) and South Eastern Europe took shape under the sphere of influence of Byzantium, which had inherited Rome's mantle in the east. . . . Modern times arrived from two directions: one was the second great expansion of the West (1500–1640) which, by stretching over the Atlantic, connected America to itself (and later absorbed Scandinavia too); the other was the great expansion of 'truncated' Eastern Europe, which created a 'complete' Eastern Europe by annexing Siberia, which stretched to the Pacific. East Central Europe got squeezed between these two regions.[1]

This latter region has been the historical intersection of Western and Eastern elements. It had the following features: (1) The bourgeoisie was weaker, there were fewer free towns and territorial autonomies, the absolute state came into being later and bourgeois society took longer to develop.[2] (2) Contrary to their Western counterparts, in these countries modern, bourgeois, capitalist and feudal societies inherited from feudalism's past lived in parallel with one another.[3] (3) In East Central Europe, however, society was not exclusively controlled by the state whereas in Eastern Europe it was (Russia, Ukraine, Belarus, Moldova), since next to the state hierarchy there also formed independent social autonomies, networks and hierarchies.

Therefore East Central Europe is to be considered a 600–700 km geographical zone rather than a historically homogeneous region. Its borderline in the West is the river Elbe and its borderline in the East is described by Szűcs as follows: 'It stretched from the region of the lower Danube to the eastern Carpathians and further north along the forests that separated the West Slavs from the East Slavs, reaching the Baltic regions in the thirteenth century. The comprehensive term used as early as the twelfth century for the region west of this line was *Europa Occidens* (Occidentalis).'[4]

This geographical zone of East Central Europe is divided into three major groups of countries. The first is in the north, incorporating the Baltic states, which belonged to the Soviet Union for fifty years and where a great number of Russian minorities still live (Estonia, Latvia, Lithuania). The second region is made up of countries lying in Central Europe in the strictest sense of the word, which were partly or wholly under German or Austrian influence and where Roman Catholicism has always played a decisive role in defining the cultural profile of the region. In effect, this region was cut into two halves by the Iron Curtain. The major part of it (Poland, Czech Republic, Slovakia, Hungary, Slovenia, Croatia and a part of Romania) lay on its eastern side, while the German- and Italian-speaking territories of Central Europe (Bavaria, Austria and the North-Eastern provinces of Veneto, Alto-Adige, and Friuli) lay on its western side. Finally, the third region is made up of South Eastern Europe, the Balkan states, which were hardly, if at all, influenced by the waves of industrialization and where the decisive influence was played by the orthodox church and in certain areas by Islam (Bosnia-Herzegovina, Serbia, Bulgaria, Macedonia, Albania and a part of Romania).

This large middle region between Eastern and Western Europe, from Finland to Greece, took on the function of *cordon sanitaire* and this function was strengthened after World War I when the Austro-Hungarian monarchy disintegrated and Poland regained its sovereignty. The creators of the peace treaty closing World War I endeavoured to create a buffer zone between Germany and Soviet Russia. Poland, with large territories in the east, received independence and the territory of the Romanian state was enlarged with the annexation of Transylvania. They also called into being state complexes such as Czechoslovakia and Yugoslavia that had never before existed. The multiethnic, non-democratic but constitutionally based dual system of the monarchy was favourable for the Hungarians and Austrians and (to a certain extent) for the Croatians. However, because of its narrow-minded ethnic minority policy it was not acceptable for the Czechs, Slovaks, Romanians and Serbs in their hope of developing into political nations.

The unacceptable nature of the Austro-Hungarian monarchy for its national minorities also created resentment against any other federate endeavours and consequently, all of them failed in Central Europe. The concept of confederacy of the Danube peoples first advocated by Lajos Kossuth in the nineteenth century and then by Oszkár Jászi after World War I was never considered by politicians as anything but a 'highbrow' utopia of intellectuals. The concept, which aimed at setting the small nations along the Danube free and furthering their cooperation, was interpreted in three different ways. One of the interpretations was that the cooperation was to be realized with the participation of the Austrians. This interpretation was received with suspicion by the anti-Habsburg theoreticians of states that had just regained their independence. According to a further interpretation, the cooperation was to rely on the small nations outside the German-speaking territories, which, in reality, nobody wanted. The third concept was substantially different from these two. It was the idea of *Mitteleuropa* worked out in Germany, projecting the image of Central Europe with German hegemony. This last theory was received with suspicion and resentment both by the elite of East Central Europe and the advocates of monarchy.

In reality the principles of US president Woodrow Wilson, deriving from nineteenth century liberal nationalism and aimed at realizing the concept of 'national autonomy', created a vacuum in the region and this vacuum was filled by aggressive ethnic nationalism or revanchism of the small nations, which turned against each other. 'The region's historical states and the framework of historical nations have broken up, and all of the borders dividing the nations have become disputed.'[5] In Romania, for instance, the idea of a homogeneous national state gained ground, aiming at quickly assimilating the national ethnic minorities. In Czechoslovakia the idea of 'Czechoslovakism' and in Yugoslavia the idea of 'Yugoslavism' was considered to serve the purpose of establishing the identity of a new and multinational state. As a result of the Versailles–Trianon peace treaties not only Germany but also Hungary and Austria were loser states and the latter two were forced to form a small state instead of the broader state bounds of the monarchy. In these countries the fight for international recognition of independence and state sovereignty was associated with the shocking experience of war defeat and territorial losses. Hungarian political and public opinion looked at the Trianon peace treaty as the dictate of brute force inflicted upon them by the victorious countries; therefore, they were unable to differentiate between the compulsory ceding of territories with other ethnic groups ready for separation and the compulsory ceding of territories with the Hungarian majority disannexed for no reason at all. As Péter Kende pointed out, the 'Trianon syndrome' that developed after the treaty survived and went on dominating the lives of Hungarians and their neighbours alike.[6] For the Hungarians the Trianon decision that subordinated one-third of the Hungarian-speaking population under the control of a foreign state lived on as an indigestible offence for a long time. For their neighbours it perpetuated fear and suspicion stemming from the assumption that the final aim of any Hungarian foreign policy could not be anything other than to enforce its territorial claims.

The 'Little entente' formed by Czechoslovakia, Romania and Yugoslavia after World War I was primarily seeking the support of France in order to be able to resist the Hungarian, Austrian and German endeavours of revanchism. It aimed to prevent a possible restoration of the monarchy. France, however, was not able to gain a firm hold over the region and so 'little entente' had lost its significance by the beginning of the 1930s. The vacuum was filled by the gathering strength of Nazi Germany through the three-power pact, the *Anschluss* and the Munich agreement. Forces supporting the sovereign Austrian state were weak and isolated and the Czechoslovakian recovery was not considered of primary importance by the Western allies. The end of *cordon sanitaire* between the two World Wars was made final by the Molotov–Ribbentrop pact in 1939 that was followed by the division and German–Soviet occupation of Poland. East Central Europe first became a German sphere of influence then after World War II it became part of the Soviet zone. Stalin did not keep his obligations made in the Yalta agreement and the East Central European *pax sovietica* did not only put an end to the sovereignty of these countries but also forced the Soviet model on their internal political–social systems. Soviet supremacy and the compulsory membership of CMEA and the WTO were most detrimental for those countries that were relatively the most developed. The Cold War and the nuclear threat drew a more clear-cut demarcation line between East and West than ever and linked Central Europe to the East for decades. Austria, with its recognized neutrality, was the only exception. Its neutrality and exclusion from the bloc were agreed upon by the great powers in a special agreement in 1955. Looking at the economic and political developments in East Central Europe during most of the twentieth century (between 1920 and 1990), one should agree with a summary which states: 'As all Central and Eastern European countries had a similar export and import pattern, they were unable to increase mutual trade. Radial and unilateral patterns prevailed until the end of World War II.' Later, being in the Soviet zone of occupation, 'unilateral trade orientation was accompanied by unilateral infrastructural development' which led to infrastructural dependence.[7]

Following decades of forced cooperation in the East and the disintegration of the Soviet world system and that of the Soviet Union, East Central Europe regained its 'in-between' position. At first the so created vacuum seemed to be filled fast by the West. It was, however, only realized in East Germany through German unification. Western countries took a more precautious political approach towards the rest of the countries and they did not seem to have any desire to enjoy the fruitful outcome of their victory in the Cold War. Newly born, newly independent or newly sovereign states had to cope with their economic inefficiency.

The peoples of East Central Europe are only connected by two things at present: on the one hand, the common historical experience and negative legacy of communism that had been forced upon them for decades; on the other, the feeling of belonging nowhere, the sour memory similar to the previous *cordon sanitaire* position. They wish to get rid of both: they want to free themselves of their fears that the one-time Eastern Empire may be revived and also of the fear of what could be caused by the territorial differences between nation and state of the neighbouring countries as the legacy of the Versailles peace treaty. That treaty accepted the idea of national sovereignty on the one hand, and created an uncertain *cordon sanitaire* position for the new states on the other. By the 1990s, nonetheless, most of the countries had set the direction of freedom towards the West and the reason was political security. The psychological moment for these countries to set themselves free from communism lent itself more to a competitive than a cooperative political strategy, which is partly due to the confinement they were previously forced to live under. Developments concerning the invitation of a few countries to NATO and to the European Union might change this situation and could bring new dividing lines in Europe to replace the old ones.

Regional cooperation or national competition: contradicting tendencies in Central European politics after 1989

Following the collapse of communism, the international political relationships between East–West and East–East can be divided into three periods. In the first period, between 1989 and 1992, Western states concentrated on the main reform countries (Czechoslovakia, Hungary and Poland) and urged their cooperation, while the Central European states were willing to act for their own benefit. In the second period, between 1992 and 1994, partly as a consequence of wars and partly as a consequence of peaceful separation, the political map not only of East Central Europe but also of Eastern Europe was re-drawn in the wake of internal processes. These changes strengthened competition between the states at the expense of earlier cooperation. The third period started in 1995 with the end of the war fought in the former Yugoslavia when the Western countries were to form more and more concrete concepts how to proceed with the process of integration and for how to select the countries to be included. This process took a more defi-nite direction in 1997 when the beginning of the NATO enlargement process was announced (entering negotiations with Poland, Hungary and the Czech Republic), and when the European Union also declared its willingness to start negotiations with six applicant countries (Estonia, Poland, the Czech Republic, Hungary, Slovenia and Cyprus). In the third period, both regional cooperation and individual competition were replaced by bilateral cooperation between the states in order to speed up their European (i.e. non-regional) integration.

The policy of cooperation in the first period between 1989 and 1992 was encouraged by Western powers, though these were intra-regional reasons as well. One new organization was the Central European Initiative (the successor of the Alps-Adria initiative, then Pentagonale then Hexagonale), established in November 1989. It aimed to cross the East–West divide by embracing Italy and Austria, as well as the Central European post-communist states. Institutionally it was a loose cooperation between those states with limited goals; that is, mainly infrastructural projects. Far more important was the establishment of Visegrád cooperation which aimed at promoting economic, political and security coop-eration between Poland, Czechoslovakia and Hungary. These post-communist democracies, however, had just regained their sovereignty and did not wish to turn 'back' too quickly to the bonds of close cooperation they had hated so much before. The Hungarian (led by József Antall) and the Polish (first led by Mazowiecki then by Bielecki and Olszewski) centre-right governments as well as the Czechoslovakian (led by Marián Calfa) centrist government coalition were engaged in finding the first steps in transforming their countries and in getting political support for the new democratic identity. In Poland, Lech Walesa, elected president in 1990, took great pains to enlarge presidential power by openly assuming Piłsudski's legacy. In Czechoslovakia, Václav Havel became president and considered himself the man to realize Tomás G. Masaryk's dreams of a 'Czechoslovak' nation. In Hungary, prime minister Antall, even before forming his government, announced that he considered himself 'in spirit the prime minister of fifteen million Hungarians', which was a message (at least for the neighbouring countries) proclaiming that the identity of democracy was to be based on the legacy of the pre-communist era. However, what brought these leaders and states together was that they all shared some basic purposes: to promote economic growth, to distance themselves from the legacy of communism, to consolidate capitalism and liberal democracy, to stabilize the region and, finally, to integrate the eastern half of Central Europe with its western half.[8]

Partly resulting from the pressure exerted by the West, but also from their common interests, in February 1991 the meeting of the heads of states and premiers of the three countries took place in Visegrád, Hungary, a symbolic place where the kings of the countries had met over six hundred years before. The resulting agreement reflected the importance of economic opening towards one another and the coordination of political actions as a part of the process towards European integration. More concretely, the parties encouraged interstate cooperation (in fields including internal security, law, education, the economy, military reform and migration policy) and promoted regional stability (with special attention to the problem of national minorities, but also to the geopolitical status of the whole region: being between a disintegrating Soviet Union and a potentially rising Germany). Most importantly, the negotiators agreed on the goal of speeding up the process of European integration and harmonizing their actions towards the European Union.[9] Western journalists started to call these three (later four) countries the Visegrád group. The Visegrád summit was followed by two others (Cracow, October 1991 and Prague, May 1992) but since then the participating states have been slowly turning away from each other and cooperation has been complemented with, or rather replaced by, competition. Retrospectively, the major institutional achievement of the Visegrád group was that it established a regional customs union, the Central European Free Trade Area (CEFTA) in December 1992. CEFTA started to operate after the break-up of Czechoslovakia (in March 1993) and proved to be attractive for other countries such as Slovenia. It also served as a pattern for multilateral trade for another region in East Central Europe, where the Baltic Free Trade Zone was established.

As early as 1991 it became obvious that the political development in the new democracies of Central Europe (including Slovenia) was taking a different course from that in South-Eastern Europe. In Central Europe the communist parties and their successors obtained a maximum of only 10–20 per cent of the vote at the first elections and they were pushed to the opposition. However, in Romania, Bulgaria, Albania, Serbia and Montenegro it was the (former) communist parties that won the first multi-party elections. The impression of a neutral political observer at the time was that while the Visegrád countries had made a clear break with the old regime, other post-communist countries still had a long transition, having being burdened with strong continuities to the past. There was a borderline where western roman and eastern orthodox christianity separated from each other and which marked the spheres of influence of the Habsburg and Ottoman–Turkish Empires. In the former region the tradition of parliamentary democracy was stronger; the agrarian population only constituted half the population and the working class movement mainly relied on social democratic traditions. It was in Central Europe that liberal, pro-independence, anticommunist movements developed in 1953, 1956, 1968, 1976 and 1980–81. It was only in these countries that underground and organized opposition came into being with the political strategy of 1976 and 1980–81. It was only in these countries that underground and organized opposition came into being with the political strategy of 'new evolutionism' and 'civil society against the state'. The party system in these countries was basically divided into left and right wings after 1989. In South-Eastern Europe, however, the parliamentary tradition was weak and, the agrarian population constituted three-quarters or four-fifths of the population. Consequently, the working class movement was not organized on a social democratic basis but on communist ideology brought into the towns by the unskilled workers flooding there from the countryside. In South East Europe the tradition of democratic opposition was also missing. Consequently, the newly formed party system was separated along the cleavage between communist and anticommunist followers.[10] By 1991 it was almost obvious that Western political organizations differentiated between their political 'favourites' (the Visegrád group) and 'stepchildren' (South Eastern countries) along the line of historically developed cultural–political differences. The 'Visegrád package', as a symbol of 'good guys' among the new democracies, was well marketed and well sold in Western European countries. In his essay, for instance, Herbert Kitschelt attributed more importance to the legacy of communism than to the traditions of the pre-communist era and took this as a basis to outline a trichotomous typology. First, in the countries of former bureaucratic–authoritarian communism (East Germany, Czech Republic) the main political cleavage was formed around socio-economic questions, and there is a revival of the classic left–right division. Secondly, in formerly national communist countries which had negotiated transition (Poland, Hungary, Slovenia) the economic policy divide between market liberalizers and socialist standpatters is less sharp; therefore the party system is tripolar (socialists, liberals, conservatives) and the main cleavage was created around cultural issues, such as morality, family and religion. Finally, in former patrimonial communist countries (Romania, Bulgaria) 'where the old elite are still entrenched in key positions in all walks of life, the big issues are law and order and de-communization'.[11] In these countries the communist–anticommunist political cleavage proved to be stronger and longer lasting than elsewhere. This approach, however, does not provide a convincing explanation of the differences between the first and second group of countries after the regime change and seems to have less explanatory power today. By the second half of 1991, several events considerably confused the initially clear picture of similarities and differences between the countries of East Central Europe, marking the beginning of a new period in the region. The abortive putsch in the Soviet Union in August 1991 was followed by a shift in power, that is to say from Gorbachev, the Soviet president to Yeltsin, the Russian president. The Baltic states had already become independent by the time of Gorbachev. Yeltsin recognized that the collapse of the Soviet monopoly and the process of democratization would sooner or later raise the question of terminating the Soviet Union, reasoning that democracy cannot keep the Soviet Union together but with the Soviet Union kept together, there would be no democracy. Bearing this in mind, Yeltsin himself urged the speeding up of the process of breaking up the empire, which was finalized by a contract signed at a meeting with the Ukrainian and Belorussian presidents in Minsk in December 1991. Also at this time, the East Slavonian conflict broke out between the Serbs and the Croatians in Croatia, which soon escalated into a war. The peaceful process of secession characterized by democratic elections and referendums which started in 1990–91 was not able to retain its 'velvet' character. The series of bloody conflicts leading to a war initiated the final disintegration of the post-Tito Yugoslavia, a country which had already functioned more like a confederation than a federation from 1980 onwards. This was followed by the 1992 Czechoslovakian election, which resulted in the victory of the conservative centre-right Civic Democratic Party of Václav Klaus in the Czech Republic and of the economically left-centred and politically nationalist Movement for Democratic Slovakia (HZDS) led by Vladimir Mečiar in Slovakia. During the negotiations between Klaus and Mečiar in 1992 the two politicians were unable to agree on confederation; Klaus was rather in favour of the idea of 'velvet separation'. Finally, this latter idea was realized on 1 January 1993. In short, the departure from communism was presented by the national elites as a departure from the former, non-democratic (con)federative structures. Contrary to their original goals, these non-democratic federations were not able 'to hold together' their peoples.[12] This was probably the only way out for the former political elite to maintain their political power as well.

The changes in 1991–92 not only re-drew the borderlines between the countries in East Central Europe but also caused a fundamental change in the international opinion, foreign political situation and character of democratic transition in this region. The new or revived national states were based on a policy of ethnic identity which gave an ever increasing impetus to nationalism and pushed the idea of political cooperation into the background. The war in the former Yugoslavia brought to the forefront a situation where the East Central European states were not seeking the possibility of cooperation and peaceful resolution of conflicts but patrons of great or medium power. The notion of *geopolitics*, which had been considered obsolete, turned up again in the political dictionary. The Croatians seemed to find their patron in Germany, the Serbs in Russia and the Bosnian Muslims in Turkey. Ethnic cleansing tore apart communities that had been living together for hundreds of years. In this war armed troops did not fight against each other but against a defenceless civil population at their mercy. Western countries were not able to enforce a lasting peace. In East Central Europe 'coalitions on instinctive attraction' were formed on the one hand between Ukraine, Hungary and Croatia and, on the other, between Slovakia, Romania and Serbia. Hungary was the first to recognize the independent Ukraine and to sign a bilateral basic treaty. Hungarian foreign policy was supposedly haunted by the fear of the one-time 'little entente' being revived.

Things got easier for the Czechs when Czechoslovakia was cut into two parts. On the one hand, they got rid of the uncertain Slovak politics and also some tensions between Hungary and Slovakia over the issue of the Gabcikovo–Nagymaros dam. On the other hand, becoming an ethnically homogeneous country, the Czechs were largely released from the acute problem of ethnic minorities. The idea of cooperation originating in Visegrád had never been unconditionally welcomed by Klaus, the Czech prime minister who later distanced his government from this regional cooperation. He refused, for instance, to mediate between the Slovaks and Hungarians in conflicts in connection with national ethnic minorities or in resolving problems such as the construction of the Gabcikovo–Nagymaros hydroelectric power station and the much disputed one-sided diversion of the Danube by the Slovaks. (His individualist stance was particularly visible in January 1994 when US president Clinton visited Prague to meet the national leaders of the Visegrád group.) Around this time, the Polish economy started growing at an ever increasing speed. Poland, that was once considered a mere 'third' in the cooperation initiated in Visegrád in 1991, had become less interested in the close cooperation by 1993, partly because of its economic achievements and partly because Russian troops had been withdrawn from its soil. In sum, at that time the Czech Republic, Poland and Hungary, rather than being like collaborators living in the same region, looked more like individual 'racers' running to come in first into the European Union. In 1994–95 all three countries submitted their application for joining the EU in the Brussels head office of the organization and all three made a declaration stating that they wanted to become members of NATO.

The war in the former Yugoslavia and the separation of Czechoslovakia considerably changed Hungary's international position. Hungary was not only looked upon as the one-time reformist country, a member of the Visegrád group, but also as a potential threat because of the Hungarian minorities in Romania, Slovakia and Yugoslavia. If observers with insufficient background information had looked at the region in the early 1990s, they might have rightly thought that all of a sudden the Balkan borderlines were pushed more to the north. Hungary, however (unlike some of its neighbours; that is, Croatia, Slovakia and the new Yugoslavia), is not a newly formed national state and therefore the European federation is a much more popular idea than the idea of an independent national state. The Antall government, which associated itself with Christian national principles, had a clear preference for a more Western orientation; partly because Christianity was also considered a Western idea. It can be assumed that Visegrád countries would have proceeded much faster towards Western integration if it had not been for the disintegration of the Soviet Union, Yugoslavia and Czechoslovakia. But given the situation that developed in 1992–93 the region was transformed into a confused territory impossible to handle because of the national and ethnic conflicts, which the Western powers started to approach with a lot more caution and uncertainty. At first, Yugoslavia was not as important for Western policy as the idea of pacifying the post-Soviet states and localizing nuclear weapons solely within Russia and preferably under central control. That is why initially they were not so eager to implement peace immediately in that troubled region. Later, nonetheless, the war in the territory of the former Yugoslavia, as well as reactivated Russian foreign policy oriented to support of Serbia, drew Western attention to the region in turmoil and strengthened its commitment to peace and stability in Europe.

The phase of an individual race for Western-oriented politics in Central Europe coincided with the change that ensued in US politics when Bill Clinton was elected president after George Bush at the end of the campaign in 1992. In 1992–93 US politics was less in a position to deal with Eastern Europe and to offer options to the East Central European countries. Because of the instability in the East, the countries in the region started to attribute a lot more significance to NATO, which they considered the only pledge of security. Feeling the increasing uncertainty of the 'race', Viktor Orbán, a Hungarian opposition politician, stated in 1994 that joining NATO was more urgent than joining the European Union because security was more important than well being. Regional foreign policy of collaborating neighbour states was, as it were, replaced by European policy and NATO policy. To sum up the developments of the second period, Valerie Bunce was right when she claimed that 'the major reason why regional cooperation among Poland, Hungary, the Czech Republic and Slovakia declined after 1992 was that the structure of power in the international system changed and, with that, the interests of the Visegrád states and the incentives they had to cooperate with each other.'[13]

In 1994–95 the beginning of a new political stage was outlined in East–West international relations, the third since 1989. Both NATO and the European Union decided to expand to the East, though without any time commitment. Western policy was partly aimed at sustaining a normal relationship with the Russians and partly at encouraging Central European countries in 'no man's land' to establish a closer relationship with the West. A part of this policy was the extension of East–West military cooperation in the framework of the partnership for peace programme, from 1994, and the organization for security and cooperation in Europe (OSCE) from 1995. The European council was also extended and even Russia was accepted as a member. The Western European Union (WEU) offered associate membership for some East Central European countries. The commitment to a future NATO enlargement was first announced at the January 1994 NATO summit. Developing the conditions for minimal cooperation also facilitated a more definite attempt to create peace in Bosnia. In Dayton, in November 1995, US foreign policy enforced a peace agreement between the representatives of Croatia, Yugoslavia and Bosnia-Herzegovina. All this made it possible to send peace implementation forces to Bosnia and Croatia which also relied on international cooperation. The Balkan war came to an end.

A more active US presence and a policy relying more on persuasion and 'gentle force' also played a part in the conclusion of the Slovak–Hungarian bilateral basic treaty in March 1995, which was ratified by the Hungarian parliament as early as the spring of 1995 and at the beginning of 1996 by the Slovak parliament. Nevertheless, the issue of the Gabcikovo-Nagymaros hydroelectric dam, that Slovakia inherited from the 1997 treaty between Hungary and Czechoslovakia, is still far from being resolved, even after the September 1997 decision of the judges in Hague, which was favourable to Slovakia. Further bilateral treaties have been signed between Romania and Ukraine, and between Hungary and Romania. Multilateral regional cooperation has been overshadowed by the newly initiated policy of bilateral treaties. Western pressure also played a part in both these events, encouraging competition and division, and in others; for example, that Greece recognized Macedonia and that the Bosnian war did not spread to Kosovo or Sandiak or to Romania, where the extreme nationalists were forced out of the ex-communist government coalition. With the victory of noncommunist centre-right parties in Romania (November 1996) and Bulgaria (April 1997) the 'long transition' of these countries ended as well. In March 1997, the European commission approved a new orientation for the PHARE programme (a project originally created to support reform in Poland and Hungary though currently it has fourteen members) in order to change it from a demand-driven programme to an accession-driven one, preparing countries of East Central Europe for membership in the EU. Together with 'technical assistance to the commonwealth of independent states' (TACIS), which is a programme for supporting reform and promoting stability in post-Soviet countries, the PHARE democracy programme for Central and Eastern Europe added up to 27 million ecus in 1996 to strengthen democratic institutions and policies.[14]

After the decision at the 1997 NATO summit in Madrid to open the doors for the three newcomers, Poland, Hungary and the Czech Republic (note that all are from the Visegrád group), efforts for cooperation were revitalized among the three. Their governments quickly agreed to hold regular meetings for foreign and defence ministers in order to harmonize the steps to take. This certainly could not have happened so fast without their previous cooperation inside the Visegrád framework as well as their entrance to the OECD, which had taken place in 1996. Other countries, such as Slovenia and Romania, continue their efforts to get closer to NATO so as to be accepted in the second round of enlargement. The NATO decision was opposed by those who feared it might further divide the region and cause unnecessary tensions. However, this proved not to be the case, since those countries which are invited and not invited were equally interested in the keeping of, or speeding up the process of, enlargement. In fact, Hungarian–Romanian foreign policy relations have never been as promising as they are today.[15] NATO and the European Union are still very popular in most of the East Central European countries as many people think that NATO guarantees peace and the European Union (in the long run) will ensure well being. Notwithstanding the pessimism which is undoubtedly present, the United States and Western Europe are also still popular; the IMF and the World Bank, however, much less so.[16] The East Central European reconciliation and cooperation process urged by the West has a good chance to come to fruition, particularly if we bear in mind the developments in the past few years. But this process is still in an inchoate stage and it is too early to judge its outcome.

The problems of integration

Obstacles in the way of the integration of European structures have different sources. The countries of East Central Europe are still struggling with the establishment of an effective administration of the state. They have to establish a modern, meritocratic civil service with well-paid professionals who are able to implement the policy of the state in an efficient and impartial manner, following rational–legal bureaucratic norms. The creation of an efficient system of local and regional government seems to be crucial as well.[17] Democratic federalism requires full internal democracy, while democracy cannot be maintained without a functioning state. Linz and Stepan are right when they say: 'Democracy is a form of governance of a state. Thus, no modern polity can become democratically consolidated unless it is first a state.'[18] State-building, however, requires an increase in social trust in the state. Without such trust the reduction of the level of corruption and the establishment of an efficient taxation system cannot be achieved, though these elements, among others, are crucial in economic stabilization as well as the popularity and legitimacy of the new democracy.

The period of state-building, a process which takes place in parallel with that of nation-building, for example in Croatia, Slovakia, Macedonia, Estonia and Moldova, is not very conducive to the construction of new federative structures. Nation-builders are not always tolerant of pluralism. The advantages of federalism are, for instance, more effective conflict management, a chance for better protection of minorities and territorial interests, respect for diversity, search for a balance between autonomy (diversity) and sovereignty (union) and, finally, a better representation of interests in society.[19] But these ideas have not been put into practice in East Central Europe so far. Most governments in East Central Europe are tending to homogenize their population's cultural and political identity instead of supporting diversity by 'federalizing' national politics. Instead of conflict management, most of them seek conflict resolution along majority principles. Instead of defending and supporting minorities by including them into the 'body politic' they emphasize the 'national' dimension of statehood by practising extremely strong internal nationalist policies.[20] The idea of consociationalism or power-sharing (which is crucial to the realization of all federal ideas), as Schöpflin points out, moves in the direction of deterritorialization.[21] However, examples from different parts of Europe show that sometimes consensual approaches, due to different local political cultures and other factors, do not work and this might lead to aggressive, exclusivist 'solutions'.[22]

In this situation ethnic minorities (especially the Roma communities) remain clearly on the loser's side. In the context of state policies which were described as 'nationalizing states and external national homelands',[23] the newly independent states try to strengthen their identity through the combination of two principles: *ethnos* and *demos*.[24] These 'ethno-democracies' (majoritarian democracy based on ethnic principles) or 'ethnocracies' (semi-democratic rule based on ethnicity) do not even seek to assimilate their minorities, as European liberal nationalists did in the nineteenth century; instead, they simply want to exclude them from 'the nation'. Consequently, by identifying the concept of nation with the state, these countries do not offer equal social status for their co-patriots as citizens of the same state with different ethnic origin.[25] The sad fact about the chances of federalism in postcommunist Europe is that as long as the idea of an internally multiethnic state is not accepted by the governments of the region (replacing the idea of ethnically homogeneous nation-states) the federalist idea will remain a dream. Presently, the major impetus for federalism comes from external, not internal, Western pressure. Federalism is practically viewed by many as a negligible part of the attractive 'welfare package' represented by the European Union.

This situation underlines the importance of a vivid civil society and the need for a democratic political culture. First, for internal reasons, because in this way citizens are able to control their own state; secondly, from the viewpoint of international cooperation, because in the temporary lack of an effective state, they can push local or regional governments to cooperate with their counterparts from another country in the border regions. Probably the most successful euro-regional cooperation can be found along the German–Polish border.[26] To give another example, but on a smaller scale, such cooperation exists between western Hungary, eastern Austria and eastern Slovenia. Beyond the existing personal labour relationships, created by Hungarians during their daily migration to different Austrian firms as well as by Austrians who are investing in Hungarian agriculture and the service sector, there are inter-regional plans to develop road and train connections and infrastructure in general. Almost all post-communist democracies in Central Europe are eager to build highways as quickly as possible in order to get 'closer' or feel themselves 'closer' to Europe. This urgency helped immensely some luckier counties, such as Győr-Moson-Sopron county in north-western Hungary, which was able to benefit from this development. This region has the lowest rate of unemployment (about 4 per cent) and one of the highest rates of economic boom in the country. Local entrepreneurs from the Western Transdanubian region of Hungary make profit from their cross-border businesses. Since Austria joined the European Union, cross-border cooperation has been encouraged even more and the INTERREG 2 – PHARE CBC programme offers Győr-Moson-Sopron, Vas and Zala counties new, coordinated developmental possibilities. 'Many microregional developmental and cooperational organisations can be found in the region, which also extend over the county borders. With changes in large and small towns in the region their dimensions are rearranged as well.'[27] The case of Hungarian-Romanian regional relations between eastern Hungary and Transylvania is becoming similar, especially since the ratification of the bilateral treaty of the two countries and the peaceful transfer of power in Romania that occurred in November 1996.[28] Some main obstacles to further regional cooperation in East Central Europe are the following: first, the relationship between East Central European regionalism and European integration is unclear, so East Central European countries are not willing to establish some forms of regional cooperation which could be used as an excuse by Western countries to keep them away from the EU; secondly, decentralization and self-governance in East Central Europe are far from the Western European level, so local governments have much more limited legal–technical grounds to act independently; and thirdly, joint members of the EU cannot receive financial resources from the EU for their own regional development and their own resources cannot allow rapid changes.[29] Moreover, the question of national minorities living outside the borders of their 'homeland' still means political tension between the given countries rather than potential for developing an economic exchange across borders. For Hungary, as for many other countries in East Central Europe which have national co-patriots outside their borders, such as Serbia-Montenegro, Croatia, Romania and Albania (not to mention Germany, Russia and Turkey), this issue could have been a destabilizing one, but it was, perhaps surprisingly, much less the case with Hungary's relationship with Romania than with Slovakia. Unlike Romania, Slovakia is a young state with a new nation-state-building identity and with less experience in independent foreign policy-making. Moreover, in Slovakia, unlike in Romania, Hungarians live in the vicinity of the common border where they compose the majority of the population, which is not as mixed.[30] They are a minority in Slovakia but a majority in the Slovakian border region of the Danube. That is probably why, especially in the first years after its regained independence, the Slovakian government felt uneasy in managing the problem of its Hungarian minority, which was regarded as a potential basis for ethnic subversion. For instance, prime minister Mečiar did not enter negotiations with his Hungarian counterpart to rebuild a bridge over the Danube between the cities of Esztergom and Sturovo, bombed during World War II, because he was not enthusiastic about facilitating transborder cooperation between minority and majority Hungarians. The solution in this case was left for the new, post-Mečiar cabinet led by Mikulás Dzurinda. The case of the Gabcikovo-Nagymaros dam was also not simply a technical or environmental issue but a symbolic, ideological and political one. For Hungarians the dam was a symbol of outdated communist prestige investments, which they were fighting during the years of the regime change, while for the Slovaks it became a symbol of national strength, independence and sovereignty. No wonder that compromise on this issue came slowly.

Despite some encouraging developments in transborder cooperation, one should not confuse the concepts of decentralization, regionalism and regional cooperation with federalism. Decentralization or regional cooperation might be a good tool for future federalization of the central power, but one cannot predict this outcome automatically. Moreover, the European Union itself was, for many years, a 'moving target' with competing and shifting identities.[31] Despite the efforts of its federalizers, Europe today is still not a federation of different, democratically organized territorial units but a confederation of sovereign, democratic states. The problem of EU enlargement and integration lies not only in the relative backwardness of the East Central European countries, but also in the willingness of the states represented at the European Union to modify their decision-making structures and so create room for the newcomers.[32]

European Union: what sort of integration?

Notwithstanding the desire for European integration and discussions about it, one question has yet to be answered: what kind of Europe is this all about? Will it be a union of states, nations or citizens? As Pierre Manent asks the question: 'Does "Europe" mean today the *depoliticization* of the life of peoples – that is, the increasingly methodical reduction of their collective existence to the activities of "civil society" and the mechanisms of "civilization"? Or does it instead entail the construction of a new *political* body, a great, enormous European nation?'[33]

Is there sovereignty beyond the nation-state? Is supranational democracy viable without nations? No doubt, contrary to the practice of confederation, the original idea of European integration was that: 'Federal institutions were to relate directly to the citizens, not just to member governments. The main powers were to be defense, currency, trade and enough tax to sustain the necessary expenditure. Other powers were to remain with the democratic institutions of the federal states: "self-rule" as well as "shared rule", now known as the principle of subsidiarity.'[34] In practice, however, the EU has a rather dualized system of governance: on the one hand it is becoming a 'multilevel bargaining system' with its principles of subsidiarity and solidarity; on the other, it is a 'market-regulatory regime' where monetary policy is strictly insulated from the political bargaining system.[35] The question remains: What shape will the structure of the European Union take when the East Central European countries want to be integrated?

The Single European Act ratified by the countries of the European Community in 1987 made an attempt to form a political community out of the member states to prepare them to realize a future European political union.[36] The Maastricht treaty has had the purpose of both accelerating and deepening this process at the same time. In the meantime the East Central European countries have become associated members of the European Union. The nature and dimension of the Union, however, have not yet been clearly defined and there are still different views as to the future of the Union. Those who were sceptical about a unified Europe believe in a European federation divided in terms of space, time or content, while others have tried to stick to the original idea. I enlist five major approaches as future perspectives.

According to an influential concept, the Union will have a hard core of those member states that can meet the requirements defined in the Maastricht treaty and an outward ring of those countries that can only later join in. This is the 'concentric circles' concept of Europe. This idea was received in Central Europe with scepticism, because it is understood as a new division between 'first class' and 'second class' Europe. The newly independent and democratic states in Central Europe need to be more convinced about the nature of Europe before they will give up some of their recent achievements in order to go 'beyond the nation-state' as the EU is presently envisaged.[37]

According to another concept, more time has to be given to those countries that are slow in catching up in such a way that does not prevent the already prepared countries from deepening their integration. This is the 'multi-speed' concept of Europe which received a more positive reaction from the candidate countries, because it might give them some time to adjust the least competitive areas of their economies.

The advocates of the third approach said that the option should be open for every member state to choose from the 'menu' of the European Union programme at their discretion, depending on the content of agreement in which they want to participate. This is the '*à la carte*' concept of Europe. This concept, however, would not be enough either for the newcomers or for the existing members of the EU. If there are no commonly accepted regulations the implementation of this approach could easily lead the Union towards disintegration.

The fourth concept is similar to the third but on the whole it could be considered as a compromise of all the concepts as it says that the Union should mean a unified market for all the member states. As far as other issues are concerned, however, it should be up to the countries whether they join the different separate agreements such as the agreement on the policy of police forces, visas or refugees (Schengen agreement), European monetary union or the common foreign and security policy. This is the 'flexible integration' concept of Europe. Judging this concept from their point of view, the countries of Central Europe were in an ambiguous position: on the one hand, they wanted to reach full membership status in order to be on the safe side; on the other, they were for a while unable to meet all the membership criteria.

Finally, the advocates of the fifth concept still emphasized the importance of rules that were generally valid for all member states. The countries of Central Europe would prefer this solution whatever its cost, while other applicant countries are more cautious. All in all, it has not yet been decided to what extent the European federation will mean an international (between states) or supranational (above states) organization. If the latter case is implemented, the question of statehood (namely, how to preserve democracy beyond states) will again come to the fore.

For a long period of time, these issues were discussed 'above the heads' of the applicant countries. During the years of accession negotiations, between 2000 and 2002, little information reached the public of these countries.

Moreover, even in the member states, contrary to original expectations, national governments and bureaucracies took a more pro-Europe stance than their citizens. The latter rather expressed their reservations and disappointment by regularly sending 'anti-European' representatives to the European parliament. For many of them, voting for the European parliament is simply a protest vote against their own government. The very concept of representation would be questionable because of the lack of responsible voting. What people knew in Central European countries was that the initial Western enthusiasm had abated and once again decisions of their concern were to be made without them.[38] Countries wishing to join the European Union were not fully concerned with issues of federation: this will most probably come only when they become fully authorized members of the Union. By joining the European Union and other Western interstate organizations for that matter, they primarily seek to find a solution to their economic and security policy problems in the long run.

Some conclusions

Due to the historical consequences of World War II, countries of Central Europe were formally members of the Soviet bloc for more than forty years. Czechs, Poles, Hungarians and Slovaks had to learn how to live and maneouvre in informal networks under the icy structures of formalities. The 'system' was above and beyond their ratio of action; they were not asked whether they liked it or not. People learned how to *survive* (and not to *live*) in the first place. Double structures of formality and informality created a systematic lack of trust in the relationship between society and an oppressive system. Those structures also made people's behaviour dishonest towards the representatives of any sort of officialdom in many respects. On the other hand, people were very trusting and honest in their own informal circles. These countries were parts of the Soviet bloc without any sense of belonging to it.

It was clearly a membership without belonging. People felt they had culturally belonged to 'Europe' and not to an empire of 'Asian despotism'. They had developed deeply sceptical and cynical attitudes to the existing 'membership' in the Soviet bloc (just as to communist party membership on an individual level), and they tried to keep hopes, respect and semi-utopian beliefs alive towards an imagined 'Europe', a place they 'truly' belonged to.

On 16 April 2003, just about thirteen years after the regime change, ten countries were officially invited to join the European Union in a political summit in Athens. All post-communist Central European states were invited, including the Czech Republic, Hungary, Poland, Slovenia and Slovakia. In the spring of 2003 several referenda were held in these countries on joining the EU. These events consistently showed low turnout but high support for EU accession. Low turnout might suggest that people sensed: these referenda are, probably, being held about 'membership' and not 'belonging'. Some analysts might think that Central Europeans are euro-sceptical but that is not true. They are just sceptical, in general, concerning any 'membership'. Nevertheless, these countries became full members of the European Union on 1 May 2004.

What Jean Monnet expressed fifty years ago for Western Europe seems to be a valid programme today for a larger Europe as well: 'There will be no peace in Europe if states reconstitute themselves on a basis of national sovereignty . . . European countries are too confined to ensure prosperity and essential social developments for their people. It follows that European states should form themselves into a federation or a "European entity" which would make them a joint economic unit.'[39]

It is not the case that Central Europe represents a 'new Europe' as opposed to the 'old' one. The idea of a 'new Europe' for the Central Europeans does not mean a divided entity but a larger, cooperative unit, the reunited and reintegrated continent.

Appendix

Central European Countries' Memberships in Different International Organizations and Initiatives (X = yes, – = no).

Country	CEFTA	CEI	SECI	Stability Pact	NATO	EU
Czech Republic	X	X	–	X	X (1999)	X (2004)
Hungary		X	X	X	X (1999)	X (2004)
Poland		X	X	–	X (1999)	X (2004)
Slovakia		X	X	–	X (2004)	X (2004)
Slovenia		X	X	–	X (2004)	X (2004)

Source: Modified from L.-A. Ghica, *Regional Intergovernmental Cooperation in Central and South Eastern Europe after 1989: The Question of Regional Identity* (MA Thesis, Department of Political Science, Central European University, 2003).

Notes

1 J. Szűcs, 'Three historical regions of Europe', in John Keane (ed.), *Civil Society and the State* (New York/London: Verso, 1988), p. 294.
2 P. Anderson, *Lineages of the Absolutist State* (London: Verso, 1979).
3 F. Erdei, 'A magyar társadalom a két háború között' [Hungarian Society Between the Two Wars] (Paper presented at the Szárszó conference of populist and socialist intellectuals, 1943). Re-published by S. Győrffy et al. (eds), *Szárszó, 1943* (Budapest: Kossuth, 1983), pp. 188–209.
4 Szűcs, 'Three historical regions of Europe', p. 292.
5 I. Bibó, 'The distress of the East European small states' [First published in Hungarian in 1946], in I. Bibó, *Democracy, Revolution, Self-Determination*, Selected Writings, edited by Károly Nagy (Boulder: Social Science Monographs, 1991), p. 58.
6 P. Kende, 'The Trianon syndrome', in B. K. Király and A. Bozóki (eds), *Lawful Revolution*

in Hungary, 1989–94 (Boulder: Social Science Monographs; New York: Columbia University Press, 1995), pp. 475–92.

7 A. Inotai, 'Past, present, and future of federalism in Central and Eastern Europe', *New Europe Law Review*, 1:1 (1993), 508.

8 V. Bunce, 'Regional cooperation and integration in post-communist Europe: The Visegrad Group' (Bratislava: paper presented at the conference on 'Europe, Central Europe, and Germany: Perspectives for the Future', Slovakia, 7–9 March 1996).

9 Ibid.

10 A. Körösényi, 'Kelet-Európa kettészakadása: körkép kommunizmus után' (A Division in Eastern Europe: Post-Communist Panorama), in A. Bozóki, T. Csapody, E. Csizmadia and M. Sükösd (eds), *Csendes? Forradalom? Volt?* [Was It a Peaceful Revolution?] (Budapest: T-Twins, 1991), pp. 57–60.

11 H. Kitschelt, 'Formation of party cleavages in post-communist democracies', *Party Politics*, 1:4 (1995), 447–72.

12 A. Stepan, 'Toward a new comparative analysis of democracy and federalism: demos constraining and demos enabling federations' (Seoul: paper presented at the 17th IPSA World Congress, South Korea, 17–21 August 1997).

13 Bunce, 'Regional cooperation and integration in post-communist Europe', p. 31.

14 A. Skuhra, 'Democratization in Central and Eastern Europe: the democracy programme of the European Union' (Seoul: paper presented at the 17th IPSA World Congress, South Korea, 17–21 August 1997).

15 R. H. Linden, 'Putting on their Sunday best: Romania, Hungary and international relations theory' (Seoul: paper presented at the 17th IPSA World Congress, South Korea, 17–21 August 1997).

16 On this issue see: P. Dunay, 'New friends instead of old foes: Hungary's relations with the West, 1989–95', in Király and Bozóki (eds), *Lawful Revolution in Hungary*, pp. 453–73; B. Greskovits, 'Good-bye breakdown prophecies, hello poor democracies. On failed predictions and Eastern transformation realities' (Chicago: paper presented at the 10th International Conference of Europeanists, 14–17 March 1996).

17 J. Eatwell et al., *Transformation and Integration: Shaping the Future of Central and Eastern Europe* (London: Institute for Public Policy Research, 1995).

18 J. J. Linz and A. Stepan, *Problems of Democratic Transition and Consolidation* (Baltimore/London: Johns Hopkins University Press, 1996), p. 7.

19 A.-G. Gagnon, 'The political uses of federalism', in M. Burgess and A.-G. Gagnon (eds), *Comparative Federalism and Federation* (New York/London: Harvester Press, 1993), pp. 15–44.

20 C. F. Juberias, 'Electoral legislation and ethnic minorities in Eastern Europe: for or against?', in R. W. Mickey and J. Stein (eds), *Ethnicity Unbound: The Politics of Minority Participation in Post-Communist Europe* (New York: IEWS, 1997).

21 G. Schöpflin, 'Culling sacred cows? State frontiers and stability', *Brown Journal of World Affairs*, 4:1 (Winter–Spring 1996–97), 197–204.

22 G. Raymond and S. Bajic-Raymond, 'Memory and history: the discourse of nation-building in the former Yugoslavia', *Patterns of Prejudice*, 31:1 (1997), 21–30.

23 R. Brubaker, *Nationalism Reframed: Nationhood and the National Question in the New Europe* (Cambridge: Cambridge University Press, 1996).

24 A. Bozóki and M. Sükösd, 'Civil society and populism in the Eastern European democratic transitions', *Praxis International*, 13:3 (October 1993), 224–41.

25 J. Kis, 'Beyond the nation state', *Social Research*, 63:1 (Spring 1996), 190–245.

26 I. Illés, 'A regionális együttműködés feltételei Közép- és Kelet-Európában' [The Preconditions of Regional Cooperation in Central and Eastern Europe], *Társadalmi Szemle*, 52:8–9 (1997), 57–65.

27 J. Rechnitzer, 'The main elements of national planning strategy in Northwest

Transdanubia', in Jody Jensen (ed.), *Transborder Cooperation Between Western Hungary and Eastern Austria* (Budapest/Kőszeg/Szombathely: Institute for Social and European Studies, 1996), pp. 24–30.

28 Linden, 'Putting on their Sunday best'.

29 Illés, 'A regionális együttműködés feltételei Közép- és Kelet-Európában', 58.

30 L. Póti and P. Dunay, 'Hungary's relations with the former socialist countries, 1989–95', in Király and Bozóki (eds), *Lawful Revolution in Hungary*, pp. 413–51.

31 T. O. Hueglin, 'The transformation of governance in the European Union: towards a federal order of Europe?' (Seoul: paper presented at the 17th IPSA World Congress, South Korea, 17–21 August 1997).

32 P. C. Schmitter and J. I. Torreblanca, 'Old foundations and new rules for an enlarged European Union', *Policy Papers*, RSC No. 97\1, (Florence: Robert Schuman Centre, European University Institute, 1997).

33 P. Manent, 'Democracy without nations?', *Journal of Democracy*, 8:2 (April 1997), 96.

34 J. Pinder, 'The new European federalism: the idea and the achievements', in Burgess and Gagnon (eds), *Comparative Federalism and Federation*, p. 45.

35 Hueglin, 'The transformation of governance in the European Union', p. 15.

36 K. Kulcsár, 'Az európai integráció és Magyarország' [European Integration and Hungary], *Külpolitika*, 1:3–4 (1995), 27.

37 M. Holland, *European Integration: From Community to Union* (London: Pinter Publishers, 1993).

38 L. Tolnay, 'A növekvő euroszkepticizmus okai' [The Sources of the Rising Euroscepticism], *Külpolitika*, 1:3–4 (1997), 146–56. A similar explanation concerning NATO enlargement can be found: L. Valki, 'A NATO bővítés kérdőjelei' [Question Marks of the NATO Extension], *Külpolitika*, 1:3–4 (1995), 97–129.

39 Quoted in Ernest Witrich, *After 1992: The United States of Europe* (New York/London: Routledge, 1989), p. 24.

Mitja Žagar

6

The collapse of the Yugoslav federation and the viability of asymmetrical federalism

Pluralism and asymmetry in multiethnic states

The spectacular collapse of the former Yugoslav federation – a state often praised for its successful management of ethnic relations – has raised the wider question of the viability of federalism as a constitutional solution for multiethnic states. Is the very existence of ethnic diversity an insurmountable problem?[1] Were there alternatives that could have saved the Yugoslav federation? In particular, was the model of an asymmetrical federation which developed in Yugoslavia in the late 1980s such an alternative?

Ethnic and cultural diversity exists in every country. Increased ease of transportation and global communication has resulted in growing internal and international mobility, thereby enhancing diversity. Constitutions and policies, however, have often failed to recognize this reality.[2] Few countries have recognized the existence of ethnic and cultural pluralism, much less developed mechanisms to regulate possible conflicts.[3]

Most states and their constitutions are still based on the concept of the nation-state, an entity forged by the historic development of Europe since the sixteenth century. Influenced by the rise of modern European nations and nationalist movements, this concept defined nation-states as ethnically and culturally homogeneous entities that can be properly described as 'single-nation-states'. Such states acquired an ethnic identity. They were perceived as instruments for the realization of national interests of 'titular' nations. The myth of ethnic homogeneity triumphed over the existing reality. Since ethnic diversity was usually perceived as a problem, national constitutions designed hierarchical and homogeneous political systems which ignored the existence of the diverse asymmetries of modern societies. Little attention was paid to citizens not belonging to the 'titular' nation or to other asymmetries inherent in any society.[4] Thus, the creation of nation-states ironically fostered ethnic consciousness of minorities and distinct communities that nation-states sought to deny.⁵

The Yugoslav state and the idea of Yugoslavia in history

The first Yugoslav state, established after World War I as the Kingdom of Serbs, Croats and Slovenes,⁶ was not an artificial entity created by great powers. The idea of Yugoslavia, and demands for a common state by its main ethnic constituents, had long existed.

The Yugoslav idea, influenced by Illyrianism and Pan-Slavism, emerged in the nineteenth century. It called for cooperation among 'brotherly' South-Slav(ic) nations and for the creation of an autonomous political unit (within existing empires) or an independent state where they could live together. Several national leaders believed that a common state would lead to national liberation and improve their future development. Two conflicting concepts of a common state existed at this time. The centralist concept advocated the creation of a unitary state, dominated by Serbs and, possibly, the formation of a single Yugoslav nation. The decentralist concept called for the recognition of ethnic diversity and autonomy and the establishment of a federation or confederation. These competing concepts were still in evidence when initiatives to create a new state of South-Slav(ic) nations intensified just before and during World War I. The creation of the Kingdom of Serbs, Croats and Slovenes marked the establishment of the unitary state based on the centralist concept. Although there was some opposition among the non-Serbian population, the fact that the Kingdom of Serbia had emerged victorious after the war, and the fear of a Soviet-type revolution in some regions of the country, combined to quell opposition.⁷

The constitutional development of the former Yugoslavia is usually divided into two main periods: (1) the period of the monarchy and (2) the period of the federal republic. The first period began with the formation of the Kingdom of Serbs, Croats and Slovenes. Its unitary and centralized political system did not reflect the incredible cultural, ethnic and regional diversities in the country, the results of the region's turbulent history. The Balkan peninsula – a natural bridge between Asia and Europe – has been a crossroads of different religions, cultures and civilizations since prehistoric times. Frequent migrations of peoples changed the ethnic composition of the region. When 'new historic peoples' came to the region, the 'old population' moved to remote areas and often managed to preserve their language, culture and identity. South Slavs settled in the territory of the former Yugoslavia in the sixth and seventh centuries. The division of the Roman Empire in the fourth century AD established a borderline, which to a considerable extent still exists, in the territory of what is today Bosnia-Herzegovina. After the schism in 1054, this border divided two Christian cultures: the Roman Catholic culture in the west and the orthodox culture in the east. The invasion of the Ottoman Turks in the fourteenth and fifteenth centuries brought the Islamic religion and culture to this region. Although Islam dominated eastern culture for five centuries, it did not eliminate orthodox Christianity. Tolerance of the Ottoman Empire enabled the coexistence of several specific – ethnic and regional – Islamic and orthodox cultures. Nevertheless, it did not eliminate occasional conflicts. The border between the Roman Catholic area and the Islamic–orthodox area stabilized along the current political borders of Bosnia-Herzegovina. Rebellions against Ottoman rule in the nineteenth century eroded the Ottoman Empire and enabled the creation of new Balkan states, including the Kingdom of Montenegro and the Kingdom of Serbia, while northern and western parts of the former Yugoslavia remained within Austria–Hungary until the end of World War I.[8]

Instead of recognizing the existing cultural and ethnic diversity, the Yugoslav constitution-makers decided to limit these differences by creating a new ethnic and national identity. The constitution of the Kingdom of Serbs, Croats and Slovenes of 1921 introduced a new concept of 'one (Serbian–Croatian–Slovenian) nation of three names' (*troimeni narod*) consisting of three historic 'tribes': Serbs, Croats and Slovenes. This concept – influenced by Serbian expansionist nationalism – denied the very existence of Macedonians, Montenegrins and Bosnian muslims/Bosnians, who were considered South Montenegro or Bosnian Serbs with specific historic characteristics. The introduction in 1929 of a new official name, 'The Kingdom of Yugoslavia', reinforced the unitary system and the goal of creating a new 'Yugoslav nation'. The constitution of the Kingdom of Yugoslavia of 1931 forbade any political association on 'religious, tribal (ethnic) or regional' grounds (Art. 13 Par. 1), thereby substantially restricting political rights, including rights to association and to gather, and freedom of speech. The only trace of linguistic or ethnic pluralism in this constitution was the definition of the official 'Serbian–Croat–Slovene' language (Art. 3) based on the recognition of the existence of, at least, three different languages.[9]

Although the constitutions of 1921 and 1931 proclaimed democratic principles and human rights, their provisions were seldom realized. Several constitutional provisions were ignored or even invalidated by subsequent legislation. Additionally, the work of the democratic institutions was often paralysed. The underdeveloped unitary monarchy dominated by the king could not be classified as a democratic state by any standards. Non-Serbian citizens became increasingly dissatisfied because of a number of factors, including the denial of the existence of ethnic pluralism, Serbian domination and expansionism, economic and social crises, restricted human rights and curtailed democracy, centralism and unitarism. Demands for the development of democracy, ethnic and social equality, social, economic and political reform, decentralization and broad autonomy, and for the establishment of federalism were ignored by the ruling establishment. Instead, the official ideology of kinship of the Yugoslav population, and repression, provided for the necessary cohesion.

In the area of federalism, the attempt to decentralize Yugoslavia by the establishment of 'Banovina of Croatia' (*Banovina Hrvatska*) in 1939 was the only important development. 'Banovina of Croatia' included most territories where Croatians formed the majority of the local population. It was established through a special decree issued by the vice-regency based upon the constitutional provisions for a state of emergency; that is, without the cooperation of parliament. This decree was the realization of the so-called Cvetković–Maček agreement (*Sporazum Cvetković–Maček*) on mutual cooperation and sharing of power between the ruling Serbian and Croatian elites. Yugoslav prime minister Dragiša Cvetković, the leading Serbian politician at the time, and Vlatko Maček, president of the Croatian peasants' party (*Hrvatska Seljačka Stranka*) and leader of 'the peasant democratic opposition', signed this agreement on 23 August 1939. It was the result of an awareness among national elites that ethnic differences would not disappear and that a new Yugoslav national identity would not be created easily. This agreement assured a special position of Croatia and Croats in the new country, but it also emphasized the equality of Serbs, Croats and Slovenes in the common state. The agreement anticipated wide autonomy and elements of statehood for ethnically defined 'Banovina of Croatia'.[10]

The formation of 'Banovina of Croatia' was very controversial. On the one hand, it was the beginning of decentralization in the highly centralized Kingdom of Yugoslavia. The implementation of the Cvetković–Maček agreement and the formation of 'Banovina of Croatia' could very well have laid the foundations for the different treatment and official recognition of ethnic diversity. On the other hand, there were several negative aspects to the establishment of the new political entity. The Cvetković–Maček agreement was an exclusive deal between two hegemonic ethnic elites that assured their domination and introduced a kind of dualism, thereby placing other ethnicities in an inferior position. The formation of 'Banovina of Croatia' decentralized the existing system to a certain degree, but this decentralization was not accompanied by democratization. Additionally, 'Banovina of Croatia' was formed by a special decree issued in an undemocratic – and possibly unconstitutional – way. Although the existing circumstances did not require the declaration of a state of emergency, the ruling regime used constitutional provisions for a state of emergency that entitled the vice-regency to issue special orders. These special orders then had to be confirmed by the People's Assembly.[11] The state of emergency declaration caused the dissolution of the People's Assembly. Elections for the new assembly were postponed for different reasons until the beginning of World War II. The People's Assembly has never confirmed the special decree on the formation of 'Banovina of Croatia'.

Were it not for World War II, other nations would certainly have issued claims for similar autonomy. The occupation of Yugoslavia interrupted these developments and prevented the full realization of the agreements for Croatia. As it was, the existence of ethnic diversity was not officially recognized in the Kingdom of Yugoslavia and there were no adequate mechanisms for the democratic regulation of ethnic relations. Democratization had not even started. The existing centralized, unitary and undemocratic political system did not provide the necessary cohesion and failed to mobilize people of different ethnic origin for the defence of the country. The institutions of the Kingdom of Yugoslavia, including its army, disintegrated within a few days of the attack on Yugoslavia in April 1941, thereby exposing the fragility of Yugoslavia's political system. The occupation ended the first phase of constitutional development.

The four-year occupation of Yugoslavia saw divisions of its territory among aggressors, the rise and fall of Croatian and Serbian puppet states, destruction and casualties. The national liberation movement united all patriots regardless of ethnic origin or political affiliation and liberated the country. The national liberation movement was an important part of the international anti-Hitler coalition. Although the communist party of Yugoslavia (CPY) led and dominated resistance to the Nazis, the national liberation war was above all a struggle for ethnic survival and liberation. The national liberation movement was by its nature multiethnic. Not only did it recognize and respect the existence of ethnic diversity, but it was organized as a coalition of national liberation movements built on the federal model. It proclaimed principles of equality, equal cooperation, 'brotherhood and unity of all Yugoslav nations'.

World War II also witnessed the first major violent ethnic conflict in this territory. The main protagonists of this ethnic war were Serbian Chetniks (*četnici*) and Croatian Ustashe (*ustaše*). Chetniks considered themselves to be the 'king's army in Yugoslavia' and operated mostly in Serbia, Montenegro and Bosnia-Herzegovina. Ustashe were the political and military arm of the Croat puppet state – the Independent State of Croatia. Both armed formations helped in the administration of occupied territories and collaborated with German and Italian occupiers of Yugoslavia in the fight against partisans. Usually, they did not fight each other directly. They terrorized local populations, mostly because of their ethnic or religious origin, but also because of their political affiliation. Ustashe tended to terrorize the Serbian and orthodox population, while Chetniks terrorized Croatians and the Catholic population. Both exterminated their political opponents and terrorized Gipsies (Roma) and Jews.

The stages of Yugoslav federalism

Federalism had already been introduced to the former Yugoslavia during World War II. The antifascist council of national liberation of Yugoslavia (AVNOJ), as the supreme authority of the Yugoslav national liberation movement, comprised representatives of all national liberation movements, and established the democratic federal Yugoslavia (DFY) by a decree adopted at its second conference in November 1943. The decree stated that the common resistance of liberation movements of all nations secured the material, political and moral conditions for the 'creation of the future brotherly, democratic, federative community of our nations' built upon the 'democratic federative principle of a community of equal nations'. DFY was defined as a state established 'on the basis of every nation's right to self-determination including the right to secession or union with other nations'. The federation ensured 'full equality of its five nations, Serbs, Croats, Slovenes, Macedonians and Montenegrins or the national states of the peoples of Serbia, Voivodina [*Vojvodina*] and Sanjak [*Sandžak*], Croatia, Slovenia, Bosnia-Herzegovina, Macedonia and Montenegro, respectively', and excluded 'every possibility of domination, privileges or majorization of one nation to the disadvantage of another, or one federal state to the disadvantage of another'. Additionally, 'all national minorities in Yugoslavia' were ensured national and minority rights by a special decree. The second conference of the AVNOJ decided the cooperation of the partisan movements and the king's government in exile. It also decided that the future form of government in Yugoslavia would be established by a public vote after the war.[12] The adoption of the first postwar constitution in the former Yugoslavia in 1946 marked the beginning of the second – federative – phase of its constitutional development.

The 1946 constitution: the Federal People's Republic of Yugoslavia

The constituent assembly of Yugoslavia was elected immediately after World War II to determine the form of government and adopt a constitution. Its bicameral structure reflected the federal structure of the country. The federal chamber was a house of representatives where one representative was elected per forty thousand voters. The chamber of nations represented federal units and the ethnic plurality of the Yugoslav community. This chamber was to ensure equality of nations (and nationalities) and federal units in the drafting and adopting of the new constitution. Each of the 6 federal units, irrespective of its size, elected 25 representatives to the chamber of nations, whereas citizens of Voivodina elected 15, and citizens of Kosmet and Metohia (Kosovo) 10.[13] The constituent assembly passed the declaration on the proclamation of the Federal People's Republic of Yugoslavia (FPRY) on 29 November 1945. This declaration determined the republican and federal form of government.

The constituent assembly passed the constitution of the FPRY in January 1946.[14] Following the Soviet example, it established a fairly centralized Soviet-type federal model and a one-party political system known as a 'people's democracy'. Nevertheless, the constitution took into account the federalism of the national liberation movement.

Despite fears of possible disintegration, the constitution defined 'the Yugoslav federal republic' as a 'community of equal nations, which, on the basis of their right to self-determination, including the right to secession, expressed their will to live together in a federative state' (Art. 1). The FPRY was composed of six constituent 'People's Republics' (PRs): Croatia, Slovenia, Bosnia-Herzegovina, Macedonia, Montenegro and Serbia with the autonomous province (AP) of Voivodina and the autonomous region (AR) of Kosovo-Metohia (Art. 2).

Neither the federal constitution nor those of the republics defined Serbia as a federation, although it included the regions of Voivodina and Kosovo-Metohia which were guaranteed autonomous rights.[15] The federal constitution treated Serbia as one of six republics with equal rights. Nevertheless, it provided for a direct representation of the AP and AR in the federal assembly, which should have strengthened the position of Serbia in the federation. Considering the centralized political process and the power of the federal leadership and CPY at the time, constitutional status, however, held little weight.

Formally, the constituent republics restricted their sovereignty only by transferring to the federation, through the federal constitution, certain rights. Competences of the federation resembled those in other federations, but in practice most relevant political, economic and social issues were decided at the federal level. The federal parliament – the People's Assembly – could change the inter-republic boundaries only with the consent of the affected PRs. The federal constitution proclaimed 'the right to cultural development and free use of their language' for all national minorities (Articles 9–13 of the constitution of the FPRY).

The People's Assembly had two chambers that were equal in their competences. In this manner, the constitution guaranteed a balance between the democratic rule of the people and the equality of the PRs and nations. The federal chamber was a house of representatives and the council of nations represented federal units. The council of nations was to ensure equality of PRs and nations. Each PR, regardless of size, elected 30 representatives, the AP elected 20 representatives, and 15 representatives were elected in the AR.[16]

In the years immediately following World War II, communist ideology dominated all spheres of everyday life, including ethnic relations. Continuing its prewar orientation, the CPY insisted on ethnic equality and protection of minorities. The existing political monopoly of power of the CPY considerably reduced the constitutionally provided autonomy of nations and PRs. The official ideology declared that the national liberation and 'socialist revolution' had resolved all ethnic and other social conflicts. Consequently, the constitution did not include provisions on the management and resolution of conflicts. The CPY and its leadership performed these functions informally when needed.

The constitutional law on the foundation of the social and political regulation of the FPRY and on the federal authority bodies of 1953 and revisions of 1954

Following the break with Stalin in 1948, the constitutional law of 1953 introduced self-management, and substantially changed the existing political system.[17] It was expected that the introduction of social self-management would eventually eliminate all social conflicts. The new self-managing system was to replace traditional political institutions and enable full direct social, economic and political participation in the development of the country. The slogan 'Factories to Workers!' was

realized by the election of workers' councils in all factories, and the same organizational concept was to be introduced in all other spheres of life. In this context,
the constitutional law abolished the council of nations as an independent
chamber of the federal assembly, replacing it with the chamber of producers. The
council of nations, as a kind of 'half-chamber' with very restricted competences,
became a part of the federal chamber (Articles 14, 44–6, 48). Representatives in
the council of nations were elected by the assemblies of the republics, by the
autonomous province and by the autonomous region.[18]

The revised constitutional law changed the political system a year later and
further reduced the role of the council of nations, which remained a part of the
federal chamber. Its role was based on the premise of the official ideology that
the national liberation war had resolved all major ethnic conflicts and that the
introduction of social self-management enabled the resolution of all potential
social conflicts. The law provided for the calling of a special session of the
council of nations upon the request of its members, but such a session has never
been convened.[19]

Self-management was developed as an alternative to the Soviet model of
development and to Soviet ideology. The formal introduction of self-management in different spheres of economic and social life and the transformation of
the 'people's democracy' into a new self-managing system demanded a different
role from the CPY. The CPY renamed itself the League of Communists of
Yugoslavia (LCY) at its 7th congress in Ljubljana in 1958 to stress its new role in
the self-managing society. Although its political and ideological monopoly was
still preserved to a large extent, and many changes were cosmetic in order to differentiate the LCY from Soviet-type communist parties, the LCY was nonetheless
quite different from traditional communist parties. The political reforms introduced by the LCY opened the door to gradual democratization. The new LCY programme adopted at this congress elaborated the policy and role of the LCY in
different fields. It stressed the importance of the principle of self-determination
of nations for the existence of the Yugoslav federation. Principles of equality and
the 'brotherhood and unity of the Yugoslav nations', and the assurance of adequate social status for ethnic minorities were declared the bases for the regulation
of ethnic relations. The LCY was aware of the importance of stable ethnic relations. The programme criticized nationalism, stressing its potential destructive
powers in a multiethnic society. Nationalism was defined as 'the remains of bourgeois nationalism' incompatible with self-management and democratic socialism. In the utopian view of the LCY, self-management would resolve all conflicts,
including ethnic conflicts, thereby surpassing the conflicting class society.[20]

The 1963 constitution of the Socialist Federative Republic of Yugoslavia

The constitution of the Socialist Federative Republic of Yugoslavia (SFRY) of
1963 was based on the ideology of social self-management.[21] It introduced a

system of 'socialist democracy' based on integrative social self-management, and changed the official name of the country to stress these developments. Although Yugoslavia was still defined as a multinational federation, the class component of the federation prevailed over the ethnic component in the constitution. The ideal was the creation of a classless society, free of economic and social exploitation. The federal constitution defined the six Socialist Republics (SRs) as 'state socialist democratic communities, based upon the power of working people and self-management' with their own constitutions, which had to comply with the principles of the federal constitution (Art. 108). Instead of different status for autonomous units, the constitution outlined the equal status of two APs, Kosovo-Metohia and Voivodina. They were defined as socio-political communities within Serbia (Articles 111–12).

The council of nations, which was to reflect a pluralistic ethnic structure and to assure equality among federal units and ethnic communities in the federal parliament, was still a 'sub-chamber' of the federal chamber in the five-chamber federal assembly. Its competences were very limited (Articles 165–6, 190–1).

Besides the general provisions on equality of languages, alphabets and nations, the constitution guaranteed the rights of members of each nation to be educated in their own language in the territory of another republic (Art. 42).[22] The constitution also guaranteed the rights of national minorities to education in their own language (Art. 43). Other minority rights were regulated by the constitutions and laws of the SRs. The term 'nationality' was employed instead of the term 'national (ethnic) minority' to express the new ethnic policy that established these minorities as equal communities. These changes actually improved the situation of ethnic minorities in the former Yugoslavia.

In response to different problems in ethnic relations, the competences of the council of nations were strengthened. Amendment I to the federal constitution, implemented in 1967, assured the equality and influence of nations, nationalities, the SRs and the APs. The council of nations was entitled to deal with all matters related to the equality of republics, nations and nationalities, or related to the constitutionally guaranteed rights of the republics. This chamber became equal to the federal chamber within the framework of its competences.[23]

Ethnic relations in the former Yugoslavia deteriorated in the late 1960s. Recognizing the importance of amicable ethnic relations and equality for a multiethnic country, a new round of federal constitutional reforms was launched. Amendments VII, IX and XII of 1968 defined the chamber of nations as the first chamber of the federal assembly and significantly strengthened its competences. The chamber of nations independently dealt with matters of equality of the republics and the autonomous provinces and other matters of common interest. As an equal chamber (to the chamber of the working communities), it decided at all instances when two-chamber decision-making was constitutionally anticipated in the federal assembly. In accordance with the specific procedure determined by the standing orders of this chamber, if ten representatives of this chamber so demanded, the chamber of nations could deal with any issue related to the equality of the republics, nations, nationalities, or with any issue which involved encroachment upon the constitutional rights of the republics and autonomous provinces. Each republic assembly elected twenty representatives to the chamber of nations, and each assembly of the AP elected ten representatives.[24]

Constitutional Amendment XVIII (1968) outlines the significance of the socialist autonomous provinces (SAPs) of Voivodina and Kosovo within the SR of Serbia for the realization of national equality and for the integral development of self-management. The rights and duties of the SAP and competences of its bodies were determined by its constitutional law in compliance with the federal and Serbian republic constitutions. Additionally, Amendment XIX granted the right to use minority languages in dealing with public institutions and in public activities, in accordance with the constitutions and laws of the republics.

Contrary to the expectations of the ruling regime, the introduction of self-management did not eliminate social conflicts. The system was very complex, thereby limiting popular participation in decision-making. Based on the ideological presumption that Yugoslavia was – or was soon to become – a conflict-free society, the political system did not develop adequate democratic mechanisms for the management and resolution of conflicts. Problems in ethnic relations and occasional nationalistic excesses persisted throughout the 1960s and 1970s. Nationalism escalated especially in Croatia, but it also grew in other parts of the country. Considering its potentially destructive power, nationalism was declared the main danger for the existence of the multinational Yugoslav federation. The leaders of Croatia, Slovenia and Serbia were replaced on the pretext of their nationalism (in combination with so-called liberalism). Lacking adequate constitutional and legal mechanisms for the management of ethnic relations and conflicts, president Tito and the communist leadership employed informal methods to handle these problems. The leadership hoped that further decentralization and the introduction of certain confederal elements into the Yugoslav federal system would prevent possible ethnic conflicts. Influenced by problems in ethnic relations, constitutional amendments in the late 1960s increased the autonomy of SRs and SAPs and stressed the importance of ethnic pluralism. However, this process of decentralization and democratization did not substantially reduce the actual power of the federal centre nor that of the LCY.[25]

The 1974 constitution of the SFRY

The 1974 constitution of the SFRY[26] continued the decentralization and democratization process lauched by the constitutional amendments of the 1960s. It emphasized ethnic and social pluralism and – to a certain degree – enabled its manifestation in the political system. The federal constitution further formally increased the autonomy and independence of federal units, the SRs and the SAPs. It was believed that further decentralization of the federation would enhance the equality of nations and federal units and reduce the possibility of ethnic conflicts.

The constitution of the SFRY defined the SRs as 'states based on the sovereignty of the people and the power of and self-management by the working class and working people'. The dual nature of republics was underlined. They were defined simultaneously as states and as 'socialist, self-managing communities of the working people and citizens and of nations and nationalities having equal rights' (Art. 3). The idea was that self-managment would slowly transform the existing models of alienated nation-states with their monopoly of power into self-managing communities based on the initiative and participation of the people. The hope was that self-management would eventually eliminate the traditional nation-state.

The SAPs within the SR of Serbia were not defined as states, but as 'autonomous, socialist, self-managing democratic socio-political communities' which were to provide for ethnic equality and for the preservation of ethnic plurality of these communities (Art. 4). Nevertheless, the SAPs were also considered constituent elements of the Yugoslav federation and the constitution provided for a direct representation of SAPs in all major federal institutions. Again, the constitution did not define Serbia formally as a federation, although Serbia included autonomous provinces which held that status of constituent elements of the Yugoslav federation.

Both chambers of the assembly of the SFRY reflected the federal concept of parity. The federal chamber was defined as a house of representatives to which each SR (irrespective of its size and number of voters) elected 30 delegates and to which each SAP elected 20 delegates (Art. 291). The chamber of the republics and provinces represented federal units composed of delegations of assemblies of SRs and SAPs. The assembly of each republic was assigned 12 delegates, and the assembly of each SAP 8 delegates. The delegates elected to the chamber of the republics and provinces retained their position in the respective republic or province assembly (Art. 292). These solutions were introduced to ensure the greatest possible measure of equality of the constituent SRs (as national states and self-managing communities) and SAPs (as specific self-managing communities) in both chambers of the assembly of the SFRY. In this context, the federal constitution defined which matters had to be decided on the basis of the consensus of all republic and provincial assemblies in the chamber of the republics and provinces. In these matters, the members of this chamber from a certain SR or SAP voted in unison (Art. 295). If a consensus was not reached, the decisions could not be adopted, unless the issue required urgent measures, but even these could not be adopted for longer than one year. A form of minority veto was given to the SRs and the SAPs to ensure their equality (Articles 289, 295–6, 298–304).

The parity structure was also introduced at the level of the presidency of the SFRY to ensure the equality of all federal units (republics and autonomous provinces), nations and nationalities.[27] Additionally, the principle was adopted that the federal and ethnic structure should be considered in the formation of the federal government called the federal executive council (Art. 348 and Amendment XLIII, 1988).

The territory of the Yugoslav federation was composed of the territories of the republics. The borders and the territory of an SR could only be changed with the consent of the affected republic (Art. 5). The borders of the republics, therefore, held legal status similar to the status of international borders.

The constitutional reform of 1974 changed the nature of the Yugoslav federation – at least formally – by introducing certain traditional confederative elements into the system. This reform not only strengthened the autonomy of federal units, but also introduced a concept of shared sovereignty. The federal constitution defined republics as nation-states of constituent nations which were based on the sovereignty of the people. Except for international independence and international legal personality, republics were given all the attributes of statehood. These attributes included constitutions that determined their political systems, coats of arms, national anthems, national official languages, public holidays, and specific educational systems and programmes. Autonomy and independence of the republics were formally limited only by the constitutional principle that the constitutions of republics should not contradict the federal constitution. Nevertheless, the constitutions of the republics introduced only a limited number of specific features into their respective systems. The constitutional and political systems of all the republics were very similar.[28]

The federal constitution determined the specific constitutional status of both autonomous provinces. Their primary role was to assure ethnic equality and to preserve ethnic plurality in these 'autonomous, socialist, self-managing democratic socio-political communities'. Although they were not defined as states, they were considered constituent elements of the Yugoslav federation. The Yugoslav constitution guaranteed them substantial autonomy and direct representation in federal bodies, in addition to the equal representation which Serbia enjoyed.

The actual level of decentralization in Yugoslavia at the start of the 1970s did not match the decentralized federal system introduced by the constitution. Yugoslavia was still rather centralized. The LCY dominated political processes and life; its monopoly of power was not questioned. When the constitution was drafted, there was even some criticism that the direct representation of autonomous provinces in federal bodies, in addition to the equal republic representation of Serbia, could favour the Socialist Republic of Serbia within the federation. The Serbian leadership, however, insisted on such an arrangement.

Following the introduction of the federal, republic and provincial constitutions in 1974, the gradual process of (formal) decentralization began in Yugoslavia. This process intensified especially after the death of president Tito in 1980 and culminated in the late 1980s and the early 1990s. Formerly, president Tito and the LCY had played the central role in political processes and had been the main integrative factors in the Yugoslav federation in the 1970s. They played the central role also in the resolution of conflicts, although their role was not determined by the constitution. The constitution – based on the official ideological presumption that Yugoslavia was a conflict-free society and that the system of self-management assured the necessary cohesion – did not create any political institutions that could have assumed the informal functions of president Tito and the LCY in the management of conflicts and in assuring the necessary cohesion within the system. This deficit became particularly evident in the late 1980s.

The process of decentralization gradually increased the actual autonomy and influence of federal units, including that of the autonomous provinces. They became important independent players at the federal level in the 1980s and their interests often conflicted with the interests of Serbia. The Serbian leadership started to complain that this situation placed the republic in an inferior position in the federation. They claimed that Serbia was unable to control its own affairs and entire territory. It should be remembered that the constitution of the Socialist Republic of Serbia of 1974 assured the direct participation and influence of both autonomous provinces within political institutions at the republic level. On the other hand, the provincial and Serbian constitutions did not regulate the Serbian republic government in its dealings with the autonomous provinces. Beginning in the 1980s, the Serbian leadership, unhappy with the existing situation and constitutional arrangements, began to demand the introduction of policies and institutional reforms that would assure the influence and control of the Serbian government over provincial affairs.

Although the constitution of 1974 did not open up the political process very much, it started the process of gradual democratization that enabled the formal introduction of democracy in the late 1980s and early 1990s. Simultaneously with decentralization, the constitution introduced the system of self-managing communities of interests that managed the existing pluralism of interests in different fields – such as culture, education, science and research, social insurance and healthcare. This concept of pluralism of self-managing interests gradually opened up the political process to different political interests. This development led to the establishment of the first opposition organizations. In Slovenia, opposition was channelled into an official umbrella socio-political organization called the socialist alliance of working people. The development of organized opposition was hampered by the escalating crisis.[29]

The social and economic crises in Yugoslavia and the 1988 constitutional amendments to the 1974 constitution of the SFRY

The economic, political and social crises in the former Yugoslavia deepened in the 1980s and the existing system was unable to deal with them. Although the ruling regime acknowledged the existence of the economic crisis, it denied the existence of the social and political crises until the late 1980s. It claimed that the only problem was the inadequate realization of the existing constitutional system.[30] By the time the regime recognized the existence of the social and political crises and the need to reform the existing political system in Yugoslavia, the consensus of all federal units necessary to amend the federal constitution no longer existed. Two opposing concepts for political reform of the federation had emerged by the late 1980s that had made global political reform impossible. The first concept advocated further decentralization and increased autonomy of the federal units, while the second concept called for a strong and centralized federation.

The adoption of constitutional amendments in 1988[31] represented a compromise, but ultimately a solution that failed to resolve the major problems of the day. Nevertheless, these amendments enabled further democratization, multiparty elections and the introduction of certain limited economic and political reforms. These reforms proposed by the federal government of prime minister Marković soon failed, however. There was neither the political consensus nor the public support necessary for successful political and economic reform.

The amendments of 1988 introduced some elements of centralization at the federal level. They assured the special stable financing of the federal Yugoslav people's army and increased the competences of the federation. They introduced minor changes in the functioning of the federal government and other institutions. Nevertheless, the centralization was much less than that advocated by the 'centralists'. On the other hand, these amendments did not include any key proposals of the 'decentralists', who demanded weaker federal institutions, further decentralization of the political and economic systems, and increased autonomy for the federal units.

In the period from 1989 to 1991, all attempts to reform the existing political system failed. The proposals to centralize the existing federal system and substantially increase competences of federal institutions advocated by the federal institutions, Serbia and Montenegro did not find the necessary support.[32] The proposal to introduce asymmetrical federalism, which would have allowed for different political systems within Yugoslavia, and the proposal of Slovenia and Croatia for a confederal Yugoslav union were also rejected.[33] Conflicts between the 'centralists' and 'decentralists' escalated in the late 1980s, until they finally paralysed the existing political system at the beginning of the 1990s.

The collapse of the Yugoslav federation

Economic, social and political differences in Yugoslavia continued to grow in the 1980s. This became especially evident in the different level of democratization and in the specific political situations in the republics and the autonomous provinces. Political systems of individual federal units began to reflect the political concept desired by their political leadership. This led to the establishment of different political systems in each federal unit. Differences between the republics and autonomous provinces increased with the introduction of political pluralism and a multiparty system. Each federal unit followed its own, specific path.

Consequently, the constitutional reforms carried out in the republics and the autonomous provinces reflected these growing differences.[34]

Constitutional reforms in the republics and autonomous provinces after World War II traditionally involved the harmonization of the constitutions of the republics and provinces with the amended or new federal constitution. Constitutional reforms in republics and autonomous provinces in the period from 1989 to 1991 substantially exceeded this traditional task. Republic and provincial constitutions introduced political concepts that were often inconsistent with the existing constitution of the SFRY of 1974 as amended in 1981 and 1988. The new constitutions in Serbia and Croatia and the amended constitution of Slovenia reshaped the federation and changed relations at the federal level, although there were no new formal changes to the federal constitution.

Slobodan Milošević, the Serbian communist leader,[35] had consolidated his political power in Serbia by 1988. He arranged for his supporters to publicly demonstrate for the replacement of the existing leadership in the autonomous provinces, and took control over both autonomous provinces. His supporters were mostly low-paid workers of Serbian nationality, who believed they were defending Yugoslavia and Serbian interests; they were an organized mob that threw their lunch – bread and yoghurt – at their opponents. For this reason their marches were called, colloquially, the 'Yoghurt revolution'. Milošević also had political ambitions as a leader at the federal level and advocated the introduction of a centralized Yugoslav federation dominated by the LCY. He envisaged that Serbia and its autonomous provinces would play a central role. Following the failure of his proposals to reform the federation and the LCY, he focused on political reforms in Serbia that would ensure his political power. In September 1990, prior to the first multiparty elections, Serbia became the first Yugoslav republic to adopt a new constitution. The constitution of the Republic of Serbia[36] introduced the (semi)presidential system, thereby replacing the former assembly system. It essentially diminished the autonomy of both autonomous provinces, which no longer had their own constitutions. These provincial constitutions, which had guaranteed a high level of provincial autonomy, were replaced by provincial statutes. The consent of the people's assembly of the Republic of Serbia was required for the adoption of the provincial statute by the provincial assembly. The new Serbian constitution abolished the presidencies of both provinces and changed the name of the autonomous province of Kosovo to the autonomous province of Kosovo and Metohia. (Articles 6, 108–12) Although the Serbian constitution encroached upon the constitution of the SFRY (1974), Serbia maintained that the federal bodies should not be changed and that the autonomous provinces, now controlled by Serbia, should remain represented in the federal bodies, thereby ensuring Serbian control over these bodies. In the area of ethnic minority rights, Serbia, at least formally, retained the regulations which were already in force. However, minority rights received less protection due to the reduction of the autonomy of the provinces.

After the first multiparty elections in 1990 the previous political opposition –

the Croatian democratic union (*Hrvatska demokratska zajednica*) – came to power in Croatia. The constitution of the Republic of Croatia[37] was adopted in December 1990, when Croatia was still a constitutive part of the SFRY. This constitution regulated the bases for the multiparty political system and introduced a specific variant of the (semi)presidential system. However, it did not define Croatia as a multinational state, which aggravated relations with the Serbian minority. Rebellious Serbs in Croatia – supported by the leadership of Serbia – demanded the status of a constituent nation and rejected being treated merely as a national minority. These conflicts resulted in a civil war (1991–92) and the temporary division of the country. During the war in Croatia, the Croatian parliament (*Sabor*) passed a special constitutional law on human rights and freedoms and on special rights of ethnic minorities. In addition to certain traditional minority rights, minorities were given the right to special cultural autonomy. Their proportional participation in the representative bodies was assured, with the possibility of founding local communities and regions with special autonomous status.[38]

Slovenia chose a different path for constitutional reform. From 1989 to 1991 the republic's assembly adopted almost a hundred amendments to the republic's constitution of 1974. These constitutional amendments introduced political pluralism, furthered political and economic democratization, strengthened the republic's autonomy, reinforced Slovenia's right to self-determination, abolished the communist political ideology in the Preamble and changed the official name of the Socialist Republic of Slovenia to the Republic of Slovenia. This gradual constitutional reform enabled a peaceful political transition, and political and social stability. The SFRY no longer existed by December 1991 when the constitution of the Republic of Slovenia was adopted.[39] Official international recognition of Slovenia's independence came in January 1992.

The process of the disintegration of ex-Yugoslavia had already started in the 1980s, long before the actual collapse and disintegration took place.[40] The existing federal constitution and the inability to reform the economy, political system and federation contributed to this.

The conflict between advocates of centralization (and initially also unitarism) and advocates of decentralization existed even before the creation of the Yugoslav state after World War I. It persisted throughout its existence, conditioned its constitutional and political development and contributed to the tragic collapse of the multiethnic Yugoslav federation. In the late 1980s two conflicting concepts emerged within the Yugoslav communist leadership. Considering social and economic differences and especially different levels of democratization in the republics and provinces, the Slovenian and later Croatian leadership called for democratization, the introduction of political pluralism (and later a multiparty political system and elections), further decentralization of the federation and stronger autonomy for federal units. On the other hand, the Serbian political leadership – with the support of Montenegro and some federal institutions – demanded (re)centralization of the federation, the reinforcement of 'democratic centralism' in the LCY and the strengthening of its political monopoly, a strong federal centre and limited autonomy for the federal units. This political conflict between the communist leadership of Serbia and Slovenia was soon perceived as an ethnic conflict. The growth of Serbian expansionist nationalism and the escalation of conflicts increased the support for decentralization of the federation in Croatia, Macedonia and Bosnia-Herzegovina at the beginning of the 1990s. As it turned out, neither of the options prevailed. Escalating conflicts paralysed the existing constitutional system, rendering it incapable of coping with the crisis.

The process of democratization in Yugoslavia proceeded at a different pace in each federal unit in the late 1980s. It resulted in the creation of political parties, the formal introduction of a multiparty system and the first multiparty elections in all republics in 1990. Political parties emerged in an environment without multiparty political traditions, where people had been used to a single-party political system. Lacking other effective possibilities, politicians in different regions used ethnicity and ethnic myths to mobilize people for their political aims. Politicians reinterpreted ethnic myths and historic events to explain their actions, proposals and political programmes and to attract support.[41] Ethnic affiliation and nationalism became important political factors in all republics and provinces. The use of nationalism and historic and ethnic myths contributed to the transformation of political conflicts into ethnic conflicts.

Yugoslavia did not become as conflict-free as the communist ideology had hoped. The existing constitutional and political system failed to provide for the necessary cohesion of the multiethnic Yugoslav community. President Tito and the LCY were very successful at the informal management and resolution of ethnic and other social conflicts after World War II due to their political and social influence. Not only did the death of president Tito in 1980 and the disintegration of the LCY in 1990 eliminate successful factors in the informal management and resolution of conflicts, but they also eliminated key informal factors that provided for the internal cohesion of Yugoslavia. The lack of formal constitutional mechanisms for the management of crises, the disappearance of effective informal mechanisms and (especially) the lack of interest in a common existence within the federation contributed to the escalation of conflicts at the beginning of the 1990s. The Yugoslav constitution of 1974 had therefore failed to perform its main task: it did not prevent the collapse of the Yugoslav federation because it failed to provide the formal democratic framework, mechanisms and procedures for the management of crises and for the peaceful resolution of ethnic and other conflicts. The failure to amend the federal constitution and reform the federation – including the rejection of the introduction of asymmetrical federation – was also an important factor in this context.[42]

The alternative of asymmetrical federation

Federalism was an important issue in Yugoslavia after World War II. The federal arrangement seemed to be the only possible 'solution' for this multiethnic country and it became a constitutional principle that found broad popular support. Federalism was taught at schools and research on federalism was encouraged.[43] When it became obvious that the existing federal model was unable to handle the growing crisis in Yugoslavia, the search for alternative solutions began. The positive aspects of the existing federal model, as well as its deficiencies, were carefully studied[44] in an attempt to develop an adequate federal model.

The concept of asymmetrical federalism emerged in Yugoslavia in the late 1980s, a few years before social asymmetries became central topics in the social sciences. The term 'asymmetrical federation' was first used by professor Peter Jambrek and the author of this chapter in a public discussion on the proposed federal constitutional reform, organized by the Slovenian Writers' Association and Slovenian Sociological Association in Ljubljana (Slovenia) in March 1988. In his discourse on existing asymmetries in complex modern societies, professor Jambrek mentioned the struggle of Quebec for the status of a distinct community within the Canadian federation. I spoke of the need for political systems to reflect asymmetrical reality considering the existing problems in Yugoslavia. We suggested a new federal model – 'the asymmetrical federation' – that would enable federal units to gain special status in certain fields in order to realize their specific interests. We argued that principles of asymmetry should also be used to reform the Yugoslav federation. In the two years following this meeting, I developed a theoretical model of the asymmetrical federation by taking into account contemporary studies and theories of federalism, the situation in the former Yugoslavia and similar developments in the world. This model offered solutions for the coexistence of different political systems in a federation.[45]

The concept of the asymmetrical federation attracted the interest of politicians in Slovenia at the end of 1988. They saw the asymmetrical federation as a decentralized alternative to the existing federal system. Discussions on asymmetrical federalism in Slovenia intensified at the beginning of 1989 when the first proposals to introduce this model in Yugoslavia appeared.[46] These discussions provoked vigorous reactions from advocates of centralization from other regions of the former Yugoslavia. They rejected any discussion of the idea that asymmetrical federalism was an alternative to federal constitutional reform. Opponents of asymmetrical federalism declared that the very initiative to discuss these issues was an attempt to destroy the existing Yugoslav federation.[47]

Nevertheless, the Slovenian political leadership officially proposed in 1989 the introduction of an asymmetrical federation. The document 'for the European quality of life', adopted by the central committee of the League of Communists of Slovenia (LCS) on 26 October 1989 reads:

> *What is the asymmetrical federation?*
> We call for the further development of the Yugoslav federation so as to assure a stable and effective federal state based on the recognition of diversity and independence of the republics. Those republics which advocate a specific decision can agree to adopt this decision for themselves [*at the level of the federation*]. They must also

assure the financing of any new activities. The decision in question is binding only on those republics which actually adopt it.[48]

At the 11th Congress of the LCS a few months later, the LCS adopted the above proposal and added the following text: 'This proposal does not undermine the functions of the federation such as international relations, defense against foreign aggression, and those functions that secure Yugoslavia as a common economic space.'[49] The Slovene political leadership and the LCS hoped that these proposals would stimulate democratic discussions which would develop compromise solutions for future constitutional reform of the federation. These hopes proved naive, as proposals for the introduction of asymmetrical federalism in Yugoslavia were immediately rejected.

Following the rejection of these proposals, the presidencies of Slovenia and Croatia went a step further and prepared a confederate proposal for reform which proposed the transformation of Yugoslavia into a community of independent states of Yugoslav nations, similar to the European Union. This proposal reflected the political sentiment of a majority of the people in Slovenia and Croatia who were unhappy with the existing federal arrangements but who still believed that their multiethnic community could be democratized and reformed.[50]

The theoretical model of asymmetrical federalism that served as the basis for the above proposals was designed to translate the asymmetries and differences that existed in Yugoslavia into a political and legal system. By establishing the procedure for asymmetrical decision-making, the constitution of an asymmetrical federation allows every federal unit to realize its specific interests within the constitutional framework. The federal constitution establishes the list of issues that are to be decided in this way.

The model of asymmetrical decision-making in federations is very different from traditional models of decision-making in federations, which tend to be based on the fixed division of competences between the federation and federal units. Traditionally, decisions made at the federal level are binding for all federal units. For the adoption of certain important decisions, federal constitutions require decisions by a specially weighted majority. Very seldom is the consensus of all federal units required, and in such cases the veto of one federal unit blocks the decision. The federal constitution in an asymmetrical federation introduces the model of asymmetrical decision-making for those issues that would usually require decisions by consensus or by a weighted majority. This model enables federal units that wish to regulate certain issues at the federal level to adopt a decision which will be binding on all federal units that adopt it. On the other hand, to protect the equality and interests of federal units, the model of asymmetrical decision-making enables individual federal units to reject such a decision at the federal level if they disagree with it. Federal units that reject the decision at the federal level are entitled to regulate this issue for themselves.

The logical consequences of the application of the model of asymmetrical decision-making are new asymmetries in the legal and constitutional systems. If the procedure for asymmetrical decision-making is employed, decisions will be binding only on those federal units that actually adopt them. Such decisions could establish new functions and powers of the federation regarding these federal units. Federal institutions could perform different functions for different federal units or groups of federal units. When federal units authorize the federation to perform certain common functions for them, they have to assure the necessary organizational structure and financial resources at the federal level. They also have to determine decision-making procedures and the framework of their cooperation. As mentioned above, federal units which do not adopt these decisions are not bound by them. They could regulate, arrange and perform these issues, functions and competences on their own.[51]

The theoretical model of the asymmetrical federation introduces a flexible division of competences and powers based on the primacy of federal units. The federal constitution determines exclusive competences of the federation by enumeration. All other competences and powers rest with the federal units. A specific feature of the asymmetrical model is that if a number of federal units decide to do so, they are permitted to transfer certain competences and powers to the federation, even if there is no consensus of all federal units. Participating federal units could establish two or more different legal and political sub-systems within the federation. This system may be useful in multiethnic and diverse countries, because it can accommodate substantial asymmetries within the constitutional system.

Critics of this model claim that it would result in a very complex and ineffective system. They fear that the asymmetrical federation would be unable to function properly and that people would not understand it due to its complexity. Such a situation, they argue, could lead to instability.

To reduce these problems, the constitutions of asymmetrical federations must precisely define the extent and content of asymmetrical decision-making within the federal system. Constitutions can limit the asymmetrical decision-making to specific issues, cases, functions and fields. It is most likely that constitutions will continue to determine the fixed common competences, powers and functions of federal institutions, and the basic relations between the federation and federal units.

The model of the asymmetrical federation can be employed to decentralize existing federal states and to increase the role of federal units within the federation. It was designed to assure equality of federal units and of distinct (ethnic) communities, regardless of their size, social power and position. The model of asymmetrical federalism may be considered to be a mechanism for the regulation of ethnic relations in multiethnic countries and for the management of social and economic crises.

This model could also have international implications. It could be used at the level of international integration – such as the European Union – as a mechanism that would assure the protection of specific interests of member states in different fields. It could also provide the formal framework for different speeds of integration and different circles of participating member states.

The asymmetrical federation was seen in Yugoslavia as a (possible) stage in the transition from a federation into a confederation (confederacy) or vice versa.[52]

The model of the asymmetrical federation has never been applied. In Yugoslavia it emerged too late to become a viable alternative. The tragic collapse of Yugoslavia was the result of the existing political system and the particular federal model that was unable to deal with the growing crisis. Nevertheless, the main reason for the collapse was the lack of interest on the part of federal units and the Yugoslav population to stay together in the future. It became impossible to mobilize people and distinct communities for active participation in the management of the crisis. Had such a mobilization been possible, elements of the model of asymmetrical federalism could have been used in combination with other proposals to address the crisis.

After the disintegration of the SFRY

The SFRY disintegrated, but federalism has not disappeared from the territory of the former Yugoslavia. Two of the five successor states are, at least formally, federations – the federal republic of Yugoslavia, which was in 2003 officially renamed Serbia and Montenegro, thereby eliminating the name of Yugoslavia from the world's political map – and Bosnia-Herzegovina, established by the Dayton agreement. Each would make an interesting case study. Although they differ substantially, both are asymmetrical and internally diverse, and both are experiencing severe problems in ethnic relations that could endanger their very existence. Their existing federal models are specific and will likely evolve substantially if they survive long enough. Without the assistance and pressure of the international community in implementing the Dayton agreement, Bosnia-Herzegovina would have already disintegrated. This federation is especially interesting, as it is an attempt to prevent future civil/ethnic wars in this territory. It consists of the Bosnian–Croat federation and the Republic of Srbska, which also represents three main ethnic communities in the country. Although the Dayton accord established Bosnia-Herzegovina as the only independent and sovereign state, it hardly exists in practice and is totally dependent on the international community, as many – or perhaps most – Croats and Serbs would prefer unification with their respective nation-state.[53]

Notes

1 Tensions among ethnic groups were evident in the 1980s and 1990s in several countries of the first, second and third world, such as Belgium, Canada, Chechnya (Russia), India, Iraq, Israel, Lebanon, Mexico, Nagorno Karabakh, Northern Ireland (UK), Peru, Rwanda, Spain, Sri Lanka, Tibet (China), USA (e.g. racial riots in Los Angeles) and the

ex-Yugoslavia (including its successor states: Bosnia-Herzegovina, Croatia, Macedonia and the Federal Republic of Yugoslavia with Kosovo, Sandjak and Voivodina). Tensions among ethnic groups and ethnic conflicts were less likely to transform into violent conflicts and (civil ethnic) wars in democratic countries with rich democratic traditions. See T. R. Gurr and B. Harff, *Minorities at Risk* (Washington, DC: United States Institute for Peace, 1993); T. R. Gurr and B. Harff, *Ethnic Conflict in World Politics* (Boulder, Colorado: Westview Press, 1994).

2 On the other hand, several authors emphasize the importance of the regulation of ethnic relations and the protection of (ethnic, national) minorities for modern democracies and their development. See F. Benot-Rohmer and H. Hardeman, 'The minority question in Europe: towards the creation of a coherent European regime', *CEPS Paper,* 55 (Brussels: Centre for European Policy Studies, 1994); F. Capotorti, *Study on the Rights of Persons Belonging to Ethnic, Religious and Linguistic Minorities* (New York: United Nations, 1991); W. Kymlicka, *Multicultural Citizenship: A Liberal Theory of Minority Rights* (Oxford: Clarendon Press, 1995); R. Stavenhagen, *The Ethnic Question: Conflicts, Development, and Human Rights* (Tokyo/Hong Kong: United Nations University Press, 1990); M. Žagar, 'Evolving concepts of protection of minorities: international and constitutional law', *Gradiva in razprave* [Treatises and Documents], 31 (Ljubljana: Institute for Ethnic Studies, 1996), 135–91.

3 The analysis of more than eighty constitutions confirms this statement. For the information on the research project 'Democratization and Resolution of Ethnic Conflict: Management and Resolution of Ethnic Conflict in Democratic Societies' sponsored by the United States Information Agency – US Congress Democracy Commission Small Grants Program and its preliminary research findings, see M. Žagar, B. Jesih and R. Bešter (eds), *Constitutional, Legal and Political Regulation of Ethnic Relation and Conflicts: Selected Papers.* (Ethnicity 2. Ljubljana: Institute for Ethnic Studies, 1999). The project's internet home-page is located at: www.unisa.edu.au/lavskis/zagar/slovenia.htm, accessed 15 December 2003.

4 For further details on nation-states and their constitutions see M. Žagar, 'Constitutions in multi-ethnic reality', *Gradiva in razprave* [Treatises and Documents], 29–30 (Ljubljana: Institute for Ethnic Studies, 1994/1995), 143–6, 152–3; M. Žagar, 'Nation-states, their constitutions and multi-ethnic reality: do constitutions of nation-states correspond to ethnic reality?', *Journal of Ethno Development*, 3:3, 1–5, 6–8.

5 See M. Keating, 'Asymmetrical territorial devolution. Principles and practice', *Project on Federalism and Compounded Representation in Western Europe – University of Western Ontario* (Oslo: Norwegian Nobel Institute, June 1996), and Chapters 3 and 10 in this volume.

6 Western parts of Slovenia, Istria and Dalmatia – that had been given to Italy by great powers for its participation in World War I – became parts of the former Yugoslavia after World War II.

7 On the creation of the Yugoslav state, see I. Banac, *The National Question in Yugoslavia: Origins, History, Politics* (Ithaca/London: Cornell University Press, 1993, 1984); D. Djordjević (ed.), *The Creation of Yugoslavia, 1914–1918* (Santa Barbara/London: Clio Books, 1980).

8 See C. Jelavich and B. Jelavich, *The Establishment of the Balkan National States, 1804–1920*, vol. 8 of *A History of East Central Europe* (Seattle: University of Washington Press, 1977).

9 On the constitution of the Kingdom of Serbs, Croats and Slovenes of 28 June 1921 (also called 'St Vitus' Constitution'[*vidovdanska ustava*]), the Law on the Name and Division of the Monarchy into Administrative Regions of October 1929 that introduced the new official name 'The Kingdom of Yugoslavia' and the constitution of the Kingdom of Yugoslavia granted by King Aleksandar in 1931 in the Serbo-Croat language, see B.

Petranović and M. F. Zečević (eds), *Jugoslovanski federalizam: Ideje i stvarnost, Tematska zbirka dokumenata, Prvi tom 1914–1943* [Yugoslav Federalism: Ideas and Reality, Thematic Collection of Documents, Vol. 1, 1914–1943] (Beograd: Prosveta, 1987).

10 For the Serbo-Croatian text of the agreement see Petranović and Zečević (eds), *Jugoslovanski federalizam*, pp. 508–10.

11 See Art. 116 of the constitution of the Kingdom of Yugoslavia of 1931.

12 The second conference of AVNOJ, held in Jajce (Bosnia-Herzegovina) on 29 and 30 November 1943, adopted the 'Decree on the Formation of Yugoslavia on the Basis of Federative Principle' that established the DFY. For the text of this and other documents of the conference (in Serbo-Croat and Slovene) see B. Petranović and M. F. Zečević (eds), *Jugoslovanski federalizam, Ideje i stvarnost, Tematska zbirka dokumenata, Drugi tom, 1943–1986.* [Yugloslav Federalism: Ideas and Reality, Thematic Collection of Documents, Vol. 2] (Beograd: Prosveta, 1987), pp. 791–801; *Prvo in drugo zasedanje AVNOJ; 26. in 27. novembra 1942 in 29. in 30. novembra 1943* [The First and Second Conference of AVNOJ: 26–27 November 1942 and 29–30 November 1943] (Ljubljana: Komunist, 1973). Citations from the decree translated by M. Žagar.

13 The law also regulated the procedures for decision-making and the required majority for the adoption of decisions. See 'Zakon o ustavotvorni skupščini' [The Law on the Constituent Assembly], *Službeni list DFJ/ Uradni list DFJ* [Official Gazette of the DFY], 63 (1945).

14 For the Serbo-Croat text of this constitution with commentaries, see *Novi ustavi: Zbirka ustava donetih posle drugog svetskog rata* [New Constitutions: A Collection of Constitutions, Adopted after World War II]. (Belgrade: Arhiv za pravne i društvene nauke, 1949), pp. 11–40, 155; Petranović and Zečević (eds), *Jugoslovanski federalizam*, Vol. 2, pp. 234–44.

15 Art. 13 of the constitution of the PR of Serbia of 1947 stated that the AP and AR had autonomous rights, ensured by the constitution of the PR of Serbia in accordance with the constitution of the FPRY. It also outlined that each autonomous unit had its own autonomous statute, sanctioning its autonomous rights. These autonomous statutes had to be submitted to the People's Assembly of the PR of Serbia for verification. See Petranović and Zečević (eds), *Jugoslovanski federalizam*, Vol. 2, pp. 245–6.

16 On the constitutional provisions for the People's Assembly, its chambers and the Presidium of the People's Assembly, see Articles 49–57, 60, 64, 70 of the constitution of the FPRY.

17 See 'Ustavni zakon o temeljih družbene in politične ureditve FLRJ in o zveznih organih oblasti' [Constitutional Law on the Foundation of the Social and Political Regulation of the FPRY and on the Federal Authority Bodies]', *Službeni list FNRJ/ Uradni list FLRJ* [Official Gazette of the FPRY], 3 (1953).

18 The federal chamber was elected by voters in general elections. They elected 1 representative per 60,000 voters (Art. 26). People's representatives, standing for the council of nations, were elected in such a way that each republic's assembly elected 10 representatives, the autonomous province's assembly 6, and the assembly of the autonomous region 4 representatives (Art. 27 of the constitutional law).

19 See: 'Zakon o spremembi 45, 46, 47, 48, in 2 odstavka 51. Člena ustavnega zakona o temeljih družbene in politične ureditve FLRJ in o zveznih organih oblasti' [Law on the Changing of Articles 45, 46, 47, 48 and Paragraph 2 Art. 51 of the Constitutional Law on the Foundations of the Social and Political Regulation of the FPRY and on the Federal Authority Bodies], *Službeni list FNRJ/ Uradni list FLRJ* [Official Gazette of the FPRY], 13 (1954).

20 See *Program Zveze komunistov Jugoslavije, sprejet na 7. kongresu ZKJ* [The Programme of the LCY: Adopted at the 7th Congress of the LCY] (Ljubljana: Komunist, 1978), especially its section 'Federation and relations between the Nations of Yugoslavia', pp. 157–66.

21 See U. Sfrj, 'Ustava Socialistične federativne republike Jugoslavije' [The Constitution of
    the SFRY], *Uradni list SFRJ* [Official Gazette of the SFRY], 14 (1963).
22 Paragraph 3 of Art. 42 introduced an exemption to the principle of equality of languages
    and scripts of the nations of Yugoslavia: In the Yugoslav people's army only the Serbo-
    Croat language was used at the level of command, in military education and in the
    administration.
23 See Amendment I (1967) of the constitutional Amendments to the constitution of the
    SFRY of 1963, *Uradni list SFRJ* [Official Gazette of the SFRY], 18 (1967).
24 The chamber of nations, with 140 representatives, was the largest of the chambers of the
    federal assembly, which had 120 representatives each. See constitutional Amendments
    VII, IX (1968) to the constitution of the SFRY, 1963, *Uradni list SFRJ* [Official Gazette of
    the SFRY], 55 (1968).
25 Historian Dušan Bilandžić claims that as early as the beginning and mid-1960s the late
    Yugoslav president Tito and Edvard Kardelj expressed their fear that ethnic conflicts and
    aggressive nationalism in Yugoslavia could endanger its very existence and cause the
    destruction of the multinational state. The solution was sought in decentralization and
    even confederalization of the state, in order to ensure greater autonomy and indepen-
    dent development for each republic. See D. Bilandžić, 'Tito je još 1962. predvidio raspad
    Jugoslavije: Nekrolog SFRJ' [Tito Foresaw the Decomposition of Yugoslavia already in
    1962: Necrology to the SFRY], *Slobodni tjednik* (Zagreb: 5 September 1992), p. 10.
26 See 'Ustava Socialistične federativne republike Jugoslavije' [The Constitution of the
    SFRY (1974)], *Uradni list SFRJ* [Official Gazette of the SFRY], 9 (1974), and corrections
    in 11 (1974). Official English translation: *The Constitution of the SFRY (With
    Constitutional Amendments I–VIII of 1981)* (Belgrade: The Assembly of the SFRY, 1981).
27 The proportional structure of the presidency of the SFRY was ensured by Amendment
    XXXIV (1971) to the constitution of the SFRY (1963). According to the constitution of
    the SFRY (1974), after president Tito's death, the president of the LCY was required to
    be a member of the presidency, together with the representatives of the republics and
    provinces, elected by the assemblies of the republics and provinces (Art. 321 and
    Amendment IV, 1981). This was changed with Amendment XLI (1988), when only rep-
    resentatives of the republics and provinces remained in the presidency.
28 See Ustav SFRJ, 'Ustavi socijalističkih republika i pokrajina, Ustavni zakoni, Registar
    pojmova' [The constitution of the SFRY, 'Constitutions of SRs and SAPs, Constitutional
    Laws (Legal) Glossary'] *Zbirka propisa* [Collection of Laws and Rules] (Beograd:
    Prosveta, 1974).
29 On the role of the federal constitution of 1974 in the process of democratization, see M.
    Žagar, 'Nekaj hipotez o kvadraturi kroga: Ustava SFRJ in proces osamosvajanja
    Republike Slovenije – Etnična dimenzija osamosvajanja Slovenije' [The Constitution of
    the SFRY and the Struggle for the Independence of the Republic of Slovenia: Ethnic
    Dimensions of the Independence], *Gradiva in razprave* [Treatises and Documents],
    29–30 (Ljubljana: Inštitut za narodnostna vprašanja/Institute for Ethnic Studies,
    1994/1995), pp. 231–60; M. Žagar, 'Ustava Socialistične federativne republike
    Jugoslavije iz leta 1974 in osamosvajanje Republike Slovenije' [The Constitution of the
    SFRY and the Independence of the Republic of Slovenia], *Slovenci in država: Zbornik
    prispevkov z znanstvenega posveta na SAZU, od 9. do 11. novembra 1994* [Slovenians and
    the State: The Collection of Contribution at the Scientific Conference at the Slovenian
    Academy of Sciences and Arts, 9–11 November 1994]. Razprave/Dissertationes 17.
    (Ljubljana: Slovenska akademija znanosti in umetnosti, Razred za zgodovinske in
    družbene vede/Academia scientiarum et artium Slovenica, Classis I: Historia et
    Sociologia, 1995), pp. 367–78. See also M. Klemenčič and M. Žagar, *The Former
    Yugoslavia's Diverse Peoples: A Reference Sourcebook.* (Santa Barbara, Ca., Denver, Co.,
    Oxford: ABC Clio, 2004).

30 See *Kritična analiza delovanja političnega sistema socialističnega samoupravljanja* [Critical Analysis of the Functioning of the Political System of Socialist Self-Management]. (Ljubljana: Zvezni družbeni svet za vprašanja družbene ureditve, Delavska enotnost, 1985).

31 See Amendments IX-XC (1988) to the constitution of the SFRY (1974), *Uradni list SFRJ* [Official Gazette of the SFRY], 70 (1988).

32 The presidency of the SFRY prepared a proposal for the reform of the federation based largely on the Serbian concept of a centralized federation, although the presidency's proposal was not as radical. This proposal supported by federal institutions, including the federal army, was supported by Serbia, which hoped to take control of the federal institutions on the basis of this proposal. See 'A concept for the constitutional system of Yugoslavia on a federal basis', *Review of International Affairs*, 41:974 (1990), 15–18.

33 See the proposal for 'A Confederate Model Among the South Slavic States' by the presidency of the Republic of Croatia and the Presidency of the Republic of Slovenia, Zagreb and Ljubljana, 4 October 1990, *Review of International Affairs*, 41:973 (1990), 11–16.

34 These differences between constitutions of SRs and SAPs grew with the adoption of constitutional amendments and new constitutions in 1989–91. See M. Žagar, *Primerjalna analiza amandmajev k ustavam SR in SAP iz leta 1989 v primerjavi z ustavo SFRJ (1974) in ustavnimi amandmaji (1981, 1988): Primerjava amandmajev k ustavi SFRJ (1988) z amandmaji k ustavam SR in SAP iz leta 1989* [Comparative Analysis of Amendments to Constitutions of SRs and SAPs of 1989 in Comparison with the Constitution of the SFRY of 1974 as Amended in 1981 and 1988: The Comparison of the Amendments to the Constitution of the SFRY of 1974 Adopted in 1988 with the Amendments to Constitutions of SRs and SAPs Adopted in 1989] (Ljubljana: Predsedstvo SRS, October–November 1989).

35 At the beginning of the 1990s, Slobodan Milošević was elected president of Serbia and served for two consecutive terms in this office. In the late 1990s he was elected president of the Federal Republic of Yugoslavia, which included Serbia and Montenegro.

36 See 'Ustav Republike Srbije' [The Constitution of the Republic of Serbia], *Službeni list RS* [Official Gazette of the Republic of Serbia], 1 (1990).

37 See 'Ustav Republike Hrvatske' [The Constitution of the Republic of Croatia], *Narodne novine RH* [Official Gazette of the Republic of Croatia], 56 (1990).

38 See 'Ustavni zakon' [The Constitutional Law on Human Rights and Freedoms and on the Rights of Ethnic and National Communities or Minorities in the Republic of Croatia], *Narodne novine RH* [Official Gazette of the Republic of Croatia], 65 (1991).

39 See 'Ustava Republike Slovenije' [The Constitution of the Republic of Slovenia], *Uradni list Republike Slovenije* [Official Gazette of the Republic of Slovenia], 33 (1991). The official English translation of the constitution was published in the autumn of 1992: Constitution of the Republic of Slovenia (Ljubljana, 1992).

40 The disintegration of the SFRY was officially recognized by the international community in January 1992, when the European Union (including some member states) and a number of other states recognized the independence of Slovenia and Croatia.

41 The medieval states of the Bosnians, Croats, Serbs and Slovenes were interpreted as direct predecessors of contemporary nation-states, although there was no such continuity. In explaining current political decisions and programmes, references were often made to specific historic events – such as the battle of Kosovo polje (Kosovo field) in Serbia or the Independent State of Croatia during World War II (totally dependent on Germany and Italy).

42 For a more detailed personal account of the Yugoslav crisis and the analysis of the collapse of ex-Yugoslavia see M. Žagar, 'Yugoslavia: what went wrong? Constitutional aspects of the Yugoslav crisis from the perspective of ethnic conflict', in M. Spencer (ed.), *The Lessons of Yugoslavia*, Research on Russia and Eastern Europe Series, Vol. 3

(Amsterdam, Toronto et al.: JAI An Imprint of Elsevier Science, 2000), pp. 65–96; M. Klemenčič and M. Žagar, *The Former Yugoslavia's Diverse Peoples*, pp. 194–366.

43 The extensive list of books on federalism by Yugoslav authors includes: M. Jovičić, *Savremeni federalizam: Uporednopravna studija* [Modern federalism: A Study in Comparative Constitutional Law] Institut za uporedno pravo, Monografije 72 (Belgrade: Savremena administracija, 1973); Z. Lerotić, *Jugoslavenska politićka klasa i federalizam* [Yugoslav Political Class and Federalism] (Zagreb: Globus, 1989); Z. Lerotić, *Načela federalizma višenacionalne države* [The Principles of Federalism in a Multiethnic State] (Zagreb: Biblioteka Globus, 1985); P. S. Nikolić, *Federacija i federalne jedinice: Uticaj federalnih jedinica na vršenje federalne vlasti. Ustavno-pravni aspekt* [Federation and Federal Units: The influence of Federal Units on the Powers of the Federal Authorities. Constitutional and Legal Issues] (Belgrade: Novinsko-izdavačka ustanova Službeni list SFR Jugoslavije, 1989); C. Ribičić and Z. Tomac, *Federalizam po mjeri budućnosti* [Federalism of the future] (Zagreb: Globus, 1989).

44 A number of foreign authors also took part in the analysis of both the positive elements and problems of the Yugoslav system and federalism in general. See B. Denitch, *Limits and Possibilities: The Crisis of Yugoslav Socialism and State Socialist Systems* (Minneapolis, MN: University of Minnesota Press, 1990); S. P. Ramet, *Nationalism and Federalism in Yugoslavia, 1962–1991*. 2nd edn (Bloomington/Indianapolis: Indiana University Press, 1984, 1992); D. Rusinow, *The Yugoslav Experiment, 1948–1974* (Berkeley, Los Angeles: University of California Press, 1977); D. Rusinow (ed.), *Yugoslavia: A Fractured Federalism* (Washington, DC: The Wilson Center Press, 1988).

45 See M. Žagar, *Sodobni federalizem s posebnim poudarkom na asimetrični federaciji v večnacionalnih državah, Doktorska disertacija* [Modern Federalism and the Applicability of the Theoretical Model of the Asymmetrical Federation in Multi-Ethnic States PhD Dissertation] (Ljubljana: Univerza Edvarda Kardelja v Ljubljani, Pravna fakulteta, 1990), pp. 325–98.

46 The first article about asymmetrical federation appeared in the daily newspaper *Dnevnik*. See M. Žagar, 'Teze o asimetrični federaciji, I' [Theses on the Asymmetrical Federation, I], *Dnevnik* (Ljubljana, 11 April 1989), 11–12, and 'Teze o asimetrični federaciji, II' [Theses on the Asymmetrical Federation, II], *Dnevnik* (18 April 1989), 12. The first book that elaborated this concept in the context of the constitutional reforms of Yugoslavia appeared soon after. See M. Žagar, *Kakšni naj bosta novi ustavi? Teze za novo slovensko in jugoslovansko ustavo ter teze listine o človekovih pravicah in temeljnih svoboščinah* [How Should the New Constitutions Look? Thesis for the New Slovene and the New Yugoslav Constitution and for the Bill of Human Rights] (Ljubljana: Komunist, 1989), pp. 38–44.

47 The opponents of decentralization and the asymmetrical federation demanded centralization, a stronger federal centre, and reduced autonomy of federal units. They thought that the best way of handling the crisis was to reduce existing differences and asymmetries in the former Yugoslavia. They usually opposed the introduction of political pluralism and a multiparty political system. (For a review of negative and positive reactions to proposals to introduce the asymmetrical federation in ex-Yugoslavia see Žagar, *Sodobni federalizem s posebnim poudarkom na asimetrični federaciji v večnacionalnih državah*, pp. 331–3, 382–5.)

48 See: *Evropa zdaj!* [Europe Now!] (Ljubljana: 2 November 1989), p. 11. (Translated by S. P. Ramet and M. Žagar; the comment in brackets added by M. Žagar.)

49 See *Za evropsko kakovost življenja, Dokumenti 11. kongresa ZKS For* [European Quality of Life, Documents of XI Congress of LCS] (Ljubljana: Komunist, 1990), pp. 43–4. (Translated by M. Žagar.)

50 Beginning in the spring of 1990, the LCS and all other parties advocated confederal (confederate) status for Slovenia in Yugoslavia. Although some opposition leaders hoped for

full international independence for Slovenia, political parties did not include such a demand in their programmes at that time. See Žagar, *Sodobni federalizem s posebnim poudarkom na asimetrični federaciji v večnacionalnih državah*, pp. 330–3.

51 The legal and political theoretical models of the asymmetrical federation are elaborated in Žagar, *Sodobni federalizem s posebnim poudarkom na asimetrični federaciji v večnacionalnih državah*, pp. 337–97.

52 See M. Cerar Jr, 'Pojmovnik: Asimetrična federacija' [The Dictionary: Asymmetrical Federation], *Teleks* (6 July 1989), 29.

53 See *The Dayton Peace Accords: General Framework Agreement for Peace in Bosnia and Herzegovina* (Vienna: USIA Regional Program Office, 1995).

PETER PERNTHALER AND ANNA GAMPER

7

National federalism within the EU: the Austrian experience

Introduction

'Federalism' is a term much used and reflected in the literature of constitutional law and political science, but it lacks a precise and universal definition.[1] Nevertheless, a common standard of minimum institutional requirements of all federal systems has been recognized;[2] namely, a distribution of powers between the federation and the constituent states, the participation of the states in the process of federal legislation, constitutional autonomy of the states, fiscal equalization and elements of cooperative federalism.

Since Austrian federalism formally features all these criteria, it is usually classified as a 'real' federal system.[3] However, this chapter attempts to show that it is not so easy to discern whether Austrian federalism really goes much beyond a strongly regionalized system. Another focus will be laid on the question of how Austrian EU membership, attained in 1995, has affected and changed the federal system.[4]

Characteristics of Austrian federalism

General remarks

The Austrian legal system is hierarchically structured, with a written federal constitution at its peak. The federal constitution does not only consist of the federal constitutional act of 1920 (*Bundes-Verfassungsgesetz, B-VG*) – although this is the main constitutional document – but also of a wide range of additional federal constitutional acts and single provisions.[5] Moreover, the B-VG alone has been amended eighty-five times so far.[6] Many of these amendments had an impact on the development of the Austrian federal system, but the need for reform has not yet been satisfied as will be shown in this chapter.

The allocation of powers

COMPETENCE CATEGORIES

The rules concerning the distribution of competences between the federation and the nine constituent states (*Länder*) are numerous and widely spread over federal constitutional law. Their main embodiment can be found in Arts 10–15 B-VG, according to which there are four general ways of allocating the legislative and administrative competences to the federation and the *Länder*, whereas judicial power is a federal competence solely:

- *Exclusive federal competences (both legislation and administration)*: More than a hundred important functions belong to this main group, which is enshrined in Art. 10 B-VG as well as several other federal constitutional acts and provisions. They include foreign affairs, defence, most matters of traffic, energy, economy and education, civil law, criminal law, water, forestry, commerce, universities, many matters relating to the environment, health and social policy, security matters, and so on.
- *Federal legislation,* Länder *administration*: Only a few matters belong to this group, which is mainly provided by Art. 11 B-VG. They include matters of nationality, traffic police, certain matters relating to shipping, environmental reviews and social welfare, housing, urban redevelopment, and so on.
- *Federal framework legislation,* Länder *implementative legislation and administration*: Here again, only a few matters belong to this group, which is mainly provided by Art. 12 B-VG. They include basic social welfare, hospitals, land reform, electricity, agricultural and forest employees, and so on. If a federal framework law has not been enacted on a certain matter, the *Länder* will be entitled to full legislation.
- *Exclusive Länder competences (both legislation and administration)*: According to Art. 15 B-VG all matters not enumerated as federal competences fall into the residuary competence of the *Länder*. Such residual competences of the constituent states are usual in most federal systems. However, their effectiveness strongly depends on the number and importance of the functions that have been specified as federal. In Austria, only a limited range of matters remains within the *Länder*'s residuary competence. They include building law, general spatial planning, nature protection, hunting, fishing, agricultural matters, youth and child welfare, sport, tourism, local police, laws on the acquisition of real estate, nursery schools, and so on.

COMPETENCE INTERPRETATION

The constitutional court has developed the rule of 'in-dubio-pro-*Länder*',[7] which means that if a doubt remains over whether the matter falls into a federal competence, a respective federal competence will have to be construed narrowly. As a consequence, the subject matter will then fall into the *Länder* competence.

Notwithstanding the theoretical importance of this rule, however, there have not been many cases where it has been applied so far.

However, other important rules on the interpretation of competences have been developed by the constitutional court: above all, the court applies the 'theory of petrification',[8] which means that a federal competence comprises only those subject matters that it was thought to comprise when the competence was enacted (regarding most competences, on 1 October 1925); that is, within the limits of the (ordinary) law regulating a certain subject matter at that time. Additional subject matters are only considered if there is a close intra-systematic relationship to the 'petrified' subject matters. Further, both the federation and the *Länder* are obliged to take each others' interests into consideration when enacting their own laws (the 'principle of mutual consideration'[9]). According to the 'rule of different aspects',[10] both the federation and the *Länder* may enact laws on the same subject matter if their respective laws concern different aspects which are covered by their respective competences. It is also noteworthy that no such rule as 'federal law breaks *Länder* law' exists (only 'federal constitutional law breaks *Länder* law').

LÄNDER INSTITUTIONS

The *Land* parliament (*Landtag*) is the organ responsible for legislation, whereas the supreme executive consists of the *Land* government (*Landesregierung*), its individual members and its presiding officer, who is called the *Land* governor (*Landeshauptmann*). Both the *Land* government as such and the *Land* governor are elected by the *Land* parliament. As a first instance, administrative matters are dealt with by district administrative authorities (*Bezirksverwaltungsbehörden*), which, from an organizational viewpoint, are *Land* agencies, but are generally vested with administrative functions both by the *Länder* and by the federation. Nevertheless, they form no territorial entity of their own within the three-layered structure of Austrian territorial organization (federation, *Länder*, municipalities).

Most of the exclusively federal matters are administered by the *Länder* (system of indirect federal administration).[11] In this case, the *Land* governor, who is constitutionally responsible for carrying out indirect federal administrative matters, is bound by instructions of the federal government or the respective federal ministers. However, under the administrative reform act of 2001,[12] which came into force in 2002, the independent administrative tribunals, which are established in each *Land*, have now become responsible for many indirect administrative matters as a second administrative instance instead of the *Land* governor.

NON-GOVERNMENTAL ADMINISTRATION

It is important to know that the *Länder* may use all forms of private law and subsidize or finance all matters without being restricted by the allocation of competences. This constitutional rule (Art. 17 B-VG)[13] serves as a 'safety valve' against the severe centralization of competences in Austria and thus is of great practical importance to the political independence and self-determination of the *Länder*.

EXECUTIVE FEDERALISM

It may be concluded that a typical feature of Austrian federalism is the predominance of federal legislation, whereas the *Länder* are mainly responsible for administrative functions.

This system of 'executive federalism'[14] may be acceptable to the administrative authorities themselves, who are thus vested with large executive powers lacking the responsibilities inherent in legislation. However, it is a dangerous way of reducing the political self-determination of the *Länder*, which not only affects the powers of *Land* parliaments, but also *Land* governments and the whole democratic (political) process of the *Länder*.[15] The *Länder* thus degenerate to regional administrative bodies, the status of which closely resembles that enjoyed by local government. Austrian membership to the EU has rapidly accelerated the development of executive federalism.[16]

The federal assembly

The federal assembly (*Bundesrat*)[17] is the second chamber of the federal parliament. Within the process of federal legislation, the federal assembly is usually entitled to object to a bill, but may be overruled by the national assembly's (i.e. the first chamber's) vote of persistence. In only a few cases does the federal assembly enjoy the right of absolute veto (e.g. if a bill intends to deprive the *Länder* of a competence[18]). The federal assembly may also set up its own standing rules, initiate drafted laws, demand a referendum in certain cases, challenge the validity of a law before the constitutional court and, in addition to these legislative functions, has several particular rights of assent and control over the executive.

Basically, the *Länder* are represented according to their population figures. Art. 34 B-VG provides certain rules of proportionality (currently, between three and twelve members for each *Land*, depending on the number of citizens). The members are elected by each *Land* parliament. They need not be members of the *Land* parliament but must be eligible for the *Land* parliament.

The federal assembly is a permanent body, as its members are not chosen in a general election but sit as long as the respective *Land* parliament is not dissolved. Since the *Land* parliaments of the nine *Länder* are dissolved and newly elected at different times, the federal assembly as such remains.

Apart from the different numbers of delegates, no *Land* enjoys a privileged position in the assembly. The position of the presiding officer circulates between the *Länder* biannually according to an alphabetic scheme.

However, the representatives stick to their respective parties, represented in the national assembly, rather than to their own *Land*. On account of these 'partisan politics' the federal assembly turns out to be a disappointingly weak organ, which has never yet made use of its right of absolute veto and has rarely objected to bills passed by the national assembly.

The constitutional autonomy of the Länder

Art. 99 B-VG empowers the *Länder* to enact their own constitutions as long as they do not violate federal constitutional law. In particular, their scope is limited, since the basic provisions concerning the democratic system and the administrative organization of the *Länder* have already been embodied in the federal constitution and must not be altered by the *Länder* constitutions (also implicit standards of homogeneity). However, the *Länder* constitutions are no longer regarded as simple 'implementation laws' as was the older doctrine and jurisdiction.[19] Instead, they may regulate all possible matters in accordance with the Austrian federal constitution, or even beyond, if the federal constitution is not affected.

Fiscal relations[20]

Art. 13 B-VG leaves it to a specific federal constitutional act to determine taxation and financial equalization. Accordingly, the financial constitutional act (*Finanz-Verfassungsgesetz*) provides different kinds of taxes; namely, exclusive federal taxes, exclusive *Länder* taxes, exclusive local taxes and shared taxes (these latter taxes are shared between the federal state, the *Länder* and the municipalities, or between at least two of them). 'Sharing' either means that all sharing entities may levy taxes on the same subjects of taxation or that the federation/*Länder* levy a basic tax, whereas the other entities are only entitled to levy additional taxes on the same subjects of taxation; or that only the federal state/*Länder* levy a tax, whereas the other entities receive part of its revenues ('joint taxes').

It is up to the financial equalization act (*Finanzausgleichsgesetz, FAG*)[21] to decide which of these taxes may be levied by which entity on which subjects of taxation. The FAG is an ordinary federal law, which is usually enacted every four years for reasons of fiscal flexibility. Traditionally, however, the federal government negotiates the act with the *Länder* and the associations of municipalities and towns. If all tiers have basically agreed on the drafted act, the FAG will be presumed not to be discriminatory by the constitutional court.[22]

The tax yield of all tiers is modified by a large number of transfers, such as grants, contributions and cost-sharing payments between the governments. In addition, there exist numerous non-official cost-sharing arrangements between the federal, *Land* and municipal governments in order to finance special projects such as roads, hospitals, schools and universities or to subsidize private expenditure.

Analysing the *Länder*'s position within the system of the current FAG, which regulates taxation and financial equalization from 2001 to 2004, one may conclude that:

- the states have no important taxes of their own;
- their main revenues derive from sharing joint federal taxes in a tripartite

system together with the municipalities, their shares being fixed by federal law;
- a substantial part of their revenues derives from federal transfers, which increases their dependence.

A substantial reverse flow of *Land* and municipal funds to the federal government is achieved by means of unofficial financial settlements. This 'grey financial settlement'[23] is regulated by contracts and other private law instruments or by political gentlemen's agreements between the governments.

One may conclude, therefore, that the Austrian *Länder* depend financially on the federal government. Notwithstanding the fact that in practice there have always been tripartite negotiations before the adoption of a new FAG, the bargaining positions of the federal government and the *Land* and municipal governments are very unequal. Indeed, the *Länder* and municipalities have no alternative but to accept that fiscal relations are determined by the federal government.[24] Moreover, the traditionally cooperative way of negotiating the FAG has increasingly given way to a top-down approach and growing isolation and particularization of the tiers' political interests.

Co-operative federalism

Whereas in other federal systems cooperative federalism has been the main instrument to overcome the strong legal position of the constituent states and to create an informal, but very efficient centralism, in Austria cooperative federalism has been important in order to unite the political power of the *Länder* and to coordinate their policies in order to prevent centralization, thus creating a strong political counterpart against the federal government's overwhelming legal powers.[25]

Instruments of cooperation are provided both on a legal and an informal basis: the most important legal instruments of cooperation are formal concordats[26] between the federation and the *Länder* or between the *Länder* themselves (Art. 15a B-VG), and all sorts of private law agreements between the three tiers of government. Either with the help of these legal instruments or by informal political agreements, a large number of joint programmes have been launched in order to perform tasks which are in the public interest (hospitals, highways, education, traffic systems, economic development of poor regions, etc.).

Furthermore, the *Länder* governors, members of the *Land* governments, the presiding officers of the *Land* parliaments and senior civil servants very often meet at joint conferences – taking place either periodically or for a special purpose. It is up to several informal agencies to prepare these interstate conferences and to render all necessary information in a professional and efficient way.[27] The most important of these is the so-called 'liaison office' of the *Länder* which is located in Vienna.[28] The most important political body of *Länder* cooperation is the conference of the *Land* governors (*Landeshauptmännerkonferenz*), which meets regularly four times a year but also for special purposes.[29]

In Austria, cooperative federalism is of great political importance. In practice, all major changes in the legal, political or financial arena are negotiated and not usually carried out without the consent of the *Länder* and municipalities. Nevertheless, the predominant role of the federal government and the dependence of all other governments on its planning and policies remain the principal features of Austrian federalism.

Asymmetric federalism

In principle, the *Länder* are equal as to their competences and their legal status as 'indestructible states' (Arts 2 and 3 B-VG). Despite this basic equality, however, there are a number of institutions and constitutional procedures leading to legal and economic differences between them.[30] The most important legal 'asymmetries' are the following:

- As mentioned above, the *Länder* may act under private law and enjoy unlimited 'spending power' without being restricted by the distribution of competences. This somehow compensates them for their inferior position within the system of allocated powers, as they are allowed to pursue all political and administrative goals by means of financial subsidies or private legal institutions – but only so far as they have sufficient funds to do so. This leads to differences between the *Länder* depending on their specific political ideas of public responsibility and on their particular economic and budgetary situation.
- Further, it has already been mentioned that the *Länder* have the power to conclude concordats with other *Länder* or with the federation (Art. 15a B-VG) and also to enter into international treaties with neighbouring states or regions within the scope of their competences (Art. 16 B-VG). Due to these treaty-making powers, a couple of special institutions of regional cooperation between certain *Länder* as well as specific joint federation–*Länder* agencies have been established. There also exist several transfrontier cooperation agencies and working groups between the *Länder* and neighbouring regions of other countries as well as numerous 'Euregios', which are smaller units of local or regional cooperation across national borders. The traditional cooperation between the Austrian *Land* Tyrol and the neighbouring provinces of Bolzano and Trentino has been institutionalized as '*Europaregion Tirol*'.[31]
- Important constitutional differences between the Austrian *Länder* concern the internationally guaranteed protection of the Slovene and Croat (language) minorities (ethnic groups) in the *Länder* Carinthia, Styria and Burgenland (Art. 7 of the state treaty of 1955 between the allied powers and Austria).[32] These (and other) ethnic minorities have the special right to use their language before the courts and administrative agencies and are guaranteed a special bilingual education system within their traditional areas of settlement.
- Due to the *Länder*'s 'constitutional autonomy' their constitutions differ, largely with respect to the system of government (proportional or majority government), to the institutions of direct democracy (referenda, people's

initiatives and petitions) and to constitutionally guaranteed principles, individual rights, social services, controlling authorities and parliamentary powers.

- Asymmetries between the *Länder* may also arise from their different ways of implementing federal framework laws as well as directives, recommendations and programmes of the EC within the scope of their competences.[33] In practice, however, these implementative laws do not differ very much, because they are usually agreed upon between the *Länder* prior to their enactment.
- According to the size of the population, differences are made regarding the *Länder*'s representation in the federal assembly and financial equalization. Finally, the capital Vienna, which is both a *Land* and by far the largest Austrian city, enjoys a special status.[34]

Austrian federalism and the European Union

General remarks
In connection with Austria's EU accession, the debate on a reform of federalism became a major topic in the late 1980s, because the *Länder* did not want to join the EU unless an internal structural reform could be achieved. In 1994 a political agreement was reached and a constitutional bill drafted. Although being repeatedly proposed to the national assembly in the following years, the bill was prevented from enactment by new coalition governments following elections for the national assembly – which made majorities for the necessary constitutional amendments impossible – and by the *Länder*'s refusal to modify the agreement in order to meet the opposition's demands.[35] Notwithstanding the failed attempt to reform the federal system, Austria joined the EU in 1995, which was made possible both by the federal parliament's consent and a successful referendum.[36]

The new role of the Land *parliaments*
However, the EU – once seen as the best chance of connecting accession with an internal reform of federalism – has weakened the position of the *Länder*, which increasingly appear to be mere administrative machines, implementing legislation made in either Brussels or Vienna.

As typical examples of how EC law reduces their legislative scope, one could mention the exclusive *Länder* competences relating to nature protection and the transfer of property. Regarding nature protection, several EC directives, including council directive 92/43/EEC of 21 May 1992 on the conservation of natural habitats and of wild fauna and flora, needed to be implemented by *Land* legislation. There not only arose a number of legal problems concerning implementation in the *Länder*'s nature protection acts, but also problems of a more political character, namely concerning the obligation to propose Natura 2000 sites. The 'Europeanization' of nature protection met much resistance from the

population, as the permanent conflict between economic and ecological interests was aggravated by the rigorous obligation to nominate certain sites.

With regard to the transfer of landed property, the respective *Land* legislation had to be amended due to EC fundamental freedoms and the jurisdiction of
the European court of justice based thereon: taking Tyrol as an example, EU
accession has even worsened the already problematic situation. Since the 1960s
there has been a dramatic increase of secondary residences and holiday homes
which well-to-do foreigners wanted to establish in the picturesque Tyrolean landscape. Even before EU accession, experts warned against a possible relaxation of
transfer restrictions, made necessary on account of the EC freedoms. In contrast
to Denmark and Finland (regarding the Åland islands),[37] Austria did not achieve
a permanent transfer restriction within EC primary law during the negotiations
preceding the accession. According to Art. 70 of the accession treaty, Austria was
simply allowed to maintain its existing legislation regarding secondary residences
for five years from the date of accession. Shortly before the end of this period, the
European court of justice delivered a fundamental judgment on the question of
compatibility between the Tyrolean *Land* transfer act and EC law.[38] The court
held that it was incompatible with EC law to be obliged to get an administrative
permit in order to acquire landed property. Even non-discriminating restrictions
of land transfer – that is, restrictions which did not differentiate between Austrian
nationals and other EU member states' nationals – were held to be in breach of
EC law under certain premises. The court argued that the aims of the Tyrolean
Land transfer act – to restrict secondary residences and to guarantee that spatial
planning is adhered to – could be realized by less restrictive means, namely a 'declaration model' combined with subsequent sanctions. In the light of this judgment and in consideration of the fact that the period of transition had nearly
come to an end, the Tyrolean *Land* transfer act was amended in order to meet
these EC requirements. Although only around 10 per cent of the Tyrolean territory is deemed suitable for permanent settlement or intense agricultural use,
Land legislation is not only prevented from restricting non-Austrian EU nationals due to the scarcity of building land, but also from enacting more restrictive, if
non-discriminating, provisions than indicated by the European court of justice.

Another severe problem lies in the complexity of EC law which, as a rule,
cannot be easily implemented in the system of Austrian federalism: since these
complex matters usually concern a number of both federal and *Land* competences,
it becomes nearly impossible to manage a clear separation between these competences when the matter is implemented. At the same time, the federation becomes
stronger, as it is vested with new powers of controlling and co-ordinating the
Länder when they implement EC law.[39]

Thus, the scope of the *Land* parliaments has become even more limited. In
order to compensate them, the *Länder* have been provided with a number of
rights under which they may either directly or indirectly participate in the EU
decision-making process and have an influence on shaping the Austrian position on EU matters. In conformity with a 'vertical' concordat between the fed-

eration and the *Länder*[40] and a 'horizontal' concordat between the *Länder* them-selves,[41] Arts 23a–23f B-VG include the mechanisms discussed below.

Direct Länder *participation*

THE DELEGATION OF *LÄNDER* REPRESENTATIVES TO THE COUNCIL OF THE EUROPEAN UNION

The federal government may empower a *Länder* representative if the subject treated in the council relates to a legislative competence of the *Länder* (Art. 23d par. 3 B-VG). However, this provision does not vest the *Länder* with a claim which would be enforceable by law. Besides, even if a member of one of the *Länder* governments represents Austria in the council, he or she will not directly represent his or her respective *Land*. Instead, the *Länder* delegate represents the member state as a whole or its central government and thus has to consider supraregional and national interests. For this reason, Art. 23d par. 3 B-VG pro-vides explicitly that the *Länder* representative must carry out his or her task in close cooperation with the competent federal minister and is responsible to the national assembly, as far as federal legislation is concerned (and to the *Land* Parliaments, as far as *Land* Legislation is concerned).

To date, this provision has never been applied: although political represen-tatives of the *Länder* have attended council meetings as members of the Austrian delegation as a whole, they have never themselves been vested with the right of representation.

THE COMMITTEE OF THE REGIONS

Austria is represented in the committee of the regions (Arts 263–265 EC treaty) by the nine *Länder* governors[42] and three communal delegates who represent the interests of towns and other municipalities and are appointed by the two Austrian municipal associations (Art. 23c par. 4 B-VG). The Austrian federal government participates in the appointment procedure of the Austrian commit-tee members, being itself bound to proposals of the *Länder* and the two associ-ations of municipalities and towns respectively.[43]

The Austrian delegation has always been headed by a top *Länder* representa-tive who at the same time is one of the committee's vice-presidents. A personal assistant of the delegation's political head, who is called the 'national coordina-tor', is in charge of the national co-ordination of the committee's activities. Before plenary meetings, preliminary internal discussions are held regularly, in which, apart from the Austrian committee members, competent civil servants of the *Länder* and municipalities participate. The *Länder*'s liaison office and the *Länder* representatives at the permanent representation of Austria in Brussels[44] are in charge of co-ordinating the delegation's work, being assisted by the offices of the two municipal associations and of the respective *Länder* liaison offices in Brussels. In order to prepare for the committee's plenary sessions, intra-delegation talks take place after the preliminary counselling of a permanent working group at civil servant level, in which both the Austrian committee members and the members of the said working group participate.

THE LIAISON OFFICES OF THE *LÄNDER* IN BRUSSELS
In addition to direct forms of participation within EU institutions, each Austrian *Land* – with the exception of Vorarlberg – has established its own liaison office in Brussels.[45] However, these so-called '*Länderbüros*' do not have any official diplomatic functions. Their activities rather operate on an informal basis and may be described as 'lobbying', including mainly:[46]

- establishing and maintaining contact networks to relevant EU functionaries, EU institutions and the representations of other member states;
- providing and promptly forwarding important information on European schemes and developments;
- the representation of specific *Länder* interests through the exertion of influence on European institutions and decision-makers;
- setting up of cross-contacts to institutions with similar interests; and
- promoting *Länder* concerns by means of public relations and providing contact services to both enterprises and individuals.

It is difficult to estimate how much influence these regional offices really have on the decision-making process. They naturally compete with dynamic lobbying activities of other interest groups and they rival the official channels of influence at the political level (permanent representation, COREPER, council working groups, ministerial contacts).

Indirect Länder *participation*
As the aforementioned forms of direct participation grant on the whole little substantial influence to the Austrian *Länder*, they have to rely all the more on effective national structures and procedures, described below.

THE *LÄNDER* PARTICIPATION PROCEDURE
Constitutional basis.   Art. 23d par. 1, 2 and 4 B-VG only enshrine the basic characteristics of the *Länder* participation procedure, leaving its more detailed concretization to the aforementioned vertical concordat of 1992, whereas the horizontal concordat, which was concluded between the *Länder* in the same year, seeks to achieve internal co-ordination.

The aim of the participation procedure is to enable the *Länder* to participate in the decision-making processes at the EU level in so far as they are concerned legally or politically, and to let them participate in the creation of community law. The intention was to offer them some compensation for the weakness of their direct powers of influence and for the loss of competences[47] connected with EU accession.

The federation's obligation to inform the Länder.   As a basic requirement, the *Länder* need to be punctually and comprehensively informed on relevant EU projects by the federation. Accordingly, the *Länder* are entitled to receive comprehensive information and are thus involved in the process of European lawmaking at its earliest stage. According to Art. 23d par. 1 B-VG, the federation 'has to inform the Länder without delay on all schemes within the framework of the European Union which concern their sphere of competences or are of interest to them'. Although there is no unanimity on the more detailed meaning of 'schemes', this provision clearly establishes a very broad and comprehensive obligation of the federation.[48] As a rule, the federation is obliged to forward information as early as it itself has been provided with official information, or, if an Austrian initiative is launched, from the very beginning; that is, even before Austria officially approaches a community organ in this matter.

Länder statements. Furthermore, the *Länder* are vested with a number of substantial participation rights, the most effective of which is the so-called 'uniform statement' on a matter pertaining to their legislative competences.[49] As the Austrian delegate to the council is usually bound to such a statement, the *Länder* may have significant influence on shaping the Austrian position in the council. Apart from the uniform statement, each *Land* may, of course, make its own and individual statement. Such a statement, however, must only be considered, and not necessarily adhered to, by the federation when it determines its position.[50]

Though basically binding, a uniform *Länder* statement is not enforceable in every case. Namely, it need not be taken account of if 'compelling reasons of foreign and integration policy' force the Austrian representative not to adhere to it when voting in the council.

From a purely legal perspective, the Austrian delegate has a relatively wide scope of discretion if he or she wants to deviate from a *Länder* statement, unless it is 'evident' that there is no 'compelling reason of foreign and integration policy' which would legitimize deviation. Practice shows, however, that *Länder* uniform statements are nearly always taken account of.

The horizontal concordat of 1992 leaves it to the *Länder* to fix the necessary organizational conditions and procedures for arranging a uniform statement, which is due to their constitutional autonomy. The *Länder*, however, had originally delegated this task to the integration conference of the *Länder* (IKL), which is a cooperative organ specifically set up by a horizontal concordat.[51] The conference consists of the federal assembly's presiding officer, the *Länder* governors and the presidents of the *Länder* parliaments. Resolutions – and thus also uniform *Länder* statements – are passed if at least five *Länder* approve and no *Land* objects to the resolution.

In practice, however, this procedure has not often taken place; indeed, since its constituent meeting in 1993 the conference has only been convened once.[52] Instead, uniform *Länder* statements have usually been arranged within the framework of traditional interstate cooperation, namely the conference of *Länder* governors, the conference of the heads of the *Länder* government offices and specific conferences of *Länder* experts. Since 1993, more than thirty uniform binding *Länder* statements, arranged in this way, have been presented to the federation. Facing this established practice, one may truly question whether an IKL resolution is the only way in which the *Länder* may legally bind the federation to their views. Whereas academics[53] deny such a possibility, practice confirms it: so far the federation has accepted nearly all uniform *Länder* statements, although they were not passed by the IKL. Thus, there has been no practical problem – a situation which could nevertheless rapidly become less satisfactory if a conflict of interests were to arise between the federation and the *Länder*.

The involvement of the Länder parliaments.   Taking in view that focus is put on the *Länder* participation procedure, the *Länder* parliaments have become afraid of losing their position as counterparts to the *Länder* governments. Six *Länder* have therefore passed specific *Land* constitutional laws in order to provide for the participation of the *Länder* parliaments in EU matters. All of them seek to bind *Länder* statements to the views expressed by the parliamentary majorities.[54] This is achieved through the *Länder* governments' obligation to inform the *Länder* parliaments on EU matters and the latters' rights to deliver statements on these matters, which may be done through parliamentary select committees on EU affairs.

Although the practical effectiveness of these models has met with some scepticism, it is obvious that the integration policy of the *Länder* governments is thus given additional democratic legitimacy and transparency.

Practical experience.   In practice, the *Länder* participation procedure has been well established. This is not least due to the fact that, much earlier on, a circular letter, issued jointly by the federal chancellor's department and the federal ministry of foreign affairs, had precisely outlined the most important intra-administrative structures and processes. Given its non-normative character, this circular letter does but contain information without binding the organs of the *Länder* or other federal ministries. Regarding the *Länder*, however, the letter seems to imply that the federation regards itself to be bound to operate and adhere to the organizational structures mentioned therein.

On the whole, uniform statements have mostly been duly represented by the federation and other kinds of *Länder* statements have been taken into account as well. However, the *Länder* are not always able to coordinate their position very thoroughly, as deadlines at the European level make it difficult for them to keep to the periods given for formulating their statements and as they depend on the federation for getting the information they need.

On behalf of the federation, the Austrian position is regularly co-ordinated by a federal ministry in charge of the matter concerned. It is not only obliged to coordinate the position taken by the federation, thus taking into account the views of all federal ministries concerned, which is indeed a time-consuming task, but also to involve the *Länder* in the national decision-making process according to the rules of the participation procedure. In particular, the obligation to inform the *Länder* of EU matters is imposed on this ministry on behalf of the federation. In addition to the written statement procedure, joint co-ordinating meetings at civil servant level often take place, including *Länder* representatives. Generally, one can observe an intense involvement of *Länder* representatives in informal consultation talks (e.g. the weekly interministerial meetings in preparation for COREPER and the preparation of council meetings) and expert working groups of the federation, which go far beyond the concrete requirements of formal *Länder* participation. Nevertheless, it is the responsible federal ministry which, considering the results of the internal decision-making process and in unanimity both with the federal chancellor's department and the federal ministry for foreign affairs, formulates the Austrian position and represents it before the EU organs.

On the part of the *Länder*, the *Länder* liaison office is mainly responsible for rendering the relevant co-ordination and information.[55]

With regard to the *Länder* participation procedure, the liaison office is responsible for forwarding and distributing all the respective documents, reports and notes which it receives from federal agencies to and among the offices of the *Länder* governments. Within the process of arranging and co-ordinating uniform *Länder* statements the liaison office is vested with essential functions of co-ordination and is responsible for forwarding the statements to the federation. Beyond that, its members represent *Länder* interests on the occasion of the aforementioned co-ordination meetings and within informal consultation groups in so far as a joint *Länder* representative is lacking.

OTHER CHANNELS OF INFLUENCE AND RIGHTS OF PARTICIPATION

The council for matters of Austrian integration and foreign policy, established at the federal ministry for foreign affairs, consists of representatives of the federal government,[56] the political parties, the *Länder* (the conference of the *Länder* governors and the *Länder* parliaments are each represented by two persons), the social partners and the two municipal associations. The council is convened twice a year and advises the federal government on matters of Austrian integration and foreign policy. It further discusses and co-ordinates decisions relating to integration policy and is responsible for distributing the relevant information. The council has to be heard on all major issues of Austrian integration and foreign policy, unless they are discussed by the national security council itself. Apart from the council, an interministerial 'working group for integration matters' has been established at the federal chancellor's office, which has to maintain permanent consultative relations with the *Länder*.

In addition to formalized *Länder* participation within the framework of statement procedures under Art. 23d B-VG and the practical involvement of the *Länder* in informal consultation and preliminary discussions at the national level, Art. 8 of the vertical concordat of 1992 provides that *Länder* representatives may join the Austrian delegations at EU level, if the subjects discussed relate to *Länder* competences or are of interest to them.[57] On this legal basis, the *Länder* had even been invited to participate in the Austrian delegations during the talks preceding EU accession. Since Austrian accession the joint *Länder* representatives have participated in a number of council working groups and the commission's advisory committees.

Formalizing well-established practice, the aforementioned vertical concordat finally entitles the *Länder* to dispatch their own delegates and staff to the Austrian permanent representation in Brussels if the federal minister for foreign affairs agrees and if they bear their own costs. On this basis, two *Länder* representatives work at the permanent representation and thus form an external branch of the liaison office of the *Länder*. They are not only responsible for representing *Länder* interests within the permanent representation, but also for forwarding information to the *Länder* via the liaison office and for representing the latter at meetings of council working groups.

LÄNDER PARTICIPATION IN THE DESCENDING PHASE OF EUROPEAN LAW-MAKING

Intense cooperation between the federation and the *Länder*, which is regularly steered by a responsible federal ministry, continues during the 'descending phase' of European law-making; that is, the implementation and execution of European legal acts by the member states. In particular, such cooperation can be observed with relation to those (numerous) acts of EC law which refer to both federal and *Länder* competences. According to Art. 23d par. 5 B-VG the *Länder* are bound to take all measures which within their autonomous sphere of competence become necessary for the implementation of EC Law.

Within the implementation procedure which, just as the *Länder* participation procedure, mainly relies on the traditional instruments of cooperative federalism, the *Länder* indirectly participate in the making of European 'secondary legislation' through the commission. It is a well-known fact that, in particular, directives confer the concretization of detailed rules to the commission and its so-called 'comitology'. The Austrian *Länder* are not only fully informed by the federation on the comitology's work if it pertains to their competences, but are involved in the national process preceding decision-making on EU matters.

It is the responsible federal ministry which – at the preliminary stages of committee meetings – seeks to bring the Austrian position in line with the *Länder* and other concerned federal ministries. This is predominantly done by means of an ad-hoc statement procedure or with specific co-ordination meetings. Moreover, a joint *Länder* representative often participates in committee meetings as a member of the Austrian delegation;[58] however, the right to vote usually remains with the federation's representative. The same applies to the participation of the *Länder* in expert working groups, that are numerously established by the commission, and to specific implementation committees at the EU level, that serve as professional forums for the exchange of experience and information regarding the national implementation procedures between the member states.

THE PARTICIPATION OF THE FEDERAL ASSEMBLY

Finally, the federal assembly enjoys a number of rights of participation in the national decision-making process relating to EU issues. Due to the federal assembly's generally weak position, however, these rights are much weaker than those granted to the federal parliament's other chamber; that is, the national assembly.[59] Thus, it is much more effective to involve the *Länder* directly so far as EU issues are concerned.

Not only the national assembly and the *Länder*, but also the federal assembly has to be informed about all schemes within the framework of the EU without delay and has to be given the right to deliver a statement (Art. 23e par. 1 B-VG). Contrary to the national assembly,[60] Art. 23e par. 6 B-VG only entitles the federal assembly to a binding statement if EU acts would need to be implemented by a federal constitutional act requiring the federal assembly's consent according to Art. 44 par. 2 B-VG (i.e. if *Länder* competences were to be diminished).

However, to date the federal assembly has never made use of its right to a binding statement which is due to the fact that EU acts, though they frequently affect *Land* Legislation, do not formally alter the national allocation of competences.

Perspectives

If one seeks to strike an overall balance in the tenth year of Austrian EU membership, the complex system of *Länder* participation turns out to work rather smoothly. The *Länder* are indeed able to represent and – under certain conditions – realize their interests at the European level.

However, these practical successes of *Länder* participation cannot make its weaknesses invisible: in several cases, the federation has shown delay in involving the *Länder*. Further, uniform *Länder* statements are not effective if the Austrian delegate pleads compelling reasons of foreign and integration policy. One could also mention the lack of opportunity for the *Länder* to contact the Austrian delegate in Brussels directly or the – so far only academic – controversy by which statement the Austrian representative should feel bound if the national assembly, federal assembly and/or the *Länder* deliver divergent views.

For these reasons, in connection with the ratification of the treaty of Nice, the *Länder* raised a couple of demands to improve their participation in EU matters.[61] In particular, they demanded a clear constitutional rule which explicitly extends the federation's obligation to inform them of Austrian EU initiatives. Further, the *Länder* should be made competent to judge for themselves if an EU scheme would be of interest to them. Regarding deviation from binding *Länder* statements, they claim to be entitled to deal with the matter anew and eventually object to the deviation, which would vest them with a similar right as the national assembly enjoys should a federal minister want to deviate from a statement of the national assembly. Most importantly, the *Länder* want a more powerful position if negotiations take place at the EU level which make an impact on their legislative competences.

Although these demands have not been met so far, they do show possible ways of a reasonable further development and of improved efficiency of *Länder* participation. The future position of the *Länder* within the system of European 'multi-level federalism' will depend on how the regions and their direct involvement in the EU decision-making process are developed and strengthened by a possible European Constitution.

Conclusion: the controversial road to reform

The conclusion to be drawn is that all elements of a federal system are formally provided and protected by the Austrian federal constitution but, in practice, turn out to be rather unsatisfactory (the major part of important competences belongs to the federation, trend to 'executive' federalism, political weakness of the federal assembly, centralistic system of financial equalization, limited ambit of the *Länder* constitutions, etc.). What may be even more alarming is the increasingly strong political trend towards centralism, which has prevented a 'reform of federalism' as it was demanded by the *Länder* in the 1990s. On the other hand, the *Länder* participation procedure in EU matters must be seen as an innovative and progressive new element of Austrian federalism, which has particularly advanced cooperative relations and co-ordination between the *Länder*.

Since the Austrian EU accession and the failure of the 'great' reform project, negotiations between federal and state governments have concentrated more on details. Since 1999 a cooperative 'mechanism of consultation'[62] has entitled the *Länder* to be consulted if the federal legislator intends to enact a bill that concerns the *Länder* financially (and vice versa). If an agreement cannot be reached despite consultation talks, the legislating authority will have to cover all expenses arising from the respective bill.

The *Länder* also agreed to a 'stability pact 2001'[63] between themselves, the federation and the municipalities. In order to meet the Maastricht criteria of convergence, the *Länder* are obliged not to run into debt but to achieve a considerable budgetary surplus, whereas the federal state may still show a deficit and the municipalities at least a balanced budget. The stability pact is an agreement under Art. 15a B-VG, which means that it could not be formally forced upon the *Länder* by the federation, since their consent was needed. Still, they were politically forced to do so, as the federal state would otherwise have imposed on them considerable penal sanctions.

Finally, a new Art. 14b was inserted into the B-VG in 2003: a central legislative competence to ensure a uniform and homogeneous procurement policy was thought convenient under the aspect of EC procurement law and was an issue of political talks between the federation and the *Länder*.[64] Following these talks, the bill received cross-party support in the national assembly as well as the consent of the federal assembly.

According to the new provision, the federation is generally responsible for procurement legislation, whereas the *Länder* remain responsible for the legislation regarding the review of procurement decisions within their ambit and have the right of consent regarding federal procurement Laws regulating matters that fall into the *Land* administration. Administrative competences are divided between the federation and the *Länder* according to their ambits.

Other parts of the 'great' reform project, especially the reform of the system of indirect federal administration, of the distribution of competences and the creation of new administrative courts in the states, are still being negotiated. Once again, the current government has expressed its aim to carry out a radical constitutional reform which would go hand in hand with at least a partial reform of the Austrian federal system. On 30 June 2003, the so-called 'Austrian Convention'[65] started to work, with its inaugural meeting on 2 May 2003. The convention consists of seventy members (political functionaries, representatives of interest groups, constitutional lawyers) who assemble in various committees, and is chaired by the president of the Austrian Court of Auditors. The convention's task is to draft a new federal constitution within eighteen months. Part of this period being already over, however, no agreement has so far been achieved with regard to a new system of federalism.[66] Since a constitutional reform would involve the revision of the federal constitution, moreover, a two-thirds majority would be required in the national assembly.[67] However, neither does the current government command such a majority, nor can the opposition, consisting of two highly centralistic left-wing parties, be expected to support the government, at least not in a way which would strengthen the *Länder*.

It is not unlikely that a future 'reform' might even weaken key elements of federalism (above all, the legislative competences of *Land* parliaments) for (perhaps) alleged reasons of economy and expediency.

Notes

1 Considering the plethora of literature on federalism, it is not possible to include all concepts of federalism. For instance, K. C. Wheare, *Federal Government* (New York/London: Oxford University Press, 1947) or, more recently, R. L. Watts, *Comparing Federal Systems*, 2nd edn (Montreal: McGill-Queen's University Press, 1999), p. 6 ff. have gained an international reputation. Even the Austrian doctrine is split: see the 'complex theory of federalism' (cf., for example, F. Ermacora, *Österreichischer Föderalismus.* (Vienna: Braumüller, 1976); P. Pernthaler, 'Der österreichische Bundesstaat im Spannungsfeld von Föderalismus und formalem Rechtspositivismus', *ÖZÖR*, 19 (1969), p. 361 ff.; T. Öhlinger, *Der Bundesstaat zwischen Reiner Rechtslehre und Verfassungsrealität* (Vienna: Braumüller, 1976) and K. Weber, *Kriterien des Bundesstaates* (Vienna: Braumüller, 1980), p. 78 ff.); further Kelsen's three-circle theory (see in particular H. Kelsen, *Allgemeine Staatslehre* (Berlin: Julius Springer, 1925), p. 163 ff.) and the related decentralization theory (see again H. Kelsen, *Österreichisches Staatsrecht* (Tübingen: J. C. B. Mohr/Paul Siebeck, 1923), p. 165; R. Walter, *Österreichisches Bundesverfassungsrecht* (Vienna: Manz, 1972), p. 108 ff.; R. Walter and H. Mayer, *Grundriß des österreichischen Bundesverfassungsrechts*, 9th edn (Vienna: Manz, 2000), p. 79; F. Koja, *Allgemeine Staatslehre*, 2nd edn (Vienna: Manz, 1993), p. 349 ff.; R. Thienel, 'Ein "komplexer" oder normativer Bundesstaatsbegriff?', *AJPIL*, 42 (1991), p.215 ff. and R. Thienel, 'Der

Bundesstaatsbegriff der Reinen Rechtslehre', in R. Walter (ed.), *Schwerpunkte der Reinen Rechtslehre* (Vienna: Manz, 1992), p. 123 ff.). See also A. Gamper, *Die Regionen mit Gesetzgebungshoheit* (Frankfurt et al.: Peter Lang), p. 15 ff.

2 See Watts, *Comparing Federal Systems*, p. 7 and R. L. Watts, 'The distribution of powers, responsibilities and resources in federations', in A. L. Griffiths (ed.), *Handbook of Federal Countries, 2002* (Montreal: McGill-Queen's University Press, 2002), p. 448 ff.

3 See e.g. P. Pernthaler, 'Verfassungsentwicklung und Verfassungsreform in Österreich', in B. Wieser and A. Stolz (eds), *Verfassungsrecht und Verfassungsgerichtsbarkeit an der Schwelle zum 21. Jahrhundert* (Vienna: Verlag Österreich, 2000), p. 100 ff. (with further references at footnote 185) and Watts, *Comparing Federal Systems*, p. 25.

4 See 'Austrian Federalism and the European Union', p. 141 ff.

5 For a general overview, see T. Öhlinger, *Verfassungsrecht*, 5th edn (Vienna: WUV, 2003); Walter and Mayer, *Grundriß des österreichischen Bundesverfassungsrechts*; L. K. Adamovich, B.-C. Funk and G. Holzinger, *Österreichisches Staatsrecht*, Vols 1 and 2 (Vienna/New York: Springer, 1997 and 1998).

6 The most recent amendment was published in the Federal law gazette as BGBl I 2003/100. Cf. the following commentaries on the B-VG: H. Mayer, *B-VG*, 3rd edn (Vienna: Manz, 2002); K. Korinek and M. Holoubek (eds), *Österreichisches Bundesverfassungsrecht* (Vienna/New York: Springer, loose leaf edition) and H. P. Rill and H. Schäffer (eds), *Bundesverfassungsrecht* (Vienna: Verlag Österreich, loose leaf edition).

7 Cf. e.g. cases VfSlg 2977/1956; 8891/1980; 9543/1982; 14266/1995.

8 See P. Pernthaler, *Kompetenzverteilung in der Krise* (Vienna: Braumüller, 1989), p. 79 ff. and B.-C. Funk, *Das System der bundesstaatlichen Kompetenzverteilung im Lichte der Verfassungsrechtsprechung* (Vienna: Braumüller, 1980), p. 69 ff.

9 Cf., most prominently, VfSlg 10292/1984 and 15552/1999. See also Pernthaler, *Kompetenzverteilung in der Krise*, p. 57 ff.; U. Davy, 'Zur Bedeutung des bundesstaatlichen Rücksichtnahmegebotes für Normenkonflikte', *ÖJZ* (1986), p. 225 ff., 298 ff. and S. Lebitsch-Buchsteiner, *Die bundesstaatliche Rücksichtnahmepflicht* (Vienna: Braumüller, 2001).

10 Cf. e.g. VfSlg 15552/1999.

11 See K. Weber, *Die mittelbare Bundesverwaltung* (Vienna: Braumüller, 1987).

12 Cf. BGBl I 2002/65.

13 See K. Korinek and M. Holoubek, *Grundlagen staatlicher Privatwirtschaftsverwaltung* (Graz: Leykam, 1993).

14 See P. Pernthaler, '(Kon-)Föderalismus und Regionalismus als Bewegungsgesetze der europäischen Integration', *JRP* (1999), p. 48 ff.; P. Pernthaler 'Mehrheitsregierung: Eine neue Chance für Demokratie und Parlamentarismus in den Ländern?', *JRP* (1999), p. 202 ff.

15 See R. Novak, 'Ist ein "Vollzugsföderalismus" noch föderalistisch?', in R. Novak, B. Sutter and G. D. Hasiba (eds), *Historische und aktuelle Probleme des Föderalismus in Österreich* (Vienna/Cologne/Graz: Böhlau, 1977), p. 27 ff.

16 See T. Öhlinger, 'Die Transformation der Verfassung: Die staatliche Verfassung und die Europäische Integration', *JBl* (2002), p. 2 ff. and below 'The new role of the *Land* Parliaments', p. 141 ff.

17 Cf. particularly Arts 34–44 B-VG. See also R. Walter, 'Der Bundesrat', in E. C. Hellbling, Mayer-Maly and H. Miehsler (eds), *Föderative Ordnung I: Bundesstaat auf der Waage* (Salzburg/Munich: Anton Pustet – Europa Verlag, 1969), p. 199 ff.; I. Kathrein, 'Der Bundesrat', in H. Schambeck (ed.), *Österreichs Parlamentarismus* (Berlin: Duncker & Humblot, 1986), p. 337 ff.; R. Walter, 'Der Bundesrat zwischen Bewährung und Neugestaltung', in H. Schäffer and H. Stolzlechner (eds), *Reformbestrebungen im österreichischen Bundesstaatssystem* (Vienna: Braumüller, 1993), p. 41 ff.; H. Schambeck,

'Föderalismus und Parlamentarismus in Österreich', in D. Merten (ed.), *Die Stellung der Landesparlamente aus deutscher, österreichischer und spanischer Sicht* (Berlin: Duncker & Humblot, 1997), p. 15 ff. and H. Schambeck (ed.), *Bundesstaat und Bundesrat in Österreich* (Vienna: Verlag Österreich, 1997).

18 Cf. Art. 44, par. 2 B-VG. See also P. Bußjäger, *Die Zustimmungsrechte des Bundesrates* (Vienna: Braumüller, 2001).

19 Cf. P. Pernthaler, 'Die Verfassungsautonomie der österreichischen Bundesländer', in *JBl* (1986), p. 477 ff.; F. Koja, *Das Verfassungsrecht der österreichischen Bundesländer*, 2nd edn (Vienna/New York: Springer, 1988); R. Novak, 'Art 99 B-VG', in K. Korinek and M. Holoubek (eds), *Österreichisches Bundesverfassungsrecht* (Vienna/New York: Springer, 1999) and A. Gamper, 'The Principle of Homogeneity and Democracy in Austrian Federalism: The Constitutional Court's Ruling on Direct Democracy in Vorarlberg', Publius (2003), p. 45 ff.

20 See P. Pernthaler, *Österreichische Finanzverfassung* (Vienna: Braumüller, 1984).

21 Cf. the recent act: FAG 2001 (BGBl I 2001/3 as amended by BGBl I 2003/71).

22 See J. Hengstschläger, 'Der Finanzausgleich im Bundesstaat', in Schambeck (ed.), *Bundesstaat und Bundesrat in Österreich*, p. 181 ff.; Pernthaler, *Österreichische Finanzverfassung*, p. 157 ff. and H. G. Ruppe, '§ 4 F-VG', in K. Korinek and M. Holoubek (eds), *Österreichisches Bundesverfassungsrecht* (Vienna/ New York: Springer, 2000).

23 See Pernthaler, *Österreichische Finanzverfassung*, p. 31 ff.

24 Ibid., p. 119 ff.

25 See Ermacora, *Österreichischer Föderalismus*, p. 148 ff. and K. Weber, 'Österreichs kooperativer Föderalismus am Weg in die Europäische Integration', in J. Hengstschläger, H. F. Köck, K. Korinek, K. Stem and A. Truyol y Serra (eds), *FS Herbert Schambeck* (Berlin: Duncker & Humblot, 1994), p. 1041 ff.

26 See T. Öhlinger, *Verträge im Bundesstaat* (Vienna: Braumüller, 1978); T. Öhlinger, *Die Anwendung des Völkerrechts auf Verträge im Bundesstaat* (Vienna: Braumüller, 1982); M. Thaler, *Die Vertragsschlußkompetenz der österreichischen Bundesländer* (Vienna/ Cologne: Böhlau, 1990) and S. Hammer, *Länderstaatsverträge* (Vienna: Braumüller, 1992).

27 See A. Rosner, *Koordinationsinstrumente der österreichischen Länder* (Vienna: Braumüller, 2000).

28 See G. Meirer, *Die Verbindungsstelle der Bundesländer oder Die gewerkschaftliche Organisierung der Länder* (Vienna: Braumüller, 2003).

29 See K. Weber, 'Macht im Schatten? (Landeshauptmänner-, Landesamtsdirektoren und andere Landesreferentenkonferenzen)', *ÖZP* (1992), p. 105 ff. and Rosner, *Koordinationsinstrumente der österreichischen Länder*, p. 15 ff.

30 See P. Pernthaler, *Der differenzierte Bundesstaat* (Vienna: Braumüller, 1993).

31 Cf. the 'Agreement on Transfrontier Co-operation within the Framework of a European Region between the Autonomous Provinces of South Tyrol-Alto Adige, Trentino and the Austrian Land Tyrol of 1998 based on the Madrid Outline Convention on Transfrontier Co-operation between Territorial Communities or Authorities'. See P. Pernthaler and S. Ortino (eds), *Europaregion Tirol: Rechtliche Voraussetzungen und Schranken der Institutionalisierung* (Bozen: Europäische Akademie Bozen, 1997) and Institut für Föderalismus (ed.), *27. Bericht über die Lage des Föderalismus in Österreich (2002)* (Vienna: Braumüller, 2003), p. 222 ff.

32 For a general overview cf. T. Öhlinger, 'Der Verfassungsschutz ethnischer Gruppen in Österreich', in H. Schäffer, W. Berka, H. Stolzlechner und J. Werndl (eds), *FS Friedrich Koja* (Vienna/New York: Springer, 1998), p. 371 ff.

33 See T. Öhlinger, 'Bundesstaatsreform und Europäische Integration', in P. Pernthaler (ed.), *Bundesstaatsreform als Instrument der Verwaltungsreform und des europäischen Föderalismus* (Vienna: Braumüller, 1997), p. 43 ff.

34 See Pernthaler, *Der differenzierte Bundesstaat*, p. 3 ff.
35 See e.g. P. Pernthaler and G. Schernthanner, 'Bundesstaatsreform 1994' and T. Öhlinger, 'Das Scheitern der Bundesstaatsreform', both in A. Khol, G. Ofner and A. Stirnemann (eds), *Österreichisches Jahrbuch für Politik 1994* (Vienna: Verlag für Geschichte und Politik /Munich: Oldenbourg, 1995), p. 559 ff. and p. 543 ff. respectively.
36 Cf. the *Bundesverfassungsgesetz über den Beitritt Österreichs zur Europäischen Union* (BGBl 1994/744).
37 See 'Protocol No. 2 on the Åland islands', *Official Journal*, No. C 241 (29 August 1994).
38 Cf. European court of justice, Case *Konle*, C-302/97.
39 See C. Ranacher, *Die Funktion des Bundes bei der Umsetzung des EU-Rechts durch die Länder* (Vienna: Braumüller, 2002), p. 208 ff.
40 Cf. BGBl 1992/775.
41 Cf. e.g. in the Tyrolean law gazette LGBl 1993/18.
42 Their deputies are either the members of the *Länder* governments (Upper Austria, Salzburg, Styria, Tyrol, Vienna), the presidents of the *Länder* parliaments (Burgenland, Lower Austria, Vorarlberg) or the members of the *Länder* parliaments (Carinthia).
43 See P. Sieberer, 'Rechtsfragen bei der Mitwirkung von Länderorganen auf EU-Ebene', *JRP* (2001), p. 209 ff.
44 See below 'Other channels of influence and rights of participation', pp. 147.
45 It is of particular interest that the Austrian *Land* Tyrol, together with the Italian provinces South Tyrol-Alto Adige and Trentino, established a transnational liaison office which is responsible for the 'European Region Tyrol' (see above, note 31).
46 Cf. in particular F. Staudigl and R. Fischler (eds), *Die Teilnahme der Bundesländer am europäischen Integrationsprozeß* (Vienna: Braumüller, 1996) and J. Unterlechner, *Die Mitwirkung der Länder am EU-Willensbildungs-Prozeß.* (Vienna: Braumüller, 1997), p. 85 ff.
47 A survey of the present extent of 'Europeanization' of *Länder* competences is given by Ranacher, *Die Funktion des Bundes bei der Umsetzung des EU-Rechts durch die Länder*, p. 86 ff.
48 Cf. T. Öhlinger and M. Potacs, *Gemeinschaftsrecht und staatliches Recht*, 2nd edn (Vienna: Orac, 2001), p. 30 ff.
49 Art. 23d par. 2 B-VG in connection with Art. 6 of the federation–*Länder* concordat.
50 Art. 5 of the federation–*Länder* concordat.
51 Art. 4 par. 4 of the *Länder*–*Länder* concordat. Accordingly, IKL statements as to schemes concerning European integration are seen as uniform *Länder* statements in the sense of Art. 23d par. 2 B-VG, if they relate to *Länder* legislative competences.
52 Namely, in 1997. The Permanent Integration Committee of the *Länder* (cf. Art. 7 of the *Länder*–*Länder* concordat), which ought to have assisted the IKL at civil servant level, was regularly convened from 1993 to 1996, but not after 1997.
53 Cf. e.g. Öhlinger and Potacs, *Gemeinschaftsrecht und staatliches Recht*, p. 33 and P. Pernthaler, *Das Länderbeteiligungsverfahren an der europäischen Integration* (Vienna: Braumüller, 1992), p. 68 ff.
54 A detailed survey and critical analysis are given by H. Schäffer, 'Landesparlamente und Europapolitik: Das österreichische Beispiel', *DÖV* (1996), p. 396 ff.; Unterlechner, *Die Mitwirkung der Länder am EU-Willensbildungs-Prozeß*, p. 107 ff. and Weber, 'Österreichs kooperativer Föderalismus am Weg in die Europäische Integration', p. 1058 ff.
55 The main functions of the liaison office are as follows: the organization of the various *Länder* conferences, the maintenance of permanent co-ordination between the *Länder* and between the *Länder* and the federation, the co-ordination and documentation of *Länder* positions and their legal acts within their own competences and, finally, serving as a joint 'post office' of the *Länder* (contact point for the issuing of statements, drafted bills, invitations, etc).

56 That is, the federal minister for foreign affairs, and a representative of the federal chancellor, of the vice-chancellor and of the federal minster for defence.

57 The *Länder* must formally apply for adequate involvement and bear the costs, under the premise that involvement is legally and practically possible (Art. 8 par. 1 of the federation–*Länder* concordat). The *Länder* representatives are nominated by the *Länder* governors, who are assisted by the liaison office of the *Länder* (Art. 8 par. 3 of the federation–*Länder* concordat).

58 According to Art. 8 of the federation–*Länder* concordat.

59 Art. 23e par. 2–4 B-VG.

60 The national assembly is entitled to a binding statement concerning all EU schemes which need to be implemented by a federal law or provoke a directly applicable legal act which relates to matters that would have to be regulated by a federal law.

61 Resolution of the conference of the presidents of the *Länder* parliaments of 3 May 2001; see Institut für Föderalismus (ed.), *26. Bericht über den Föderalismus in Österreich (2001)* (Vienna: Braumüller, 2002), p. 244f.

62 Cf. BGBl I 1998/61 and BGBl I 1999/35; see J. Weiss, 'Der Konsultationsmechanismus als Instrument zur Reduzierung der Folgekosten gesetzgeberischer Maßnahmen', *JRP* (1997), p. 153 ff.; E. G. Primosch, *Stabilitätspakt – Konsultationsmechanismus* (Vienna: Verlag Österreich, 2000); P. Bußjäger, 'Rechtsfragen zum Konsultationsmechanismus', *ÖJZ* (2000), p. 581 ff.; P. Pernthaler and E. Wegscheider, *Der Konsultationsmechanismus in der österreichischen Finanzverfassung* (Innsbruck: Institut für Föderalismus, 2000); K. Weber, 'BVG Gemeindebund', in K. Korinek and M. Holoubek (eds), *Österreichisches Bundesverfassungsrecht* (Vienna/New York: Springer, 2000).

63 Cf. BGBl I 2002/39 and A. Gamper, 'Der Stabilitätspakt 2001 im Spannungsfeld von Budgetkonsolidierung und Finanzausgleichsgerechtigkeit', *JRP* (2002), p. 240 ff.

64 BGBl I 2002/99. Cf. e.g. R. Klaushofer, 'Art. 14b B-VG', *ZfV* (2003), p. 630 ff. and C. Kleiser, 'Die neue Kompetenzverteilung im Vergaberecht', *ÖJZ* (2003), p. 449 ff.

65 Several law journals have meanwhile published special issues treating the constitutional convention: See issue 11/1 of *JRP* (2003) and issue 1/2 of *Forum Parlament* (2003). Cf. also H. Hösele and K. Poier (eds), *Österreich-Konvent, Politicum* 94 (2003).

66 See the interim committee reports at www.konvent.gv.at.

67 Further to that, the consent of the federal assembly will probably be needed, and a referendum is likely to be held as well for political reasons, even if the proposed constitutional amendment did not involve a 'total revision' of the recent constitution (compulsory referendum).

Jens Woelk

8

Farewell to the 'unitary federal state'? Transformation and tendencies of the German federal system

Stable but protected system facing new challenges

For four decades (Western) Germany enjoyed a period of relative tranquillity. Mainly concentrating on the economic reconstruction after World War II this 'economic miracle' was partly due to a specific form of social and economic cohesion, the 'social market economy', which had been supported by all political forces. Political stability was seen as an important precondition and thus also became an institutional objective. The outstanding economic success was not matched by a proportional increase of political power: Germany was a divided country at the front line of the Cold War and the period of tranquillity was paradoxically due to its artificial and particularly protected situation.

The end of the Cold War, symbolized by the sudden and spectacular fall of the Berlin Wall on 9 November 1989, ended this period and opened the road to unexpected re-unification: a historical chance, but also a necessity due to the fast erosion and implosion of the German Democratic Republic (GDR) (with the resulting need for overall reconstruction). In addition, the acceleration in the European integration process, marked above all by the completion of the single market and the Maastricht treaty, raised important questions about the future of this very process and Germany's role in it. After focusing almost totally on these two issues in the first half of the 1990s, a more global perspective has been added to the inward-looking and European-centred approach of German politics and reform: Germany has become a 'normal' state like many others, while remaining one of the world's most important economies; thus limited sovereignty and division were no longer an excuse for half-hearted action in the international sphere.[1] However, recently the pace of economic growth has almost come to a stop, raising difficult questions regarding Germany's capacity to modernize in order to adapt to the challenges.[2] The federal system, so far seen as one of the elements guaranteeing political stability, is now increasingly criticized as not very efficient and a major obstacle to reform.

This chapter focuses on the recent evolution of German federalism as a reaction to the mentioned internal, European and global changes. After a short illustration of the various faces of German federalism with particular focus on historical continuity, the re-unification process is analysed from the perspectives of administrative cooperation and financial solidarity. The huge amount of money needed for the reconstruction of the former GDR and the obligation of consolidating the budgets of all public bodies leading to reductions in the welfare system, raise the important question of the sustainable degree of homogeneity or differentiation. In addition, German federalism has to adapt to the transfer of more and more powers to the European level, with the resulting risk of leaving the *Länder* in the role of mere decentralized implementation agencies, far from their claim to be 'states'. Can more participation as compensation for lost powers really be considered a valid and working alternative, or is it simply the only possible solution? Considering these challenges, it is understandable that issues related to globalization in a wider sense have been discussed only quite recently. However, an active 'foreign economic policy' of the *Länder* had already been a consolidated practice for some time. More controversial are the reactions to changes in society, especially with regard to citizenship and immigration. Again, the underlying question is the very fundamental one for each federal system: where lies the balance between homogeneity and differentiation, that is, unity and diversity? Can a new balance be found by mere adaptation or is there a need for major reform? The frequent calls for institutional reform seem to suggest that the time is ripe for a new 'formative period' in which some structural limits of the current system have to be changed, just as happened in the late 1960s in the period of the 'grand coalition', which produced profound changes in the fields of cooperative federalism and financial redistribution.

Various faces of federalism in the 'unitary federal state'

German federalism used to be described as a mixture and combination of three models: the classic dual model, the unitary model and the cooperative model, all of them to some extent present in the framework of the German basic law (GG).[3] However, a true American-style dual federalism with spheres of powers and activities – at least by tendency – strictly separated, has never been realized in Germany. The German federal system is, on the contrary, characterized by interdependence and constant mutual influence between Federation and *Länder*.

The evolution towards a federal system with strong unitary tendencies in post-World War II Western Germany reflected a general expectation of German citizens (the mixture of population, integration of refugees, reconstruction and 'economic miracle' after World War II certainly had an important impact in this regard). Its origin and justification are to be found in the numerous interdependencies in social and economic life as well as in a standardization of products and services, in faster communication and higher mobility and an increasing demand on the state as service-provider, corresponding to the logic of the welfare state (in line with the principle of the 'social state' in Art. 20 GG) and creating an overriding imperative of homogeneity of living conditions throughout the entire federal territory.[4]

This has led to intensive horizontal and vertical cooperation and coordination (i.e. between the *Länder* and between Federation and *Länder*), even in sectors which are by tradition considered a domain of the *Länder*, in particular complex matters which cannot be limited to the territory of one single *Land*, such as protection of the environment, regional planning and education. However, the resulting co-ordination and cooperation by means of informal mechanisms, co-decisions, accords and treaties always depend on the weakest link of the chain (i.e. negotiations must continue until all participants are satisfied in order to prevent vetoes), thus often being an obstacle on the way to necessary innovation.

In the name of unitary requirements, the Federation has also expanded its legislative powers by the extensive use of so-called 'concurrent powers' (Art. 72 GG), thus emptying the sphere of differentiated *Länder* legislation. The Federation can, in practice, bind a major part of the *Länder* legislation very efficiently by means of its far-reaching legislative powers, and has increasingly done so.[5] In addition to the 'concurrent' legislative power, the federal framework legislation influences the administrative sphere of the *Länder* and the judicial system (which is organized by the *Länder* with the exception of supreme federal courts and federal legislation on procedure). There are also strong federal influences in the financial and fiscal sphere.

According to so-called 'executive federalism', the *Länder* do not only implement their own legislation, but are also responsible for implementing federal legislation in their own right (Art. 83 GG).[6] This not only corresponds to historical experience, but should also avoid the establishment of a costly parallel federal administrative structure. It also leads to the necessity of *Länder* participation in the federal legislation (as the same *Länder* would have to implement most of the federal laws in their own right).

This structural interdependence is strengthened by various interconnections between the different spheres of government due above all to the parallel structures of political parties in the Federation and in the *Länder*. The general result is a much greater power of the Federation in the German federal system than originally foreseen. It is only limited, and not fully counterbalanced, by the increasing influence of the federal council (*Bundesrat*, Art. 50 ff. GG).[7]

The gradual loss of their powers has been compensated by an evolution towards 'participatory federalism'; that is, more frequent (and more efficient) participation of the *Länder* in the federal legislative process. The federal council, whose members, nominated by the *Länder* governments and depending on their directives, represent the *Länder* interests by exercising far-reaching rights of approval or even veto, has become the pivotal institution of the whole federal system: if the federal council opposes a bill which necessitates its approval, the only way to pass it is via a compromise in the so-called 'mediation committee' (*'Vermittlungsausschuss'*, Art. 77 par. 2 GG) equally composed of members of the federal parliament and the federal council. If such a compromise cannot be found or is not accepted by parliament or the federal council, the law cannot enter into force.[8] Originally, only thirteen matters were subject to the federal council's approval, by contrast with roughly two-thirds of all federal laws today.[9]

The peculiar composition of this federal institution (members representing the *Länder* executives) reflects the specific institutional logic of German federalism with a preponderance of government bureaucracies and intergovernmental relationships. These features have their origins in the formative period of German federalism, especially in the Bismarck period, but institutional continuity can be found from the seventeenth century up until today.[10] The strength of traditional patterns of intergovernmental bargaining and accommodation through negotiation is a direct result of the fact that in Germany the process of state-building was based not on the national, but on the territorial level:[11] The Bismarck Empire was a federation of twenty-five states of which Prussia was the dominant entity. The states continued to possess considerable territorial autonomy and formed the federal council as the supreme sovereign institution corresponding to the principle that territorial interests are represented by the sovereign in negotiation with other sovereigns.

After the interruption of this continuity during the formally federal Republic of Weimar and the highly centralized third Reich, the federal structure after World War II was primarily (re-)established as a reaction to the experience of this totalitarian regime: federalism should above all provide for a system of checks and balances by means of a vertical separation of powers and thus strengthen democracy. This was deemed to be much more important than the guarantee of diversity between the *Länder* (given that in most cases these were new creations); on the contrary: as shown, economic reconstruction and recovery together with the build-up of the welfare state further shifted the balance in favour of unitary elements.

This is best illustrated by the numerous joint and co-ordinated projects between Federation and *Länder*. To guarantee a certain degree of homogeneity even in the financial sphere, the so-called 'joint tasks' (*Gemeinschaftsaufgaben*, Art. 91a GG, introduced by a whole set of amendments in 1969) have developed into a kind of 'benevolent federal dictatorship' by means of offering federal financial grants for projects in the *Länder* (guaranteeing federal influence on the projects). Originally, these grants should have – for a limited period – helped to create politically active entities and contribute to structural innovation. However, due to the inherent tendency of becoming independent structures, these mechanisms resulted in declaring nearly two-thirds of the federal territory as 'disadvantaged areas', thus creating an excess of infrastructures (e.g. in the hospital sector). Instead of separated tasks and functions and a clear distribution of financial resources, today in a number of sectors a shared (political and financial) responsibility of Federation and *Länder* can be found. These overlapping interrelations between federal and *Länder* powers and finances have additionally strengthened the unitary element.

However, this development is in line with the second important element of institutional continuity peculiar to German federalism: the responsibility for policy implementation in most fields is and remains vested with the *Länder*, especially in the administrative sphere. The resulting polycentric structure is deeply rooted and can be traced back to the pre-modern Roman Empire of the German Nation. On the one hand, in postwar Western Germany, it had a remarkable impact on the spatial growth patterns of the economy, mitigating tendencies towards spatial concentration of economic activity and strengthening polycentric regional policy networks.[12] On the other, it created an inherent and structural interdependence of federal and *Länder* bureaucracies and contributed to the intensive vertical and horizontal cooperation and co-ordination.

The resulting '*Politikverflechtung*' (interlocking policies)[13] has proved to be nearly immune to all attempts at reform. On the one hand, cooperation in terms of self-co-ordination is a useful means of avoiding the centralization of functions (as requested by the economic theory of federalism);[14] on the other, the influence (and control) of political parties is better guaranteed by co-ordinated action and the resulting mobilization of financial resources for specific purposes (it might even be used as an excuse for not responding to financial demands of single interest groups).[15]

Re-unification and the core issues of solidarity and homogeneity

With the incorporation of the five Eastern *Länder* which had been (re-)constituted in the German Democratic Republic,[16] on 3 October 1990 the German basic law became the definitive and legitimate constitution of Germany as a whole.[17] It had been a deliberate – and much criticized – choice in the treaty of unification to include the new Eastern *Länder* by extending the basic law's sphere of application (according to Art. 23 GG) rather than drafting a new constitution as foreseen in Art. 146 GG. Only the well-experienced and generally appreciated basic law (its general acceptance is best illustrated by Dolf Sternberger's fortunate expression of 'constitutional patriotism' as opposed to national patriotism or, worse, nationalism) seemed to offer a guarantee of German reliability in front of its neighbours as well as a solid constitutional base for the difficulties and time constraints of the re-unification process. However, besides these important advantages, Eastern Germans saw virtually everything they had known turned upside down and transformed according to Western patterns which created a psychological problem not yet overcome. Moreover, old problems of the (Western) federal system, such as the negative effects of cooperative federalism, were far from being resolved and even stressed during the process of re-unification.[18]

A federal 'trust' for the new Länder instead of reform

Besides the largely passive attitude of the Länder governments, the federal council had fallen under social democratic majority control and chancellor Helmut Kohl preferred to keep the – generally more sceptical – opposition as far out of the negotiating process as possible.[19] Apart from the procedural aspects of re-unification (in particular the non-participation of the Länder), the transitional provisions had been heavily criticized:[20] some authors were even asking, provocatively, whether Germany could still be categorized as a 'federal state', given the further weakening of the (already fragile) 'statehood of the Länder', which touched the very substance of federal statehood.[21]

The crisis of the federal system was not only due to the huge disparities between the Western and the new Eastern Länder, but also to a tendency to let the Federation take care of the resolution of the resulting problems, a kind of 'federal trust': for a limited period of time the Federation acted as a 'trustee' in favour of the new Eastern Länder without any express legal title for doing so: a clear sign that the classic and experienced mechanisms of cooperative federalism were on the whole not sufficient for managing the necessary and extraordinary efforts during the re-unification process.[22] A remarkable innovation, however, easing the transition at the administrative level, were the sponsorships Western Länder assumed for the Eastern ones. By assigning civil servants for direct assistance in setting up the new administrative structures, the Western Länder guaranteed a minimum of administrative autonomy of the new Länder, thus avoiding a system of indirect federal administration by federal civil servants which would have further weakened the federal system.[23]

An important exception, securing the extraordinary influence exercised by the federal government, regarded the system of mutual financial assistance between the Länder, which was not extended to the new Eastern Länder until 1995. The Western Länder argued that the obligation to fully integrate the latter would have been too much of a financial burden for them. Instead, a specific fund for German unification (Fonds für deutsche Einheit) was established, financed by the federal government and, to a minor extent, by the Western Länder.[24] Even after the end of this exceptional system, the Eastern Länder received special, favourable treatment, predominantly through vertical (i.e. federal) instead of horizontal transfers: to cover the costs of political management, reconstruction and privatization of formerly state-owned enterprises and industries.[25] An additional 'solidarity tax' has been levied on the income tax for bearing the enormous costs of the re-unification and reconstruction process, but also the Western municipalities contributed by a reduction of their share in the corporation tax (thus easing the pressure on Federation and Länder).

Despite numerous requests for reform (seen by many as a substitute for a new constitution), no major constitutional changes occurred. Although its mandate expressly mentioned the issue of the relations between Federation and *Länder*, not even the joint commission for constitutional reform established by the unification treaty came up with any important proposal for changes in the federal system.[26] It became clear that the Western *Länder* had used the chance of re-unification (through the need for their approval via the federal council) to strengthen their own interests, putting them even before the interests of the unified country. As a result, only minor constitutional amendments were adopted in 1994,[27] regarding above all the concurrent legislative powers (Art. 72 GG, see below), the introduction of a federal (concurrent) power regarding state liability (Art. 74 c. 1 Nr. 25 GG) and the framework legislation (Art. 75 GG), which has been transformed into a kind of legislation via directives. These constitutional amendments are far from reaching the importance of those approved by the grand coalition in the period 1968–69, which is particularly astonishing considering the historical importance of re-unification.[28] The major issues can thus be considered still open.

'Equality' or 'equivalence' of living conditions?

The major change introduced by the aforementioned constitutional amendments in 1994 concerns the concurrent legislative powers in Art. 72 GG, the most important powers in practice. The rich catalogue, often amended and enriched, comprises roughly thirty subject matters of *Länder* powers (in Articles 74 and 74a GG) which are, however, open to federal legislation if specific preconditions are met. According to the previous wording of Art. 72 GG (second paragraph), three cases permitting federal legislation can be distinguished:

> The Federation has legislation insofar as a need for federal legislation arises because 1) a substance matter cannot be effectively regulated by legislation of the respective *Länder* or 2) regulating a substance matter by the law of one *Land* might infringe on the interests of other *Länder* or the whole or 3) this is needed for the preservation of legal and economic unity, particularly the preservation of *equal* living conditions beyond the territory of one *Land*. (Emphasis added)

The establishment or the creation of equal living conditions has never been a general constitutional objective, but only the precondition allowing for federal legislation in the fields of concurrent legislative powers. But in practice, and in the context of an expanding welfare state and accentuated social rights of citizens, this open clause provided for unlimited political discretion of the federal government and thus led to a nearly total absorption of the concurrent powers by the Federation. Moreover, from the very beginning, the federal constitutional court proclaimed any controversy about these criteria to be a political question not to be decided by the court,[29] thus leaving the *Länder* without any means of control.

Consequently, the *Länder* used the minimal constitutional amendments of 1994 in an attempt to contain this centralizing mechanism, mainly by imposing different preconditions for federal legislation and by obliging the federal constitutional court to deal with controversies arising from the use of these powers.[30]

The new formulation of the second paragraph reads: 'In this field, the Federation has legislation if and insofar as the establishment of *equivalent* living conditions in the federal territory or the preservation of legal and economic unity *necessitates*, in the interest of the state at large, a federal regulation' (emphasis added). Besides the change from *equal* to (the wider formula of) *equivalent* living conditions as a criterion, a mere need (*Bedürfnis*) for federal legislation is no longer sufficient, but there has to be a true necessity (*Erforderlichkeit*) for justifying a federal regulation. In addition, a new paragraph 3 determines that the power can be transferred back to the *Länder* if the preconditions permitting federal legislation are no longer given: 'A federal statute can stipulate that a federal regulation for which the conditions of Paragraph 2 no longer hold true is replaced by law of the *Länder*'. Finally, Art. 93 GG (controversies before the federal constitutional court) now expressly comprises the obligation of the federal constitutional court to monitor the exercise of the concurrent powers in case of claims stating the non-existence of the preconditions for federal legislation.[31]

The shift in the criterion from equal to mere equivalent living conditions has been approved with the political intention of permitting more diversity and differentiation between the *Länder*.[32] The practical consequences of the reform have not been very spectacular, so far. Rather than being intended to serve as an operational provision, the reform of Art. 72 GG represents a fundamental political and symbolic turn: for the first time ever, a constitutional amendment regarding the relations between Federation and *Länder* will stop and invert centralizing tendencies instead of promoting them. This symbolic act stands for a recent tendency to underline the importance of (more) competition for the future development of German federalism. It has been advocated, above all, in the field of financial relations, especially with regard to horizontal equalization payments.

Fiscal federalism between solidarity and (more) competition

Related to the logic of equal living conditions, the fiscal and financial system established by the constitutional amendments of 1969 also aims at a generally equal distribution of fiscal obligations over the whole federal territory. The legislative powers regarding finances and taxation are vested primarily with the Federation, leaving only a few residual powers as the responsibility of the *Länder*. In terms of financial arrangements, the basic law provides that the most important tax revenues are shared between the Federation and the *Länder*: income and corporation tax are shared equally, the value-added tax (VAT) is shared on the basis of a periodical adjustment.[33] Other tax revenues are apportioned either to the Federation (e.g. excise duties) or to the *Länder* (e.g. property, inheritance, motor vehicle and beer taxes).

Horizontal and vertical mechanisms of financial equalization (i.e. transfers among the *Länder* as well as complementary support from the Federation to the *Länder*, Art. 107 GG) shall guarantee the unitary objective of uniformity of living conditions in the federal territory (Art. 106 par. 3 GG). More specifically, these equalization mechanisms are the expression of a tension between the contrasting principles of autonomy, responsibility and the safeguard of the existence and individual decisions of each entity on the one hand and the solidarity and co-responsibility of the other members of the Federation on the other. The tension between these two contrasting positions is inherent in all federal systems. It cannot be resolved once and for all, but has to be balanced and to be adjusted from time to time. In the decades before re-unification, the German fiscal and financial system had led to a far-reaching levelling of the economic and financial conditions of the *Länder*.[34] Considering the financial constraints of the re-unification process and the huge money transfer into the Eastern *Länder*, it was only a question of time as to when the issue of redressing the balance would come up again,[35] especially after the transitional system for the Eastern *Länder* and Berlin had ended in 1995.

In three important judgments, the federal constitutional court has dealt with the delicate issue of financial equalization and the resulting need to find a balance between solidarity and responsibility.

First, in a decision of 1986 the principle of a community based on solidarity was considered as fundamental and as providing guidance for the whole system of equalization between the *Länder*.[36] The court underlined the existence of an obligation of the richer *Länder* to assist the poorer *Länder* financially, despite their sovereignty and financial independence from each other. As financial equalization can be considered a (political) compromise establishing the concrete balance between autonomy and self-responsibility of the single *Land* and the solidarity-based co-responsibility for the existence and autonomy of the other *Länder*, the 'federal principle of mutual responsibility' not only provides for the justification (and the base) for financial obligations in favour of the poorer *Länder*, but also for their limits: assistance has to be granted as long as it is necessary and sustainable.[37] In a further judgment (1992) the court stated that any existing *Land* has to be able to fulfil its tasks and functions in organizational and financial terms; (only) if this is not possible, the other members of the solidarity-based community have to assist.[38]

Following increasing criticism against the system of financial equalization, and after futile attempts to come to a political solution, Bavaria, Baden-Württemberg and Hesse claimed the unconstitutionality of the system before the federal constitutional court. Their main criticism was directed against the ordinary law of financial equalization (which at that time fixed the degree of horizontal equalization at 95 per cent).[39] Of course, this law could have simply been changed by parliament (i.e. *Bundestag* and approval of the federal council). The fact that it has not been possible to find a political solution (as would have been typical in the logic of cooperative federalism) is a clear sign of the beginning of a period characterized by a more competitive and conflicting relationship in the different context after re-unification.

In the judgment of 11 November 1999,[40] the federal constitutional court declared the 1993 federal law on horizontal financial equalization unconstitutional and – though very prudently – indicated the principles such as transparency and responsibility which should inspire not only the financial equalization, but also the entire financial policy. The court added clear time-lines for implementation, deciding that the federal law on financial equalization could continue to be applied transitionally until 2004, requiring the federal legislator to define and to determine general criteria for the equalization until the end of 2002. Regarding rationality and transparency, the concrete mode of equalization ought to be redefined in a separate federal law on its general parameters (*Maßstäbegesetz*): all financial rights and obligations ought to be based on an express motivation and the distribution of the fiscal income should be periodically planned on a midterm basis. This procedure offers the advantage of separating the discussion on the (legitimization of) rights and obligations from the concrete financial negotiations. The long-term binding effect of this law should serve the rationality of the parameters.

Underlining again the fundamental character of the principle of solidarity between Western and Eastern, but also between richer and poorer *Länder*, the court did not follow the richer *Länder* completely in their argument. However, for the first time the importance of competition in the economic politics of the *Länder* was mentioned expressly and certain differences in their respective economic performance were not only seen as a natural consequence but also as necessary (this might confirm the mentioned thesis of Art. 72 GG as a general guiding principle for interpretation rather than a concrete norm for implementation).

After long and controversial negotiations between Federation and *Länder*, a compromise was found for a new regulation of the equalization system (from 2005 to 2019) reducing the total sum of financial transfers as well as the thresholds, thus providing for more incentives. Until 2019 the Eastern *Länder* will receive additionally roughly 150 billion Euro directly from the Federation. In July 2001, the federal parliament adopted the required law on parameters, determining the new general criteria for the shares in VAT, for the financial equalization between the *Länder* and for additional federal transfers to *Länder* in financial difficulties.

The crisis of fiscal federalism and redistribution as a consequence of the huge regional disparities after German re-unification risked seriously affecting the federal balance. It is generally agreed upon that the 1999 judgment marks an important step away from the previous 'tranquil', inherently cooperative and proceduralized system towards more competition and conflict. However, it also marks another step to an increasing 'judicialization' of politics: in times of increasing conflict, participatory procedures alone no longer guarantee political compromise, so the federal constitutional court has to step in. The implementation of the judgment, necessarily again by compromise, which was finally found, seems to confirm the trend towards greater differentiation and more competitive elements.

EU integration: more 'participatory' federalism

In the 1990s, after the creation of the single market and due to the increasing number of competences and sovereign powers transferred to the European level (which very often concerned *Länder* powers), the question of how to organize internal participation in the decision-making process became more and more pressing. Under Art. 24 GG, the previous constitutional base for German participation in European integration, the limitation and transfer of sovereign rights were exclusively decided by the federal government. Independently of the internal distribution of powers and responsibility, this applied to the resulting obligation of implementing EC law as well, and thus led to claims of the *Länder* being involved in the decision-making process at European level.[41] After the ratification of the Maastricht treaty (and the necessary approval by the federal council), the *Länder* succeeded in having their demands transformed into a constitutional guarantee of participation rights in the new Art. 23 GG, known as the 'European clause' (*Europaartikel*).[42]

In its first paragraph, the new article on European integration declares European unification an objective of the state and explicitly permits the transfer of sovereignty rights to the European Union, but it also contains a so-called 'structural guarantee' by expressly listing the structural principles of the German basic law with which the European Union has to comply.[43] Being in its formulation very similar to the fundamental structural principles listed in Articles 20, 28 and 79 par. 3 GG (including the federal principle) and adding the principle of subsidiarity, the drafters' intention is clear: Germany continues to participate actively in the European integration process, but – at least at this stage – cannot be merged into a fully fledged European state. This purpose of the 'structural guarantee' clause, setting a constitutional limit, was confirmed by the much disputed federal constitutional court's decision on the Maastricht treaty only a few months later.[44] Much emphasis has been put on the protection of the federal principle. Participation of the *Länder* is now guaranteed by paragraphs (2, 4, 5 and 6) of the 'European clause'.

Participation of the Länder *in EU affairs*
Following the already existing statutory practice, guiding principle is the – at least partial – compensation for the loss of *Länder* competences as well as for the loss of competences of the federal council by strengthening their participation in the exercise of rights by the federal government at EC level. Thus, the new article does not introduce an entirely new set of procedures, but rather 'constitutionalizes' the already established, so-called '*Bundesrat* procedure',[45] putting the institutional participation through the federal council at the centre.[46]

The different degrees of participation, ranging from information and consultation to rights of direct representation at community level, correspond to the domestic distribution of competences. The implementation, a detailed regulation in the 'Law on the cooperation between the Federation and *Länder* in affairs of the European Union' (EUZBLG), further integrated by an agreement between the federal government and the *Länder* governments,[47] considerably extend the already existing obligation of the federal government to keep the *Länder* informed on European affairs: information about all preparatory acts and proposals of potential *Länder* interest is included as well as the possibility of direct participation of a *Länder* observer in the negotiations in Brussels.

According to Art. 23 par. 4 GG, the participation of the federal council (in the form of a deliberation) is necessary, if it would be required for similar decisions or issues in the domestic sphere, or if the sphere of *Länder* competences is affected according to the internal distribution of competences: the concrete forms of participation range from consultation (par. 4) to procedures of internal co-decision (par. 5). The federal government has to 'consider' the opinion expressed by the federal council on behalf of the *Länder* when taking a decision at community level. The meaning of 'consider' ('*berücksichtigt*') in this context is to be understood as the obligation to examine the *Länder* position thoroughly and to take it into account – although it has no binding effect; it applies not only to sectors of concurrent powers or federal framework legislation, but also extends to areas of exclusive federal competence, at least in so far as a proposal also affects *Länder* interests.

If a proposal predominantly concerns matters of *Länder* competence, their administrative organization or structure or their administrative procedures, the opinion is of binding character: in these cases, according to a qualified co-decision procedure, the federal government has to follow the federal council's opinion, presenting it as its own at community level (Art. 23 par. 5 GG). The opinion's binding power is limited only by the overall responsibility the Federation bears for the federal republic (in particular for reasons of foreign policy, defence or requirements resulting from European integration) or in case of possible financial burdens for the Federation.

The *Länder* are further protected by the requirement of their approval (through the federal council) of all proposals based on Art. 308 TEC which affect their interests.[48] They can raise alleged violations of their guaranteed participatory rights before the federal constitutional court.[49]

In the case of proposals made at community level which affect the substance of 'exclusive legislative competences' of the *Länder*,[50] direct representation as the highest degree of participatory rights is the consequence (Art. 23 par. 6 GG): in the negotiations at community level a representative of the *Länder* will act on behalf of the federal republic. Representing the position of the *Länder* majority as established within the federal council,[51] this representative is authorized to bind the federal government (according to the condition in Art. 203 TEC).

Although there is thus no final federal 'filter', not even in these cases does a complete transfer of the power of external representation take place: the federal government continues to be head of the delegation and therefore remains ultimately responsible in the negotiations at European level; there is always a federal civil servant present acting as an 'assistant'. All strategies of negotiations have to be co-ordinated with the federal government. A compromise procedure avoids the paralysis of the federal republic's capacity to act at community level in case of objections by the federal government to the request of direct representation or to strategies. So far, substantial agreement has always been possible.

In addition to the participatory rights, direct contacts with community institutions (in particular the commission) are important independent sources of information and decisive for lobbying activities. For some decades already, a specific observer (*Länderbeobachter*) sent by the authorities of the German *Länder* has been working in the permanent representation of the federal republic in Brussels. He or she is even allowed to participate in the meetings of the community institutions as an observer; that is, without the right to actively intervene. The practice of liaison offices, run by all *Länder* in Brussels in forms of private or public law, has been put on an explicit legal base.[52] In addition, all *Länder* participate with their representatives in the committee of the regions, much criticized because of its 'mixed' (local and regional) composition, as well as in various regional initiatives and associations.

Evaluation of participation as compensation for lost powers

The participatory rights are rather unspectacular in terms of their constitutional legitimacy: due to its prevailing powers for external affairs, the federal government's autonomous final say is safeguarded, at least substantially (even though taking a different position from a binding opinion expressed by the federal council can only be seen as a means of *ultima ratio* and thus as a serious exception). Therefore, the principles of integration, of the separation of powers as well as the autonomy of the federal government in the sphere of external relations and foreign power are respected.

The concentration of the formal side of participation in the federal council as the pivotal institution for all participatory instances must be considered as a unique situation. The transformation into an institutionalized 'participatory' federalism is expressed by a high degree of formalization in the legal procedures of participation. Equally important are the often informal procedures for co-ordination, based on a continuous and reciprocal circulation of information at all levels of government, as well as the involvement of the *Länder* in the various preparatory stages.

Despite an overall positive evaluation the basic problem remains: the *Länder*, deprived of some of their powers and responsibilities for own action, receive a mere right to participate in the action of others as a substitute. Even worse, this participation is only indirect, as it is filtered through the federal council, in which each single *Land* has to look for allies in order to form a majority for the defence of its own rights and interests. This often causes a strong pressure for compromise in this federal institution. Thus, in the council the *Länder* representative does not represent the genuine interests of one *Land*, but their joint position as the position of the member state of Germany. In the end, the political symbolism of direct representation in the council does not correspond to substantial, direct political influence.[53] However, considering the reality and the nature of the decision-making process at European level, in which the Federation limits sovereignty and transfers powers, no other solution was considered to be equally practicable.

'Foreign policy' by the *Länder* and changes in society

Besides the more and more frequent participation of Germany's armed forces in a number of foreign missions (currently in Bosnia and Herzegovina, Kosovo and Afghanistan),[54] two more direct consequences of the various globalization processes lead to a further opening of German statehood and also affect the federal system: the 'foreign (economic) policy' of the *Länder* as well as recent legislation regarding citizenship and immigration (although the latter does not affect the federal system in the first place, it introduces a higher degree of diversity into society and challenges the homogeneity scheme).

In foreign policy matters, responsibility constitutionally belongs to the federal government (Art. 32 GG). However, there are some noteworthy foreign activities by the *Länder*, especially in the economic and cultural fields. Besides cross-border cooperation in the strict sense (i.e. cooperation with direct neighbours), such as numerous relationships between German and foreign local bodies across the German borders, almost all *Länder* have signed partnership agreements also with foreign entities abroad (e.g. with American cities and states, Chinese provinces and Russian republics). Bavaria, for instance, nurtures continuous relationships with Austrian *Länder*, provinces in northern Italy and South Africa, departments in southern France, and the government of Québec. Since 1990 support for Central and Eastern European countries has constituted an additional and important dimension of *Länder* foreign relations.[55]

As far as their legislative powers are concerned, the *Länder* may conclude, with the consent of the federal government, treaties with foreign states or their entities (Art. 32 par. 3 GG). Insofar as they are responsible for the exercise of their rights and the discharge of their duties, the *Länder* can, with consent of the federal government, even delegate sovereign powers to institutions for areas at their borders (Art. 24 par. 1a GG).[56] The prior approval should guarantee that there is no discrepancy in the international obligations taken by the federal government and the *Länder*. In practice, however, the *Länder* have transferred their (limited) powers to conclude international treaties on matters of their powers to the Federation on the condition that their position is duly taken into consideration by the negotiating federal government.[57]

There is no single model of how the *Länder* manage their foreign representations.[58] Problems related to the management of foreign policy lie in its complexity and difficult implementation rather than *Länder* contesting the federal government's authority over the question or attempts by the federal government to curb *Länder* activities.

The other side of globalization is the need for measures of integration of Germany's ca. 10 per cent of foreign residents. During the economic boom of the 1960s Germany badly needed skilled foreign workers: the '*Gastarbeiter*' (i.e. guest-workers), came, but most often did not leave after their job had been done. A number of them did not even leave Germany for retirement and most of them made their families join them. In consequence, there are a lot of younger people who have grown up and live in Germany, but still do not possess German citizenship.

The debate on the integration of foreign residents began in the late 1980s with a discussion on the right of foreigners to vote in elections at municipal level as a means of fostering their integration. The introduction of such a right in two *Länder* was held incompatible with the basic law by the federal constitutional court.[59] However, in order to accommodate the new obligation stemming from primary community law to grant such a right to all EU citizens (Art. 19 par. 1 TCE, formerly Art. 8b), the basic law was changed.[60]

On 1 January 2000, the new law on citizenship entered into force, providing for a double citizenship for children of foreign residents who are born in Germany according to the *ius soli* principle. The period of residence in Germany which has to pass before foreign adults can ask for German citizenship has been reduced. These changes provoked a controversial discussion (after all, the previous law on citizenship had been from 1913!) on the (difficult) integration of foreign workers, who are often muslims. They were opposed by the conservative opposition who asked for a (German) *Leitkultur* (guiding or dominant culture) as the guiding concept for integration. Another debate followed, this time on the project of facilitating the arrival of foreign computer-specialists (especially from India) on the German labour market by means of a special permits, a German 'green card'. The lack of some twenty to thirty thousand information technology workers should have been resolved in this way. Interestingly, there have been attempts by some *Länder*, especially Bavaria (governed by the conservative opposition, but with a number of high-tech industry companies), to go even further by introducing their own 'blue cards'. The project of a federal law on immigration, adopted in parliament in March 2002, had been stopped by the federal constitutional court in December 2002 because of procedural mistakes. A comprehensive and modern concept for immigration and integration of the foreign residents in Germany is still absent.[61]

Stability and uniformity versus (more) flexibility and differentiation?

It has been rightly stressed that 'co-operative federalism in Germany is much more flexible and open to institutional adaptation and policy change than is often assumed. The German federal state has to be acknowledged as a dynamic system.'[62] Its evolution is mainly characterized by centralization and participation; that is, federal legislation with participation of the *Länder* and their (full) responsibility for implementation. Alternatively, in order to avoid centralization in some fields and to safeguard the autonomy in the organizational domain of the *Länder*, the strategy of consensual unitarization through substantive and procedural harmonization based on horizontal cooperation was chosen, thus creating more and more interdependence and 'interlocking policies' (*Politikverflechtung*).

This evolution corresponds to the specific institutional logic of German federalism with its preponderance of government bureaucracies and (horizontal and vertical) intergovernmental relationships.[63] The victims of these executive-controlled policies are above all the *Länder* parliaments, which are at the brink of an almost total loss of influence and importance.

The cooperative model of the last decades has certainly permitted relatively homogeneous living conditions throughout the entire federal territory (at least until re-unification), the realization of social rights and the creation of a stable political system based on consensus and avoiding radical solutions. Although this consensus has been very important for the acceptance and stability of the whole system, the vertical and horizontal fusion of – legislative and executive – powers creates a vicious circle by requiring always more consensus for decisionmaking. The 'interlocking policies' are increasingly criticized as much slower and less efficient than a dual or separated federal system. Moreover, cooperative federalism has not been able to manage the complex situation after re-unification. Calls for reform, suggesting a more competitive approach between the members of the Federation as well as a reform of the participatory rights of the federal council, have thus become louder and more frequent.[64]

More competition?
The call for more differentiation, as a means of reviving incrusted federal structures allowing for experiments and for comparisons of best practice, is linked to the crisis of the continental European welfare state, which makes more flexibility of the federal system necessary and desirable.[65] The secret of success and of political stability in the old federal republic might be summarized by the concept of 'German consensus' (since the 1950s basically the agreement on a system of 'social market economy'). But today, the disparities and differences after unification and the recent difficulties in the economic situation leading to cuts in the welfare state system make far-reaching reforms necessary and the consensus-based procedures alone seem too slow for a reaction to profound changes.

A number of proposals and initiatives for reform can be summarized by the label of 'competitive federalism'.[66] Starting from the observation that the dynamic potential within the German federal system could and should be better used, and based on the economic theory of federalism, the common feature of these proposals is that the value of competition as an incentive for innovation through experiments should be rediscovered. For in doing so, the need for striking a different balance between integration and subsidiary has been advocated.[67] These demands correspond to the economic responses to the globalization processes – more responsibility of the concerned, more differentiation – and attempts to apply them to the federal system. The main demand is to restore the link between decision-making power and political responsibility for the consequences, which, in many fields, has been made unrecognizable by the 'interlocking policies'.

Critics of the concept of 'competitive federalism' point to the north (and east)–south divide between the supporting and the sceptical *Länder:* as more competitive elements have been expressly asked for by the richer *Länder*, especially in the equalization proceedings, they are consequently regarded with suspicion by others. Critics argue that the simple transfer of economic concepts to the federal system cannot work due to the different context, which – at least in part – guarantees equal chances and services for all citizens.[68] However, most reform proposals aim at introducing greater separation in the field of legislative powers (with compensation through a parallel reduction of *Länder* participation through the federal council), as well as at a new regulation of financial relations (including equalization, but also increased *Länder* powers in tax and fiscal legislation).

Although the reform of Art. 72 GG offers new room for manoeuvre and the 1999 judgment on financial equalization seems to support the strengthening of competitive elements, there is currently no form of authentic normative competition between the *Länder:* 'competitive federalism' still waits for implementation on a wider scale. The precondition is that differentiation and in particular different standards of living conditions have to be at least tolerated or, better, judged positively. 'Competitive federalism' is certainly no substitute for cooperative federalism, but it might give new impetus for regaining greater flexibility through (more) subsidy. Applied as a guiding principle for interpretation, it might counterbalance a legal doctrine which, by strongly supporting the normative role of the 'equality of living conditions' without questioning the theoretical foundations and the systematic context, tends to idealize the necessities of unity in the legal system.[69] Of course, its implementation depends on the political will of all actors.

Another periodically discussed recipe for reform regards the territorial redesign of the federal republic: the sixteen current *Länder* should be merged into fewer, greater and economically more viable units. However, even though economists and other experts seem to enjoy drawing new maps according to economic and financial criteria, their scenarios have never had any success: so far, all plans and attempts at reform have failed, from the Luther commission in the 1950s and the Ernst commission in the 1970s up to the refusal of Brandenburg's citizens to approve the fusion with Berlin in 1996.[70] Thus, the detailed provisions for territorial changes in Art. 29 GG have never been applied; all successful territorial fusions (e.g. the 'South-Western State' Baden-Württemberg) have been based on specific constitutional provisions.[71]

Of course, criteria such as real economic capacity and guarantee of the respective tasks and functions are important, but any proposal has to respect public identification with the *Länder* (which, at least in Western Germany, rests on five decades of their own history). Together with the reaction to the over-centralized socialist system, this explains why in 1990, despite Western fears regarding their sub-optimal scale, the five Eastern *Länder* had been restored instead of creating two or three bigger ones or simply transforming the GDR into the twelfth *Land*, both more reasonable alternatives in terms of financial and administrative resources.[72] Today, a reduction of the number of *Länder* does not seem possible; it might not even be the adequate solution for the problems created by the 'interlocking policies' and overlapping powers of Federation and *Länder*.

The pivotal role of the federal council: strength or obstacle?

Recently, the federal council has become the institutional target for the widespread criticism of participatory federalism. Until today, continuous enlargement of its veto power and at the same time progressive harmonization, in particular of administrative rules and operating procedures, have characterized the participation of the *Länder* at federal level. In addition, more often the political parties which form the opposition (in the *Bundestag*) control the majority of votes in the federal council, permitting the opposition to block governmental policies according to party lines rather than serving *Länder* interests. This new kind of *cohabitation à la allemande* bears the risk of a deliberate blockade in the negotiation process and might even lead to a change of the organ's institutional role:[73] the federal council might less serve its original function as an organ of institutional representation of *Länder* interests at federal level, becoming increasingly similar to a second chamber with exclusively political functions.[74]

The climax of this evolution was reached with the vote on the immigration law in March 2002, which led to a 'constitutional crisis' and could only be resolved by a decision of the federal constitutional court. The case illustrates the dilemma of the institution very well. In the federal council the votes of each *Land*, representing its interests, can only be cast as a block vote (Art. 51 par. 3 GG). Due to the majority situation, Brandenburg's four votes were decisive for the adoption of the much disputed federal immigration bill proposed by the federal government and passed by the majority of social democrats and greens in the *Bundestag*. Considerable pressure had been placed on Brandenburg's grand coalition government in which the social democrats supported and the Christian democrats opposed the bill. Although the leader of the Christian democrats had expressed his opposition in the voting procedure, the vote of Brandenburg was counted in favour of the bill, after the council's president (Berlin's mayor and a social democrat) had asked the president of the *Land* (a social democrat) for a second time to cast Brandenburg's vote (this time without explicit protests by his coalition partner). The bill was saved and adopted, but the delegations of the *Länder* ruled by Christian democrats protested and finally asked for a decision by the federal constitutional court. On 18 December 2002, the court declared the immigration law to be unconstitutional, because (in the first round) the vote had not been cast as a block vote and was thus not valid.[75]

This case shows the increasing pressure on the federal council exerted by the political parties which wish to prevail over the representation of *Länder* interests. Usually, coalition agreements provide for abstention, if there is dis-agreement between the political partners. However, in case of important deci-sions and narrow majorities, an abstention can easily have the effect of a 'no' vote, which explains the readiness to engage in conflict. As the *cohabitation à la allemande* has become a frequent situation, the temptation to 'abuse' the federal council's veto power is certainly getting stronger (as well as a further 'judicial-ization' of politics).

Consequently, the most radical proposals for reform even call for a trans-formation of the organ into an elected senate. But especially from a comparative perspective, this seems too risky: apart from being probably unconstitutional,[76] these proposals do not sufficiently consider the advantages of the concentration of *Länder* participation in one institution (in which majority and not consensus is the operative voting rule). Moreover, cooperative procedures involving the *Länder* executives are deeply rooted in the German system and are an essential part of the legal and constitutional culture. Despite the prevailing centralization of the past, the federal council is certainly a flexible and not necessarily 'one way' institution. It has the potential to adapt to greater decentralization of powers, provided that reforms taking this road find a majority (above all among the financially weaker *Länder*).

Perspectives for reform

Reforms of the federal system are necessary. The debated issues are much older than the process of re-unification and some issues were debated as far back as the 1960s. They have come to the fore again because they were left unresolved after the constitutional model of the old federal republic had been simply extended to the whole, unified Germany. However, as all reforms have to pass the federal council, they will have to find the approval of the *Länder*. Therefore much depends on the public's readiness for reform (which seems to be greater today than just a few years ago).

The main proposals agree on the importance of greater separation of powers and responsibilities: they comprise the concentration of elections in order to avoid the situation of a permanent election campaign as well as a redis-tribution and clear assignment of powers and responsibilities, reducing or even abolishing the federal framework legislation. The new formulation of Art. 72 GG should be used as a flexible means of the functional assignment of powers – in both directions. In addition, opening clauses in federal legislation could create room for diverging legislation at *Länder* level. Institutionally, the federal council would be much less entangled in the political combat zone if participa-tion were restricted to matters of important *Länder* interests. The cautious re-ordering of the financial equalization system after the judgment of 1999 introduced incentives for efficient administration of resources and limits the degree of levelling of financial capacity.

The German experience shows that the importance of stability, justified by the situation of reconstruction after World War II, might – in a different context and without adjustment – even risk destabilizing a political system through political inflexibility combined with an overbearing and unmanageable welfare system which does not fit into present times. Co-operative federalism is in part structurally inherent in the German federal system, but works due to a considerable degree of homogeneity (as well as sufficient resources for redistribution). The widespread agreement on the need for reform (above all in the welfare system and also because of budgetary constraints) should facilitate a fundamental shift to more differentiation and competition within the system, permitting more flexibility for experiments and innovative spirit through larger manoeuvral space for the single *Länder*. 'Competitive federalism' should not be interpreted in a darwinistic sense as the domination of the strongest (i.e. richest) *Länder*. Solidarity and integration always remain essential elements in a federal system. But a functional and complementary ingredient to counterbalance the cooperative and participatory elements in German federalism might be the right recipe for the future: the aim of the necessary reforms should therefore be to allow for more 'diversity' in 'unity'. Perhaps already the coming months will show whether a – partial – farewell to the 'federal unitary state' will succeed.[77]

Notes

1 In fact, complete sovereignty over the German territory was only achieved by the treaty on the final status of Germany of 12 September 1990 (cf. Art. 7 s. 2), Federal Official Gazette (*BGBl.*), II (1990), p. 1318.

2 See the survey on Germany: 'The uncertain giant', *The Economist* (7 December 2002).

3 P. Häberle, 'Die Schlußphase der Verfassungsbewegung in den neuen Bundesländern (1992/93)', *Jahrbuch des öffentlichen Rechts (JöR)*, 43 (1995), 355–418; at p. 408 ff.

4 This goes far beyond the so-called homogeneity clause (Art. 28 GG), according to which the constitutional order of the *Länder* has to conform to basic principles, such as fundamental rights, democracy and the rule of law; in addition it has to provide for directly elected political representation of citizens. However, there are also exceptions from the imperative of homogeneity of living conditions: despite efforts of coordination, differentiation between the *Länder* is still quite remarkable in the systems of local government, regulation of media and the educational system.

5 K. Hesse, *Grundzüge des Verfassungsrechts der Bundesrepublik Deutschland*, 20th edn (Heidelberg: C. F. Müller, 1995), p. 116. Despite the general presumption in favour of *Länder* legislative power, Articles 30 and 70 GG and the explicit catalogue of federal powers, Art. 71–75 GG.

6 In fact, there are only very few examples of direct federal administration: the diplomatic service, the army, border control, air traffic and federal finances including customs.

7 K. Hesse, *Der unitarische Bundesstaat* (Karlsruhe: C. F. Müller, 1962).

8 Less frequent (in practice) is the second category of federal legislation where the parliament can, by an absolute majority, override the opposition of the *Bundesrat* and pass the bill.

9 Also due to the jurisprudence of the federal constitutional court, according to which a law is subject to approval even in case of only a single article concerning *Länder* interests; Decisions of the Federal constitutional court (BVerfGE) 8, 274 (294).

10 G. Lehmbruch, 'German federalism and the challenge of unification', in J. J. Hesse and V. Wright (eds), *Federalizing Europe? The Costs, Benefits, and Preconditions of Federal Political Systems* (Oxford: Oxford University Press, 1996), pp. 169–203, at p. 171 ff. See for a brief overview R. Hrbek, 'Germany (Federal Republic of Germany)', in A. L. Griffiths (ed.), *Handbook of Federal Countries 2002* (Montreal & Kingston/London/ Ithaca: McGill-Queen's University Press, 2002), pp. 148–60, at pp. 148–50.

11 Lehmbruch, 'German federalism and the challenge of unification', p. 179.

12 Ibid., p. 178 ff.

13 See the fundamental study by F. W. Scharpf, B. Reissert and F. Schnabel, *Politik-verflechtung: Theorie und Empirie des kooperativen Föderalismus in der Bundesrepublik,* Vol. 1 (Kronberg im Taunus: Scriptor Verlag, 1976) and, more recently, F. W. Scharpf, *Optionen des Föderalismus in Deutschland und Europa* (Frankfurt a.M./New York: Campus, 1994).

14 According to the main thesis of this theory, competition always leads to an efficient order, not only between private subjects but also in the public sphere; that is, among states or territorial bodies; see e.g. D. Wellisch, *Dezentrale Finanzpolitik bei hoher Mobilität* (Tübingen: Mohr & Siebeck, 1995).

15 F. W. Scharpf, 'Zur Wiedergewinnung politischer Handlungsfähigkeit', in Bertelsmann Foundation (ed.), *Demokratie neu denken. Verfassungspolitik und Regierungsfähigkeit in Deutschland* (Gütersloh: Bertelsmann Foundation, 1998), p. 61 ff.

16 The five *Länder* had been abolished in 1952 and replaced by fourteen districts; their restoration, backed by strong political support, was an autonomous decision of the new political elite of Eastern Germany (as well as the introduction of a parliamentary system).

17 Thus it had lost its provisorial character, which was particularly evident in the re-formulation of the preamble (which saw the obligation to strive for unification cancelled) and in Art. 146 GG. On German re-unification see P. Zelikow and C. Rice, *Germany Unified and Europe Transformed* (Cambridge, MA: Harvard University Press, 1995); C. Jeffery (ed.), *Recasting German Federalism: The Legacies of Unification* (London/New York: Cassell, 1999).

18 See for example R. Arnold, 'Problems of federalization in Germany after the unification', in S. Bartole, S. Ortino and G. Conetti (eds), *Federalismo e crisi dei regimi comunisti* (Torino: Giappichelli, 1993), pp. 95–109; A. Benz, 'Neue Formen der Zusammenarbeit zwischen den Ländern', *Die öffentliche Verwaltung (DÖV)* (1993), p. 85 ff.; R. Herzog, 'Deutschland nach der Wiedervereinigung', in J. Hengstschläger, H. F. Kock, K. Korinek, K. Stern and A. Truyol y Serra (eds), *Für Staat und Recht. Festschrift für Herbert Schambeck* (Berlin: Duncker & Humblot, 1994), p. 701 ff.; and – more recently – U. Volkmann, 'Bundesstaat in der Krise', *DÖV* (1998), p. 613 ff; as well as E. Klein (ed.), *Die Rolle des Bundesrates und der Länder im Prozeß der deutschen Einheit* (Berlin: Duncker & Humblot, 1998).

19 Lehmbruch, 'German federalism and the challenge of unification', p. 183.

20 Especially the (temporary) exclusion of the new *Länder*, see in particular Benz, 'Neue Formen der Zusammenarbeit zwischen den Ländern', p. 85 and, for the transitional provisions, U. Häde, *Finanzausgleich: die Verteilung der Aufgaben, Ausgaben und Einnahmen im Recht der Bundesrepublik Deutschland und der Europäischen Union* (Tübingen: Mohr & Siebeck, 1996), p. 257 ff. and J. Hidien, *Handbuch Länderfinanzausgleich* (Baden-Baden: Nomos, 1999), p. 558 ff.

21 H.-P. Schneider, 'Die bundesstaatliche Ordnung im vereinigten Deutschland', in J. Huhn and P.-C. Witt (eds), *Föderalismus in Deutschland, Traditionen und gegenwärtige Probleme* (Baden-Baden: Nomos, 1992), pp. 239–61, at pp. 243 and 251; Volkmann, 'Bundesstaat in der Krise', p. 613 ff. and, from a comparative perspective, S. Ortino, *Diritto costituzionale comparato* (Bologna: Il Mulino, 1994), pp. 100–17.

22 The expression '*fiduziarischer Föderalismus*' (federal trusteeship) has been coined by

Häberle, 'Die Schlußphase der Verfassungsbewegung in den neuen Bundesländern', p. 410 ff.

23 Lehmbruch, 'German federalism and the challenge of unification', p. 187. As an additional effect, cross-cutting linkages between East and West have been created.

24 Altogether *ca.* 57.5 billion Euro (of which 10 billion were directly provided by the Federation, the rest jointly by Federation and *Länder*). The funds had been foreseen in Art. 7 of the treaty of unification (*Einigungsvertrag* of 31 August 1990, *BGBl.*, II, p. 889); see Schneider, 'Die bundesstaatliche Ordnung im vereinigten Deutschland', p. 239 ff.

25 A special public law body, the Federation-owned *Treuhandanstalt*, has guided, monitored and – in part – actively promoted and managed the process of privatization in the former GDR.

26 Art. 5 of the treaty of unification provided the legislative organs of the unified Germany with a mandate to 'resolve in terms of amendments of the Basic Law, within two years, all issues raised in the context of German unification', in particular the relationship between the Federation and the *Länder*. Cf. M. Kloepfer, *Verfassungsänderung statt Verfassungsreform. Zur Arbeit der Gemeinsamen Verfassungskommission* (Berlin: Berlin Verlag, 1995), p. 100. Most importantly, various proposals to reform the so-called 'financial constitution' had not been realized.

27 42nd Amendment, 27 October 1994 (*BGBl.*, I, p. 3.146), entered into force on 15 November 1994.

28 Kloepfer, *Verfassungsänderung statt Verfassungsreform*, p. 149.

29 BVerfGE, 2, 213.

30 See for the new version Kloepfer, *Verfassungsänderung statt Verfassungsreform*, p. 103 ff.

31 Art. 93 par. 1 no. 2a GG: 'The Federal Constitutional Court decides … in case of differences of opinion on the compatibility of federal law with Article 72 (2), at the request of the Federal Council, of a *Land* government, or of a *Land* parliament'. See C. Neumeyer, *Der Weg zur neuen Erforderlichkeitsklausel für die konkurrierende Gesetzgebung des Bundes (Art. 72 Abs. 2 GG)* (Berlin: Duncker & Humblot, 1999); C. Calliess, 'Die Justiziabilität des Art. 72 Abs. 2 GG vor dem Hintergrund von kooperativem und kompetitivem Föderalismus', *DÖV* (1997), p. 889 ff.

32 In strict legal terms, paradoxically, the reform might even make federal legislation easier as the threshold for federal intervention is now even lower (from 'equal' to 'equivalent' living conditions). The drafters' intention had been, however, to make federal legislation more difficult; cf. Calliess, 'Die Justiziabilität des Art. 72 Abs. 2 GG vor dem Hintergrund von kooperativem und kompetitivem Föderalismus'.

33 Every three years by federal legislation subject to the *Bundesrat*'s approval. The financial and fiscal relations are regulated in the so-called 'financial constitution', Articles 106, 107 and 104a GG.

34 For more in-depth information on fiscal federalism in Germany, see D. Carl, *Bund-Länder-Finanzausgleich im Verfassungsstaat* (Baden-Baden: Nomos, 1995); Häde, *Finanzausgleich*; Hidien, *Handbuch Länderfinanzausgleich*; and, from an interdisciplinary perspective, G. Färber, *Probleme der regionalen Steuerverteilung im bundesstaatlichen Finanzausgleich* (Baden-Baden: Nomos, 2000).

35 In fact, the issue was a subject of the annual debate of Germany's constitutional scholars; see the publication of the proceedings in Peter Selmer and F. Kirchhof, 'Grundsätze der Finanzverfassung des vereinten Deutschlands', *Veröffentlichungen der Vereinigung der Deutschen Staatsrechtslehrer* (VVDStRL), Vol. 52 (Berlin: de Gruyter, 1993), as well as, from the perspective of a richer *Land*, the recent brochures on the system of equalization with statistical data, '*Der bundesstaatliche Finanzausgleich*' and '*Der neue Finanzausgleich ab 2000*', edited by the Bavarian Ministry of Finances, www.stmf.bayern.de/finanzpolitik/laenderfinanzausgleich/, accessed 12 December 2003. In 2001, all horizontal and vertical transfers together made up nearly 30 billion Euro.

36 BVerfGE 72, 330 (402), together with the principle of responsibility for the other members of the community (i.e. *Länder*) as a direct consequence from Art. 107 par. 2 GG.

37 BVerfGE 72, 330 (387).

38 BVerfGE 86, 148 ff. According to this judgment (confirming the earlier cases), the financial and budgetary emergency in the two tiny *Länder*, Saarland and Bremen, in the late 1980s could not be resolved by simply starving these *Länder* to their financial ruin. The constitutional court underlined that territorial redesign as a political decision could not be *de facto* provoked by the refusal of financial assistance.

39 This led to a gigantic redistribution, in 1999, of around 7.5 billion Euro. In 2000, only 5 *Länder* payed 8.2 billion Euro into the equalization fund from which 11 *Länder* profited, which understandably raised some doubt as to whether this could still be called a 'solidarity-based' system; see F. Kirchhof, 'Die Finanzen des Föderalismus', in Europäisches Zentrum für Föderalismus-Forschung (ed.), *Europäischer Föderalismus im 21. Jahrhundert* (Baden-Baden: Nomos, 2003), pp. 48–64, at pp. 56 and 58.

40 BVerfGE 101, 158.

41 These claims had their first success in the course of the ratification of the Single European Act. The federal Law of Ratification of the Single European Act of 1986 (EEA-G, *BGBl*, II (1986), p. 1102, abolished by Art. 15 EUZBLG) contained a procedure for cooperation between Federation and *Länder* in European matters.

42 38th amendment to the basic law, 21 December 1992 (*BGBl*, I, p. 2086).

43 The clause, addressed to the organs of the German state which participate and contribute to the European Union, demands that the EU should fulfil 'democratic, social and federal requirements whilst operating under the rule of law, is governed by the principle of subsidiarity and guarantees the protection of human rights to a standard that is, in essence, equivalent to the standard of the basic law'.

44 BVerfGE 55, 155 ff. In this decision the BVerfG explicitly reserved the competence to control whether Community acts were *ultra vires* or within the domain of Community competence.

45 For a description of the participation procedure established by Art. 23 GG see R. Lang, *Die Mitwirkungsrechte des Bundesrates und des Bundestages in Angelegenheiten der Europäischen Union gemäß Artikel 23 Abs. 2 bis 7 GG* (Berlin: Duncker & Humblot, 1997); S. Oberländer, *Aufgabenwahrnehmung im Rahmen der EU durch Vertreter der Länder. Theorie und Praxis im Vergleich* (Baden-Baden: Nomos, 2000); D. König, *Die Übertragung von Hoheitsrechten im Rahmen des europäischen Integrationsprozesses* (Berlin: Duncker & Humblot, 2000); U. Kalbfleisch-Kottsieper, 'Föderaler Kompetenzverlust durch Überkompensation? Eine kritische Bilanz der europapolitischen Mitwirkung der deutschen Länder insbesondere mit Blick auf den Bundesrat', *Jahrbuch des Föderalismus 2001. Föderalismus, Subsidiarität und Regionen in Europa* (Baden-Baden: Nomos, 2001), pp. 168–87

46 In the same way, the federal government has to inform the *Bundestag* (House of Representatives), but the participatory rights of the directly elected chamber are much weaker (Art. 23 par. 3 GG). In the federal council, for cases of particular urgency the *Europakammer*, a committee in which each *Land* is represented by only one delegate, has been established. It has deliberation powers and can, if necessary, even substitute for the federal council (Art. 52 par. 3a GG).

47 Implementing Art. 9 EUZBLG, cf. text in Oberländer, *Aufgabenwahrnehmung im Rahmen der EU durch Vertreter der Länder*, pp. 214–16.

48 Though only at the level of ordinary law, Art. 5 par. 3 EUZBLG.

49 The *Länder* can address the court indirectly through the federal council (controversy between constitutional organs, Art. 93 par. 1 no. 1 GG) and directly (competence conflict between Federation and *Länder*, Art. 93 par. 1 no. 3 GG). Apart from one landmark

case (though still decided on the basis of the former procedure of participatory rights under ordinary law) regarding the TV directive, BVerfGE 92, 203 (227 and 230), there has been no jurisdiction so far.

50 This is a new concept, different from the system of competences in German basic law and has to be interpreted (negatively) in the sense that any action of the Federation is excluded; König, *Die Übertragung von Hoheitsrechten im Rahmen des europäischen Integrationsprozesses*, p. 361, and Oberländer, *Aufgabenwahrnehmung im Rahmen der EU durch Vertreter der Länder*, p. 44 ff.

51 This is no representation in institutional terms: the federal council only nominates the representative. Although no statistical data are available, direct participation in the council is a rather frequent and consolidated practice.

52 Art. 8 EUZBLG.

53 For a comparative analysis see J. Woelk, 'A place at the window: regional ministers in the council', in R. Toniatti, M. Dani and F. Palermo (eds), *An Ever More Complex Union. The Regional Variable as a Missing Link in the EU Constitution* (Baden-Baden: Nomos, 2004).

54 The armed forces have always been a very delicate issue in postwar and divided Germany. Thus, until 1989, any mandate of (Western) Germany's armed forces was limited to the defence of German territory. Beginning with the AWACS missions over the Adriatic Sea including German soldiers during the Balkan wars and the participation in the UN peacekeeping mission in Somalia in 1994, this taboo has been broken, but was not undisputed. In its jurisprudence, the BVerfG has established the principle of parliamentary approval for such missions. There are discussions on a federal law establishing general criteria for missions in foreign countries ('*Entsendegesetz*'), so far without concrete results.

55 See T. Fischer, 'Die Außenbeziehungen der deutschen Länder als Ausdruck "perforierter" nationalstaatlicher Souveränität? Transföderalismus zwischen Kooperation und Konkurrenz', in H.-G. Wehling (ed.), *Die deutschen Länder. Geschichte, Politik, Wirtschaft* (Opladen: Leske & Budrich, 2000), pp. 355–76, at p. 355 ff.; N. Michaud, 'Federalism and foreign policy: comparative answers to Globalisation', in Griffiths (ed.), *Handbook of Federal Countries 2002*, pp. 389–415, at p. 405.

56 Paragraph inserted by 38th Amendment (21 December 1992).

57 In the treaty of Lindau (14 November 1957), cf. text in Michael Sachs (ed.), *Grundgesetzkommentar* (München: C. H. Beck, 1996), p. 853 f. There are doubts about the constitutionality of this treaty as there is no constitutional clause allowing for such a shift of powers by simple agreement and no formal constitutional amendment has taken place. However, according to the predominant view in constitutional doctrine, the treaty does not confer a new power to the Federation, but merely confirms and specifies its existing general one for foreign affairs (Art. 32 par. 1 GG); see e.g. F. Palermo, *Die Außenbeziehungen der italienischen Regionen in rechtsvergleichender Sicht* (Frankfurt a.M.: Peter Lang, 1998), p. 233 ff.

58 See, for instance, F. Gress and R. Lehne, 'Länder governance in a global era: the case of Hesse', *Publius: The Journal of Federalism*, 29:4 (1999), 79–97.

59 BVerfGE 83, 37 ff. (Schleswig-Holstein) and 60 ff. (Hamburg), with an exception (after a respective constitutional change) for EC nationals (at 59), as the introduction of a right to vote in municipal elections had already been discussed.

60 Art. 28 par. 1 s. 2 GG. The 38th Amendment (21 December 1992) was adopted before the Maastricht treaty was ratified.

61 However, considerable differences between the various *Länder* can be seen, above all in various policy fields, for example school (lessons on Islamic religion) and local government (consultative councils elected by foreign residents).

62 A. Benz, 'From unitary to asymmetric federalism in Germany: taking stock after 50 years', *Publius: The Journal of Federalism*, 29:4 (1999), p. 56 ff.

63 Lehmbruch, 'German federalism and the challenge of unification', p. 172.
64 See the proceedings of the debate of German constitutional scholars in R. Dolzer and M. Sachs (eds), 'Das parlamentarische Regierungssystem und der Bundesrat – Entwicklungsstand und Reformbedarf', *Veröffentlichungen der Vereinigung der Deutschen Staatsrechtslehrer (VVDStRL)*, 58 (Berlin: de Gruyter, 1999). Very instructive for an understanding of the critical positions is the study-proposal drafted by the Bertelsmann Foundation (ed.), *Demokratie neu denken*. See also A. Benz, 'Politikverflechtung ohne Politikverflechtungsfalle – Koordination und Strukturdynamik im europäischen Mehrebenensystem', *Politische Vierteljahresschrift*, 39 (1998), p. 558 ff. and Volkmann, *Bundesstaat in der Krise*, p. 613 ff.
65 See in particular P. Pernthaler, *Der differenzierte Bundesstaat. Theoretische Grundlagen, praktische Konsequenzen und Anwendungsbereiche in der Reform des österreichischen Bundesstaates* (Vienna: Braümuller, 1992).
66 U. Münch, 'Konkurrenzföderalismus für die Bundesrepublik: Eine Reformdebatte zwischen Wunschdenken und politischer Machbarkeit', *Jahrbuch des Föderalismus 2001. Föderalismus, Subsidiarität und Regionen in Europa* (Baden-Baden: Nomos, 2001), pp. 115–27, at p. 118 ff.; D. Sauerland, *Föderalismus zwischen Freiheit und Effizienz: der Beitrag der ökonomischen Theorie zur Gestaltung dezentralisierter Systeme* (Berlin: Duncker & Humblot, 1997); S. Oeter, *Integration und Subsidiarität im deutschen Bundesstaatsrecht* (Tübingen: Mohr & Siebeck, 1998); and – from an interdisciplinary perspective – U. Männle (ed.), *Föderalismus zwischen Konsens und Konkurrenz* (Baden-Baden: Nomos, 1998).
67 Oeter, *Integration und Subsidiarität im deutschen Bundesstaatsrecht*, p. 565.
68 Kirchhof, 'Die Finanzen des Föderalismus', pp. 48–64, at p. 50 ff.; Münch, 'Konkurrenzföderalismus für die Bundesrepublik, pp. 120 and 125 ff.
69 'The traditional paradigm of unity in German federal thought is based on the misunderstanding of taking unity for justice, organisational dimension for efficiency in the performance of functions, and imposed hierarchical predomination in the fulfilment of public functions for efficacy.' Oeter, *Integration und Subsidiarität im deutschen Bundesstaatsrecht*, p. 14.
70 Although the two parliaments had already approved the merger, cf. U. Keunecke, *Die gescheiterte Neugliederung Berlin-Brandenburg* (Berlin: Duncker & Humblot, 2001), p. 431. See for the various proposals of territorial redesign, W. Rutz, *Die Gliederung der Bundesrepublik Deutschland in Länder. Ein neues Gesamtkonzept für den Gebietsstand nach 1990* (Baden-Baden: Nomos, 1995); and S. Greulich, *Länderneugliederung und Grundgesetz. Entwicklungsgeschichte und Diskussion der Länderneugliederungsoption nach dem Grundgesetz* (Baden-Baden: Nomos, 1995).
71 See Art. 118 for the creation of Baden-Württemberg, Art. 118a GG for Berlin and Brandenburg.
72 See Lehmbruch, 'German federalism and the challenge of unification', p. 184 ff., who also points out the additional problem of the small-scale organization of local government in Eastern Germany which urgently needed reform.
73 See the debate of Germany's constitutional scholars regarding the role of the federal council in Dolzer and Sachs, *Das parlamentarische Regierungssystem und der Bundesrat*.
74 The federal constitutional court had denied the federal council's legal nature as a second chamber, BVerfGE 37, 363.
75 BVerfG (2 BvF 1/02), judgment, 18 December 2002 (www.bverfg.de/).
76 Art. 79 par. 3 GG, the so-called 'eternity clause', explicitly mentions the 'participation on principle of the *Länder* in [federal] legislation' as one of the limits for constitutional amendments.
77 A recent position paper by the federal government ('Renovierung eines Erfolgsmodells: Modernisierung der bundesstaatlichen Ordnung', www.Bundesregierung+

zur+Modernisierung+der+bundesstaatlichen+Ordnung.pdf, 15 July 2003). On 7 November 2003, a joint commission of *Bundestag* and *Bundesrat*, established for the modernization of the federal system, met for the first time (meetings are planned until the end of 2004); see the documentation on the website (www1.bundesrat.de/coremedia/generator/Inhalt/DE/; and in R. Hrbek and A. Eppler (eds), *Deutschland vor der Föderalismus-Reform – Eine Dokumentation* (Tübingen: Europäisches Zentrum für Föderalismusforschung, 2003).

FRANCESCO PALERMO

9

Italy's long devolutionary path towards federalism

Introduction

Since the mid-1970s, Italy has faced a permanent increase in the power of its regions. The path has been anything but straightforward and coherent, and very much influenced by constitutional adjudication. The process ended up in an overall constitutional reform in 2001, whose implementation is taking much longer than expected and it seems that a reform of the reform will be approved before the previous constitutional amendment will be fully enacted. The process is thus far from being complete and Italy will certainly be subject to several other changes where the relationships between the layers of government are concerned.

Such a complex and unfinished 'regionalizing process' makes the case of Italy an outstanding example of the quick, asymmetric, rather unsystematic evolution of decentralized (federal and regional) forms of government. From a legal point of view, it helps in detecting the (mainly procedural) instruments that best serve the modern requirements of territorial reconfigurations taking place throughout Europe and worldwide.

This chapter briefly examines the evolution of Italian regionalism from the highly centralized administration of the past to the present 'quasi-federal' setting. The most relevant aspects of the system will then be outlined, ranging from the asymmetry of powers and procedures to the main strengths and deficits of the present setting.

The role of the European integration process on Italian regionalization will be illustrated, arguing that some indirect but remarkable influence has been exercised by very membership of the EU.

Finally, the chapter will focus on the most relevant institutions and procedures for differentiation, arguing that some of them are common to most of the decentralizing experiences analysed in this volume. It points out the (to some extent involuntary) modernity of a regional system lacking a real centre and based on procedures rather than institutions for its further implementation.

Genesis and the early stage of Italian regionalism

The original constitutional design
In spite of a multi-century history of regional division, Italian regionalism is, from a legal perspective anyway, quite a recent phenomenon. Since the achievement of national unity, completed only in the second half of the nineteenth century, the Italian constitutional and administrative system has been modelled on the French tradition of a unitarian, centralized and bureaucratic form of government. Thus, no sub-national entities were established after the unification, although 'regional' diversities (in economic, social, political, even linguistic terms) have always been very strong. For a long time the sole form of decentralization was municipal self-government, but then the mayor used to be both a locally elected figurehead and the representative of the state at local level.

The Kingdom of Sardinia and Piedmont initiated the unification of the different states which, until halfway through the nineteenth century, made up the Italian peninsula. Act No. 4671 of 17 March 1861, granting Victor Emmanuel of Savoy the title of king of Italy, formally instituted the Italian kingdom, which took as its constitution the statute conceded to Piedmont by king Charles Albert in 1848. The Albertine statute was a flexible constitution, one that could be amended through the same procedures as ordinary laws and one which extended to the whole of Italy the model of parliamentary monarchy provided for therein. In its fundamental characteristics the statute was based on the Belgian constitution of 1831, from which it drew both the determination of the form of government and the typical features of the unitarian state with a strongly centralized administration. The resulting state took its inspiration from the model of the French administrative state; that is, both centralized and unified.

The extension of the Piemontese constitution to the newly founded kingdom of Italy dashed the expectations of the federalist movement which, in the previous decades, had envisaged Italian unity in the framework of an institutional system respecting the marked regional diversities of the country. Theoreticians such as Carlo Cattaneo and Giuseppe Ferrari, who upheld the need to bring about a federation of the various Italian states within the framework of a unitarian constitution, saw their hopes overruled by the requirements of *Realpolitik*. They yielded to the political and military supremacy of Piedmont which, in accordance with its own political and constitutional traditions, was unlikely to recognize territorial autonomies. The political class that won the battle for unification, the 'moderates', imposed its absolute conception of national unity, overcoming that held by the minority of democrats and federalists. In 1865, the parliament of the united Italy also rejected the proposals for strengthening municipal and provincial autonomy and rebutted the idea of

creating regions with some political autonomy. Following the defeat of the federalist option, upheld by an absolute minority in society as a whole, any regionalist ideas and, more generally speaking, support for the territorial division of
power were subsequently abandoned. In the decades following the unification
of Italy, as in France, national unity was seen as a supreme principle and any
territorial autonomy, other than that of a merely administrative kind, was
regarded as a potential threat to the value of that unity, which was achieved with
such difficulty.

Centralization reached its peak during the fascist regime (1922–43), when
even the mayor was appointed by the state. Surprisingly, however, the idea of the
present regions dates back to the 1930s, when regions were 'invented' for statistical purposes, without following the borders of historical geographical units.

The republican constitution, which came into force on 1 January 1948, had
to face a complex situation where regional diversity was concerned. On the one
hand, international obligations imposed by the peace treaty (such as the
Degasperi–Gruber agreement on the protection of the German-speaking
minority in South Tyrol)[1] had to be taken into account;[2] on the other hand, concrete fears for the secession of parts of the national territory (especially Aosta
Valley and Sicily[3]) as well as for geographical reasons (Sardinia), made the establishment of a strong sub-national level of government in at least five areas inevitable: Trentino-South Tyrol, Aosta Valley, Friuli-Venezia Giulia, Sicily and
Sardinia. In order to avoid too strong an asymmetry between these areas and the
rest of the country, and to experiment with a 'third way' between a federal and
a unitarian system, regions were foreseen for the whole country, although enjoying a much lesser degree of autonomy than the five named above.

For the first time, the idea was presented that unity did not necessarily have
to mean centralization and that national unity was still possible even if some
political autonomy was granted to the regions themselves. In constitutional
terms, this principle is stipulated in Article 5 of the constitution which states that
'the Republic, one and indivisible, recognizes and promotes local autonomy'.

The constitution thus establishes twenty regions (Art. 131), five of which
enjoy a higher degree of autonomy (Art. 116).[4] These five so-called 'special' or
'autonomous' regions had their own 'basic law', approved as a constitutional law
of the State; they also received much more legislative, administrative and financial autonomy, and could negotiate their own by-laws directly with the national
government, bypassing the national parliament. In addition, the powers of each
region and, to some extent, even the governmental structure, were different in
each special region.[5] The remaining fifteen – so called 'ordinary' – regions had
only limited legislative power in specific fields listed by the national constitution
(Art. 117) and a very similar, if not identical, governmental structure. Moreover,
they remained on paper for more than twenty years: it was only in 1970 that the
first laws were established; and only in 1972 were the first laws devolving some
legislative powers enacted. Finally, it was only in 1977 that effective powers
began to be transferred to the ordinary regions.

The devolutionary process and recent constitutional reforms[6]

LEGISLATIVE (AND ADMINISTRATIVE) VERSUS CONSTITUTIONAL
'FEDERALISM'

Since the 1980s many things have changed. Apart from the special regions, which were able to negotiate (in a more or less satisfactory way) their own destiny with the central government, big problems arose for the 'ordinary' regions immediately after their establishment. These regions lacked a political culture as well as governmental experience, and the sharing of power between State and regions designed by the constitution showed its inadequacy, especially in terms of division of competences. All this led to a profound cleavage between the constitutional provisions and reality.[7] The more active regions tried to 'force' the central government towards a more benevolent interpretation of the constitution and more autonomy, whereas the weaker regions were left behind. Thus, the case law of the constitutional court became much more relevant in determining the real powers of the regions than the laws and the wording of the constitution itself.

In other words, it became immediately clear that the real rules on the relationship between the levels of government were not to be found in the constitution, but rather in ordinary legislation and administrative acts, and, primarily, in the constitutional adjudication. As a consequence, the regional interests could not be guaranteed by the constitution, and each region had to actually negotiate them with the central State. This on the one hand strengthened the asymmetrical features of Italian regionalism, but on the other made a reform of the constitutional provisions on the regional system necessary.

The political consensus over the need to strengthen the system of regional government was growing. The creation and growth of federalist parties have been both the cause and effect of parliamentary activity, giving rise so far to three committees with a remit for working out a proposal for reforming the organizational section of the constitution, in addition to numerous other initiatives. The first bicameral committee (1982) produced modest results from a legal point of view, was given little political support, and therefore failed to drum up the political will needed to bring its proposals to fruition. The second committee (1992) led to far more concrete conclusions, which were also politically plausible. The suggestions were not acted upon only because of the early dissolution of parliament. A third committee (1997) seemed to produce more concrete results, at least in terms of the successful outcome of its work, but the parliamentary approval of its proposals was suddenly stopped for political reasons. On 2 June 1998, the fifty-second birthday of the Italian Republic, the bicameral committee was declared dead, and never restarted. There have been other institutional initiatives, however, including numerous study sub-committees established by parliament in the 1980s and 1990s, and governmental proposals.

None of these proposals, however, came to fruition. The political support for creating a system of regional self-government was increasing but did not produce practical results in terms of constitutional changes.

However, many very important laws reforming public administration and the system of self-government have been approved since the late 1980s. What could not be achieved through a (politically impossible) constitutional reform was rather successfully pursued by means of legislation. The legislative reforms succeeded in modifying the general administrative structure, thus encouraging regions to develop their potential for self-government. The largest set of reforms began with the law on re-organization of ministerial bureaucracy (act no. 400 of 1988), rationalizing numerous decision-making procedures and formalizing the role of the 'Standing Conference of the state and regions', a cooperative body established to discuss decisions with regard to matters of regional interest. This law was followed by the reform of local self-government (act no. 142 of 1990), containing a number of groundbreaking provisions to improve the efficiency of municipalities and provinces. Closely connected with that law was the new set of rules on administrative procedures (act no. 241 of 1990), simplifying and rationalizing the functioning of state, regional, provincial and municipal administrations. Act no. 81 of 1993 was politically a very significant step towards raising awareness of local self-government, with the introduction of direct elections for mayors and provincial presidents. Act no. 46 of 1995 then introduced a technically complicated and overall totally impractical arrangement, nonetheless introducing a direct popular vote for regional presidents too.

Also the political attitude towards decentralization changed radically, and the 'regional issue' was put back on the political stage. Considering the political obstacles for constitutional reforms, in 1997 a different way was chosen: instead of amending the constitution, four ordinary laws (i.e. not requiring a qualified majority for approval) were passed by the center-left majority, reflecting a real revolution in the relationship between the State and the regions (so-called 'Bassanini laws'). These laws constituted not a formal, but certainly a substantive constitutional change, especially because they redesigned the division of legislative and administrative competences, enumerating the State's competences and making the regions responsible for the remainder.

CONSTITUTIONAL 'FEDERALISM'

The introduction of a *de facto* federal system by means of parliamentary (and to some extent even governmental) legislation bypassed some political problems, but obviously created legal ones. In particular, the constitutionalization of the new principles was necessary. Giving up – for political reasons – on the attempts for an organic amendment of the constitution, single constitutional laws have been approved, modifying specific aspects of regional self-government. Constitutional law no. 1/1999 changed the regional form of government, introducing the direct election of the presidents of the regions,[8] and constitutional law no. 2/2001 did the same with regard to the autonomous regions.[9] Finally, in March 2001, in a highly contentious political atmosphere, constitutional law no. 3/2001 was approved, which succeeded in amending the entire part of the constitution dealing with the relationship between national and sub-national levels of government. Since it was approved only by simple majority, the constitutional amendment could enter into force only on 7 November 2001, after having been approved by a nation-wide referendum.[10]

This recent reform finally gives constitutional coverage to the principles already enshrined in the 1997 legislation as well as in the case law of the constitutional court: most of the rules provided by the reform were already contained in the 1997 legislation, although some additional principles have been added. The new system considerably limits legislative and administrative powers at the national level, abolishes state control over regional legislation and puts the presumption for general regional legislative competence in the constitution. It also establishes a more cooperative regionalism, by creating new bodies for the cooperation between regions and State, although not transforming the senate into a chamber of regions, as advocated by the majority of scholars. Regions are now also enabled to conclude international agreements (although only with the consent of the State) and can freely determine their own form of government. In particular, they can decide how to appoint the president of the region (in almost all regions the president is now directly elected by the people and no longer nominated by the assembly) and can approve their own electoral law. As to competences, the regions not only received the general legislative competence in all matters that are not explicitly reserved for the state, but they can also get some additional powers in the fields of culture and security by means of a new negotiation procedure with the state.[11] Last but not least, ordinary regions are now entitled to approve their own *statuti* (constitutions) while respecting the limits imposed by the national constitution and by EU law: this represents a decisive step, at least from the formal point of view, towards federalism.[12]

The new constitutional framework thus makes the Italian regional system so close to a federal setting that it is almost impossible to draw a line between the two concepts. Nevertheless, the reform still contains many aspects that must be clarified in practice, will need to be specified by additional legislation and will most probably be newly amended within a short time.[13] Above all, the reform (as well as the possible 'reform of the reform') will be substantially interpreted by the constitutional court, which again will play the key role in determining the real contents of the new system.[14]

The current constitutional scheme and its implementation

The constitutional system of intergovernmental relations after the reform of 2001 can be divided into three parts. The first contains the provisions that are immediately enforceable: apart from the organization of their own form of government, the regions immediately acquired new legislative powers in a number of matters. However, even in these cases, the state contested many regional laws adopted on the basis of the new powers, challenging them in front of the constitutional court. The political strategy was easily predictable: to keep legislating as if the reform had not taken place. In practice, very little has changed in terms of the concrete use of the new powers of the regions, and again the only improvements have come from the jurisprudence of the constitutional court, which again has been the regions' best ally.[15] However, after two years of timid implementation of the reform, in October 2003 the constitutional court delivered a landmark judgment on the division of powers between the state and the regions (no. 303/2003), stating in sum that the material criteria laid down in Art. 117 of the constitution are merely indicative and do not prevent the state from attracting regional competences or vice versa. Thus in future the crucial element will have to be found in the agreement between the State and the region(s), which could even derogate from the division of powers provided by the constitution![16] In other words, the court found a way of making a rigid system of division of legislative powers much more flexible, based on the requirement of an agreement between the involved actors.

The second part of the reform is that requiring legislative implementation. Many articles of the constitutional text provide for a law that should establish the concrete procedures for their implementation. This is particularly the case for the cooperative procedures between the state and the regions (also where the regional relations at international and EU level are concerned); the fora for the cooperation; the concrete scope of the principle of subsidiartity; and the division of administrative powers between the State, the regions and the municipalities. It took almost two years to pass the by-law of the reform.[17] Moreover, the by-law will require further implementation by means of secondary legislation of the government,[18] and its intention is clearly to undermine the reform, waiting for a new constitutional change.

The third part of the reform cannot be implemented as long as the regions do not pass their own new constitutions (*statuti*). The exercise of the new legislative powers, the regulation of the administrative powers (to be divided between regions and municipalities), international and EU relations, the institutional structure, and so on, must now be decided by the regions. However, where the approval of their own constitutions is concerned, the regions show immense difficulties, mostly because of the lack of political maturity. As of July 2004, only two regions had approved their own constitution (and one of them has been declared unconstitutional),[19] and very few had elaborated proposals to be submitted to the respective assemblies,[20] and it can be easily predicted that the process will last for years. For this reason, a considerable part of the responsibility for the scarce improvement of regional autonomy after the profound constitutional changes of 1999 and 2001 remains with the regions. If they were more active in adopting their own constitution, they could more substantially benefit from the newly conferred opportunities.

In the following pages, the most controversial aspects of the present Italian constitutional regional system will be highlighted. Special attention will be paid to the elements that might serve as hints for further discussion in other countries experiencing the 'changing faces' of their federal/regional system.

Municipalism, regionalism and participation in decision-making

One of the main defects of the new constitutional setting is the uncertain definition of the constitutional roles of the provinces and municipalities vis-à-vis the regions. The determination to grant the municipalities greater autonomy risks with these rules making the whole reform inefficient. The contradiction crops up in the first article of the amended part of the constitution (Art. 114), which reads as follows: 'The Republic comprises the municipalities, the provinces, the regions and the State.' It asserts, however, that 'the municipalities, the provinces and the regions are autonomous entities with their own powers'. This provision has been sharply criticized by scholars, pointing out that either the regions, provinces and municipalities are all constitutive elements of the republic, and therefore federal entities, each with their own constitutional autonomy and with a presumption of residual power, or they are all merely entities of administrative decentralization and, therefore, the republican order cannot be a federal one.[21] However, although vaguely formulated, the provision aims at creating a double set of residual powers or, in figurative terms, two levels of federalism: where legislation is concerned, residual powers are vested in the regions and the federal relationship only affects the regions and the state. As to administration, residual powers shall be vested in the municipalities, on the basis of the principle of subsidiarity. This might be seen as a step forward towards a more modern, reticular form of government[22] and as a reasonable compromise between 'regionalist' and 'municipalist' positions. What the reform totally omitted to consider, however, is that whereas differentiation among regions is constitutionally provided for, all the eight thousand and more municipalities are supposed to be legally equal, regardless of their variable size, economic and geographic conditions, and political and administrative capacity.

The contrast between regionalism and municipalism is evident also in the maintenance of the legislative power of the State to regulate 'electoral law, governmental bodies and fundamental functions of the municipalities' (Art. 117 par. 2 lit. p). This gives rise to a continuity in the traditional manner of Italian decentralization: an alliance between state and municipalities, detrimental to the regions. On many points of the reform, doubts remain about the functionality of the model, and it is no coincidence that those parts of the text where the greatest clarity and institutional coherence are found are those where such ambiguities were overcome (as in the case of relations between the regions and the EU as well as foreign countries). There is no doubt that the constitutional reform leaves many of certain regions' expectations of autonomy unsatisfied, gives rise to uncertain provisions, and contains technical and constitutional shortcomings of considerable importance.

The failure of a clear 'pro-region' choice is connected with the (lack of) representation and regional participation at the central level, which forms the weakest point of the whole reform. The composition of the senate has not been changed, in spite of the unanimous calls by scholars. In the future also, the relations between the levels of government will thus be developed by a number of cooperative bodies and procedures, ranging from the so-called 'permanent conference between the State and the regions' to other conferences including provinces and municipalities, to special procedures from the autonomous regions to countless ad-hoc fora.[23] The same goes for the establishment in each region of a 'Council of local autonomies' (Art. 123 constitution), aimed at granting to the municipalities an institutionalized participation in the decision-making process at regional level.

Beside the increasing confusion in terms of applicable procedures and enforceability of the agreements agreed upon in merely consultative bodies, at least one involuntary aspect of this situation will be outlined: the organs and procedures for an intense institutional cooperation are countless. On the one hand, this will increase confusion and uncertainty, but on the other hand it is almost certain that every claim for participation and cooperation will find a procedural way to be taken into account.

Subsidiarity: towards a governance-based form of government?

The reform also introduces at constitutional level the criterion of subsidiarity as a guidance parameter for the system of division of power, establishing that subsidiarity must operate both vertically (i.e. between public bodies) and horizontally (between private and public authorities) (Art. 118). This provision reflects a clear choice in favour of a system where public authorities intervene only where necessary, leaving the rest to private initiative.[24] From that point of view, we cannot but note a radical innovation vis-à-vis the 1948 constitution which, particularly in economic matters, was strongly interventionist in its approach. On the basis of this programming provision, it might in the future prove problematic to reconcile 'statist' regulations on material matters contained in Part I of the constitution with the new regulations.

Where 'vertical' subsidiarity is concerned, Art. 118 par. 1 of the constitution provides that 'administrative functions are attributed to the municipalities', and only if it is more appropriate in order to ensure the unity of the system, can they be 'conferred to provinces, metropolitan cities, regions and state, based on the principles of subsidiarity, differentiation and adequacy'. It is obviously far from easy to define the specific meaning of the criteria mentioned. However, especially considering that the long and detailed list of competences enshrined in Article 117 contains a lot of matters that cannot be easily identified,[25] the criteria for concretely determining who does what become crucial. It might be argued that the criteria of subsidiarity, differentiation and adequacy might become hazardous, being the result of excessive confidence in a concept as legally insignificant per se as subsidiarity.[26] On the other hand, however, these criteria might constitute the procedural ground for a 'relational regionalism', governed by procedures (subsidiarity and adequacy) and based on the differential use of them (differentiation), in order to better accommodate the specific interests at stake. Subsidiarity, adequacy and differentiation 'work as a lift':[27] they are criteria for moving the competences from one level of government to the other, depending on functional criteria.[28] This seems now to be confirmed by the aforementioned decision no.

303/2003 of the constitutional court, which applied these criteria not only to the administrative, but also to the legislative division of powers.

Subsidiarity necessarily makes the competence fields 'soft' and elastic,[29] and establishes the procedural parameters for a functional governance. The instrument of this type of governance-based form of government would be a network of the levels of government instead of the division of powers among them. The network, forced by the criteria mentioned, has been defined as an 'overwhelming procedural and occasionally institutional instrument by means of which the functional complementary relationship between a plurality of public and private actors jointly manages common interests'.[30] Thus, the criteria, intended as procedures regulating the interactions of spheres that necessarily overlap, become crucial. Since almost all the competence fields cross-cut, there is a need for identification criteria and this might be the role of the procedures laid down in Article 118. Subsidiarity, in other words, might display an integrative role in managing the coordination between the various actors involved in a complex decision-making process. It can help, particularly in some delicate matters, to design in a procedural, dynamic way the relationship between the spheres of government. It is thus in first place a principle for decision-making (directed to public and private actors, to the legislature and the administration), and only in second place is it a principle for judicial adjudication.[31] Nevertheless, because it is procedural, the violations of the procedure might be challenged in the court system and thus become also a criterion for adjudication.

Financial autonomy

As far as financial relations are concerned, the reform is quite innovative compared with the previous situation. Article 119 of the constitution provides for financial autonomy not only for the regions but also for the provinces and the municipalities. Again from this point of view, therefore, municipalities and provinces are put on an equal footing with the regions. Apart from financial autonomy, or rather self-sufficiency of revenue vis-à-vis expenditure, all the local and regional authorities also enjoy fiscal autonomy, or the authority to impose their own taxes. The principles for the coordination of public finance are determined by a state law. The system becomes more complex with regard to the criteria for achieving the regions' financial self-sufficiency and determining the fiscal capacity of the different regions. In this way, those regions with greater financial resources, in other words the richer regions, obtain a lower quota of all tax revenue, for which reason the degree of financial autonomy will vary in practice from one region to another.

This system also provides for the establishment of an equalization fund guaranteeing support for the regions whose fiscal capacity is lower than the parameters to be established by law. The law for determining the forms of and limits on financial and fiscal autonomy is the unknown factor in an overall convincing system. After all, the practical execution of the constitutional provisions will depend on that law, whose approval is, in any case, postponed. It is definitely too early to assess the issue of financial autonomy, and this issue will prove to be crucial for the concrete development of the 'federalizing' dynamic of the Italian constitutional system.

Relations with the EU and international activities of the regions

A clear-cut innovation can be detected in the constitutional text with regard to the new relationship with the European Union as well as, more broadly, to regional foreign powers. The reform introduced new elements vis-à-vis the previous text but, in reality, is greatly limited to constitutionalizing what was already provided for in the previous order, including, textually, the regulatory provisions and the effects of constitutional case law on this point.[32]

From the constitutional point of view, the reform fulfils two tasks. On the one hand, it takes account of the work already concluded in the process of European integration, incorporating into the constitution provisions specifically dedicated to that, as well as what has already been accomplished by the constitutional legislators of many European countries (Germany, Austria, France and Spain). Secondly, the reform also takes account of the multi-tiered structure of the Italian constitutional order and enables the regions to have a say over community questions, establishing that they participate in direct decision-making for drafting community acts and see to their execution and implementation. It also provides a state power to intervene, should the regions be inactive (Art. 117 par. 5). Nonetheless, the procedural arrangements for putting these principles into practice will call for additional legislation.[33]

The impression given by these provisions is twofold. On the one hand, it reveals how much is already provided for by the existing ordinary law; in other words the power of the regions to execute community acts within the scope of their own powers. On the other hand, its scope is limited, since it only provides for a legal reserve in respect of the regional participation in the procedure for taking decisions in this area. The decision on how to regulate that participation and, therefore, the practical formulation of the new regional powers in this area will, therefore, be delayed.

The partisans of this bill would have shown more courage if they had taken note of what has happened, in particular, in Germany and Austria (see chapters 7 and 8), namely new sections 23 GG and 23a–f B-VG on the procedure for participation by the German and Austrian *Länder* in community matters. However, a historical perspective in this case too allows for a more positive assessment as to the degree of difference of the order under examination. Whereas Germany and Austria have a more advanced federal system, endowed with a greater tradition, in Italy reform is a matter of constitutionally formalizing what has already been created in recent decades. All of what follows, in the form of a constitutional base, and therefore made easier than before, will nonetheless be tantamount to a step forward on the road to an evolution of regional powers in community matters too.

A further and important aspect of projecting the regions beyond their own territory is the new constitutional framework of their foreign powers. The new

provisions provide for a genuine (albeit obviously partial) international subjec-
tivity of the regions. According to Art. 117 par. 9, the regions will be able to conclude agreements with foreign states or their local and regional authorities, or in
the framework of general principles set by law in the national parliament. Here
too, apart from constitutionalizing what already exists, progress is being made
by granting the regions the power to regulate their own foreign affairs, although
under State supervision. The progress achieved by the Italian regions in this area
is surprising when we consider that the first explicit recognition of any of their
powers by the constitutional court goes back only to 1987.[34] This means that in
barely fifteen years, powers have been built up almost from scratch and are now
likely to be one of the strong points of the future federal constitution.[35]

A devolutionary asymmetric federalism in the making: three lessons

In brief, after the recent constitutional reform, Italian regionalism can be defined
as 'devolutionary asymmetric federalism in the making'. Even though there
seems to be no substantial difference between the present regional system and a
more 'consolidated' federal system, it is worth noting that in the reformed constitution the term 'federalism' never appears, thus indicating the self-perception
of the Italian constitutional system as a transitional and open-ended one, which
will need to be determined step by step, starting with the approval of the new
'constitution' (*statuto*) of each region.[36]

It will be up to the regions to adopt homogeneous constitutions or to differentiate among them. Under the present system, all the regional *statuti* are almost
identical, and so are governmental structures, especially where ordinary regions
are concerned, whereas a higher degree of asymmetry can be observed between
the special regions, which already have different powers and different legitimization by the government (direct election of the president or his or her appointment by the assembly).[37]

Asymmetry in Italian regionalism is thus not only a consequence of historical developments, political negotiations and the existence of more or less consistent minority groups, but also a constitutional 'duty' for some regions[38] and
now an opportunity for all of them. One of the most innovative provisions of
the reformed constitution is, in fact, enshrined in Art. 116 par. 3, which provides
the constitutional base for additional differentiation between ordinary regions.[39]
If regions take advantage of this asymmetrical opportunity, they could improve
their own degree of self-government, especially in fields closely related to minority protection, such as education, culture and the environment.[40]

This opportunity will give rise to a highly differentiated, asymmetrical
regional system, clearly inspired, in its structure as well as in its procedures, by the
Spanish model.[41] At a first level there will be the special regions, each of them
different from the others in terms of powers, governmental structure and capacity of self-government. At a second level there will be the ordinary regions, making

use of the new opportunity to achieve more powers in the areas discussed (most probably the richer industrial regions of the North). At a third level, there will be the ordinary regions that will not acquire more powers but will nevertheless be able to accommodate their special needs by approving their own constitution.[42]

The near future of Italian regionalism will thus have its strong blueprint in its asymmetrical nature. For our purposes, this has at least three fundamental constitutional and political consequences.

First, most of the exclusive powers retained by the State are not competences in the strict sense of the term. Issues such as relations with the EU, competition protection, civil and criminal law, and basic level of benefits relating to civil and social entitlements where civil and social rights are concerned (Art. 117 constitution) are above all policy fields which, depending on the political development of Italian regionalism, can either limit in a substantive way the realm of regional self-government, or, on the contrary, accommodate the regional differences. The new system will thus be a very flexible one, distinguishing between macro-policies (reserved for the State and, even more, for the EU) and micro-policies, in which regional diversity can come to the fore.

Secondly, the Italian case shows the importance of the political perception of the sub-national self-government. Not all the regions provided with more autonomy were able to take advantage of it, and not all the 'ordinary' regions are in fact weak political units. It can easily be said that one of the deficiencies of Italian regionalism has been (until now) the lack of true, locally developed regional policies. Apart from some special regions – in particular, again, South Tyrol and Aosta Valley – the political discourses and the political careers of regional politicians were dominated by national politics. Thus, apart from small and peculiar realities (mostly determined by the very existence of ethnic minorities, as in South Tyrol, Aosta Valley and, to a much lesser extent, Friuli-Venezia Giulia), the regional policy has been shaped by the national one: for example, many regional presidents resigned to become members of the national parliament.[43] Direct election of the 'governors' is gradually making regional policy stronger and less dependent on national policy, thus contributing to the perception of the role of regions not only on paper but in everyday life. Such a self-consciousness of the importance of regional policy was, on the other hand, always a prerogative of some autonomous regions, in particular those where minorities are settled. Thus, indirectly, the very existence of minorities contributed in a relevant manner to the development of a regional political conscience.

Thirdly, the type of federalism which is gradually developing after the reform is of a procedural and conflictive nature. Procedural because of the previously mentioned criteria for determining the concrete power-sharing between the spheres of government. Conflictive because the procedures inherently contain the possibility to judicially challenge the procedure followed in the specific case. In particular, if central government continues to advocate a reductive interpretation of the reform (as has been the case in the first year after the reform entered into force), the only means for the regions to assess their newly acquired powers is constitutional litigation. In this respect, a continuity with the previous situation must be noted. More generally, this is a tendency common to all the 'devolutionary' federal systems; that is, the constitutional systems that became federations by means of devolution of powers from the centre to the periphery and not by federalizing already sovereign entities. Constitutional litigation shows its ability to become the tool for evolution and stabilization of constantly changing federative processes. As a consequence, 'litigating federalism' seems to be a generalized outcome of the modern federal reconfiguration of many States.

Concluding remarks: a new federative paradigm

In conclusion, we should try to summarize some of the most interesting elements for an overall new theory on modern federalism emerging from the Italian experience. The highlighted aspects are peculiar to the Italian case, but they seem to be applicable, to a variable degree, to other constitutional changes taking place in Europe and elsewhere.

First, Italian federalism developed from the 1990s onwards for a number of reasons, one of them being what has been described as 'federalism by giving up'.[44] An increasing number of tasks and functions have been transferred to regions (and municipalities) as a means of reducing the State's expenditure. This became particularly evident when limited financial resources made clear the necessity (also in economic terms) of a decentralized management of public tasks. Decentralization was thus not a consequence of a change in the political culture, but rather an economic necessity. However, this Italian peculiarity has to do with the overall process of redefinition of the role of States, ceasing to be providers of services and gradually becoming regulatory bodies.[45] Consequently, the concrete duties to be performed need to be transferred to lower levels of government. This shifting in the functions of the State is common to all Western democracies, but is particularly evident in the case of Italy because of the rapidity of the process, caused by the necessity to catch up after a historical delay. If this is true, it is easy to detect the big weakness of the Italian constitutional reform: the underdevelopment of cooperative procedures under the reformed constitutional system. In fact, since the role of the state has become the setting up of standards for activities to be performed by other, normally lower levels of government, it is crucial for the latter to have the ability to participate in the decision-making where the general rules and standards are elaborated; that is, at national and European level. Whereas the reform provides for a consistent improvement in regional relations with the EU, it is somewhat lacking where relations with the state are concerned, although this chapter has demonstrated that cooperative procedures are nevertheless established and somehow working.

Secondly, the regionalization was consequently driven also – though indirectly – by membership of the EU. The need for an advanced regionalism within member States has been intensified by the joint effect of the 1988 reform of the structural funds and the 1992 single market programme. In the 1990s, in fact, regions became increasingly involved in and responsible for the management of community transfers and for the implementation of EC legislation. In addition, while promoting the free movement of economic factors and the efficient allocation of resources, the creation of the internal market increased regional disparities, its benefits not being uniformly distributed throughout the EC.[46] With many national governments pressured both by the stability and growth pact and the Maastricht criteria, the competence on policies for economic development and investment attraction had to be transferred to the lowest levels for increasing their effectiveness. An additional incentive for the adoption of the regional model was introduced with the creation of the EU cohesion policy. In fact, specific provisions of structural fund regulations require regional-based structures for eligibility to EU financing, thus leading to the creation of regional units in many centralized states and affecting the constitutional morphology of candidate countries.[47] In simple words, there is a demonstrable link between regionalization and a more efficient use of EU resources, which makes it logically necessary for the member States to decentralize.[48]

Finally, the Italian case provides an example of how a quasi 'anarchical' federal structure can work due to the presence of functional elements. It has been pointed out above that the amended constitution gets rid of the former hierarchic structure, providing that all the constitutive elements of 'the Republic' (municipalities, provinces, regions and the state) have equal dignity – though obviously not equal powers – in the new constitutional frame (Art. 114). Such a provision creates a system where all the 'spheres of government'[49] shall be involved in the process of elaboration and implementation of the policies. The rules according to which this will happen are partially enshrined in the constitution, and to a greater extent devolved to the by-laws of the constitutional reform as well as to the future regional constitutions. The system is thus far from being complete, but it reveals some tentative answers to modern challenges of federalism: how to combine a complex system of government overcoming hierarchies by promoting the government by networking. The institutions of the new Italian federalism are not completely formalized yet – compared with other systems the procedures for transferring powers from the State to the regions and vice versa are less sophisticated[50] – but the tendency is already clear. Functionalism, procedures instead of (or parallel to) institutions, cooperation instead of hierarchy, criteria for rapidly shifting the territorial level of competence are increasingly becoming general features of modern federalism.

Notes

1 According to the agreement (1946), which was attached to the Paris peace treaty between the allied powers and Italy (1947), 'German-speaking inhabitants of the Bolzano Province . . . will be assured a complete equality of rights with the Italian-speaking inhabitants, within the framework of special provisions to safeguard the ethnical char-

acter and the cultural and economic development of the German-speaking element'. On the legal protection of minorities in South Tyrol see below.

2   A subsequent treaty dealt with the particular situation of the Free Territory of Trieste, which was governed by an international regime until 1954, providing special protection for the Slovenian-speaking population.

3   Fears of secession arose in Aosta Valley (a small region in the north-west of the country which had a long tradition of self-government and which had already set out a plan for strong autonomy in 1943) and in Sicily, which set out its own constitution as a possible independent state in 1946, before the Italian constitution was drafted.

4   Sicily, Sardinia, Trentino-Alto Adige/South Tyrol, Friuli-Venezia Giulia and Aosta Valley/Vallée d'Aoste. These are the three smaller regions of the alpine area, characterized by the presence of consistent national minorities, and the two main islands, whose special autonomy was for different reasons: nevertheless in both Sicily and Sardinia small minority groups have settled (Albanians in Sicily, Catalans in Sardinia), and the Sardinians themselves are often regarded as a minority.

5   Moreover, the region Friuli-Venezia Giulia (in the North-East) was only established in 1964, after the final settlement of the Trieste situation. In 1972 the autonomous region of Trentino South Tyrol was redesigned, transferring almost all substantial powers to the two provinces of which it consists: Bolzano/Bozen (South Tyrol), where the majority of the population is German speaking, and Trento, almost exclusively Italian.

6   It must be pointed out that the term 'devolution' in this context refers to the historical process of decentralization by means of transfer of powers from the centre to the periphery. V. Bogdanor, *Devolution in the United Kingdom* (Oxford: Oxford University Press, 1999), p. 2, has defined devolution as 'the transfer to a subordinate elected body, on a geographical basis, of functions at present exercised by Ministers and Parliament'. In this sense, in the theory of federal processes, 'devolutionary' federalism is opposed to 'aggregative' federalism. Whereas the latter was the rule in the historical formation of most of the federal countries, in more recent times new federations are evolving from previously centralized states. This is not only the case for Italy, but also, and even more so, for Belgium and Spain, and to a lesser extent the UK and France. See the respective chapters in this volume.

7   R. Bin, 'Veri e falsi problemi del federalismo in Italia', in L. Mariucci, R. Bin, M. Cammelli, A. Di Pietro and G. Falcon (eds), *Il federalismo preso sul serio* (Bologna: Il Mulino, 1996), p. 68.

8   It is not by chance that the newly directly elected 'presidents of regions' (this is now the official name) are normally referred to, in the political discourse and in the media, as 'governors', underlying the (supposed) analogy with the American governors because of their popular election (europe-wide, this is the only case of popular election of president of sub-national entities). The regions are now free to determine the rules for the election of the president. They are thus theoretically free to decide that the 'governor' shall be appointed by the assembly. Politically, however, this is nearly impossible: not only the direct election of the presidents was introduced in the constitution on request of the regions, but this reform is also very popular. When a region (Friuli-Venezia Giulia) tried to re-introduce the indirect election of the president, the proposal was rejected by an overwhelming majority in a referendum on 29 September 2002.

9   Apart from the autonomous province of Bolzano (South Tyrol) and the autonomous region of Aosta Valley. In every case, special regions were enabled to decide their own form of government and the State rule only applies as long as the regions do not pass their own legislation on this topic.

10 Amendments to the Italian constitution 'shall be adopted by each House after two successive debates at intervals of not less than three months, and shall be approved by an absolute majority of the members of each House in the second voting. Amendments are submitted to a popular referendum when, within three months from their approval, a

request is made by one-fifth of the members of a House or five hundred thousand voters or five regional assemblies. A referendum shall not be held if the amendment has been approved in the second voting by each of the Houses by a majority of two-thirds of the members' (Art. 138 constitution). Until the reform of 2001, a conventional constitutional rule prevented use of the second amending procedure, which in practice makes it possible to modify the constitution by majority. The center-left government wanted to approve the reform before the elections held in May 2001, and so it did. The center-right parties, who opposed the change, called therefore for the confirmative referendum, and so did the center-left parties, being sure that the reform was desired by the citizens. The large majority of voters voted in favour of the reform, although less than 30 per cent participated in the referendum.

11 Art. 116 par. 3 of the constitution (see below).

12 For details on the changes introduced by the reform see T. Groppi and M. Olivetti (eds), *La Repubblica delle autonomie*, 2nd edn (Torino: Giappichelli, 2003) and B. Caravita, *La costituzione dopo la riforma del titolo V* (Torino: Giappichelli, 2002).

13 Proposals for amending the amended constitution have been presented, particularly by the center-right government, aiming at changing some features of the 2001 reform. A new division of powers is proposed by the government (draft bill no. 3641), commonly called 'devolution'. Again, as in the case of 'governors', this is a (misleading) copy of terminology. Here the term underpins the devolution taking place in the UK. The English word is particularly *en vogue* within the circles of the *Lega Nord* (the Northern League), the party advocating stronger autonomy for the North and claiming a sort of 'mystical' analogy with Scottish nationalism.

14 In the ten months following the entrance into force of the reform (November 2001–September 2002) the constitutional litigation between State and regions increased by 400 per cent compared with the previous ten months!

15 Among the numerous decisions that could be mentioned in this regard, no. 282/2002 deserves special mention. This was the first decision in which the court was called to interpret the scope of the reform: the government contested a regional law on the basis of the previous criteria and the region claimed its newly acquired power to legislate on health care and doctors' admissions. The court recognized the new constitutional frame and the decision was a landmark for subsequent judgments on the issue of division of powers. See also the comments by R. Bin, 'Il nuovo riparto di competenze legislative: un primo, importante chiarimento', *Le Regioni*, 6 (2002), p. 1445 and by A. D'Atena, *La Consulta parla . . . la riforma del Titolo V entra in vigore*, in www.associazionedeicostituzionalisti.it.

16 See for details A. Morrone, 'La Corte costituzionale riscrive il titolo V', *Quaderni costituzionali* (4/2003), p. 818.

17 The law was approved only in June 2003 (law no. 131/2003) and is also known as law '*La Loggia*'. Many parts of it were challenged by the special regions, but the constitutional court substantially upheld the law (judgment no. 238/2004).

18 It establishes that the national government (!) shall determine, within one year, the general principles on the relations between State and regions in the various competence fields.

19 The constitutional court struck down the constitution of Calabria because the election of the president was found in contrast with the provisions of the national institution on the regional form of government (judgment No. 2/2004).

20 See on this process M. Olivetti, *Nuovi statuti e forma di governo delle regioni. Verso le costituzioni regionali?* (Bologna: Il Mulino, 2002).

21 See S. Bartole, R. Bin, G. Falcon and R. Tosi, *Diritto regionale. Dopo le riforme* (Bologna: Il Mulino, 2003), p. 47. The authors thus argue that there is a substantive continuity between the old and the reformed constitutional design in this respect.

22 For a positive evaluation of the provision see S. Ortino, 'Guardare avanti, guardare indie-
tro: il dilemma della bicamerale', *Rassegna Parlamentare*, 2 (1998), p. 319 ff.

23 For an overview see I. Ruggiu, *Istituzioni del federalismo e rappresentanza territoriale*
(Cagliari: University of Cagliari, 2001).

24 A. M. Poggi, *Le autonomie funzionali 'tra' sussidiarietà verticale e sussidiarietà orizzontale*
(Milano: Giuffrè, 2001).

25 They have been defined as 'matters–non matters'. A. D'Atena, 'Materie legislative e tipo-
logia delle competenze', *Quaderni costituzionali*, 1 (2003), p. 19. Fields such as 'environment' (Art. 117 par. 2 lit. s), 'zoning and planning' (Art. 117 al. 3), 'education' (Art. 117
par. 2 lit. n), 'social security' (Art. 117 par. 2 lit. o), 'determination of the essential levels
for civil and social right' (Art. 117 par. 2 lit. m), and so on, cannot be defined as clear competence matters and thus need criteria for the allocation of the power to intervene.

26 A literal interpretation of this rule could, for example, give the municipalities administrative powers in matters such as justice, the armed forces or currency.

27 See R. Bin and G. Pitruzzella, *Diritto costituzionale* (Torino: Giappichelli, 2000), p. 95.

28 S. Ortino, *Per un federalismo funzionale* (Torino: Giappichelli, 1994).

29 O. Chessa, 'La sussidiarietà (verticale) come "precetto di ottimizzazione" e come criterio
ordinatore', *Diritto pubblico comparato ed europeo (DPCE)*, IV (2002), p. 1448.

30 R. Toniatti, 'Il regionalismo relazionale e il governo delle reti: primi spunti ricostruttivi',
in S. Gambino (ed.), *Il 'nuovo' ordinamento regionale. Competenze e diritti* (Milano:
Giuffrè, 2003), pp. 167 ff.

31 J. Isensee, 'Subsidiarität – das Prinzip und seine Prämissen', in P. Blickle, T. O. Hueglin
and D. Wyduckel (eds), *Subsidiarität als rechtliches und politisches Ordnungsprinzip in
Kirche, Staat und Gesellschaft* (Berlin: Duncker & Humblot, 2002), pp. 129 ff.

32 Art. 117 par. 1 finally mentions the EU legal system in the text of the constitution. Italy
was the only member state of the EU that did not amend its constitution in order to
accommodate the relationship between the domestic and the community legal system.
The mention of the legal system of the EU in Article 117 of the constitution, however, is
just a partial recovery. The community law serves as a limitation of the legislative powers
of State and regions (thus indirectly recognizing the principle of supremacy of community law), but the basic principles of the relations between domestic and community law
are still to be found in Article 11 of the constitution, which does not mention the EU.

33 The concrete rules according to which the regions, 'in their respective competence fields,
participate in the elaboration of the normative acts at community level and implement
international agreements and community law' have to be determined by a law of the state
(Art. 117 par. 5).

34 Judgment no. 179/1987.

35 In this sense it is interesting and perhaps paradoxical that, just after the reform, we
should be discovering the considerable potential of the previous constitutional setting.
The ever-evolving case law of the constitutional court concerning relations between the
state and the regions and the various pieces of reform legislation passed in the 1990s are
finally executing the 1948 constitution at the very moment when it had to be reformed.
The text produced by the reform, in other words, constitutes at the same time a stock-
taking of the evolution of relations between the centre and the periphery, as they have
developed over the last fifty years, and a stronger base for their later development, due
to mature in the years to come.

36 At the time this chapter was completed (July 2004), the process of elaboration of the new
regional constitutions was progressing very slowly. Only one region (Puglia) has already
a new constitution. As to the others, only some regions (among them Calabria, Liguria
and Veneto) have appointed special commissions for the preparation of the draft documents. A couple of more regions have already completed the process of drafting their new
constitutions. All in all, however, it seems that all the regions prefer to start with the

approval of their own laws on the form of government (election of the president, electoral system for the assembly, rules on regional referenda, etc.), whereas the approval of the new constitutions will certainly take a much longer time.

37 However, only in South Tyrol and in Aosta Valley is the president appointed by the assembly. All other presidents are now directly elected by the citizens.

38 The right of the special regions to be different and to enjoy a higher degree of autonomy is considered by most scholars one of the basic values of the constitution and thus not subject to constitutional reform. The constitutional court, in fact, has stated that the very fundamental principles of the constitutional system (such as the democratic principle, the openness towards international law, etc.) cannot be changed, not even by means of a formal constitutional amendment: in such a case, the court would declare the constitutional law unconstitutional because of the breach of the fundamental principles (see judgment no. 1146/1988). See V. Onida, 'Le costituzioni. Principi fondamentali della costituzione italiana', in G. Amato and A. Barbera (eds), *Manuale di diritto pubblico*, Vol. I (Bologna: Il Mulino, 1997), in particular p. 112, and S. Labriola, 'Il principio di specialità nel regionalismo italiano', in S. Ortino and P. Pernthaler (eds), *La riforma costituzionale in senso federale. Il punto di vista delle autonomie speciali* (Bolzano/Trento: Regione Autonoma Trentino-Alto Adige, 1997), p. 84. This means that there is a constitutional privilege for the regions to be treated differently. This opinion is shared by the constitutional court (see e.g. judgment no. 213/1998, in *Giurisprudenza costituzionale*, 1998, p. 1667). For a more detailed analysis see L. Antonini, *Il regionalismo differenziato* (Milano: Guiffrè, 2000).

39 Art. 116 par. 3: 'Additional special forms and conditions of autonomy, related to the areas specified in article 117, paragraph three and paragraph two, letter l) [administration of justice] – limited to the organizational requirements of the Justice of the Peace – and letters n) and s), [education, culture and environment] may be attributed to other regions by State law, upon the initiative of the region concerned, after consultation with the local authorities, in compliance with the principles set forth in article 119'. It must be noted, however, that the government's draft constitutional bill for the 'reform of the reform' eliminates this provision.

40 The central government has recently proposed a bill in order to add to the subjects mentioned some other powers to be 'negotiated' by the regions with the State, including police, social and health care and additional sectors of the educational sphere (proposal to the senate, draft bill no. A.S. 1187). If this proposal is approved (although is does not seem that there will be the political consensus to reach the majority required for amending the constitution), the mentioned tendency towards asymmetrical devolution of powers will increase even more.

41 See chapter 10 in this volume.

42 This structure is in the end quite similar to the solution adopted in Spain with the 1978 constitution and its further implementation. Interestingly, Italian regionalism, whose only (theoretical) source of inspiration was the Spanish 1931 constitution, has played an important role in influencing the present Spanish constitution of 1978 in this regard, and now again it is the Spanish model that is used as a guide to the evolution of the Italian transition towards an 'asymmetric federalism'. It is not by chance that both the Italian and the Spanish regional systems are to a large extent derived from and shaped by goals of minority protection.

43 This example shows the low political importance of the regional level for a political career. See Bin, 'Veri e falsi problemi del federalismo in Italia', p. 70.

44 F. Pizzetti, 'Brevi spunti di riflessione sull'esperienza di un trentennio di regionalismo', in A. Ferrara and V. Visco Comandini (eds), *Regionalismo, federalismo, welfare state* (Milano: Giuffrè, 1997), p. 260.

45 For this evolution see A. La Spina and G. Majone, *Lo Stato regolatore* (Bologna: Il Mulino,

2000). See also G. Majone, 'The rise of the regulatory State in Europe', *West European Politics*, 17:3 (1994), p. 78.

46 S. Mazey, 'Regional lobbying in the new Europe', in M. Rhodes (ed.), *The Regions and the New Europe: Patterns in Core and Periphery Development* (Manchester: Manchester University Press, 1995), p. 81 ff.

47 European Parliament, *Regionalisation in Europe, Working Paper* (abridged edition) (Luxembourg: EC Publication Office, 1999).

48 See for a recent example on the English regions, M. Burch and R. Gomez, 'The English regions and the European Union', *Regional Studies*, 36 (2002), p. 767 ff.

49 The term 'spheres of government' is used in Article 40 of the South African constitution of 1996, indicating the same tendency towards the elimination of hierarchy in favour of a government by network, inspired by the principles of the 'cooperative government'.

50 See e.g. the procedures laid down in Article 72 of the German constitution or in Article 140 and following of the Spanish constitution, where the procedure for the transfer of powers is laid down in detail. However, in these countries also, many informal channels are used parallel to the constitutional ones.

BRUNO DE WITTE

10

Regional autonomy, cultural diversity and European integration: the experience of Spain and Belgium

Introduction: why Spain and Belgium?

Spain and Belgium, considered in the context of this volume, have common characteristics which distinguish them from the rest of Western Europe. They are the two countries in the European Union which in the last two decades have most clearly experienced the opposite pulls of internal federalization and European integration. These forces have caused significant changes to the institutions of these previously unitary nation-states. The timing of these developments was not the same for both countries; Belgium was transformed into a federal state when already part of the European Community, whereas Spain's devolution preceded its integration into Europe.

Both countries have a regional tier of government (the autonomous communities in Spain, the communities and regions in Belgium) with legislative and executive powers and important financial resources. Spain and Belgium do not usually appear in comparative studies of federalism. They tend rather to be considered as prime examples of a new institutional category that caught the attention of scholars in the early 1980s: the regional state.[1] Since then, Belgium has moved on. In 1993, on the occasion of the last of a series of five constitutional reforms which had started in 1970, a new Article 1 was introduced into the Belgian constitution which declared Belgium to be a 'federal state, composed of the communities and the regions'. There is no such self-definition in the Spanish constitution. The Spanish state is variously called an *Estado de las autonomías* (which is somewhat tautological) or an *Estado compuesto* (the rather abstract wording preferred by the constitutional tribunal). It may be 'a federation in the making',[2] but there is a general consensus among Spanish politicians and academics that it would be improper to call it a federal state at present.

To be sure, the difference between federal states and regional states should not be exaggerated. There is, in fact, a debate among comparative constitutional lawyers on whether there are two separate forms of state organization which can be called 'federal state' and 'regional state' or, rather, a sliding scale of national situations without firm categorical distinctions.[3] A comparison of Belgium and Spain supports the latter view; the self-definition of those two states may well put them in two different constitutional categories, but this nominal difference is overshadowed by the many political and institutional features of divided government which these two countries have in common. The most important of these features is that both the Belgian and the Spanish autonomous institutions have exclusive legislative powers in the fields delineated by the constitution, and that policing of the boundaries between central and autonomous powers is entrusted to a neutral arbiter, the constitutional tribunal in Spain and the court of arbitration in Belgium. Therefore, unlike a more modest regional system such as that found in France, the scope of the autonomous powers is constitutionally guaranteed and cannot be changed unilaterally by the national institutions.

These features are shared by other countries in the European Union as well, including Germany, Italy and Austria. What distinguishes the systems of divided government in Belgium and Spain from these other countries is that they came about primarily as a *response to internal cultural diversity* with nationalist overtones. Cultural diversity was not just the triggering factor of devolution in Belgium and Spain – it has also remained a driving force in the troubled evolution of their regional/federal systems ever since.

Another characteristic shared by Spain and Belgium is that their regional systems are *asymmetrical*. This feature is not unknown elsewhere and, in fact, some measure of differentiation is unavoidable in any regional or federal system.[4] Asymmetry is much more prominent in Spain and Belgium and is, indeed, one of the essential characteristics of their system of regional government. In both countries, this asymmetry is closely related to their cultural diversity. In Spain, the three so-called 'historical nationalities' (Catalonia, Basque Country and Galicia) were initially established as autonomous communities with a higher degree of autonomy than the others. Even if some measure of 'equalization of powers' has occurred, there are still two classes of autonomous communities.[5] Even the privileged class is not homogeneous. The Basque Country, in particular, has a highly specific regime of autonomy, in part due to the constitutional recognition of the 'historical' rights of the Basque provinces.[6] It is likely that one of the main obstacles to the fully fledged federalization of the Spanish state will be the insistence by the historical regions that they should retain their own distinctive, and distinctly higher, degree of autonomy.

In Belgium, asymmetry is even more striking, as this country displays the unique feature of possessing two superimposed sets of sub-national institutions: the three regions (Flanders, Wallonia and Brussels) with autonomous powers in fields such as environmental protection, regional development, housing, employment and transportation, and the three communities (Flemish-, French-

and German-speaking communities) with autonomous powers in fields such as education, culture and social services. Both sets of autonomous institutions are territorially based but their respective territories do not entirely overlap. This institutional oddity is due to the pattern of language use in the country. Indeed, the four constitutionally entrenched language areas (the Dutch, French and German language areas and the bilingual French/Dutch area of Brussels) form the territorial basis for both the communities and the regions, but in different combinations. The Flemish region and the Flemish community are based on the Dutch language area in the north of the country. In addition, the Flemish community exercises its powers on the territory of Brussels but only with respect to the Dutch-language institutions situated there. The Walloon region and the French community are both based on the French language area in the south of the country. The French community is also responsible for the French-language institutions situated in Brussels. The Walloon region comprises the German language area in the south-east, which is considered too small to form a region of its own but which has a community of its own, reflecting and protecting the cultural distinctiveness of the area. Finally, Brussels was established as a separate region but not as a separate community: the Flemish and the French communities are concurrently responsible for education, culture and social services in the territory of the capital of Belgium.

There is further asymmetry at a second level as neither the three communities nor the three regions have identical powers. The small German-speaking community lacks some of the powers possessed by the two larger ones, and the two larger regions, Flanders and Wallonia, have broader autonomy than the smaller region of Brussels. A third and final source of diversity is the fact that the Flemish community and region are served by a common government and assembly, whereas the Walloon region and French community have not merged to the same extent.[7]

The similarities between Spain and Belgium should not hide the fact that there are also important institutional and political differences between their systems of territorial government. A few of these differences are highlighted below.

Whereas the Belgian system is based on an almost utopian effort to affirm the mutually exclusive nature of federal and member state powers, exclusive powers for the Spanish autonomous communities are much less numerous than their *shared powers* in which the central state is free to intervene in order to define the broad framework. This separation of powers leaves to the autonomous communities only the task of adopting implementing legislation. Moreover, the Spanish central state possesses some redoubtably broad 'transversal' powers, particularly in the field of economic policy, which allow it to make inroads into autonomous competences.

The degree to which the sub-national units participate in central government is different as well. Neither of the two countries has a true 'federal chamber' comparable to the German *Bundesrat*. Their second chambers (called 'senate' in both countries) serve only to a limited extent as a forum for expression of the interests of the sub-national level of government.[8] Belgium, however, has functionally equivalent legal and political mechanisms. There are mechanisms of cooperative federalism (primarily, as will be explained below, in relation to European affairs); there are rules guaranteeing equal representation of the two principal language groups in federal institutions;[9] there is, above all, the fact that all leading political parties are organized along language lines, so that, politically speaking (if not in formal constitutional terms), the central state is actually dominated by the 'periphery'. The Belgian system resembles a dyadic federation with the strong confederal features that dyadic federations often display.[10]

In Spain, there is no comparable compensation for the absence of a true 'federal chamber'. Cooperative federalism is less prominent than in Belgium because of the broad horizontal powers which the central state possesses and which make it, formally at least, less dependent on the collaboration of the autonomous communities. The fact that a cooperation mechanism between state and autonomous communities in European affairs was so tardily concluded is confirmation of this observation (see p. 00). On the other hand, the leading nationalist political parties of Catalonia and the Basque Country have sometimes played a strategic role in central government affairs, but this is a recent and contingent phenomenon which is primarily due to the fact that their votes have occasionally been needed to ensure a majority for the government's policies. The ordinary autonomous communities, however, are entirely without influence in central government affairs.

So much for the general features of the regional systems of government in Spain and Belgium. The rest of this chapter will focus on two particular aspects of those systems. These aspects may be of more general interest as a point of comparison with other member states of the European Union, and in light of the future accession of Central and Eastern European countries to the European Union. The first aspect is the *interaction between regional autonomy and membership of the European Union*: are these mutually reinforcing or contradictory developments (see p. 205) The second aspect is the *interaction between cultural diversity* (which underlies regional autonomy in both countries) *and the European integration process*: are they compatible or conflicting (see p. 215) These two questions are related but do not entirely overlap. Indeed, for some of the regions (in fact, for most of the Spanish autonomous communities), cultural distinctiveness is not an important political consideration. Similarly, culture is only one of the arenas in which other regions have entered a triangular contest with their own state and with the European Union; to date, it has not even been the main arena, due to the paucity of powers of the European Union in the field of culture.

Regional autonomy and European integration

The 'twin challenge' to the nation-state
The coincidence of growing regional autonomy and deepening European integration has led many commentators to observe that the nation-state in Western

Europe is faced with a twin challenge to its role, and even to its existence. It is difficult to say whether, beyond the chronological coincidence, there is also a causal link between these two phenomena. There has been ample speculation on the combined *effects* of those processes on the state. In this respect, two opposing hypotheses can be forwarded, which Michael Keating has formulated as follows. The first hypothesis is that regionalism and European integration 'will weaken the state by eroding its authority and functional competence simultaneously from above and below'; the second hypothesis is that regionalism and European integration 'serve to strengthen the state by off-loading the less gratifying functions and externalizing difficult tasks'.[11]

For a long time, the latter hypothesis seemed the more plausible. Despite recurrent dreams of a 'Europe of the regions', history does not demonstrate that the process of European integration has strengthened the position of the regions vis-à-vis the central government of their countries. To some extent, the contrary has happened, as the institutional system of the European Community has been biased against regional governments. Both the central state and the autonomous regions or local governments have seen a gradual erosion of their powers through European integration. Central governments were able to compensate for this by playing a decisive role in European decision-making through their presence in the council. The regions were excluded from the institutional structure of the European Community, and yet they have to comply with European policies which they did not help to shape. The impressive degree of 'normative supranationalism' promoted by the European court of justice's case law on the direct effect and supremacy of EC law has been accompanied by a strong intergovernmental pattern in decision-making, with the council (hence: the national governments) controlling the development of European Community activity. The same balance of losses and gains did not apply to the regions. From their perspective, every advance in European integration constituted a net loss in terms of power and influence. Throughout the years, the European Community system had failed to provide a formal role for regional and local authorities, despite the fact that regional autonomy – which at the time of drafting the EEC treaty in 1957 was a peculiarity of Germany – had become in the mid-1980s a feature of the constitutional system of at least four member states: Germany, Italy, Spain and Belgium – one could add France, but the French regions, while wielding important budgets, did not, and do not, have genuine legislative powers.

Recognition of the regions in the European institutional system: Maastricht and beyond

An informal 'Europe of the regions' has been emerging since the mid-1980s through horizontal contacts between regional institutions of the various countries, but the member states of the EEC (as it then was) continued to prevent direct institutional links between the supranational and the sub-national levels of government. The Single European Act of 1986 did not alter that situation. It introduced a reference to the regions as the *object* of the Community's regional development policy (see Articles 130A and 130C of the EC treaty), but it did not provide the regions with a role as *actors* in the Community policies which affect them. Granted, the reform of the European structural funds of 1988 provided for 'partnership' between the Community and regional and local authorities in the implementation of EC regional development policies, but it was specified that this would only happen if the single member states were prepared to accept such partnership.

From the mid-1980s, the regions of Europe started to insist more strongly on the need for institutional recognition in the Community system. Many of them took the initiative to establish offices for the representation of their interests in Brussels,[12] but these offices serve primarily as information and lobbying bodies; they are not formally integrated in the European institutional system.

The Maastricht treaty on European Union, concluded in 1992, was a turning point. It finally gave to the sub-national level of government a distinctive, if still limited, role in the EU decision-making process. The Maastricht treaty can therefore be said to mark, within the history of European integration, the passage from functional regionalism to institutional regionalism. The decisive factor in bringing about this change was the claims for recognition made especially by the German *Länder* and, in their own more modest way, by the Belgian communities and regions. In the years preceding Maastricht, the *Länder* had gradually developed a coherent model of the European Community as they fancied it. They were able to obtain the support of other regional and local authorities in Europe for their views, by means of discussions within the European-wide associations of regional governments, such as the Assembly of the Regions of Europe. The German and Belgian delegations to the Inter-governmental conference on European political union, which took place in 1991, tried to persuade the other countries' governments to support their view. The other countries were at first somewhat reluctant to burden the institutional structure of Europe with a new regional dimension, but, in the end, two forms of institutional recognition of regional government emerged from the Maastricht treaty: the committee of the regions and the modification of the rules on the membership of the EU council.

THE COMMITTEE OF THE REGIONS

Towards the end of the 1980s, the *Länder* and their allies in other countries proposed the establishment of a true 'European senate of regions', in the form of a third chamber which would exercise legislative powers jointly with the council and the European parliament. This claim was doomed to failure, if only because a mere four countries of the European Community had regions with legislative powers. It would be unthinkable to grant partial legislative powers to a new EC institution composed of, for the most part, representatives of regions or local authorities which do not possess legislative powers in their own country. A 'senate of regions' would furthermore have made European decision-making even more complicated and inefficient than it presently is.

However, a watered-down version of this idea was approved by the member states in the framework of the treaty on European Union. Agreement was reached on the creation of a committee with consultative rather than decision-making powers, on the model of the economic and social committee which has represented employers, trade unions and other interest groups in the EC system since 1958. The proposal received strong backing from Belgium and Germany and, eventually, from Spain and proved acceptable to countries such as France and the United Kingdom which had been reluctant.

Since 1 November 1993, the date of entry brought into force by the treaty on European Union, this committee of the regions has been called to provide its opinion on a number of issues of Community policy, such as education, culture, public health, cohesion and regional development. The underlying principle is presumably that the committee is to be involved in the formation of European Community policy in those areas where regional and local governments have special interests, if only because those governments will be called, in some countries at least, to implement EC policy once it is adopted.

Among the first generation of members of the committee there were some high-powered politicians from Belgium and Spain, such as the prime minister of the Flemish community, Van den Brande, the president of the Catalan government, Pujol, and the mayor of Barcelona, Maragall, who was for some time the chairman of the committee. Many of their fellow members have less political clout. They often represent local rather than regional institutions, or come from countries where the regional tier of government does not exist. In addition, much of the advisory work of the committee is rather mundane, so that the political rewards of membership appear less attractive than they might have seemed at first. However, the committee is permitted to 'issue an opinion on its own initiative in cases in which it considers such action appropriate' (Art. 265 par. 5 EC treaty). The committee has used this window of opportunity to express its views on matters of general political interest, such as the regional dimension of subsidiarity or the revision of the EC and EU treaties. It is not, however, a major player in the European decision-making process.[13]

The revision of the EC treaty carried out by the treaty of Amsterdam (which entered into force in 1999) led to an increase in the number of policy areas in which the committee of the regions must be heard. The committee's position in the overall institutional framework of the EU, however, was not fundamentally altered. Its opinions continue to lack binding force for the 'true legislators' of the European Union: the commission, the council and the European parliament. The treaty of Amsterdam did not even offer the committee the symbolic gratification which it had requested, of being added to the list of major institutions of the European Community in Art. 7 of the EC treaty. However, in the context of the current debate on the constitutional future of the European Union, that was launched by the declaration of Nice in December 2000, the regional 'lobby' is again trying to upgrade the institutional role of the committee of the regions and, more broadly, to reinforce the regional dimension in the EU constitutional system.[14]

SUB-NATIONAL REPRESENTATION IN THE EU COUNCIL

Sub-national representation in the council of ministers is a second element of institutional regionalism developed by the Maastricht treaty which, in contrast to the committee of the regions, affected only a few countries in the Community. This innovation was enacted through a rather sibylline change of the rules on the composition of the EU council. The old version of the treaty held: 'The council shall consist of representatives of the member states. Each government shall delegate to it one of its members.' This meant that national delegations in the council had to be headed by a member of the national government; representatives of the regions might also be present in the discussions but did not have an autonomous right to vote. The new Article of the EC treaty as amended in Maastricht, states: 'The council shall consist of a representative of each member state at ministerial level, authorized to commit the government of that member state' (Art. 203 EC). Thus, the treaty implicitly allows for the possibility that members of a regional government may represent their state in a meeting of the council, vote and undertake obligations in its name. The treaty obviously does not impose this formula, and it is up to each country's internal arrangements whether direct regional participation in the council will be allowed, and for which matters.

It is clear that EU member states are not allowed to split their vote. This means that regional ministers always represent their country as a whole, which in turn presupposes some coordination of views between the regional and central governments of each country, the latter continuing to bear the global responsibility for European affairs. To date, only Germany and Belgium have used this new opportunity and have organized a system of representation by regional ministers in (some meetings of) the council.

Regional participation in European policy-making in Spain and Belgium[15]

The manner in which each member state of the European Union defines its input in EU decision-making is an internal matter which depends on the constitutional rules and practices of each country; this is the principle of *institutional autonomy*.[16] From this constitutional perspective, every country viewed the question of the role of the regions in European affairs as part of the broader question of the organization of foreign affairs. Both Belgium and Spain started from this perspective, but their present positions are different. In today's Belgian federalism, the leading principle is that of the *parallel nature* of internal and external powers. In the areas in which the regions and communities have internal competences, they also have the corresponding foreign relation competences. The Spanish constitution, on the contrary, defines foreign affairs as a separate subject matter which is globally attributed to the central state. With respect to the European Union, this means that the Belgian regions and communities represent the Belgian state in all EU matters related to their own domestic competences, whereas European Union affairs are, in principle, the *domaine réservé* of the central state in Spain.

Upon closer examination, the contrast between the two countries is less stark, if only because it has proved necessary, in both countries, to introduce mechanisms of cooperation between state and regions in EU affairs. Nonetheless, the distance between the respective constitutional starting points remains visible in many respects, as will be demonstrated below.

Germany's regions have traditionally served as a model for regions in the other member countries of the EU, and continue to do so for the Spanish autonomous communities. The role of the *Länder* in European affairs has been recognized since the beginning of the EEC, but has been considerably strengthened in the last decade. The new Article 23 of the German constitution, adopted as part of the ratification of the treaty of Maastricht, has constitutionally entrenched extensive participation rights for the *Länder*.[17] The present regime in *Belgium*, however, though less publicized abroad, is even more 'advanced' than that of Germany. For a number of years, the communities have had important powers in international relations. The most striking aspect of these powers was, at first, that international agreements concluded (by the state) on subjects coming within the internal competence of the Belgian communities must be *approved* by the community councils. This rule was applied to the treaty of Maastricht. Because that treaty recognized new European Community powers in fields such as culture and education which fall within the exclusive legislative competence of the communities, it had to be approved by a record number of six assemblies. In addition to the two chambers of the national parliament, the treaty was also approved by the councils of the Flemish-, French- and German-speaking communities, as well as the joint community commission of Brussels-capital (which is a mixed body exercising the powers of the communities as far as the bicultural institutions of Brussels are concerned).

The constitutional reform of May 1993 went one important step further by granting to both the communities and the regions the power to *conclude* treaties themselves, on matters falling within their competences (Art. 167 of the constitution), and by denying the federal government the right to enter into treaties on those same matters. No federal constitution has ever gone this far.[18] In practice, there are many multilateral treaties which straddle the Belgian constitutional boundary between federal and member state policy competences. Such treaties must be concluded as 'mixed agreements', where both the central state and the communities and/or regions appear as contracting parties. The first example in the EU context was the signing of the treaty of Corfu on the accession of Austria, Sweden, Finland and (as originally envisaged) Norway to the European Union. Belgium declared the signature of its representative committed to the federal, regional and community authorities of the country.

As far as day-to-day decision-making in the European Union is concerned, the same principles apply. In areas falling within the domestic competence of the regions or communities, the regions or committees determine the position to be adopted by Belgium. Of course, EU business cannot be neatly subdivided along the boundary lines of Belgian federalism. The constitution itself provides, therefore, that the respective roles of the various levels of government in European affairs are detailed in a cooperation agreement between them. This 'cooperation agreement on coordination and representation in EU affairs', signed by the state, the communities and the regions, was adopted on 8 March 1994.[19] As its title indicates, it deals with two interrelated questions: coordination and representation.

As far as *coordination* is concerned, all matters brought before the EU council are discussed within a coordination committee, run by the ministry of foreign affairs, at which all interested ministerial departments, both central and sub-national, are represented. In the case of mixed subjects, straddling the line between federal and member state competence, the Belgian position must be determined by consensus among them.

As for the symbolically important question of *representation* in the EU council, a distinction is made between four types of council meetings: those dealing with subjects coming exclusively within federal competence (for instance, external relations of the EU, justice and home affairs, EMU); those dealing with subjects of a mixed character with a federal predominance (internal market, environment); mixed subjects with member state predominance (research, industrial policy); and those falling within exclusive member state fields of competence (culture, education). In the latter two types of council meetings, Belgium is represented by a member state minister who speaks for the country as a whole. This minister is sent by a region or a community depending on the subject, and the positions rotate among the various regions and communities every semester.[20]

The input of the *Spanish autonomous communities* in the European decision-making process is much more modest than that of their Belgian counterparts. Recent hard won arrangements for their participation are restricted to the internal preparation of EU negotiations. Representatives of autonomous communities are not allowed to speak for Spain directly at the European level.

The general framework of internal coordination is the conference for European affairs (*Conferencia para Asuntos Relacionados con las Comunidades Europeas*) established informally in 1988, and then officially in 1992. Its role is to provide a forum for a global dialogue between the central state and the autonomous communities on developments in European integration. One of the main achievements of this conference was the elaboration of a mechanism for the involvement of the autonomous governments in day-to-day European decision-making. On 30 November 1994 (i.e. roughly nine years after Spain's entry into the EU), the central government and the governments of all autonomous communities represented in the conference (except the Basque Country[21]) signed a formal *acuerdo* which considerably upgraded the position of the autonomous communities. On the basis of this agreement, specific EU business is discussed in seventeen sectoral conferences (*Conferencias sectorales*) each covering a sector of EU activity. A distinction is made, similar to the Belgian case, between three types of European policy areas:

1   Policy areas involving exclusive state competences. There, the autonomous governments are merely to be kept informed about developments.
2   Policy areas involving exclusive autonomous competences. Here, the autonomous governments should adopt a 'common position' (*posición común*) which must be 'compellingly taken into account' (*tenida en cuenta de forma determinante*) by the central government during European negotiations.
3   Finally, there is a large area of Community policy involving shared competences of the central state and the autonomous communities. Here, the autonomous governments are meant to draw up a common position, and then search for an agreement with the central government on the Spanish position to be defended in the EU arena.

Although the agreement of 1994 certainly improved the position of the autonomous governments, it has weaknesses.[22] First, it creates a very cumbersome process requiring successive stages of coordination (first among the autonomous communities, then between them and the central government) in a political culture which is less consensus oriented than that of, for example, Germany, and in the framework of a European negotiation process which requires speed and flexibility on the part of national delegations. Secondly, the agreement uses a number of ill-defined notions; both the typology of Community policy areas and the corresponding duties of the central government are vague. Thirdly, it is an arrangement among executive organs, entirely excluding the national and regional parliaments. This is similar to Belgium but unlike Germany, where the *Bundesrat* is given an important role in European policy-making (one should not forget, though, that even if the *Bundesrat* is formally a parliamentary institution, its membership consists of representatives of the *Länder* governments). Finally, the agreement fails to deal with the question of the direct presence of representatives of the autonomous communities in EU bodies.

On the last point, an additional commitment was forced upon the government in 1996 by the so-called 'investiture and governability agreement' (*Acuerdo de investidura y gobernabilidad*) between the Partido Popular and the Catalan nationalists (the agreement which gave the political 'green light' for launching the first Aznar cabinet). In accordance with the promise made at that time, the government created the position of 'councillor of autonomy affairs' within the Spanish permanent representation in Brussels. This civil servant keeps the autonomous communities informed and consults their Brussels offices about European Union matters.[23]

The regions and the implementation of Community policies
The principle of institutional autonomy also applies to the implementation of Community measures once they have been adopted. Many of these measures require some action on the part of EU member states (either implementing legislation or simply administrative application and enforcement), and it is up to each state to organize itself according to its own constitutional rules. However,

the end result of ensuring compliance with European legal obligations must be achieved. National governments cannot justify the fact that a European directive was not fully and correctly implemented by arguing that a region had failed to take the necessary action. In other words, the principle of institutional autonomy is complemented by a principle of *global responsibility* for the effective enforcement of European Community obligations.

In Belgium, the implementation and enforcement of Community policies follows, again, the lines of the internal distribution of powers between the federal and member state levels. It therefore happens that action, or lack of action, by the regions and communities causes a breach of Community law, for which Belgium as a whole is held responsible. More concretely, the European commission sometimes brings infringement proceedings against the Belgian state in cases where its respondent (the ministry of foreign affairs) is unable to remedy the situation because the competence to do so lies with the communities or the regions. To deal with this situation, the constitutional reform of 1993 provided a specific power for the central state to *substitute* its action for that of the member state, but only if Belgium has been found in breach of its international obligations by the European court of justice.[24] Because of this restrictive condition, the federal power of substitution is largely symbolic; it has not been used to date and one may wonder whether it will ever be used.

During the first years of Spanish membership of the (then) EEC, the central government tended to deny to the autonomous communities the power to take any initiatives for the implementation of EC law, by claiming that the implementation of EC policies fell within its 'reserved domain' of foreign affairs. The autonomous communities opposed this view and brought numerous appeals before the constitutional tribunal on this question. Initially, the tribunal supported the approach taken by Madrid, but in a series of judgments between 1989 and 1993, it gradually reversed its position and insisted that implementation of EU policies could not be considered as 'foreign affairs' but should occur along the normal lines of the domestic division of powers.[25] If autonomous communities had been granted by the constitution law-making powers in the field of environmental protection, for example, then those law-making powers would not apply merely to purely internal environmental matters, but also to the implementation of European Community directives on environmental protection.

Conclusion: practical and symbolic functions of European integration for the regions
The demands of membership of the European Union have, both in Belgium and in Spain, forced the central and sub-national governments to cooperate willy-nilly with each other.

As the Spanish constitution was adopted years before the country entered the EU, the need to organize such cooperation in external affairs was ignored at that time. For a long time, successive governments in Madrid insisted that European policy was 'foreign affairs' and therefore, according to the constitutional division of powers, their exclusive preserve. Only very gradually did the central state decide to allow a greater input from the autonomous communities in European decision-making. One factor in this evolution was purely coincidental: from 1993 onward, the national governments had to rely on the support of the nationalist parties of Catalonia and the Basque Country, a situation which allowed these parties to lobby for their own interests and, accessorily, for the improvement of the position of the other autonomous communities as well. A second factor in the evolution is less contingent in nature; most European policies require implementation into domestic law. In many matters, including major EU policies such as agriculture and the environment, this requires action by the autonomous communities rather than, or in addition to, action by the central parliament or government. Because of this, the central government realized that effective application could not be separated from policy formulation, and that allowing for the participation of the autonomous communities in EU policy *making* was convenient because those same communities were called to *implement* those policies once they were decided in Brussels. European affairs are thus spearheading the diffusion of a culture of 'cooperative federalism' in the Spanish state and thereby indirectly contributing to the cohesion of that state.

The same is true for Belgium, even though, since the 1993 revision of the constitution, the practice of cooperative federalism in European affairs is more firmly institutionalized.[26] Unlike in Spain, the regions and communities can speak 'as equals' on European affairs, although the political reality is that the central government still takes a clear policy lead on 'Europe'. There are various reasons for this. One is that most of the important European policies are still, from the Belgian constitutional perspective, federal rather than member state matters. A second reason is that specialized expertise is concentrated in federal organs such as the ministry of foreign affairs, the ministry of finance and, above all, the Belgian permanent representation at the EU which, despite the fact that it represents Belgium as a whole and that it comprises civil servants sent by the communities and regions, displays a strong federal ethos.

By and large, the channels for the representation of sub-national institutions in Spain and in Belgium have been developed, both in the EU institutional system directly and in the national organization of European affairs. In practical terms, the sub-national authorities have become meaningful players in the European process, thus lending support to some recent models of EU politics which emphasize the tendency towards *multi-level governance.*[27] At the same time, the growing importance of Europe has preserved, to date, the role of the central state as the main intermediary between the EU and national societies, and as the main spokesman for the national interests.

There is, however, another dimension to the triangular relationship between Europe, the central state and the sub-national institutions. This dimension is not about practical conflicts and forms of collaboration, but about the symbolic meaning of European integration for the dynamics of regional devolution. Neither in Belgium nor in Spain (particularly in the case of the Basque Country) is the threat of separatism and secession altogether absent. Membership in the European Union affects separatism in contrasting ways. On the one hand, establishing nominal sovereignty by means of the creation of a new state is even less meaningful in the European Union than elsewhere in the world, because the scope for effective national autonomy is reduced. On the other hand, this anchoring in Europe also means that the nation-state can no longer deliver many of the benefits it traditionally delivered. In an 'area without frontiers', national borders have largely become irrelevant and the political impulse towards secession is no longer restrained by fear of economic or welfare costs. Scottish nationalists may argue that if Ireland and Luxembourg can be member states of the European Union, why not Scotland? And if Estonia were invited to become a member state of the EU, why not Euskadi as well? Needless to say, European Union institutions themselves have always carefully avoided interfering with such delicate 'internal affairs'. In fact, the European integration process, by promoting a habit of 'loyal cooperation' both in EU decision-making itself and in the related national-level coordination, arguably has a restraining effect on separatist tendencies.

Cultural identity and European integration

Cultural identity was an important factor in triggering the process of regionalization in Belgium and Spain. Cultural policies (including media regulation, education and language planning) have been a bone of contention between central and regional levels of government in the past two decades. The Belgian communities have obtained exclusive powers in the field of culture. In Spain, the division of powers is more complex, but the 'historical three' autonomous communities (Catalonia, Basque Country and Galicia) have actively sought to use their available powers to protect and strengthen the cultural distinctiveness of their region. The 'language normalization' programmes are perhaps the most visible and controversial features of these cultural policies.[28]

Cultural policies, for these Belgian and Spanish communities, are symbols of their autonomy and distinctiveness. What is the impact of the European integration process on this aspect of regional autonomy? Culture would seem to be an appropriate policy area in which to test the hypothesis that European integration has seriously reduced the scope of autonomous action for regional governments, and that the growing participation of the regions in the *elaboration of EU policies* (as illustrated in the preceding section) is a (limited) compensation for losses in the *scope for their autonomous policy-making*. This issue is also of interest for other, present and future, EU member states, especially those that are most concerned with the preservation of their cultural identity. The role of the European Union can be seen, in this context, as part of the general discussion about the effects of globalization on cultural distinctiveness.

Conversely, it could be argued that the large amount of cultural diversity which exists among and within the member states of the European Union is a potent force preventing the transformation of the EU into a federation, or, at the very least, that further moves towards the federalization of Europe would have to be designed so as to avoid further costs to cultural diversity.

Economic integration and the preservation of cultural diversity

The economic integration of Western Europe in the 1950s aimed at increasing the economic welfare of the participant states, but also, undoubtedly, at achieving political objectives, such as the preservation of peace, the encapsulation of Germany and (more broadly) an 'ever closer union among the peoples of Europe'. Closer union did not imply, in the minds of the founding fathers, *cultural* assimilation. There was no obviously dominant national culture and none of the founding states of the European Community harboured thoughts of cultural expansionism by means of economic integration. One might even say that the European Community system, as it was established, was marked by a clear but unexpressed resolution to separate the economic and the cultural spheres, and to launch a process of economic unification which would leave national cultural identities unaffected. In this respect, as in many others, European integration can be seen as a highly original political process involving a break with earlier traditions of nation-building where political and economic unification were accompanied by efforts at cultural homogenization. The guiding image of Europe was – and still is for most of its citizens – that of a community of interests respecting existing cultural patterns rather than that of a new nation-state following the nineteenth-century model.

This starting point can also be expressed in legal terms. The European Community was created by an international treaty containing specific rules binding the contracting states and attributing specific powers to the Community institutions. Apart from these enumerated rules and powers, the member states have retained their sovereignty. As the EEC treaty did not formulate a Community cultural policy (by not providing to Community institutions explicit powers to adopt rules in this area), the logical conclusion would seem to be that Community rules simply could not affect the cultural policies of the member states.

This simple picture was never entirely true, however, and requires serious qualification today. Economic integration of the member states into a common market has proved to have indirectly affected their established cultural patterns. As a result, culture is no longer a sector excluded from Community activity, and has indeed emerged in recent years as a significant dimension of EU policy. In the treaty of Maastricht, as will be seen in the next section, the member states have formally recognized this evolution by including specific provisions on culture and attempting to strike a balance between the need for further economic and political integration and the need for preserving cultural diversity.

The evolution of market integration since the 1950s, through the political action of the European institutions and the judicial interpretation of the treaty provided by the European court of justice, has shown that there can be no neat separation between economy and culture, and that the economic-sounding concepts used in the EC treaty could affect cultural goods and activities in so far as these have an economic dimension (which most of them do). The EC treaty could, in fact, be said to have had an implicit `cultural programme' from the very beginning: the elimination of national obstacles to the free flow of cultural goods and activities within the territory of the community. Thus, the *free movement of goods* applies, in principle, to cultural goods as it does to other goods. To be sure, Art. 30 allows an exception for free movement for reasons of 'protection of national treasures possessing artistic, historic or archaeological value', but there would have been no need for a provision excepting a limited category of cultural goods if the basic principle of free movement did not apply to all cultural goods in the first place. Indeed, the court of justice confirmed at an early stage that all products forming the object of a commercial transaction (including works of art, musical recordings, newspapers or books) come under the rules on free movement of goods, whatever their other qualities. The same subsumption of culture under general economic concepts occurs with the *freedom to provide services*, which, according to the European court of justice, includes the cross-border distribution of broadcasts. This ruling enabled the European commission to launch an ambitious project to (de)regulate transfrontier broadcasting, which led in 1989 to the adoption by the EC council of a directive on 'television without frontiers', which contains cultural policy provisions. Similar stipulations have been instituted regarding the free movement of persons: *freedom of establishment* in other EU countries is, in principle, guaranteed to professionals and to self-employed operators or firms in the cultural and educational sector as in any other sector of economic life. The *free movement of workers* entails the right to work in the cultural or educational sectors. Community nationals, for instance, cannot be excluded from employment as teachers in the national educational system or as musicians in a national orchestra.

Over the years, several situations have arisen, often by means of judgments of the European court of justice, whereby apparently *bona fide* member state cultural policies seemed to clash with these principles of market integration. The Belgian communities were confronted directly with this in the field of broadcasting regulation. Belgium was found in breach of Community law by the European court of justice on two occasions, in 1994 and 1996, both times because legislation by the Flemish and French Communities (not the central state) contained protectionist elements restricting the distribution of television programmes originating from other European countries. Regulation of language use is another delicate matter where tensions between Community legal principles and regional cultural policies occur. Language requirements imposed on access to public employment may not have a discriminatory effect on citizens of other EU countries. Language requirements for the labelling of consumer products should respect the EU legal framework based on the need to ensure the free movement of goods within the internal market.[29]

The impact of European law on cultural policies is not limited to so-called 'negative integration'; that is, the process of abolition of existing national barriers to the mobility of goods, services and persons. Beyond that, the Community institutions have also brought about 'positive integration' by adopting legislative acts which harmonize national rules or create entirely new Community rules. Negative and positive integration often go hand in hand, as can be illustrated by the example of the directive on 'television without frontiers' which was first adopted in 1989 and revised in 1997. Its primary purpose is one of negative integration: to create a European market for broadcasting services by eliminating national rules (particularly rules relating to cable distribution) impeding the free provision of broadcasting services from other EU countries. The member states represented in the EU council were prepared to accept this deregulation of national media regimes, however, only if it were accompanied by some measure of European re-regulation of broadcasting standards on such issues as the amount and content of advertising, the protection of children against harmful content, and the guarantee of a quota of 'European' works on each television channel.[30]

The growing entanglement of the European Community with culture and education provides an excellent illustration, and partial vindication, of functionalist theories of integration. 'Spillover'[31] into the cultural sphere takes place, roughly speaking, as follows. Market integration for economic activities implicitly but directly affects culture in its material form, thereby indirectly affecting its symbolic significance. National cultural policies are effectively limited by those rules on market integration. This limitation of national powers may, in turn, lead to the perception that some fields of regulation must be dealt with at the European level, so as to counterbalance the effects of market integration. This is a dynamic process which does not represent a perfect equilibrium between the 'negative' and 'positive' dimensions of integration, but instead is marked by major integration deficits which fuel the process.

A new deal for culture in the treaty of Maastricht?

European developments, as presented in the preceding section, have diluted the original separation between the economic and the cultural spheres. The EEC treaty did not, however, until 1993, provide adequate 'constitutional' resources for dealing with this phenomenon and for striking a considered balance between the distinct needs of both spheres of activity. Indeed, a common criticism made in the literature has been that the European Community viewed cultural activities through an economic prism, with a corresponding neglect of the cultural values served by those activities.

The fact that the cultural sector was being 'pulled into' the European integration process attracted public awareness only in the late 1980s. This greater awareness resulted in the elimination of the lingering discriminatory and protectionist measures. At the same time, there arose a concern that 'Brussels' might start dictating cultural policies and eventually threaten cultural diversity. This distrust was most visible among the smaller cultural communities, particularly those that were more heavily exposed to foreign influences by their geographical location. In the difficult process of adjusting national identity to internationalizing trends, culture became a key variable and a matter of contention. The fear emerged that successful economic integration might, after all, cause cultural assimilation, and that some of the smaller national languages (such as Dutch or Danish) might be reduced to the status of quasi-dialects while one or a few 'national' language(s) of Europe would emerge. To this was added the concern of *regional institutions* – particularly, at first, the German *Länder* – that the growing involvement of the EC with culture would erode their autonomous legislative powers. It is therefore understandable that some of the sharpest criticism of Community cultural policy came from the German *Länder*, whose 'core business' today is cultural policy.

Beyond the specific situation of the small cultural communities and the regions, there were more widespread misgivings, in political and academic circles, about the economic undertones and the market-oriented outlook of Community interventions in the field of culture, and the lack of sensitivity which they showed to the values protected by national cultural policies. This appeared to be at odds with the role of the state as the protector and promotor of cultural development, which finds recognition not only in continental European legal doctrine and political philosophy, but also in the constitutions of most European states. These states declare the protection of cultural heritage to be one of the duties of government. In view of the nature of the European Union's political system, one would expect these national policy preferences and constitutional values to be reflected at the European level. Indeed, respect for, and promotion of, cultural and linguistic diversity became undisputed policy goals of the member states and Community institutions, and were often celebrated in European Community documents from the late 1980s onward. These values were then solemnly enacted in the treaty of Maastricht (1992), which provided a new constitutional foundation for the cultural law and policy of the European Community, without reversing altogether the earlier links between economic integration and cultural policies.

The treaty of Maastricht was not a *tabula rasa* in the field of culture. The provisions of that treaty dealing with culture can be said to serve two distinct purposes: *codification* and *containment*.[32] The first of these purposes was achieved by the new Art. 128 of the EC treaty (since renumbered as Art. 151), which provided a legal basis for many informal developments that had occurred in the interstices of the earlier treaty system, and hence put an end to certain controversies about Community competences in the field of culture. Art. 151 defines the areas in which the Community may develop its activities as the 'improvement of the knowledge and dissemination of the culture and history of the European peoples; conservation and safeguarding of cultural heritage of European significance; non-commercial cultural exchanges; artistic and literary creation, including in the audiovisual sector'. Those areas correspond, in part, to the domains covered by earlier funding programmes of the community. To this extent, Art. 151 may be seen as codifying these programmes and transforming the earlier 'pilot actions' into stable elements of Community policy. Also, the need to keep these programmes very small, which was a direct result of their dubious legal basis, no longer exists. In 2000, the EC transformed the various small cultural support programmes into a global *Culture 2000* action programme, the budgetary allocation to which is, however, still rather limited.[33]

Apart from providing a legal basis for existing Community financial subsidy schemes, Art. 151 also (and, perhaps, above all) seeks to *contain* the expansion of Community activity in this field, to restore the balance between the logic of economic integration and the specific features of cultural activities, and to formulate clearer roles for member states and the Community in the field of culture. The effort at containment is particularly visible in the general formulation of the role of the European Community. Art. 151 states that the central purpose of EC action in this field is not the development of a European culture, but rather the protection and promotion of cultural diversity. The first paragraph directs the community to 'contribute to the flowering of the cultures of the Member States, while respecting their national and regional diversity and at the same time bringing the common cultural heritage to the fore'.

Insistence on the need to preserve cultural diversity is related to a principle which has come to play a central role in the European debate post-Maastricht: the principle of *subsidiarity*. This principle, defining the appropriate division of responsibilities between levels of government, is formulated in general terms in Art. 5 of the EC treaty, as added by the Maastricht treaty. It has become, in post-Maastricht discussion, the almost miraculous response to the fear that 'more Europe' will lead to the assimilation of national and regional specificities. Art. 151 on culture contains a specific formulation of the general principle of subsidiarity. While allowing for Community action in a field which is widely defined, it also constrains such action by imposing the preservation of cultural diversity as an overall aim, and by limiting the range of available legal instruments for Community action. As to the latter, par. 5 of Art. 151 states that Community institutions may adopt *incentive measures* complementing national policies (this means, in practice, financial support schemes), but they are expressly denied the power to *harmonize* national laws and regulations in the field of culture. Such a 'negative competence clause' is new in EC law; until Maastricht, the absence of any explicit denial of powers to the Community meant the possibility of the dynamic expansion of a range of new Community policies beyond the express wording of the treaty. The purpose of the prohibition in Art. 151 was clearly to preempt any further expansion of Community involvement in the field of culture. A further guarantee was sought in the procedure for the adoption of the incentive measures. Such measures have to be decided according to the so-called 'codecision procedure', which closely associates the council and the European parliament, and has the unusual requirement of the council's unanimous vote. This unanimity requirement was inserted on the initiative of the German government acting on behalf of the *Länder*. Moreover, some regional governments with legislative powers in the field of culture, namely those of Germany and Belgium, are closely associated with decision-making on cultural matters, as they now represent their country in the meetings of the EU council (see above). They could be expected to act as jealous guardians of their autonomous powers against EC encroachments, as indeed has happened with the German representatives in the council who, in the decade since Maastricht, have adopted restrictive views of Community projects and expenditure in this field.

The exact scope of the prohibition of harmonization contained in Art. 151 remains in doubt. Community action with strong cultural implications, but which finds its legal basis in other chapters of the EC treaty, is still allowed. The directive on television without frontiers, for instance, was a measure legally based on the need to facilitate the free movement of services. Similarly, a directive from 1993, providing for the return of works of art illegally exported from their (EU) country of origin, was justified by the need to eliminate obstacles to the intra-community trade in goods.[34] A more recent directive of 2001 harmonized the national rules concerning the resale rights of artists (i.e. their right to obtain a percentage of the proceeds of any later sales of their work). Indeed, the law-making powers of the European Community connected with the smooth functioning of the internal market were not altered by Art. 151, so that European cultural policy 'through the backdoor' is still legally possible. Any measures of harmonization in the cultural field, however, while still possible under headings other than Art. 151, are subject to the so-called 'integration clause' (also contained in Art. 151) stating that 'the Community shall take cultural aspects into account in its action under other provisions of this treaty, in particular in order to respect and to promote the diversity of its cultures'. This seems to be a somewhat veiled recognition of the need to mitigate the full effect of economic integration by giving due consideration to its cultural and linguistic consequences.

Conclusion

The treaty of Maastricht has tried to correct certain defects of the original EEC treaty. The EEC treaty's main shortcoming, on the question considered here, was that a number of economic principles of Community law applied to cultural activities, but there was no satisfactory legal mechanism for recognizing and protecting the specific nature of those cultural activities. The European constitution, as rewritten in Maastricht, offers better institutional conditions for striking a balance between economic and political integration, without jeopardizing cultural heritage, pluralism of the media, or the linguistic identity of the nations and regions of Europe. Still, a decade after the entry into force of the Maastricht reform, it remains to be seen whether cultural diversity is merely to be celebrated in official European discourse, or whether it is really becoming part and parcel of the daily activity of the European institutions.

Whereas the main responsibility in the field of culture remains with each member state (and, in countries such as Belgium and Spain, with sub-national authorities), there is also, arguably, a positive role for Europe in the field of culture. One important task of the European Union could be to contribute more actively to the protection of cultural pluralism against external threats which the smaller cultures cannot effectively face on their own. Indeed, some national governments, and even more regional governments, have irremediably lost some of their capacity for action in this field, which is partly due to the European principles of market integration, but also, and more importantly, to the growing internationalization of the economy and of social life and the cultural changes caused by these processes. More particularly, it is now for the European Community, rather than its member states, to protect cultural policy values in global trade negotiations within the context of the World Trade Organization.[35]

Notes

1 A pioneering work in this field was the book edited by Y. Mény, *Dix ans de régionalisation en Europe* (Paris: Cujas, 1982). Others have proposed to use the Spanish denomination as a new general category: C. Bidegaray (ed.), *L'État autonomique: forme nouvelle ou transitoire en Europe?* (Paris: Economica, 1994).

2 See J. J. Solozábal, 'Spain: a federation in the making?', in J. J. Hesse and V. Wright (eds), *Federalizing Europe?* (Oxford: Oxford University Press, 1996), p. 240.

3 On this question, see the excellent synthesis by C. Grewe and H. Ruiz Fabri, *Droits constitutionnels européens* (Paris: Presses Universitaires de France, 1995), pp. 314–55.

4 See, for instance, the discussion of Austria by P. Pernthaler, *Der differenzierte Bundesstaat* (Vienna: Wilhelm Braumüller, 1992), p. 46 ff. For a comparative study of the asymmetrical features of current federal and regional systems, see E. Fossas Espadaler, 'Autonomía y asimetría', *Informe Pi y Sunyer sobre Comunidades Autónomas 1994* (Barcelona: Fundació Carles Pi i Sunyer, 1995), p. 890.

5 For reflections on the evolution of the distinction between 'first rate' and 'second rate' autonomous communities in Spain, see J. Corcuera Atienza, 'La distinción constitucional entre nacionalidades y regiones en el décimoquinto aniversario de la Constitución', *Documentación Administrativa*, 232/233 (1993), p. 13; J. García Roca, 'Asimetrías autonómicas y principio constitucional de solidaridad', *Revista vasca de administración pública*, 47:2 (1997), p. 45; and L. López Guerra, 'Modelo abierto y hecho diferencial', *Revista vasca de administración pública*, 47:2 (1997), p. 97.

6 The special legal regime of the Basque Country is very complex. For recent presentations, see J. M. Castells Arteche, 'El hecho diferencial vasco', *Revista vasca de administración pública*, 47:2 (1997), p. 113; Rafael Jiménez Asensio, 'El sistema de fuentes del derecho de la Comunidad Autónoma del País Vasco como "ordenamiento asimétrico"', *Revista vasca de administración pública*, 47:2 (1997), p. 127. A short survey in English is provided by A. Saiz Arnaiz and J. Bengoetxea Caballero, 'The Basque Country: Basque law in Spain', in E. Örücü, E. Attwooll and S. Coyle (eds), *Studies in Legal Systems: Mixed and Mixing* (The Hague: Kluwer Law International, 1996), p. 35.

7 All this is, needless to say, extremely perplexing to the foreign observer (and to the Belgian citizen). For clarification, see the following works: V. Bartholomée, 'L'asymétrie', in F. Delpérée (ed.), *La Belgique fédérale* (Brussels: Bruylant, 1994), p. 61; W. Pas and J. Van Nieuwenhove, 'La estructura asimétrica del federalismo belga', *Informe Pi y Sunyer sobre Comunidades Autónomas 1994*, p. 936. On Brussels, see M. Monnier, 'Le statut de Bruxelles', *Revue du droit public* (1994), p. 1037, and P. Nihoul, 'Les autorités bruxelloises', in Delpérée, *La Belgique fédérale*, p. 142; on the German-speaking community, see K.-H. Lambertz, 'Les autorités germanophones', in Delpérée, *La Belgique fédérale*, p. 161.

8 This shortcoming often draws criticism in the literature. On the composition and role of the Belgian senate, see E. Colla and J.-C. Scholsem, 'La réforme du système bicaméral

belge de 1993', *Administration publique trimestriel* (1994), p. 205. On the Spanish senate, see A. Saiz Arnaiz, 'El Senado y las Comunidades Autonomas', *Revista vasca de administración pública*, 41 (1995), p. 293.

9 X. Delgrange, 'Le fédéralisme belge: la protection des minorités linguistiques et idéologiques', *Revue du droit public* (1995), p. 1157, at pp. 1173–7.

10 See I. D. Duchacek, 'Dyadic federations and confederations', *Publius: The Journal of Federalism*, 18 (1988), p. 5.

11 M. Keating, 'Europeanism and regionalism', in B. Jones and M. Keating (eds), *The European Union and the Regions* (Oxford: Oxford University Press, 1995), p. 1, at 9–10.

12 There has been a multiplication of such offices since the late 1980s; see the survey and evaluation proposed by G. Marks, F. Nielsen, L. Ray and J. E. Salk, 'Competencies, cracks and conflicts: regional mobilization in the European Union', *Comparative Political Studies* (1996), 164.

13 For first evaluations of the record of the committee of the regions, see J. Loughlin, 'Representing regions in Europe: the Committee of the Regions', in C. Jeffery (ed.), *The Regional Dimension of the European Union* (London: Frank Cass, 1997); R. E. McCarthy, 'The Committee of the Regions: an advisory body's tortuous path to influence', *Journal of European Public Policy* (1997), p. 439; and various contributions in J. Bourrinet (ed.), *Le Comité des Régions de l'Union européenne* (Paris: Economica, 1997).

14 For a survey of this discussion, written in the summer of 2002 (as the EU constitutional reform debate was in full swing), see L. Domenichelli, 'Le Regioni nel dibattito sull'avvenire dell'Unione: dalla Dichiarazione di Nizza alla Convenzione europea', *Le Regioni* (2002), 1239.

15 For introductory surveys in English, see F. Morata, 'Spanish regions in the European Community', in Jones and Keating (eds), *The European Union and the Regions*, p. 115; and L. Hooghe, 'Belgian federalism and the European Community', in Jones and Keating (eds), *The European Union and the Regions*, p. 135.

16 For a general explanation of the meaning of this concept in the constitutional system of the EU, see L. M. Diez-Picazo, 'What does it mean to be a state within the European Union?', *Rivista italiana di diritto pubblico comunitario* (2002), p. 651, at pp. 655–61.

17 There is a vast body of literature on the role of the German *Länder* in European affairs. See, among many others, C. Jeffery, 'Farewell the third level? The German Länder and the European policy process', *Regional & Federal Studies* (1996), p. 56; V. Nessler, 'Die "neue Ländermitwirkung" nach Maastricht', *Europarecht* (1994), p. 216; G.-B. Oschatz and H. Risse, 'El Gobierno federal encadenado a los *Länder*? Acerca de la participación del *Bundesrat* en la politica europea', *Informe Pi i Sunyer sobre Comunidades Autónomas 1994*, p. 979.

18 For a general presentation of Belgian external relations law after the constitutional reform of 1993, see Y. Lejeune, 'Le droit fédéral belge des relations internationales', *Revue générale du droit international public* (1994), p. 577; and various contributions in a special issue of the *Revue belge du droit international* (1994), 1, 'La Belgique fédérale et le droit international'.

19 See J.-V. Louis and A. Alen, 'La Constitution et la participation à la Communauté européenne', *Revue belge du droit international* (1994), p. 81, at 94–6.

20 See the detailed study by B. Kerremans, 'Determining a European policy in a multi-level setting: the case of specialised co-ordination in Belgium', *Regional and Federal Studies* (2000), 36. For the broader context, see Y. Lejeune (ed.), *La Participation de la Belgique à l'élaboration et à la mise en oeuvre du droit européen* (Brussels: Bruylant, 1999).

21 The Basque Country had concluded a separate, bilateral, arrangement with the central government in 1995; for further details see L. Burgorgue Larsen, 'Espagne', in J. Rideau (ed.), *Les États membres de l'Union européenne. Adaptations – Mutations – Résistances* (Paris: LGDJ, 1997), p. 135, at pp. 168–9.

22 See R. Bustos Gisbert, 'Un paso más hacia la participación autonómica en asuntos euro-peos – El acuerdo de 30 de noviembre de 1994', *Revista española de derecho constitu-cional*, 45 (1995), p. 153.

23 See, for a comprehensive view of the question, E. Albertí Rovira, 'La posición de las Comunidades Autónomas en la fase ascendente de la formación del Derecho comunita-rio europeo', *La participación europea y la acción exterior de las Comunidades Autónomas* (Madrid: Marcial Pons, 1999).

24 Art. 169 of the constitution. See Louis and Alen, 'La Constitution et la participation à la Communauté européenne', pp. 97–103.

25 See Florestano Ruiz Ruiz, 'Las competencias de la Comunidades Autónomas en el desar-rollo normativo y la ejecución del derecho comunitario europeo – Análisis de la juris-prudencia constitucional', *Revista española de derecho constitucional*, 45 (1995), 279, 297–302.

26 For a general analysis of the institutions of cooperative federalism in Belgium, see J. Poirier, 'Formal mechanisms of intergovernmental relations in Belgium', *Regional and Federal Studies* (2002), 24.

27 A representative expression of this school of thought in European integration studies is G. Marks, L. Hooghe and K. Blank, 'European integration from the 1980s: state-centric v multi-level governance', *Journal of Common Market Studies* (1996), 341.

28 On the concept of 'language normalization' and for a short description of the policies involved, see J. Cobarrubias, 'The protection of linguistic minorities in the autonomous communities of Spain', in P. Pupier and J. Woehrling (eds), *Language and Law* (Montreal: Wilson & Lafleur, 1989), p. 399. For a comprehensive analysis of language law and policies in Spain, see G. Poggeschi, *Le nazioni linguistiche della Spagna autonomica* (Padova: CEDAM, 2002). For recent studies of the Catalan case, see A. Miliani Massana, *Público y privado en la normalización lingüística. Cuatro estudios sobre derechos lingüísti-cos* (Barcelona: Atelier Editorial, 2000), and E. Roller, 'The 1997 *Llei del Català*: a Pandora's box in Catalonia?', *Regional and Federal Studies* (2001), 39.

29 On the impact of EC law (and European court cases in particular) on regional and minority languages, see B. de Witte, 'The impact of European Community rules on lin-guistic policies of the Member States', in F. Coulmas (ed.), *A Language Policy for the European Community: Prospects and Quandaries* (Berlin/New York: Mouton de Gruyter, 1991), p. 163, and F. Palermo, 'The use of minority languages: recent developments in EC law and judgments of the ECJ', *Maastricht Journal of European and Comparative Law* (2001), p. 299. For a recent comprehensive analysis, see N. Nic Shuibhne, *EC Law and Minority Language Policy: Culture, Citizenship and Fundamental Rights* (The Hague: Kluwer Law International, 2002).

30 The imposition of a duty on European broadcasters to transmit a major proportion of European-made fiction (the famous 'European quota' rule) is a clear example of European cultural policy. See the discussion in B. de Witte, 'The European content requirement in the EC television directive – five years after', *The Yearbook of Media and Entertainment Law* (1995), p. 101.

31 For a general discussion of the phenomenon of 'spillover' in European integration, see R. O. Keohane and S. Hoffmann, 'Conclusions: community politics and institutional change', in W. Wallace (ed.), *The Dynamics of European Integration* (London: Pinter Publishers, 1990), p. 276.

32 See J. M. G. Loman, K. J. M. Mortelmans, H. H. G. Post and S. Watson, *Culture and Community Law* (Deventer: Kluwer, 1992), p. 195.

33 See the text of the action programme in *Official Journal of the European Communities* (2000), L 63/1.

34 For further details, see B. de Witte, 'The cultural dimension of Community law', *Collected Courses of the Academy of European Law*, 4:1 (1995), 229, 237–46.

35 For a reflection on the issues of cultural diversity arising in that context, see B. de Witte, 'Trade in culture: international legal regimes and EU constitutional values', in G. de Búrca and J. Scott (eds), *The EU and the WTO – Legal and Constitutional Issues* (Oxford: Hart Publishing, 2001), p. 237.

Giovanni Poggeschi

11

The United Kingdom and France: a stronger decentralization or just an institutional 'maquillage'?

Introduction

The United Kingdom and France were until recently considered two of the most centralized systems in the world. A dogma of uniformity has ruled the political and institutional life of both countries. In the United Kingdom this uniformity has been directed by the idea of the supremacy of the crown, and then of the cabinet system which links the executive and the legislative in the name of this royal function.[1] The welfare system has followed this pattern of uniformity, with some slight (but very interesting for this chapter) exceptions regarding Scotland. In France the rule of law, the expression of the common will of the French,[2] has been the means of assuring uniformity of law and is connected to the idea of equality and liberty. The system of codification is a result of this idea.

Thus, in ways that reflect the individual history of each country and their institutional principles governing constitutional practice, the United Kingdom and France have become models of efficient unitarian states with a strong centre (nevertheless the most important federal systems outside Europe derive from English rule, which allowed, like most of the Empires, a certain degree of self-government to the local entities. Neither has France's centralism been absolute, allowing municipalities and departments to enjoy some self-government.) The Westminster model has served as an example for many countries, which have adopted some features of it (especially the alternation in power and the trust relation between the parliament and the government),[3] even if sometimes distorting it. And the uniform system of administration in France has been the example for most of the European countries – from the Prussia of Frederic the Great to post-unification Italy.[4]

Currently both the United Kingdom and France are experimenting with a process of decentralization which looks like a revolution for those countries, especially from the symbolic point of view (but not only, as will be seen in the following pages). Devolution in the UK officially started in 1998[5] with the White Paper on Scotland and with the following Scotland Act. It is one of the most important constitutional reforms which has modern roots that can be traced back to the 'Irish question'.

The Act of Union of 1707 had abolished both the separate parliament of England and the separate parliament of Scotland, and brought into existence the parliament of the United Kingdom and, from a legal point of view, the United Kingdom of Great Britain itself. Dicey stressed that:

> In 1603 James VI of Scotland succeeded on the death of Elizabeth to the English crown as James I of England. Hence arose the so-called union of Crowns. Under this union the King of England was the same person as the King of Scotland. But, as King of England, he had, constitutionally, no authority in Scotland, and as King of Scotland, he had no authority in England – hence it resulted that no law passed by the English Parliament had operation in Scotland, and no law passed by the Scottish Parliament had operation in England.[6]

Thus the parliament of Scotland has been restored after nearly three centuries and perhaps now seems an appropriate time to draw some conclusions. A similar case affects Wales. Not forgetting Northern Ireland, which presents different features because the process of devolution seems above all linked to the need for pacification (nevertheless the so far unlucky 'Stormont agreement' contains very interesting and original solutions regarding communal consent and proportional power-sharing in regional government, and cross-border institutions).[7]

France enacted a constitutional revision on 29 March 2003. This revision is the starting point of a reform which puts decentralization among the fundamental principles of the republic. Art. 1 of the constitution now states that its organization is decentralized. Many other articles of the constitution have been affected: we can quote Art. 72, very complex in its new form, which foresees the possibility, for regions and other local entities, to use certain legislative power (*power of derogation*), under the control of the national parliament.

It is too soon to assess the effectiveness of the French reform (and also in the light of the unsuccessful referendum in Corsica on Corsican autonomy held on 6 July 2003), but it seems that the government of Jean-Pierre Raffarin has set a system which gives a strong degree of (asymmetrical) local self-government.

Both the United Kingdom and France are thus experimenting with new and elaborate forms of self-government in their regional entities. This chapter will try to discover the common features of this trend, after having analysed the legal basis of the decentralization of each system. The analysis on the United Kingdom will cover mainly devolution to Scotland, with some mention of Wales, Northern Ireland and the project of regionalization of England. Most of the attention will be focused on Scottish devolution, because it has been shown to be the most relevant of the projects aiming to create a strong level of territorial self-government.

The analysis of France will explore the question of Corsica and the constitutional reform of March 2003 on decentralization.

The British case: Scottish and Welsh devolution and the regionalization of England

Before tackling the issue of devolution in its fundamental aspects, it is important to underline how devolution and regionalism are not synonymous, even if some authors tend to mix the two concepts. Devolution consists of 'the transfer to a subordinate elected body, on a geographical basis, of functions at present exercised by ministers and parliament'. This definition takes into consideration the functional side of devolution more than the 'identitarian side' which is the ground for the entire process of devolution in Scotland, Wales and Northern Ireland, and which makes the question of regionalization of England so different.[8] In the United Kingdom devolution affects historical entities which may be called 'nations without a state'. With regionalization we mean the giving of more power to administrative entities which reflect, more than an 'identity' question, the need for rationalization and modernization of some areas, in order to improve their economic capacity for competing in the global market,[9] and which is expressed, from the legal point of view, by the White Paper of regionalization of 2000.

Devolution[10] is one of the most important constitutional reforms of the twentieth century in the United Kingdom. Although it is true that Britain has always been an officially multinational state, where the different histories and identities of Scotland, Wales and Northern Ireland were recognized, the predominance of the English element was nonetheless reflected in all of its institutions, from the crown to Westminster and the government, even if it has to be remembered that 'the long but intermittent process of achieving complete political integration throughout the United Kingdom over the course of at least 500 years was driven more by a sense of strategic necessity (from the French threat) and political expediency than by constitutional principle or ideological conviction'.[11]

Whereas the rearrangement of minor authorities was achieved (albeit with delays and contradictions)[12] throughout the 1960s and 1970s, Scottish and Welsh devolution did not take place. On the other hand, extensive decentralization was carried out in six of the nine Ulster counties belonging to the British crown, by means of the Northern Ireland constitution act of 1973. The Scotland and Wales devolution bill was 'unexpectedly torpedoed',[13] in 1977, thanks to the 'betrayal' of forty or so labour members of parliament who either voted against it or abstained.

As with today's devolution, the labour government's desire to grant wide-ranging powers to the 'historical nationalities' coincided with the electoral successes scored by the Scottish and Welsh nationalist parties throughout the 1960s.[14] The term 'historical nationalities' recalls Art. 2 of the constitution of

1978 of Spain, which uses the terms 'nationalities and regions' without establishing first which are nationalities and which are regions. 'Historical nationalities' is a more political concept, but it is obvious that Catalonia, the Basque Country and Galicia are considered historical nationalities, even if only the statute of Galicia contains the full expression *'nacionalidad histórica'*: the statutes of Catalonia and the Basque Country just speak about *'nacionalidad'*, which sounds even more ambitious than *'nacionalidad histórica'*; nevertheless, some statutes of autonomous communities which were not originally considered 'historical' claim that their *Comunidad Autónoma* is a 'historical' one, even if not in an explicit way: for instance, Asturias, which uses the expression 'historical community' and Aragon, which uses the expression 'historical identity as a nationality'.[15]

It would, however, be reductive to dismiss the plan to grant wide-ranging autonomy because of 'threatening' electoral successes. In reality, the success of the nationalist or regionalist parties can be explained by the outlet they provided for the need for a political representation which is closer to the citizen and, in certain areas such as Scotland and Wales, to reflect their own identity. Devolution and the success of regionalist parties are coincidental phenomena ascribable to the same changing historical climate in Europe, where traditional-style nation-states no longer satisfy all current social demands. Moreover, devolution will continue its process also after the 'little failure' that the nationalist parties had in the Scottish and Welsh elections of May 2003.

Devolution reflects an evolution rather than a revolution, not only from the procedure which has served it, both conciliatory and negotiating, but also from the historical perspective: one can say that the British constitution has become familiar with the principle of the 'division of sovereignty' through its experience over many centuries.[16] It should be recalled that many of the most pertinent experiences of federal states can be found in former British colonies: the United States of America, Canada and Australia, as well as India, South Africa, Malaysia and Nigeria. This fact would seem to confirm the American school of thought according to which the type of organization to be found in the British Empire favoured the development of federalism in its colonies, in view of the existence of a two-tier authority exercised by those colonies and the mother country.

The last time that a possible limit was placed on Westminster's powers was the occasion of the European community act of 1972. Accession to the European community and the consequent direct applicability of community law meant for the United Kingdom not so much a possible limitation on parliamentary sovereignty, but the fact that it might no longer be able to establish its own powers in the future. The solution adopted for overcoming the problem of safeguarding the dogma of parliamentary sovereignty has been to recognize the supremacy of community law over parliamentary acts 'if and until when the latter cannot be recognised as a deliberate disavowal by parliament of the treaties themselves'.[17]

The two pillars of devolution in Scotland are the *White Paper* and the *Scotland Act*.[18] The first was presented in July 1997 by the labour government of Tony Blair, and is a result of the strategy of the shadow cabinet during the conservative governments of Margaret Thatcher and John Major, which were (and still are, even if the attitude may have changed a little)[19] against the idea of devolving power to the peripheral areas. It is a political document whose contents derive mainly from the *Claim of Right for Scotland* of 1989, which founded the *Scottish Constitutional Convention*. The convention was addressed not only by the labour party but also by many other organizations which expressed a need for modernization in the frame of a more autonomous Scotland.[20] Thus the White Paper is not a pure party document, although it has the nature of a programme-of-government document, clear and optimistic. A referendum with two questions was then held in September 1997 'and the degree of public endorsement for the policy was persuasive in Scotland',[21] where on a turnout of around 60 per cent, 71.4 per cent voted for a Scottish parliament and 63.5 per cent voted for giving it tax-varying powers.[22]

With this popular support, the government was thus able to enact in 1998 the Scotland Act, which is a much more juridical tool than the White Paper. The restored parliament of Scotland is composed of 129 members, 73 elected from single-member constituencies and 56 through proportional representation. This mixed system has caused a need for parliamentary coalitions, an event that does not normally occur in Westminster.[23] The Scottish executive is tied to the parliament by a fiduciary relationship. The experience has shown that the Westminster model, based on the supremacy of the parliament, and at the same time on the central role of the cabinet, has been followed in its key elements, with the notable exception of a stronger governmental instability, nevertheless mitigated by the continuing leading role of the labour party.

As Forman states, the most distinctive characteristics of Scottish devolution under the 1998 Scotland Act are the real restrictions, both theoretical and practical, upon the scope for Scottish politicians seeking to stretch the devolution settlement too far in the direction of national autonomy and independence for Scotland.[24]

Let us analyse in more detail how those features are sketched in the two documents and then also the concrete functioning of the institutions of devolution.

Section 28 of the Scotland Act states that the Scottish parliament has the power of primary legislation in the matters not reserved to Westminster, which are listed in schedule 5 of the act: here we find obviously defence, foreign affairs, economic, monetary and fiscal policy, immigration and nationality and all dealings with the European Union. However, there are other items that could be treated by the Scottish authority (of course with a kind of 'supervision' from London, following the Italian example of Art. 117 of the constitution or Art. 79 of the German *Grundgesetz*), for example, telecommunications and an energy policy, infrastructural aspects of transport policy, employment, and health and safety issues.

But the most binding principle to the Scottish primary legislative power is declared in section 29 of the Scotland Act, according to which 'an act of the Scottish parliament is not law so far as any provision of the act is outside the legislative competence of the parliament'. The second line adds that a provision *is* outside that competence if it relates to matters reserved to Westminster. If this prerogative, which fosters the already mighty power of Westminster, is endorsed by the courts, the role of the Scottish parliament will be definitely reduced.[25]

Maintaining Westminster sovereignty is explicitly stated in the White Paper on Scotland in the chapter entitled 'New constitutional provisions'. Section 2 of this chapter stipulates that the parliament of the United Kingdom is and shall remain sovereign in all matters, but that, pursuant to decisions taken by the government to modernize the British constitution, Westminster must choose to maintain that sovereignty while devolving legislative responsibilities to the Scottish parliament, without its own powers in any case being diminished. Thus it is possible to define Scottish devolution as 'a flexible model with the prevailing of the centre'.[26]

This primacy of Westminster is even more effectively specified in the *Memorandum of Understanding and Supplementary Agreements* between the British, Scottish and Welsh administrations which was published in October 1999. The most relevant passage is that dealing with 'parliamentary business', according to which:

> The United Kingdom parliament retains authority to legislate on any issue, whether devolved or not. It is ultimately for parliament to decide what use to make of that power. However, the UK government will proceed in accordance with the convention that the UK parliament would not normally legislate with regard to devolved matters except with the agreement of the devolved legislature. The devolved administrations will be responsible for seeking such agreement as may be required for this purpose on an approach from the UK government.[27]

In this passage we can find the core of the actual practice of devolution in Scotland and, to a lesser extent, in Wales. The possibility of Scotland to enact primary legislation has been overtaken by the consultative role of the Scottish institutions regarding the Westminster legislation related to devolved matters. This participation of the Scottish institutions in the British legislation is one of the numerous cooperative procedures and practices which have marked relations between London and Edinburgh in the first years of devolution in Scotland. This practice, described in the following, seems to recall the model of cooperative federalism in Germany.[28]

The most visible outcome of these cooperative procedures is the so-called 'Sewel convention'.[29] This procedure, which has been developed by Lord Sewel, similarly to an old commission established at the beginning of the twentieth century for Northern Ireland, is working as a compensation for the lack of utilization of the legislative function which the Scottish parliament enjoys but that, for several reasons, it has not taken the chance to exploit. One of those reasons, the supremacy of Westminster, is stressed in several documents which influence the practice; another reason may reside in the need for all the devolved powers to get used to the new possibilities.

When a bill under discussion in Westminster touches on devolved matters, the Scottish parliament is invited to express its consent through the approval of a 'Sewel motion'. This procedure is a kind of 'peculiar constitutional convention' because it has been created *ad hoc* and it is very recent.[30]

Another legal ground for the Sewel convention is section 6 of the White Paper, according to which it will be up to the house of commons to take account of Scottish affairs in future legislation.

An example of the faith of the White Paper in the ability of the Scottish and British institutions to cooperate is section 15, according to which (only occasionally, in keeping with the optimism of the document's draftsmen) should there arise different opinions as to how to interpret the acts of Scotland's legislative powers, the procedures for identifying and resolving any possible difficulty of this type will more easily succeed since the government believes that, given the open and constructive relationship between the government of the United Kingdom and the Scottish executive, problems will normally be resolved quickly and amicably.[31]

If this agreement is not reached, then the role of the courts will have to take the place of the friendly settlement and cooperation. The judicial committee of the privy council will be the body for deciding how to solve any conflicts that might arise between the Scottish parliament and the British government. This committee has been in existence since 1833 and acted as an arbiter in disputes that arose in the empire or, later, in the commonwealth.

The judicial committee will take action should the procedure provided for in that section be properly implemented, which consists in allowing a certain lapse of time to take place between approval of the law by the Scottish assembly and the royal assent, in order to see whether there might not be reason for the British government to oppose a given law. This judicial committee, which might in certain cases meet in Edinburgh if the senior law lord so decides, will be composed of the so-called 'lords of appeal in ordinary'. At least five law lords will have to be present. The judicial committee is not only entrusted with the prior examination of the legitimacy of the law in question, but it can also examine any subsequent conflict of powers relating to the laws and acts of the Scottish parliament following the royal assent, according to the bill.

The possibility of judging on a question regarding devolution is given to all courts, and this judicial review can be asked by any person who is affected by the case. Thus the judicial committee of the privy council acts as the highest court, like the supreme court of USA, but also as a constitutional court, not only because it has competence on constitutional issues, but also because it has to function as a previous judge on the constitutionality of the Scottish acts.[32]

From this role similar to a constitutional court of the judicial committee of the privy council has arisen a debate about the opportunity to create a real constitutional court on a continental (Austrian) model. This solution has not been chosen, but it is necessary to review some of the rules of the British courts which do not yet seem to feel wholly comfortable with dealing with new issues such as devolution and the Human Rights Act of 1998.[33]

The lack of opportunity for the Scottish institutions to tackle the acts of Westminster is another factor which puts the balance in favour of the centre.[34] So far devolution, especially in Scotland, has been marked by a 'consociational model' with a prevailing of the centre, but a certain degree of stronger self-government for Scotland has been developed. This result has been possible also because of the presence of the same ruling parties in London, Edinburgh (and Cardiff). Probably, with other combinations, it would be more difficult to reach a consensus which would be at the same time satisfactory for the need for autonomy of Scotland (and Wales) and good for keeping the unity of United Kingdom.

The weakest point of devolution seems to be the financial aspect. The seventh chapter of the White Paper opts for the continuation of the 'block and formula' system in force since the end of the 1970s, strongly characterized by rigid central control. According to that, the Scottish (like the Welsh) budget consists of a given quantity (block) which is changed on the basis of the numerical fluctuation of the population (formula). A limited power of the Scottish parliament to raise taxes without being able to set local authority taxes is added to the system already in existence without altering its spirit.

The approach used to fix the exact amount of the quotas earmarked for Scotland and Wales is the 'Barnett formula'. This came into effect in 1978 and took on the name of its creator, the Labour MP and now member of the house of lords, Joel Barnett. It aimed at balancing the Scottish economy vis-à-vis the English economy, which at that time was considerably stronger. Since the Scottish economy is now largely on an equal footing with the English one, according to the formula Scotland now receives more than it would if a purely redistributive calculation were to be applied.

Thus there continues to be a 'paternalistic' vision of largely 'derived' finances. The only relevant novelty consists of the amount allocated to the Scottish and Welsh assemblies instead of to the corresponding secretaries of state, and the discretionary powers on how to spend funds received from the centre.

One of the questions that is now arising is the risk of an overlap in financial issues by some devolved politics, for example, the care of the elderly. This important Scottish reform, launched on 1 July 2002, and which constitutes a concrete success of the Scottish institutions, is a typical case of policy divergence within a state which has clear effects also on the financial aspect.[35]

Devolution to Wales has features which differ considerably from Scottish devolution; the main one is the lack of primary legislation power, and the mere possibility to regulate the devolved matters through executive acts. Even so, the assembly of Wales has been capable of developing important policies on matters such as agriculture, economic development, environment, fishing, housing and local authorities in the spirit of cooperation with London already described in the stronger Scottish devolution.

The practice of devolution in Wales seems to be marked by a stronger separation of powers which takes the assembly in a parliamentary direction.[36] Also the linguistic policy on the Welsh language has been fostered during the last few years. Wales, or *Cymru* in the Welsh language, is certainly demanding in matters of the country's cultural and linguistic identity. Following the decline of Breton, Welsh is now the world's best surviving Celtic language, with more than 500,000 speakers, albeit concentrated in certain areas in the west of the country, not coincidentally where the devolution referendum received in 1997 the most resounding 'yes' vote (still alive but far less widespread is the Scots Gaelic language, which probably has around 50,000 speakers left).

The success of devolution in Scotland and, to a lesser extent, in Wales, could create a knock-on effect on other regions with a less marked identity but which desire more self-government. A similar occurrence took place in the special Italian regions which, in the construction of the regional state, were taken as models for the ordinary regions instituted in the early 1970s. This was also the case in Spain, where the autonomous communities of Catalonia and the Basque Country, through their activity but also because of political contingencies, often benefited those other autonomous communities with a less marked sense of national identity. But this evolution looks more difficult in England. In fact there is only a project, a project that looks to be much less supported by public opinion than was devolution, about the general regionalization of England.[37] The main legal tool about the project of regionalization in England is the White Paper *Your Region, Your Choice*, released in March 2002.

To draw a partial conclusion, it can be assumed that devolution in Scotland and Wales, six years after publication of their White Papers, is a reality. It has shown different paths and choices in those two devolved areas (Northern Ireland is a different and less successful case), and further evolution is to be expected in the future. What is certain, nevertheless, is that devolution has been a constitutional success. It is true that formally the parliament of Westminster could cancel it, but most of the doctrine agrees on the impossibility of abolishing the Scottish parliament and revoking the Scotland Act, because it has been approved through referendum – and thus is a reinforced act[38] – and mainly because it would be politically very difficult to cancel all the institutions and practices set up in those five years.

France: the constitutional revision of 29 March 2003 and the case of Corsica

Among the adjectives quoted by Art. 1 of the constitution of the Fifth French Republic of 1958 we may find 'indivisible' (the others are 'secular', 'democratic', 'social' and, after the revision of March 2003, 'decentralized').[39] This seems to have hindered the development of ideals and practices of regionalism and federalism.[40] The indivisibility had already been achieved in 1791, and federalism was so prohibited that one could be sentenced to death if accused of this crime.[41]

The national ideal in France is linked to a conception which was enhanced by the Jacobins, who used the set of ideas elaborated by the enlightenment and above all by the encyclopaedists.[42]

To return to the more recent roots of French regionalism, it is important to remember the result of the referendum on the senate and the consequent creation of regions of 1969: this reform was strongly promoted by General De Gaulle, but on 27 April 1969 the French rejected the proposal, leading to the withdrawal of De Gaulle.[43] The project was rather ambitious, including constitutional, organic and ordinary laws. The regions had to be included in the list of the territorial entities of Art. 72 (this goal was fulfilled with the constitutional revision of March 2003), and Art. 2 of the project (an ordinary law) would have stated that 'The region is a territorial entity ['*collectivité territoriale*'] with the aim of contributing to the economic, social and cultural development and also to the care of the corresponding part of the national territory'. Other provisions foresaw a complex system of transfer of competences from the state to the regions and the way the regions could exercise self-government.

In 1972 the regional reforms started again, but it was in 1982 that decisive reforms on the issue were carried out with strong governmental support and will. The regional reform was part of those that president Mitterrand wanted for the renewal of the country, and it followed the very relevant reform of the 'nationalizations' enacted in February 1982. The regional reform was enhanced by means of an ordinary law, according to the provision of Art. 72 of the constitution stating that 'a new territorial entity must be created by the law'.[44]

In a different way from Italy, Germany and Spain, French regions are not considered a higher level vis-à-vis the departments, 'the same way departments are not a hierarchical authority vis-à-vis the municipalities'.[45] This leads to a weak position of the region in relation to other territorial entities,[46] and it consists above all as a means to develop and modernize the economy.

Thus not until 2003 were French regions constitutionally recognized entities, and they were not entitled to legislative power. The best French doctrine stresses that this lack of autonomous legislative power determines 'the border between a divisible and an indivisible state'.[47] This idea hides the fear that a strong decentralization, and above all federalism, may lead to the dissolution of the country: French scholars and politicians are still aware of this, but it seems it is now time not to take too seriously this hypothetical fear,[48] since experience has shown, as in Italy and above all in Spain,[49] that a strong legislative power exercised by the regional level does not necessarily mean a danger for the unity of the country. French regions have shown, in spite of their lack of legislative power, a strong dynamism and a capability to use the large resources they have at their disposal. Their visibility and the perception of the people are getting stronger every day, especially since the reform of 1982, according to which the election of the president of the regions is direct. This growing perception of the role of the region, and at the same time of its president, has been witnessed by the career of the prime minister, Jean-Pierre Raffarin, who showed his political capacities when he was president of the region Poitou-Charente.

The *Conseil constitutionnel* indicated some guidelines that the reform of 1982 and its attachment about Corsica[50] had to respect (let us remember that the

constitutional council functions *a priori*, before the law is in force, when a parliamentary minority, or the president of the republic, or the prime minister, refer
the draft law to the constitutional council). Judgment no. 82-138 of 25 February
1982 says that 'the fears of the MPs proposing the *saisine* are not founded. They
are afraid that the notion of special statute, which Corsica may enjoy, could dan-
gerously dislocate the national unity.' This statement is one of the few expressed
by the constitutional council which is favourable to regionalism and decentralization. In fact the state must prevail over the *collectivités territoriales*, and a
federal or quasi-federal evolution, similar to the kind Spain and Italy have
known, is firmly to be rejected. The judgment has now two categories of territorial collectivities, one with constitutional relevance and the other with only
legislative status (the new regions).[51]

It is true anyway that, within the system of French legal sources, the lack of
an autonomous legislative power of the regions, as of any other territorial collectivity, is not too relevant, because this power belongs only to parliament;
according to Art. 34 of the constitution: 'All legislation shall be passed by parliament'. Art. 3 declares that 'national sovereignty belongs to people who exercise it through its representatives and through referendum. No section of people
may be given this right.'

It has to be underlined that the primary normative power, which includes
both regulations, issued from the executive power, and laws, issued by the legislative power, leans more towards the former, and this means that within the
French system, the legal sources must be detected not from the point of view of
the hierarchy, but from the perspective of the competence.[52]

Using powers of regulation to their maximum, regions could thus already
exercise a strong self-government and the 'coexistence of the hierarchical criterion with the competence criterion in the field of legal sources is typical of the
federal or regional states'.

> [T]he only difference between those systems and the French situation is the criter-
> ion of the competence to distribute the primary normative power [after the consti-
> tution] acts within the federal states between different juridical persons, the central
> state and the member states or the regions. In the French system, they act between
> organs of the same juridical person, the parliament and the government'.[53]

So, keeping in mind that this distinction was made between the regulation
power and the legislation power, it could be used also for a division of competences between the central state and the territorial collectivities, especially the
regions, regarding both the laws and the regulations.

The reform of March 2003 opens new opportunities for the regions: a first
interpretation of it states that the territorial collectivities are vested in an 'experimental derogation power', according to the renewed Art. 72. Before analysing in
detail the provisions of the recent constitutional reform on decentralization, it is
worthwhile tracing the history of the autonomy of Corsica, which could be considered to be a 'general rehearsal' for the decentralization of the whole country.

Corsica

Corsica (*Corse* in French) has been the leader among the French regions in the demand for a stronger autonomy, and related to this feeling is also an institutional primacy in trying new solutions of self-government (together with the overseas territories). Its territory has belonged to France since 1768, after three centuries of rule of the Republic of Genua, just one year before Napoleon, the most famous Corsican (and Frenchman) in history, was born.

The statute of 1991 was questioned by judgment of the *Conseil Constitutionnel* no. 91-290 of 9 May 1991. Many provisions of this statute, the '*Loi portant statut de la collectivité territoriale de Corse*', were analysed by the constitutional council. Most of those provisions were 'saved', but not that which declared the existence of a 'Corsican people'.

Article 1 of the law in fact stated that:

> The French Republic will guarantee to the living historical and cultural community constituting the Corsican people, composed of the French people, the rights to the preservation of its cultural identity and to the defence of its specific social and economic interests. Those rights related to insularity will be exercised within the respect of national unity, in the frame of the constitution, of the laws of the republic and of this statute.

The constitutional council denies the existence of a portion of people inside France who differ from the rest of the French people. This idea is linked to a rigid application of the principle of equality, because the French constitution treats its citizens regardless of their origin, race or religion. Thus, with a reference to the declaration of 1789 and to the constitution of 1958, the principle of the indivisibility of the French people is stressed, and this has been considered by an author a very original feature of the French constitutional system vis-à-vis many foreign constitutional systems.[54]

The constitutional council admits that Art. 53 of the French constitution of 1958 quotes the 'affected populations' of a territory, but it does not use the notion of people for regional entities, even if they are inside the French Republic. It is a firm refusal of any kind of federalism; the French people is an *unicum*, not the sum of different peoples. The reasoning of the constitutional council is built on two propositions: the constitution only knows one people; and this people is composed of 'citizens', that is to say of 'differentiated individuals'.[55] The proposition could be also be reversed: all are citizens, who all together make only one people.

After more than ten years, ten years marked by bloody events and scandals on the island, a new statute of Corsica has been enacted, in January 2002. The *Conseil Constitutionnel*, with its judgment of 17 January, had previously curtailed some of the 'boldest' provisions of the statute. To summarize, the power of regulation with which the assembly of Corsica is vested has been declared legitimate, but the very innovative power of legislative derogation was declared unconstitutional. Art. 4 of the statute, stating that

> when the assembly of Corse believes that the legislative provisions or the drafts
> present some difficulties in being applied to the special features of the island, it may
> ask the government that the legislator gives it the possibility to do some experiments
> which allow some derogations to the rules in force, waiting for the parliament to
> regulate the issue by an appropriate law

was not saved by the constitutional council.[56] The request of this 'adaptation' to the peculiarity (*specificité*) of the island had to be made by the assembly of Corsica through motivated deliberation, and the state law had to fix the nature and the significance of these experiments, and also the conditions and the terms within which the powers of Corsica may have acted. The evaluation would have been carried out by a parliamentary commission with proportional representation of the groups.

This reform would have meant a real change in the French legal system, because it would have led to a kind of 'experimental derogation power' embedded in the assembly of Corsica. This 'experimental derogation power' figures among the most relevant new features of the constitutional revision of decentralization of 29 March 2003, and is regulated by the reformed Art. 72.

The combination of Art. 3 and Art. 34 of the French constitution of 1958, without this last constitutional reform, prohibited any legislative power vested in a territorial collectivity.

However, the draft law of the statute of autonomy of Corsica has made it possible for the local assembly to 'adapt' the general state legislation to local needs. It means that a kind of legislative power is given to the region of Corsica. This is very usual in the case of federal and regional states, but it is exceptional in the case of France.

Anyway, the question of Corsica has shown that times were ripe for a political proposal which allowed a deeper level of regionalism: it must not be perceived with surprise that the most peculiar and innovative features of the new reform issued by the constitutional revision of March 2003 are very similar to those of the draft statute of Corsica which were declared non constitutional by the judgment of the *Conseil Constitutionnel* of 17 January 2003. The clear example is exactly the 'power of adaptation', or the 'experimental derogation power' that the powers of the territorial collectivities may use, according to Art. 72 of the constitution.

A surprise, on the contrary, was caused by the result of the referendum held in Corsica on 6 July 2003: with a tiny majority of around 1000 votes, corresponding to 50.8 per cent of the vote, the 'no' to the statute won.[57] The result was a deep disappointment for prime minister Raffarin and the minister of interiors Sarkozy, who had invested a lot of effort and expectations in this reform. The results show that the 'nos' had been numerous in the two towns, Ajaccio and Bastia, where many people who are not native Corsicans live. But also some Corsican nationalists may have found some ambiguity in the reform, or perhaps they considered it a little too ambitious.

This result may lead to a dangerous radicalization of the struggle for autonomy of Corsican nationalists, but from a more juridical point of view it is more relevant to read this result in the light of the general reform of 2003. If Corsica, which had to be the '*chef de file*' of the regionalization project, does not want to exploit this possibility, what will the other, 'less identitarian' regions do?

The constitutional revision of March 2003

The revision which took place on 29 March 2003 on decentralization has already been analysed, mainly in the light of the unexpected defeat of the referendum for Corsican autonomy.[58]

The most important changes reside in Articles 1 and 72 of the constitution.

According to Art. 1, which lists some principles which all the public powers must follow – the indivisibility, the secular and social character and the principle of equality – France is now a country whose organization is decentralized.

The new Article 72 is redacted as follows (first section):

> The territorial units of the republic shall be the communes, the departments, the regions, the special-status areas and the overseas territories to which article 74 applies. Any other territorial unit shall be established by statute, in appropriate cases in place of one or more units provided for by this paragraph.
>
> Territorial units may take decisions in all matters that are within powers that can best be exercised at their level. In the manner provided by statute, these units shall be self-governing through elected councils and have power to make regulations.
>
> In the manner provided by institutional act, where the essential conditions for the exercise of public liberties or of a right secured by the constitution are not affected, territorial units or associations thereof may, where provision is made by statute or regulation, as the case may be, derogate on an experimental basis for limited purposes and duration from provisions laid down by statute or regulation governing the exercise of their powers.
>
> No territorial unit may exercise authority over another. However, where the exercise of a power requires the combined action of several territorial units, one of those units or one of their associations may be authorized by statute to organize their joint action. In the territorial units of the republic, the state representative, representing each of the members of the government, shall be responsible for national interests, administrative supervision and the observance of the law.[59]

The significance of this article will be specified by organic and ordinary laws. It is too soon to predict what the outcomes will be; nevertheless it appears that the French constitution has designed an articulated system which presumably will function in an asymmetric way. Some provisions of Art. 72 ('*ont vocation*', '*selon le cas*') may sound indefinite, and experience has shown that usually, in these cases, the primacy falls on the state level, which has more refined tools to grant its power.

In fact parliament then enacted an organic law in the summer of 2003, about 'experimentation by the territorial entities'. This law, which allows the regions and the other territorial entities to carry out experiments in order to adapt the national normative to local needs, has been declared legitimate by the constitutional council through its judgment 2002–478 of 30 July 2003.[60]

Conclusion

One common feature of the regional and devolution trend in France and in the United Kingdom seems to be a certain 'vagueness'. This feature has also been reproached by some authors on another relevant regional reform, that enacted in Italy with the constitutional reform.[61]

But, at least for Scottish and Welsh devolution, which can already be judged after some years of functioning, this constitutional vagueness must not be confused with the sense of pragmatism. The process of Scottish devolution – it is always important to underline that it is a process, by its nature long and not regular in its path – has been since the beginning marked by the need for consensus, reached by friendly negotiations between London and Edinburgh. This agreement seems to be much easier to reach when the majorities in the two assemblies belong to the same party (in the present case labour). Experience will show if this consensus among the British and the Scottish institutions will be the same when the ruling parties are different and (which is the same thing) the majorities in the assemblies are not the same.[62]

Time will tell us how the regional reform in France is applied. It is impossible to make realistic prophecies about its future evolution, especially in the light of the British experience. Who could foresee in 1998 that the Scottish parliament would not have exploited to the full its autonomous legislative power and on the contrary would have developed, under the auspices of the Sewel Commission, a special form of 'agreed Westminster legislation on devolved (or related to devolved) matters'? What we may be rather sure to foresee is that in France the *Conseil Constitutionnel* and the *Conseil d'Etat* will play a decisive role in clarifying some of the provisions that the new constitutional text contains. Expressions such as '*ont vocation de*' ('they are called to') and also the complex provisions on derogatory power need to be interpreted.

What seems certain is that the process of regionalization in France and the process of devolution (and also regionalization, if we want to keep the two phenomena separated) in the United Kingdom are strongly linked to the process of European integration. Is this what forces states to create or to foster an effective regional level? Not necessarily. Some European states are still reluctant to create a strong regional level (Sweden, Greece and most of the new members). What is sure is that the European integration process helps states to apply the principle of subsidiarity, so, when a state has a strong regional level, it is sufficient to use another stake of territorial power; those which prevail will be determined case by case, according to the internal division of competences between Europe, the state and the regional (or even municipal or other) level, and following, if possible, a very flexible technique.

Reversing the concept, it is possible to state that the existence of a strong regional level makes participation at the European level easier. The public institutions, especially those of the central state, are already 'trained' in the loss of power in exercising their policy. From the point of view also of the perception of public opinion, this loss of sovereignty vis-à-vis Europe is a tragedy if this sovereignty is already eroded from the bottom; that is to say, from the regions.

The trend for stronger regionalization is common throughout Europe: we can quote as recent examples the reform of the Italian constitution of October 2001,[63] and outside the European Union the regional reform of Croatia of 2000. Countries such as Germany, Austria, Belgium and Spain already have settled integrated systems with a strong emphasis on the regional element, with all their differences and the obstacles that decentralization must face.

Nevertheless, in some cases this regionalization faces many difficulties in finding an effective outcome: this is the case in Italy, where the regions are still, in the middle of 2003, after almost two years from the constitutional revision, writing their statutes of autonomy. The reality shows that we usually find a strong and effective self-government of the sub-national *niveau* in places where the sense of regional, or even national, identity is strong: this is the case in Catalonia and the Basque Country, which had nevertheless a domino effect on the other *comunidades autónomas* in Spain; this is the case of Trentino–Alto Adige/*Südtirol*; this is the case in Scotland, which we have seen has developed an interesting system of strong and peculiar 'shared self-government' with the central state.

But this statement could be contradicted in the future if the French regions with a low degree of historical identity take the chance offered by the constitutional reform to enhance their self-government. This chance was refused by the electors of Corsica on 6 July 2003: if Bourgogne or Provence-Côte d'Azur, to quote two regions with a medium or low sense of identity, decide on the contrary to exploit the 'power of administrative and legislative derogation' deriving from Art. 72 of the constitution, this will mean that a regional strong self-government will not only be linked to a historical feeling, but also to a functional perspective. Nor will it mean that those regions have become strongly 'identitarian', at least from the historical and cultural point of view. It has taken centuries to create a Scottish or Catalan identity. Anyway, it is possible to forge an institutional sense of identity detached from the identitarian one, even if undoubtedly the sharing some of common values and feelings, which is a *condicio sine qua non* to make a political community function, is easier in places such as Scotland and Catalonia than in Devon or Provence-Côte d'Azur. The consequence of what has been said would be a confirmation that the work of the comparative lawyer needs to stress all the differences that contemporary legal systems know and the difficulty of labelling various phenomena.

The role of the central parliaments will also have to change in the UK and France. This is already happening in Westminster, although less than was expected, due to the cooperation procedures between Edinburgh and London that have been so far developed. But if the future is to present a totally devolved and regionalized United Kingdom, then it will be natural for Westminster to intertwine not only with a few devolved administrations, but with a dozen. And the house of lords too, which was reformed in 1999, could be composed taking into consideration the regional and devolved units.

A decisive role will be played by both the courts of France and the United Kingdom in determining the evolution of regionalism. In complex systems the task of clarifying the meaning of the norms enacted at the various territorial levels is left more and more to the constitutional courts. The French *Constitutional Council* and even more the judicial committee of the privy council are very atypical constitutional judges. This nature may give innovative solutions which will add new features to the already interesting and peculiar French and British regional systems.

Notes

1 W. Bagehot, *The English Constitution*, 1st edn (Oxford: Oxford University Press, 1867), re-edited 1928, chapter 1.
2 The classic essay is R. Carrè de Malberg, *La Loi, expression de la volonté générale* (Paris: Economica, 1984), last printing.
3 P. Pernthaler, 'The English roots of European and global Constitutionalism' (Bari: paper presented at the International Meeting the 29 and 30 May 2003, *La Costituzione britannica/The British Constitution*), stresses 'the English roots at the onset of a *European Constitution* in both its pillars, namely the European Union and the European Convention of Human Rights'.
4 Another French institution which has been imitated is the semi-presidential system, especially in the countries of Central and Eastern Europe after 1989: but Sergio Ortino warns about the usefulness of the notion of 'semi-presidentialism': S. Ortino, *Diritto costituzionale comparato* (Bologna: Il Mulino, 1994), pp. 332–3.
5 A. Torre, 'On devolution. Evoluzioni e attuali sviluppi delle forme di autogoverno nell'ordinamento costituzionale britannico', *Le Regioni*, 2000/2 (2000), 207–19.
6 A. V. Dicey, *Thoughts on the Union Between England and Scotland* (London: Macmillan and Co., 1920; reprinted Westford, CT: Greenwood Press, 1971), p. 5.
7 For the question of Northern Ireland I suggest a book which has recently been published: *Peace Process through Constitutional Arrangements in Northern Ireland*, 44 (EURAC Bolzano/Bozen: Arbeitshefte/Quaderni, 2003), with essays by A. Alcock, T. Hadden, E. Craig and J. Cushnahan, and with an introduction by G. Poggeschi.
8 V. Bogdanor, *Devolution in the United Kingdom* (Oxford: Oxford Paperbacks, 1999), p. 2. The statement is far from being a critique of the definition of Bogdanor, which does not take into consideration the identity issue: in fact the quoted book has been written from a very complete analysis of nationalism in Scotland, Wales and Northern Ireland.
9 This idea of regions, thought of as poles for an economic and human development, has been developed by the historian and urban planner L. Mumford, *The Culture of Cities* (New York: Hartford, Brace and Co., 1938).
10 The Italian journal *Le Regioni*, 2000/2, has devoted to British devolution the two most complete essays so far published in the Italian language: Torre, 'On devolution'; and P. Leyland, 'L'esperimento della devolution nel Regno Unito: uno sconvolgimento dell'assetto costituzionale?' According to Bogdanor, *Devolution in the United Kingdom*, p. 1, 'devolution is the most radical constitutional change this country has seen since the Great Reform Act of 1832'.
11 F. N. Forman, *Constitutional Change in the United Kingdom* (London/New York: The Constitution Unit, 2002), p. 34.
12 A radical restructuring of the local political and administrative bodies was carried out but it should be remembered that the demands of direct democracy were often sacrificed

for the sake of efficiency. See C. Bonomi, 'L'evoluzione politico-legislativa della riforma del governo locale in Gran Bretagna – dal Redcliff–Maud report al Local Government Act 1972 ed alla ristrutturazione del National Health Service' [The Legislative and Political Development of the Reform of Local Government in Great Britain: From the Redcliff–Maud Report to the Local Government Act of 1972 and the Restructuring of the National Health Service], *Rivista trimestrale di diritto pubblico*, 2 (1975), p. 729.

13 J. D. Stewart, 'The local government approach to devolution', *The Political Quarterly* (1977), 440.

14 A. Smith, *The Ethnic Revival* (New York and Cambridge: Cambridge University Press, 1981); focused on the three more important 'nations without a state' in the Western world is M. Keating, *Nations against the State: The New Politics of Nationalism in Quebec, Catalonia and Scotland* (Basingstoke: Palgrave, 2001).

15 For Spain, see chapter 10 of this book and also, among the huge literature, E. Aja, J. Tornos, T. Font, J. M. Perulles and E. Albertí, *El sistéma jurídico de las Comunidades Autónomas* (Madrid: Tecnos, 1985); J. J. Solozábal Echevarría, *Las bases constitucionales del Estado autonómico* (Madrid: McGraw Hill, 1998).

16 On this issue see C. J. Friedrich, *The Impact of American Constitutionalism Abroad* (Boston: Boston University Press, 1966).

17 'If and until when United Kingdom judges do not feel obliged to apply Acts of Parliament resolutely opposing and manifestly contrasted with Community law'; Ortino, *Diritto costituzionale comparato*, p. 162.

18 See N. MacCormick, 'The English constitution, the British state, and the Scottish anomaly', *Scottish Affairs. Special Issue. Understanding Constitutional Change* (1998). In Italian and in German see G. Poggeschi, 'La devolution in Scozia', *Le istituzioni del federalismo*, 5 (1998), 937–60; R. Grote, 'Regionalautonomie für Schottland and Wales – das Vereinigte Königreich auf dem Weg zu einem föderalen Staat', *Zeitschrift für ausländisches öffentliches Recht und Völkerrecht*, 58/1 (1998), 109–46.

19 The programme of the Tories concerning Scotland can be seen in the White Paper *Scotland in the Union – A Partnership for Good*, of 1993, and in J. Major, *Scotland in the United Kingdom* (London, 1992).

20 L. Paterson, *The Autonomy of Modern Scotland* (Edinburgh: Edinburgh University Press, 1994), p. 176.

21 Forman, *Constitutional Change*, p. 88.

22 C. Pattie, D. Denver, J. Mitchell and H. Bockel, 'The 1997 Scottish referendum: an analysis of the results', *Scottish Affairs*, 22 (1998).

23 For instance, in Scotland the government before the elections of May 2003 was a coalition of labour and liberal democrats. Labour had 14 ministers, including the prime minister, Jack McConnell, and the liberal democrats 4: see J. Mitchell and the Scottish Monitoring Team, *Third Year, Third First Minister*, in R. Hazell (ed.), *The State of the Nations 2003. The Third Year of Devolution in the United Kingdom* (Exeter: Imprint Academic, 2002), pp. 119–39.

24 Forman, *Constitutional Change*, p. 89.

25 Leyland, 'L'esperimento della devolution nel Regno Unito', pp. 353–4.

26 T. Groppi, 'Conflitti devolutivi: nuovi percorsi per il judicial review of legislation?' (Bari: paper presented at the International Meeting held the 29 and 30 May 2003, *La Costituzione britannica/The British Constitution*), p. 3.

27 The entire text can be found at www.scotland.gov.uk/library2/memorandum/: accessed 16 December 2003.

28 See chapter 8 of this book; among the huge literature see U. Männle, *Föderalismus zwischen Konsens und Konkurrenz* (Baden-Baden: Nomos, 1998).

29 Groppi, 'Conflitti devolutivi', p. 6.

30 A very detailed analysis of traditional constitutional conventions, among which the

Sewel convention could hardly find a place, is in A. V. Dicey, *Introduction to the Study of the Law of the Constitution*, chapters XIV and XV, 8th edn (London: Macmillan, 1915). There is also an excellent recent translation of this book in Italian, made by A. Torre (who has also written the introduction to the book): *Introduzione allo studio del diritto costituzionale* (Bologna: Il Mulino, 2003).

31 Other ways to reach the consent among the devolved administrations and London are the *Joint Ministerial Committees* and the *Concordats*: about this procedure see A. Trench, 'Intergovernmental relations: officialdom still in control?', in Hazell (ed.), *The State of the Nations 2003*, pp. 145–8.

32 P. Craig, *Administrative Law*, 4th edn (London: Sweet & Maxwell, 1999), p. 203.

33 Leyland, 'L'esperimento della devolution nel Regno Unito', pp. 370–5.

34 Another factor of maintenance of the primacy over Scotland from the centre is the role of the *Secretary of State for Scotland*: see M. Mistò, 'I problemi di rappresentanza politica e responsabilità politica connessi al ruolo costituzionale dei Secretaries of State territoriali: alcune osservazioni concernenti il caso scozzese' (Bari: paper presented at the International Meeting held the 29 and 30 May 2003, *La Costituzione britannica/The British Constitution*).

35 For a more detailed comment on this issue, see R. Simeon, 'Free personal care: policy divergence and social citizenship', in Hazell (ed.), *The State of the Nations 2003*, pp. 215–35.

36 R. Hazell, 'Introduction', in Hazell (ed.), *The State of the Nations 2003*, pp. 3–5.

37 A very complete set of essays is collected in *Regional Studies* (the Journal of the Regional Studies Association), in the special issue *Devolution and the English Question*, 36:7 (October 2002).

38 Groppi, 'Conflitti devolutivi', p. 3.

39 A. Viola, *La notion de République dans la jurisprudence du Conseil Constitutionnel* (Paris: LGDJ, 2002), pp. 117–18, states that through the interpretation of the constitutional council the notions linked to the idea of Republic has been juridicized, and thus have lost some of the symbolic value they carried when the legal consequences were not so clear.

40 D. Rousseau, *Droit du contentieux constitutionnel*, 6th edn (Paris: Montchrestien, 2001), pp. 235, 321 ff. (mainly about Corsica). On regionalism in France, see also Y. Meny, *Dix ans de régionalisation en France* (Paris: Cujas, 1983).

41 G. Carcassonne, *La Constitution*, 5th edn (Paris: Seuil, 2002), p. 40.

42 Y. Plasseraud, *Les minorités* (Paris: Montchrestien, 1998), p. 90, reminds us that the definition of the nation of Diderot and Alambert is one of a 'population of one State, regardless of its characteristics and feelings'.

43 The text of this reform can be found in J. Godechot (ed.), *Les Constitutions de la France depuis 1789* (Paris: Flammarion, 1995), pp. 457–90.

44 L. Favoreu, 'Décentralisation et Constitution', *Revue du droit public et de la science politique en France et à l'étranger*, 4 (1982), 1263.

45 C. Chabrot, 'L'organizzazione territoriale', in D. Rousseau (ed.), *L'ordinamento costituzionale della Quinta Repubblica francese* (Torino: Giappichelli, 2000), p. 354.

46 A. Mabileau, *Le Système local en France* (Paris: Montchrestien, 1994), p. 64.

47 Favoreu, 'Décentralisation et Constitution', p. 1277.

48 If there is such a fear, it is then understandable that the constitution contains clauses which explicitly forbid the dissolution of the country, like Article 2 of the Spanish constitution.

49 French literature puts Spain between the unitarian and the regional state, because the autonomous communities are entitled to normative power but not to constituent power. This distinction nevertheless does not seem too relevant. The more decisive one is between unitarian states and federative states: Ortino, *Diritto costituzionale comparato*.

50 Favoreu, 'Décentralisation et Constitution', p. 1261, uses the image of the wagon.

51 *Ibid.*, pp. 1267–8.

52 Ortino, *Diritto costituzionale comparato*, p. 322. The rank of regulation is considered by some authors the main one, at least from the practical point of view, and the legislative competence works just as an exception: C. Leclercq, *Droit constitutionnel et institutions politiques* (Paris: Litec, 1999), pp. 526–7.

53 Ortino, *Diritto costituzionale comparato*, p. 322.

54 D. G. Lavroff, *Le Droit constitutionnel de la Ve République* (Paris: Dalloz, 1999), p. 228.

55 L. Favoreu and L. Philip, *Les Grandes Décisions du Conseil constitutionnel*, 11th edn (Paris: Dalloz, 2001), p. 764.

56 A. Viola, 'Le Conseil constitutionnel et la langue corse', *Revue française de droit administrative*, 3 (2002), 474–8.

57 'Corse: un petit non et une grande claque', *Libération* (7 July 2003).

58 'Décentralisation: le grand projet vire au grand flop', *Libération* (8 July 2003).

59 The translation in English is taken from www.assemblee-nat.fr/english/8ab.asp, accessed 16 December 2003.

60 J.-M. Pontier, 'La loi organique relative à l'expérimentation par les collectivités territoriales', *Actualité juridique droit administratif*, 32 (2003), 1715–23.

61 A. Ruggeri, *'Itinerari' di una ricerca sul sistema delle fonti*, 1 (Torino: Giappichelli, 2003), pp. 1–35.

62 It may be interesting to quote some data about Spain, which has chosen regionalism using a totally different approach, based on the maximal exploitation of the autonomous legislative power: from the beginning of the 1980s to 22 February 2000, 3,158 laws of the autonomous communities have been enacted! The data are found in R. Jiménez Asensio, *La ley autonómica en el sistema constitucional de fuentes de derecho* (Madrid: Marcial Pons, 2001), p. 22, note 3.

63 See chapter 9 of this book.

GABRIEL N. TOGGENBURG AND ORSOLYA FARKAS*

12

Some first reflections on the 'treaty establishing a constitution for Europe'

Introduction

The European Union now faces one of its most intense periods of change: with the eastern enlargement in 2004 the number of its members increased to twenty-five and the intergovernmental conference (IGC) could provide Europe with a new constitution. Although the final version of the constitution largely depends on the outcome of the political negotiations at the IGC started on 4 October 2003, major future changes can already be described on the basis of the draft 'treaty establishing a constitution for Europe' as elaborated by the European Convention.[1]

The treaty is supposed to consist of four parts. Part I holds no denomination and is subdivided into nine titles, which more or less contain the substantive structure and principles of the Union ('Definition and objectives of the Union'; 'Fundamental rights and citizenship of the Union'; 'Union competences'; 'The Union's institutions'; 'Exercise of Union competence'; 'The democratic life of the Union'; 'The Union's finances'; 'The Union and its immediate environment' and 'Union membership') consisting of Articles I-1 to I-59. Part II has as its title 'The charter of fundamental rights of the Union' and incorporates the charter as adopted by the European council in Nice at the end of 2000 and consists of Articles II-1 to II-54. Part III contains 'The policies and functioning of the Union' and consists of Articles III-1 to III-342, whereas Part IV contains the 'General provisions governing the interpretation and application of the charter' consisting of Articles IV-1 to IV-10. If not otherwise indicated, we refer in the following to the draft constitutional treaty when quoting articles.

Five protocols have been attached to the treaty: the first on the 'role of national parliaments in the European Union'; the second on the 'application of the principles of subsidiarity and proportionality'; the third on the 'representation of citizens in the European parliament and the weighting of votes in the

European council and the council of ministers'; the fourth addresses the 'Euro Group'; and the last one focuses on the amendment of the treaty establishing the European atomic energy community.

This chapter will touch numerous topics, albeit not in detail, such as the institutional design, the division of competences between European and national levels, the issue of the convention method as a constitution-making process and that of membership. All these issues will be recalled with the aim of speculating whether the forthcoming amendments will bring about qualitative changes in the European integration process.

The activity of the convention has been accompanied by high scientific interest and the main expectations regard the elaboration of a constitutional treaty with which European citizens can identify themselves and which limit the complexity of the existing treaties by answering the issues raised in the Laeken declaration.[2] Two-thirds of citizens in the enlarged EU support the idea of a European constitution, but overall awareness of the questions involved remains very low.[3] To better understand the need for a stable constitutional framework for the European integration process it is worthwhile recalling the chronology of the treaty modifications.[4] In the 1950s three European organizations were established with the aim of economic integration: the European coal and steel community (ECSC, 1951),[5] the European economic community (EEC, 1957) and the European atomic energy community (EURATOM, 1957). The three communities had partly distinct institutional set-ups and it seemed to be reasonable to simplify the institutional structure: besides the court and the parliamentary assembly which were already unique, the Merger treaty (1965) provided for a single commission and a single council for the three communities. The merger meant only institutional unification; the competences remained separate for each of the three communities. The first modification of the EEC treaty occurred in 1986 with the Single European Act.[6] Most of the amendments served the completion of the internal market: the removal of the remaining technical, fiscal and administrative obstacles on the common market; the increased possibility of qualified majority voting in the council – instead of unanimity – for the adoption of measures necessary for the functioning of the internal market; and the introduction of a new policy concerning the economic and social cohesion in order to redistribute the costs and benefits of a more intensive economic integration process.

The Maastricht treaty in 1992 established the European Union based on three pillars: the community pillar including the ECSC, EURATOM and the EEC which changed its denomination to European community (EC); the common foreign and security policy pillar, and the justice and home affairs pillar. The last two pillars function on an intergovernmental basis. The provisions of the community pillar were amended and supplemented in particular due to the achievement of economic and monetary Union (EMU). Among others, the principle of subsidiarity and that of proportionality were introduced into the treaty, indicating the need for a better control of the exercise of the European decision-making power vis-à-vis the member states' competences. The Maastricht treaty itself foresaw an intergovernmental conference with the task of strengthening the political union and preparing the Union for the eastern enlargement, which at that time was not precisely scheduled regarding the date or number of the acceding countries. The Amsterdam treaty was signed in 1997 and entered into force in 1999, but it did not manage to fulfil its task of preparing the Union for the forthcoming enlargement, although it introduced some not negligible amendments such as respect for the principles of liberty, democracy, human rights and fundamental freedoms and the rule of law (Art. 6 TEU); the possibility of imposing sanctions by the council in case of a serious and persistent breach by a member state (Art. 7 TEU); the new title on employment; and closer cooperation, making possible two-speed integration. In addition to the substantial changes the Amsterdam treaty re-numbered the articles of the treaty on European union and the treaty establishing the European community (TEC) and edited a consolidated version. Since the Amsterdam treaty failed to address the issue of the institutional reforms, a new IGC was convened to propose a solution to the so-called 'left-overs' of the previous IGCs (i.e. mainly the composition of the commission, the vote-weighting in the council and the expansion of qualified voting in the council). The Nice treaty, which entered into force on 1 February 2003, makes technically possible the functioning of a Union of twenty-five member states, but its solutions are far from satisfactory. Suffice it to say that the discussion among the heads of state and government at the Nice European council in December 2000 was so intensive that the final text was signed only in February 2001. As an illustration of the lack of popular support for the Nice treaty the first Irish referendum can be mentioned which failed to ratify the treaty.[7] Consequently, the issues raised at the Laeken European council at the end of 2001 and the call for a convention on the future of Europe, and successively for a new IGC, were quite reasonable.[8]

As this short historical overview shows, the EEC treaty was first modified after nearly thirty years, whereas between 1990 and 1999 three modifications were made. The amendments brought about important changes in the structure of the community pillar: its decision-making and institutional system have been adjusted from time to time, doing the least possible in order to adapt the community to an increasing number of member states and keep it functioning. Under this aspect the simultaneous occurrence of constitution-making and enlargement can produce effects of mutual reinforcement: the accession of ten new countries requires a qualitatively new institutional and decision-making system.

Institutional design

The proposals set out in the draft constitution regarding the institutional arrangements are not revolutionary, but they take the first steps towards a substantial institutional reform. The provisions laid down in the text are the fruits of compromises; in some cases future conflict scenarios are easily recognizable, in others further reforms and institutional developments are predictable. In the following pages some of the most important innovations will be recalled in particular with regard to the political institutions.

First of all, the institutional framework has become more simple. The entire European Union, the so-called 'three pillars' set up by the Maastricht treaty, has been unified. Consequently, the draft constitution puts an end to the division between the European council and the institutions of the European community (Art. 4. TEU and Art. 7 TEC). According to the draft, the institutions of the European Union are now listed together and comprise the European parliament, the European council, the council of ministers, the European commission and the court of justice (Art. I-18 (2)). In addition the European central bank was for the first time included in the list. In the final version, however, the present distinction in the European community between the European institutions, on one side (Art. 7 TEC) and the European central bank, on the other side (Art. 8 TEC), was confirmed.[9]

The European council maintains its fundamental functions of stimulating the development of the Union, by defining its general political directions and priorities. Formally its composition slightly changes. Beside the heads of state, governments of the member states and the president of the commission, it shall consist also of a president directly elected by the European council itself, by qualified majority, for a term of two and a half years, renewable once. The establishment of the position of the president of the European council, incompatible with national mandate (Art. I-21), represents one of the biggest innovations – very much discussed during the work of the convention.

Furthermore, a new 'union minister for foreign affairs' (Art. I-27), also elected by the European council with the same majority and the agreement of the president of the commission, 'shall take part' in the works of the European council (Art. I-20 (2)). As the draft of the constitution explicitly establishes that within the European council, its president and the president of the commission do not vote (Art. I-24 (2)), and as the expression 'shall take part' referred to the new union minister for foreign affairs and seems to exclude his or her right to vote in this body, the intergovernmental character of the European council's composition has not been modified. According to Art. I-20 (4) decisions in the European council continue to be taken by 'consensus', 'except where the constitution provides otherwise'.

Because of the establishment of the new union minister for foreign affairs, national ministers for foreign affairs do not assist regularly the European council meetings as happens now; albeit the draft constitution sets out that national ministers may assist the members of the European council. The text confirms what has been a practice so far: the European council meets quarterly. The union minister for foreign affairs is the result of a merger between the external relations commissioner and the high representative for the common foreign and security policy, which role is now exercised by the secretary-general of the council. The tasks of the union minister for foreign affairs, as described in the text of the draft constitution (Art. I-27), can raise some elements of conflict with other organs competent for foreign affairs. In particular, the tasks of the union minister for foreign affairs carry a possible conflict between this organ and the president of the European council. In fact, the president, among his other tasks, ensures the external representation of the Union on issues concerning its common foreign and security policy. Although the text itself underlines the respect for the responsibilities of the union minister for foreign affairs, it remains difficult to imagine how the two activities can be carried out without overlaps and, consequently, conflicts. The union minister for foreign affaires is also vice-president of the commission and responsible for handling external relations and for coordinating other aspects of the Union's external actions, and he shall conduct the Union's common foreign and security policy.

The amendments regarding the council of ministers bear signs of simplification. The Seville European council on 21–22 June 2002 had already diminished the council configurations to nine from the previous fifteen;[10] the draft constitution mentions only three configurations: legislative, general affairs and foreign affairs councils, adding that the European council can establish further formations in which the council of ministers may meet (Art. I-23 (3)). The rotating presidency of each formation, with the exception of the foreign affairs' formation, is expanded to at least one year instead of the present six month system, which will probably increase the programmability of the council's work.

As a general rule, the council decides by qualified majority, which majority shall consist of the majority of the member states representing at least three-fifths of the population of the Union. Where the council may act on its own initiative without proposal of the commission or of the Union minister for foreign affairs, the majority shall consist of two-thirds of the member states, representing at least three-fifths of the population of the Union. It is mainly up to Part III of the constitution to decide which issues continue to require unanimity in the council; that is, in which cases national interests can be expressed as an ultima ratio by veto. The lower the number of these issues, the more the Union can be described by the characteristics of a federal organization. In any case the abandonment of vote-weighting in the council from 2009 onwards will ease the formulation of coalitions among the member states before a vote takes place in the council, whereas the vote-weighting under the Nice system is highly complex in this respect (Art. I-24). It remains to be seen, however, whether Spain and Poland, which would have to give up their relatively strong position under the Nice system, will succeed in reintroducing the weighing of votes in the council in the course of the IGC.

The draft constitution foresees the possibility to ease the procedures concerning respectively the adoption of legislative measures and the voting system for single decisions in specific areas. The European council may decide that the council of ministers acts according to the ordinary legislative procedure instead of a special one (after consulting the European parliament and informing the

national parliaments), or that it decides by qualified majority instead of unanimity (after informing the national parliaments no less than four months
before any decision is taken on it) (Art. I-24(4)). Such a facilitation presupposes
that all member states agree with the proposed legislation, since the decision in
the European council is taken by unanimity.

The convention had to find a solution to the issue left open by the Nice
treaty concerning the reduction of the members of the commission. According
to the draft constitution the commission shall be composed from 1 November
2009 of a president, a vice-president and thirteen commissioners, selected on a
rotation system, and of other non-voting commissioners coming from those
member states which are not represented in the college. The system of rotation
will be elaborated by the European council and must reflect the demographic
and geographical range of the member states. There must also be strictly equal
treatment among the member states as regard the determination of the sequence
of and the time spent by their nationals as members of the college. The objections to the introduction of 'second class' commissioners which hold no voting
right represent a central issue within the intergovernmental conference. In particular, the smaller states and the commission itself want to stick to the status
quo and guarantee thereby a fully fledged commissioner per each member state.
The European parliament gains slightly more weight in the election of the president of the commission: the European council, deciding by qualified majority,
puts to the European parliament its proposed candidate for the presidency of the
commission. The European parliament elects the candidate by the majority of
its members. For the nomination of the European commissioners, each member
state, determined by the system of rotation, establishes a list of three persons, in
which both genders are represented, whom it considers qualified to be a
European commissioner. It enters into the competence of the elected president
to choose the thirteen European commissioners. Then, the president, the nominated commissioners, the union minister for foreign affairs and the non-voting
commissioners are submitted collectively to a vote of approval by the European
parliament. Compared with the procedure laid down in the Nice treaty, one can
note two main differences: the first is that the candidate for the presidency of the
commission is elected by the European parliament on the proposal of the
European council, whereas the Nice treaty uses the terminology of 'approval';
the second difference regards the nomination of the members of the college:
only the elected president acts, choosing among the persons proposed by the
member states, whereas the Nice treaty previews that the council of ministers
acts by qualified majority by common accord with the nominated president.

The European parliament, according to Art. I-19 of the draft constitution,
jointly with the council, enacts legislation and exercises the budgetary function,
as well as functions of political control and consultation. As indicated above, the
European parliament elects the president of the commission, albeit on the proposal of the European council, which acts by qualified majority. Easily recognizable in these new amendments is the attempt of the draft convention to

introduce the fundamental characteristic of a federal state (created for the first time in modern history by the US constitution of 1787), consisting in the presence of two branches of the legislative body (US senate and house of representatives: EU council of ministers and parliament), as well as the German version of a parliamentary system where the low chamber (GG – Bundestag, EU – parliament) elects the prime minister (GG – Bundeskanzler, EU – president of the commission) on proposal of the head of state (GG – Bundespräsident, EU – European council). Notwithstanding these attempts, it is difficult to imagine that the future functioning of the European institutions will look like that of a traditional federal state.

The competences of the Union

The repartition of power between the Union and its member states determines to what extent the member states limit their own sovereignty, empowering the Union's institutions to act instead of, or, alongside them. As set out in Art. 1 of the draft constitution:

> Reflecting the will of the citizens and states of Europe to build a common future, this constitution establishes the European Union, on which the member states *confer competences* to attain objectives they have in common. The Union shall coordinate the policies by which the member states aim to achieve these objectives, and shall exercise in the community way *the competences they confer* on it.[11]

The common objectives of the Union are set out in Art. I-3, but what is more important from the point of view of the issue at stake is the way in which the Union can exercise the power. According to Art. I-9 it must respect three principles: the principle of conferral (referred to twice in Art. I-1), the principle of subsidiarity and the principle of proportionality. These principles were already laid down in the EC treaty (Art. 5 TEC), but the text of the draft constitution is more elaborated. With regard to the principle of conferral it specifies that the competences not conferred upon the Union remain with the member states. Concerning the principle of subsidiarity, reference is now made not only to the activity of a member state at its central level, but also to the regional and local levels, if, by reason of the scale or effects of the proposed action, the objectives of the intended action can be better achieved. This reference, however, does not mean a modification of the relations within the single member states between the central government and the local bodies. This possibility is determined by the constitutional arrangements of each member state. Regarding both the principle of subsidiarity and that of proportionality, the draft constitution recalls the protocol on the application of the two principles, which is annexed to the constitution.

The draft constitution states that the constitution and law adopted by the Union's institutions in exercising competences conferred on it, shall have primacy over the law of the member states (Art. I-10). This provision has a fundamental importance: it does not constitute a novelty in its content, but in its codification, since it was elaborated by the court of justice throughout its jurisprudence. The European Court of Justice, in interpreting the treaties and community legislation, has created a set of rules and principles which ensures the uniform application of EU law and which activity contributed to a large extent to the development of a European constitutional order. By the codification these concepts became also formally recognized.

The draft constitution defines the categories of competences conferred upon the Union (Art. I-11). It distinguishes between three types of competences: exclusive competence, shared competence and a competence in order to undertake actions of supporting, coordinating or complementing the activities of the member states in specific areas. The IGC will probably modify the list of areas sharing these categories according to the interests of the member states. It is clear that in the case of an exclusive competence only the Union may legislate, but the reference made in the text to the role of the member states in the exercise of competence is useful, inasmuch as the explanation renders more comprehensible and transparent the EU system of competences. In the case of the shared competences it is not very clear where the power of the Union ends and where the power of the member states starts. As a general principle, the draft constitution states that 'The member states shall exercise their competence to the extent that the Union has not exercised, or has decided to cease exercising, its competence' (Art. I-11 (2)). The solution seems to be easier if the Union expressly ceases exercising its competence. Further problems emerge in the case of specific categories of the shared competences. In Art. I-11(3, 4) it is stated that: 'The Union shall have competence *to promote and co-ordinate* the economic and employment policies of the member states; and *to define and implement* a common foreign and security policy, including a *progressive framing* of a common defence policy.'[12] Although specific provisions are provided for each policy field in Part III, the content and interpretation of the above phrasing remain doubtful. One example can be given from the field of employment policies, where the community, according to Art. 125 TEC, together with the member states shall work towards developing a coordinated strategy for employment, as introduced into the treaty at Amsterdam (1997). However, at the centre of this coordination there are common guidelines and the European employment strategy's feature suggests the process is more convergence than co-ordination.[13] A process of convergence presupposes a common core of objectives, priorities and targets to which member states' policies can converge, whereas a mere activity of coordination does not require such a common core. This example leads us to conclude that the interpretation of categories such as promotion, coordination or framing might be uneasy, in particular when the competences of the Union *versus* member states are at stake.

Finally, it is worth highlighting the introduction in this matter of the flexibility clause. Art. I-17(1) states that if action by the Union should prove necessary within the framework of the policies defined in Part III of the draft constitution to attain one of the objectives of the Union, and the draft constitution has not provided the necessary powers, the council, acting unanimously on a proposal from the commission and after obtaining the consent of the European parliament, shall take the appropriate measures. This sort of power is already contemplated by Art. 308 (ex 235) TEC. The novelties are represented by the new competence of the European parliament to consent to the exercise of the power to the council and the paramount area of intervention, no more limited to the common market only, as it is at present, but including all the objectives of the Union.

Reforming the treaty revision procedure

It is well known that what stood and stands at the centre of the discussion on the nature of the European communities and the European Union is the procedure to revise the treaties. This is not something peculiar to the discussion surrounding the process of European integration, but derives from the general conviction that the fact, whether a Union between states is based on a treaty which is revisable by (qualified) majority or – to the contrary – exclusively by unanimity, is decisive for the legal nature underlying that Union.[14] In the latter case one would tend to qualify the union at stake as confederation whereas the former case would indicate that we are confronted with a federation.[15] Some qualified – in the context of the European convention – this at first glance technical detail as the decisive element for differentiating a state from a non-state.[16] Others again see in the requirement of unanimity even the 'essential difference between contract and constitution'.[17]

The Union built and still builds on strict unanimity when it comes to amending the treaties 'on which the Union is founded', providing thereby every single member state with an absolute veto power in moments of 'constitutional change'(Art. 48 TEU).[18] As far as single provisions do not foresee special procedures, any treaty amendment has to be subject to the following procedure: the government of any member state or the commission (but not the parliament) may submit to the council proposals for amendment. If the council (after consulting the European parliament and, 'where appropriate', the commission[19]) delivers a positive opinion, the president of the council shall convene 'a conference of representatives of the governments of the Member States' which has the purpose to determine 'by common accord the amendments to be made'[20] to the treaties. These amendments enter into force only after having been ratified by all the member states in accordance with their respective constitutional requirements – providing thereby the risk of vetoes exercised by sub-national units (in the case of a federal system such as Belgium) or the respective national peoples (in the case of referenda).[21] This current procedure gives strongest evidence of what is meant when speaking of the member states as the 'masters of the treaties'. It is they who entirely dominate the revision procedure. They hold (admittedly, next to the commission[22]) the monopoly to initiate the procedure. At the intergovernmental conference itself the driving momentum lies with the member states alone – the commission and other community institutions functioning in the best case as observing guests. The past decade showed, however, that at least on a *de facto* level the influence of the community institutions as well as overall participation and transparency in the course of the respective IGCs are constantly growing.[23] Nevertheless, the decisions taken in the framework of the IGC have to be ratified by *all* the member states (but *not* by the European parliament).[24] The member states are free to redefine 'their Union' during these moments of constitutional modelling in one or the other direction.[25]

Besides this general revision procedure, which is very rigid, long winded and state-centred, the treaties do know certain elements of flexibility. Some few provisions allow for a certain 'autonomy' of the EU institutions vis-à-vis the general 'masters' of the treaties by granting the council the power to amend certain specific features of the constitutional EU skeleton outside the framework of the cumbersome exercise of convening an IGC. These special amendment procedures have therefore been labelled [26] as '*autonomous*'[27] and '*quasi autonomous*'.[28] In the former case the amendment takes place without the council having to recommend the measure to the member states for adoption in accordance with their respective constitutional requirements (avoiding thereby the risk of vetos and delays at national level). In the latter case (the quasi-autonomous procedure), amendments have to be ratified by all the member states (but even here no intergovernmental conference has to be convoked). However, these special procedures apply only in very rare cases and, moreover, cannot do away with the need to find a consensus between the governments as the council decides by unanimity. Therefore, with every new IGC the need to reform the treaty revision procedure became more and more evident.

The convention method – used for the first time for the elaboration of the charter of fundamental rights in 2000 – was soon labelled as the new 'good' method of constitutional engineering able to defeat the deficiencies of the old 'bad' method, namely the traditional IGC.[29] The quadripolar composition of the convention (build-up by representatives of the national parliaments, the European parliament, representatives of the national governments and the commission), its time schedule (the conventions were both working over a year) and the considerable potential for interaction with civil society provided an until then unknown degree of legitimacy, transparency and efficiency of the EU revision procedure.[30] However, the application of the convention method could not hide the fact that in the end it was the IGC (2000 and 2003/4), and thereby the member states' political consensus, which determined the destiny of the treaty revision. The convention method might reduce the transparency and legitimacy gap of the current treaty revision procedure. But as long as the final decision about even most minor changes in the treaties requires an overall consensus among the European leaders, treaty revision will continue to risk ending in a horse-trading exercise directed versus the lowest common denominator.

In order to circumvent this weakness, at least for those parts of the 'constitution' which might be considered less fundamental in the eyes of the member states, the discussion focused on the idea of so-called 'treaty splitting'.[31] Certain parts of the treaties could be made accessible to an amendment procedure which is not subject to the unanimity requirement. Such a development would put the Union, on the one hand, in line with many other international organizations, such as the United Nations, the World Trade Organisation, the World Health Organization and the International Labour Organization, and even a regional organization such as the council of Europe, which all provide (at least formally) for an amendment of their respective statute by majority decisions. On the other hand, and somehow paradoxically, it is exactly its supranational character which makes it difficult for the Union to apply a modus of treaty revision which would be more supra than international in its character: to give away the veto-power of the member states even in crucial moments of 'constitutional crisis' means for many to push the Union definitely into the form of a proper federal state. However, it is submitted here that the idea of treaty splitting is a valid response to these legal concerns. Providing a possibility to change the constitutional treaty by a (super)qualified majority only in those cases where the provisions at stake are not crucial for the states' identities and the power-sharing (between the states and the Union's institutions) can hardly be seen as a challenge to the current legal identity of the Union. Rather, such a development would be nothing more than a constitutional engineering towards more efficiency which, by the way is already known from the increasing transition from unanimity towards qualified majority voting within the council – a process which also somehow 'split' the treaty in provisions which remain under the regime of unanimity and those whose transferral under the majority-regime appeared politically digestible (admittedly this 'split' is different in nature and of less constitutional relevance as it regulates daily legislative business and not the sensible moments of 'constitutional crisis').[32] Moreover, one can think of many mechanisms which could protect a potentially overruled minority within the council – a fact which should, politically speaking, render the introduction of a super-qualified majority in the course of treaty revision more acceptable.[33] The idea of 'treaty splitting' failed however in the European convention. The commission repeats therefore in its opinion on the IGC 2003 its wish to render the method of revision more flexible in order to avoid '*total paralysis of the Union*'. It proposes that amendments to Part III of the constitution should only require a five-sixths majority of the member states.

The convention remains – with regard to the treaty revision procedure – on traditional grounds.[34] According to the proposal the whole text of the constitution is subject to one single revision procedure. The latter is in principle the same as the existing one and remains dominated by the unanimity requirement. The IGC remains the central forum for any treaty amendment and possibilities for autonomous or quasi-autonomous treaty amendment remain a rare exception.[35] Nevertheless, the draft comes up with three new elements (Art. IV-7). Firstly, the right of initiative to convene an IGC is granted also to the parliament.

Moreover, national parliaments are also peripherally involved in the treaty revision procedure as they shall be informed about any proposal to amend the constitution. Secondly, the European convention becomes a general prae-phase in every treaty revision procedure. A convention is summoned by the European council (simple majority vote) after consulting not only the parliament, but also the commission. However, the European council may decide by simple majority, after obtaining the consent of the European parliament,[36] *not* to summon a convention '*should this not be justified by the extent of the proposed amendments*'. In any case the convention has only the right to adopt '*by consensus a recommendation to the conference of representatives of the governments*'. It remains therefore the usual IGC which determines '*by common accord*' the amendments to be made to the treaty. Just as before, these amendments have to be ratified by the member states and not by the European parliament. Thirdly, the draft treaty provides for a mechanism which is obviously supposed to respond to problems emerging during the process of ratification. If after two years a treaty amending the constitution has not been ratified in one or more member states, then '*the matter shall be referred to the European council*' – if at least four-fifths of the member states have already ratified it. This however cannot be considered to be a solution to such a deadlock. Rather, it raises the question of what the European council is supposed to do with such a failed project of treaty amendment.[37] What seems clear, however, from the text is that if less than four-fifths of the states have ratified the amending treaty, the latter is to be considered a political dub and to be erased from the political scene.

In conclusion, regarding the procedure for future treaties *amending* the EU constitution not much has been gained here in terms of EU efficiency – rather, a big chance has been lost. The discussion on the 'entry into force' of the treaty *establishing* the EU constitution gives a taste of what this omission might mean for the future. As the European council took in Copenhagen in December 2002 the (political) decision to first enlarge the Union and only then deepen it – that is, to take in new member states before signing the new EU constitution – the new treaty will have to be signed after 1 May 2004 by up to twenty-five EU member states.[38] The view to a plethora of potential hurdles in the course of this ratification marathon gave birth to a 'refoundation theory' which tries to get rid of the strict chains of Art. 48 EU (calling for unanimity when amending the current treaties).[39] International law forbids *inter se* modifications of a multilateral treaty if these affect the rights of those parties of the modified agreement which do not sign the new modifying agreement – an effect which indeed would occur in the case of the draft treaty establishing the EU constitution.[40] In order to 'ease the birth' of the 'new' Union some seem tempted to see in the new treaty not an amendment of the existing treaties but an *aliud*. In a first secret then prominent, but never official, document (the so called 'non-paper' Penelope) the Commission proposes an elaborated '*innovative solution*' to this '*thorny problem*'.[41] According to this paper the states are supposed to sign besides the treaty also an agreement on the entry into force of the treaty on the constitution.

This agreement is to enter into force before the constitutional treaty and is supposed to provide overall acceptance between the states about the entry into force of the latter. According to the agreement the constitutional treaty enters into force after three-quarters have made a '*solemn declaration*' which confirms the will to join the Union. The agreement provides that those who do not come up with such a declaration shall leave the Union on the date of entry into force of the new constitutional treaty.[42] However, the problem which the agreement is meant to resolve arises again with regard to that very agreement itself – the need for ratification by all the states.[43]

Interesting in this respect also is the position of Giscard d'Estaing, who warned those states that fail to ratify the new treaty by saying that there will be '*no existing structure for them to cling to*'.[44] Views like this seem to assume that those states which do not sign the new constitutional treaty will be left out of the new common European house without having the possibility to make usage of the old building of the EU. In order to justify such a position one might take recourse to the concept of 'constitutional rupture' as elaborated by Carl Schmitt. According to the latter a constitutional rupture ('*Verfassungsdurchbrechung*') represents a moment evidencing the supremacy of essential *de facto* pressures over mere normativity ('*bloße Normativität*').[45] Indeed, one can think of 2004 as a moment of major constitutional crisis and it seems therefore not absurd to call for a constitutional move compromising the existing rules on treaty revision in order to save the integration process as a whole. But since the idea of an 'EU *Verfassungsdurchbrechung*' is closely linked with an absolute vision of sovereignty, one should be cautious in exporting hastily a concept such as the '*Verfassungsdurchbrechung*' from the national to the supranational context.[46] What, in any case, can be said is that the new constitutional treaty is a reformed version of the old treaties sharing with the latter a common legal genome. It forms no revolutionary *aliud* and any departure from the treaty revision procedure as outlined in Art. 48 EU constitutes therefore a serious legal challenge. From the legal perspective the remove of the twenty-five states from the old EU house to the new EU house presents a picture which diverges from d'Estaing's vision as quoted above.[47] If a 'non-willing' state fails to ratify the new constitutional treaty, it is not its membership in the current EU which is hindered, but the membership of all the 'willing' states in the reformed EU.

Membership of the Union

The issue of membership raises three main questions: what are the conditions for becoming a member state, when and to what degree can the rights linked to EU membership be suspended during membership, and can membership be terminated (either via voluntary withdrawal or expulsion)? The work of the convention did not touch upon the first question, hardly upon the second, but quite significantly on the last.

There has been a long-standing and intensive debate in the literature on the possibilities of terminating membership. The treaty was traditionally silent on this topic. The only indication given was that the treaties were *'concluded for an unlimited period'*.[48] The academic discussion surrounding this issue usually takes recourse to a *rebus sic stantibus* argument and accepts expulsion (exclusively) as a mean of *ultima ratio* in order to react to extreme cases such as the rise of dictatorial regimes within a member state. In general the position in the literature vis-á-vis the legality of a unilateral withdrawal is even more sceptical.[49] The hope that the Amsterdam treaty would clarify these open points by drawing – with the insertion of the suspension mechanism in Art. 7 TEU[50] – *'a clear line'*[51] proved to be premature. Art. 7 EU allows the Union to impose sanctions against a member state which breaches the values listed in Art. 6 par. 1 EU, namely *'the principles of liberty, democracy, respect for human rights and fundamental freedoms, and the rule of law, principles which are common to the Member States'*. The sanctions may consist of the suspension of certain of the rights deriving from the treaty, including voting rights in the council (Art. 7 par. 3 EU). However, when it comes to discussing the possibility of expulsion or unilateral withdrawal, the new suspension mechanism can be used as an argument by both opponents and advocates: those opposing the possibility of withdrawal/expulsion can now invoke the treaty as a monopolizing 'self-contained regime' which foresees an exhaustive list of sanctions. Those upholding the possibility of withdrawal or expulsion can invoke the treaty by stating that these two means are an expression of the same principle which is now enshrined in the suspension mechanism, namely the principle of efficient loyal cooperation aiming at preservation of a smoothly functioning community of values.[52] Nevertheless, the sanction mechanism was hailed as one of the most innovative and prominent outcomes of the 1996 IGC. The mechanism filled a vacuum in the EU legal order, if compared with other international organizations that have long-standing mechanisms for the suspension of membership rights.[53] On the eve of enlargement, it represented an attempt to guarantee future respect for the EU constitutional values (Art. 6 par. 1 EU).[54] After the experience of the so-called 'Austrian crisis',[55] the treaty of Nice added a new paragraph 1 to Art. 7 EU containing a procedural mechanism which operates prior to the 'breach determination' procedure. This new monitoring procedure allows one-third of the member states, the commission or even the parliament to submit to the council a *'reasoned proposal'*, whereupon the council, acting with a majority of four-fifths of its members[56] may determine that there exists *'a clear risk of a serious breach'* by a member state of the Art. 6 (1) TEU principles and, additionally, may *'address appropriate recommendations'* to that state.[57] Moreover, the council *'may call on independent persons to submit within a reasonable time limit a report'* on the situation. This possibility of calling upon independent experts to submit reports on the situation in the member state in question has clearly been inspired by the Austrian crisis.

With regard to this sanction apparatus the convention changed the status quo of Nice in two ways. Regarding the possible reaction of the Union against 'value-threatening' states, the constitutional treaty erases the institution of the *comité des sages* from the text. This might reflect a politically cautious stance vis-à-vis any sort of monitoring position exerted by the EU in the sensitive field of human rights. On the other hand, the constitutional treaty slightly changed the wording regarding the factual preconditions for any EU reaction as the new wording of Art. 2 (the Union's values) is not identical to the former Art. 6 (1) TEU.[58] Art. 2 adds that these values '*are common to the Member States in a society of pluralism, tolerance, justice and non-discrimination*'. This addition seems, however, rather to describe the aforementioned values than to establish new European values such as a compulsory 'pluralistic society'.[59]

More far reaching are the changes proposed by the European convention with regard to the expulsion/withdrawal debate. The convention proposed to regulate *expressis verbis* at least the case of voluntary withdrawal. The proposal states that '*any Member State may decide to withdraw from the European Union in accordance with its own constitutional requirements*'.[60] Such an intention has to be notified to the European council, which '*shall examine that notification*'. The European council will then provide '*guidelines*' which form the basis of an agreement which has to be negotiated and concluded with the Union. This agreement has to set out the arrangements for the withdrawal, '*taking account of the framework for its [the former member state's] future relationship with the Union*'. The agreement is concluded on behalf of the Union by the council, acting by a qualified majority, after obtaining the consent of the European parliament.[61] The constitution shall cease to apply to the state in question from the date of entry into force of the withdrawal agreement or, failing that, two years after the notification referred to above, unless the European council, in agreement with the member state concerned, decides to extend this period.

In conclusion one can say that regarding membership the constitutional treaty provides for an asymmetric solution. It becomes possible for individual states to get rid of the Union without other member states being able to unilaterally veto such a decision. On the other hand, there is no mention of any possibility for a collective (of states) to get rid of single member states. This situation confirms the sovereignty of the member states, which, on the one hand, cannot be forced to share the destiny of the Union and, on the other hand, cannot be expelled from it. However, read against the equally 'sovereignty friendly' provisions on the treaty revision procedure, one might wonder whether the provision on withdrawal is of major importance: such a clause would have been of substantial importance if it had come along with an amended treaty revision procedure putting member states at the risk of being 'constitutionally overruled'. By leaving any treaty revision under the Damocles sword of the veto of every single member state, it is more the question of expulsion which arises and less the question of withdrawal.[62] Expulsion was, however, left to the academic speculations of experts in international law.

Both the discussions, that surrounding treaty revision and that surrounding withdrawal and expulsion from the Union, indicate that the future might

offer hybrid forms of 'non-member memberships' to the Union situated somewhere half the way out of an existing European Union (in the case of withdrawal) or half the way into a newly changed European Union (in the case of
troubled treaty revision). The exact legal position of such hybrid *stati* will have
to be defined by agreements with those respective states which are to 'fade out'
from or to 'fade into' the Union. This experience will not be entirely new to the
Union as there exists already a variety of forms of 'EU affinities' outside strict
membership. The gravitation field of the Union shows states simply applying EU
law for economic convenience,[63] groups of states[64] or single states[65] 'bridging' on
to the Community in order to participate in the internal market and, finally,
'applicant states' sitting in the waiting room for true EU membership holding a
'structured relationship' with parts of the political decision-making machinery
within the Union[66] and participating in the internal market.[67] However, one can
assume that future forms of 'fading out' from EU membership may result in legal
positions which raise more complex questions than those related to the nowadays 'fading in' phenomenon.[68]

This potential of growing 'external asymmetry' in the future has to be seen
in connection with a European Union of twenty-five proper member states,
which will also provide for enhanced 'internal asymmetry'. The fact that the
number of member states is nearly doubled will give life to those Amsterdam-
and Nice-born provisions which established the figure of the so-called 'enhanced
cooperation'. Enhanced cooperation allows the building of subgroups of
member states which foster integration in certain areas – a potential which up to
now has remained a sleeping beauty.[69] According to the proposed constitutional
treaty which simplifies the existing set of provisions,[70] the council – on the basis
of a proposal of the commission[71] – can authorize cooperation between some
member states as a last resort *'when it has been established ... that the objectives of
such cooperation cannot be attained within a reasonable period by the Union as a
whole, and provided that it brings together at least one third of the Member States'*
(Art. I-43 (2)).[72] Whether future EU internal asymmetry and 'enhanced cooperation' between subgroups of states will impinge on the character of the Union is
of course difficult to predict. However, one can say that flexibility and asymmetry can be found in various federal systems and do therefore not *per se* exclude
looking at the European Union as a federal and strong entity.[73] Nor would it be,
legally speaking, convincing to argue that flexibility necessarily pushes the institutional balance within the EU towards a more confederal balance.[74] However,
one has to admit that, politically speaking, excessive flexibility could lead to the
weakening of the Union as a whole.[75] Nevertheless, it is submitted that flexibility
within the Union is a necessary tool which might function as an alternative valve
offering potentially frustrated members an 'integration friendly' alternative to
withdrawal from a system which makes constitutional changes at the overall level
increasingly difficult. In any case a more diverse future will have to place special
weight on the preservation of the necessary degree of unity.[76] The principle of
loyalty will under these new circumstances have to fulfil new tasks.[77] Loyalty

seems the most appropriate legal ground for hosting future parameters when intervening in conflicts of interest between the various 'in' and 'out' groups or between the community interest and subgroups of member states.

Concluding remarks: a change of face or of character?

By being 'sui generis' in nature the European communities became a permanent provocation for those who wanted to find the right label for the EC (and, later, the EU). The latter keeps oscillating between a statal unit and a non-state, a 'Bundesstaat' and a 'Staatenbund'. It is somehow an international organization and at the same time it is not. 'Hybrid' is also the legitimation of this entity which is drawn from both the national (via the council) and the European level (via the elections to the parliament). Wittgenstein rightly noticed that often the 'limits of [our] language mean the limits of [our] world' and, indeed, the fact that the community seemingly existed somewhere in between and beyond established federal paradigms created a degree of uncomfortable insecurity and endless academic discussion.[78] Especially in Germany even the term 'constitution' seemed to many out of the reach of the Union.[79] This overall dogmatic insecurity was augmented by the fact that the Union is not a static but a quickly moving target which – to make things even worse – cycles in order not to fall (to use Walther Hallstein's famous picture) without being equipped with a clear 'finalité politique'. Looking at this 'unidentified integration object' through the glasses of traditional public law reminds us of Werner Heisenberg, who said – looking at something quite different, namely electrons – that '[t]he more precisely the position is determined, the less precisely the momentum is known in this instant, and vice versa'.[80]

At the background of this insecurity the community was labelled, from an integration-friendly perspective, as a sui generis entity, from a more sceptical view, as mostro simile or – in order to find peace with the strange object – as a Verfassungsverbund. However, old headings continued to be used for new contents and there is still a lack in those theoretical academic tools which would allow us to fully grasp the European reality as that which it is: an arising postnational constitutional reality. Using traditional patterns when describing new realities can easily lead to the establishment of paralysing 'constitutional taboos' which are more likely to be politically misused than legally founded.[81] Indeed, it does not seem useful to keep here elaborating which elements qualify the treaty for being a constitution,[82] the community for being a state, or the community system and its member states for being a Bundestaat (or a Staatenbund).

Rather, it seems appropriate to ask whether the new treaty establishing the European constitution will result in a mere change of face or a change of character. As the parliament has put it nicely, the European Union has already now 'a kind of Constitution in the form of the treaties, but that Constitution is piecemeal, nameless, unreadable and invisible'.[83] The new treaty will equip the European Union with an openly declared 'constitution',[84] which is indeed much more 'visible' in many of its aspects than it used to be. This is true when looking at the provisions categorizing the competences or those on the principles of the Union which even spell out the principle of supremacy.[85] The constitution will also become more readable as the pillar structure has – formally at least[86] – disappeared and the treaties are merged into one single text. The 'constitutional chaos' has therefore been reduced.[87] On the other hand, it is obvious that the new constitution is a product of a 'legal recycling process'. In particular, Part III of the constitution lacks a convincing systematic order. The fact that the charter has been incorporated unchanged in Part II of the constitution provides for repetitions and inconsistencies.[88] Moreover, important provisions such as on subsidiarity or on the role of national parliaments have been delegated to protocols and, on the other hand, superfluous provisions or provisions of seemingly minor importance kept as parts of the constitution.[89] Even if the text is improved,[90] it will hardly become a concise and clear-cut constitution. In this sense one might conclude that the convention succeeded in rendering the Union slightly more visible and in slightly reducing the constitutional chaos but failed in drafting a fully fledged and concise 'constitution for the European citizen'.[91]

Other tasks set by the Laeken declaration have, however, been achieved. Most importantly the Union can be said to have become more 'democratic' under the new treaty as the European parliament has been considerably strengthened,[92] and the national parliaments have been equipped with a control function regarding the principle of subsidiarity and the citizen with a right of initiative.[93] Qualified majority voting and co-decision have become the ordinary legislative procedure (however, the commission calls for further areas to be moved into qualified majority voting).[94] From a procedural perspective the Union could become on the basis of the proposed treaty more 'federal' but also more transparent. However, it is difficult to foresee whether the new decision-making modus in the council will survive, since it meets serious resistance in the IGC. The same goes for the overall institutional structure such as the presidency of the council and, especially, the composition of the commission, which might still be the object of major changes in the course of the IGC.[95]

Nevertheless, it seems not too brave to risk the judgment that the Laeken-induced improvements will not substantially impinge on the constitutional dialogue between the Union and its 'integrated' states. It is not without reason that it is less the vertical power game (member states vis-á-vis European level) which stands at the centre of current attention but the two aspects of the horizontal power game (namely, member states versus member states and European commission versus (European) council). The outcome of the intergovernmental conference will show where the balance will be found alongside these lines of horizontal tensions. Regarding the member states' autonomy, it is hard to see this new treaty as an additional threat to sovereignty which would lay the ground for a future 'American *dejavu*'.[96] The proposed constitutional treaty establishes 'united in diversity' as the Union's constitutional 'motto' and lists it among the five 'symbols' of the European Union.[97] This evidences that the pondering process between the dedication to the common European interest and identity on the one hand, and to the (p)reservation of national interest and identities on the other, stands at the core of the European Union. Every step in one direction calls for counterbalancing measures in the other. Whereas confederal elements in the EU system (such as the powers of the council) guarantee the preservation of national interests and identities and assure thereby the legitimacy of the European project among the member states, the federal elements within the EU system (the powers of the parliament and the commission) aim at and guarantee the efficient and impartial fulfilment of the EU's tasks in a hopefully ever more democratic and transparent way. The outcome of the European convention, and especially the provisions on membership and the treaty revision method, confirm the expectation that the Union is to continue its existence as a 'strange dog' rather than being 'big banged' into a federal state such as a sort of United States of Europe.

Notes

*   Farkas is responsible exclusively for the following parts: 'Introduction', 'Institutional design' and 'The competences of the Union'. Toggenburg is responsible exclusively for the following parts: 'Reforming the treaty revision procedure', 'Membership of the Union' and 'Concluding remarks: a change of face or of character?'.

1 CONV 850/03, *Official Journal*, C 169 (18 July 2003), 1–105.

2 In December 2000 the European council raised in the declaration on the future of Europe four major issues, namely the distribution of competences, the status of the charter of fundamental rights, the simplification of the treaties and the role of national parliaments. A year later the Laeken declaration added more than fifty questions, calling for a major brainstorming on the Union's overall future shape and function.

3 Compare the latest (November 2003) Eurobarometer results on this issue: http://europa.eu.int/comm/public_opinion/flash/fl142_2_convention_en.pdf. Only five countries out of twenty-five have more than 50 per cent of respondents who state that they have heard about the convention.

4 The ink had not yet dried on the final draft of the constitution, when Jean-Luc Dehaene, vice-president of the convention challenged before the press Giscard D'Estaing, president of the convention's claim, that the constitution will last for half a century, stating that the text could come up for revision as early as 2006 (*European Voice*, 3–9 July 2003).

5 The ECSC treaty was signed for fifty years. As the ECSC was set up in 1952, it ceased to exist in 2002 and its tasks were overtaken by the EC.

6 Originally two distinct texts were supposed to be elaborated: one modifying the EEC treaty, the other on political cooperation in matters of foreign policy, which started functioning on an intergovernmental basis in 1969. Ultimately the two texts were merged.

7 Needless to recall that also the Maastricht treaty was rejected by the first Danish referendum. In the end the treaty was approved by all the member states (twelve at that time); nonetheless Denmark, together with the United Kingdom and Sweden, made use of the opting out clause established by the treaty, and did not enter into the Eurozone.

8 Already Protocol No. 23 of the Nice treaty indicated the necessity of a new IGC for 2004.

9 On the possibile consequences of the different position of the European central bank

with respect to the other Community institutions, see S. Ortino, 'International and Cross-border Co-operation among Banking Supervisors. The Role of the European Central Bank', *European Business Law Review*, volume 15, 4 (2004).

10 Presidency Conclusions – Seville, Annex II.

11 Emphasis added.

12 Emphasis added.

13 M. Biagi, 'The European Monetary Union and industrial relations', *IJCLLR*, 16 (2000), 43–5.

14 Compare in this context e.g. Art. V of the US constitution.

15 See e.g. S. Ortino, *Introduzione al diritto costituzionale federativo* (Torino: Giappichelli, 1993), p. 273.

16 See D. Grimm, 'Zukunft der EU: Bitte keinen Europäischen Staat durch die Hintertür', *Die Zeit*, 17 (2003), p. 10.

17 See H. Abromeit and T. Hitzel-Cassagnes, 'Constitutional change and contractual revision: principles and procedures', *European Law Journal*, 5:1 (March 1999), 23–44, at p. 31.

18 To be more precise one has to underline that this goes only for those 'constitutional changes' which come into being through formal treaty amendment. One might very well see – from a more substantial perspective – 'constitutional changes' also in developments induced through mere institutional *usus* or through pronounced exercise of judicial powers, such as happens when the court develops common principles of law.

19 If the parliament is not informed the resulting amendments of the revision procedure are to be considered illegal. See W. Meng, 'Art. 48', in H. von der Groeben, J. Thiesing and C.-D. Ehlermann (eds), *Kommentar zum EU-/EG-Vertrag*, Vol. 5 (Baden-Baden: Nomos, 1997), p. 1124.

20 The European central bank shall be consulted in the case of institutional changes in the monetary area (see Art. 49 EU).

21 Such referenda can be imposed by the respective constitution or induced by an ad hoc political decision. The currently discussed constitutional treaty is likely to undergo a national referendum in 2004/2005 in about a third of the twenty-five states at stake. For up to date information see www.european-referendum.org/countries/index.html, 17 December 2003. The positions of the various political players in the various countries regarding a referendum are depicted in A. Maurer and S. Schunz, 'Ratifikation durch Referendum?' (Stiftung Wissenschaft und Politik Berlin, discussion paper, November 2003): www.swp-berlin.org/pdf/brennpunkte/referendumratifikat_mrr_schunz_031103.pdf, 17 December 2003.

22 If the initiative comes from the commission the procedure can be stopped by the council as it is a positive avis of the latter – preceded by the possibility for the parliament and, eventually, the commission to be heard – which forms the compulsory basis of the decision of the presidency (of the council) to convene the IGC.

23 See in detail on the nature of the IGC procedure B. de Witte, 'The closest thing to a constitutional conversation in Europe: the semi-permanent treaty revision process', in P. Beaumont, C. Lyons and N. Walker (eds), *Convergence & Divergence in European Public Law* (Oxford: Hart Publishing, 2002), pp. 39–58.

24 Furthermore, it has been argued that the member states could escape to the usage of a multilateral treaty concluded between the member states outside the prescribed revision procedure. Others have sustained that the treaty could also be changed through customary law. For the arguments used and references to the respective literature see H.-J. Cremer, 'Art. 48 TEU', in C. Calliess and M. Ruffert (eds), *Kommentar zum EU-Vertrag und EG-Vertrag* (Neuwied: Luchterhand Verlag, 1999), pp. 242–6. The court, however, rejected these attempts which would have given even more flexibility to the member states in what regards the revision of the EU system. Quite to the contrary, the court gave

impetus to another, quite opposed, debate, namely whether the member states have to respect certain substantial limits when revising the treaties: in its opinion of 14 December 1991, ECR I-6079, the court *inter alia* replied to the commission's suggestion to change what was then Art. 238 (conclusion of association agreements) in order to make the draft on the EEA compatible with the EC treaty. The fact that the court said that such an amendment would not cure the 'incompatibility with Community Law [namely Art. 164 TEU] which establishes the monopoly of the Court to ensure interpretation of the treaty of the system of Courts to be set up by the agreement', led some authors to maintain that there are implicit limits to the amendment of the founding treaties. See, however, the rather convincing (dismissive) position in this context laid out by Nuino Picarra and J. L. Cruz Vilaca, 'La revision de los tratados europeos', *Revista de Derecho Politico* (1992), 445. An example of such an '*acquis fundamental matériel*' could be the irreversibility of the process of an 'ever closer Union' or 'hyperconstitutional values' such as the free market character of the economies, human rights or the rule of law. However, one is far from any consensus in this respect. The court never further elaborated on this and the literature remains divided on this topic. Compare in this respect e.g. B. de Witte, 'Rules of change in international law: how special is the European Community?', *Netherlands Yearbook of International Law*, 25 (1994), 299–334.

25 Note, however, that the '*dejavu*' clause in Art. 48 (2) TEU contained – seemingly – a sort of limitation: 'A conference of representatives of the governments of the Member States shall be convened in 1996 to examine those provisions of this Treaty for which revision is provided, in accordance with the objectives set out in Articles A and B' (Article A TEU referred to the concept of an 'ever closer Union' and Art. B TEU listed the objectives of the Union).

26 See in this context the study by the European University Institute, 'Reforming the Treaties' amendment procedures', delivered to the European Commission 31 July 2000, http://europa.eu.int/comm/archives/igc2000/offdoc/repoflo_en2.pdf, 17 December 2003.

27 The best known example in the TEC is that the number of commissioners can be changed by the council deciding alone (see Art. 213 par. 2 EC). Similar goes for the organization of the court (see Art. 221 par. 4; 222 par. 3; 245 par. 2; 225 par. 2 EC – the latter provision calls also for a consultation of parliament and the commission). Note that the treaty of Amsterdam introduced two new cases of autonomous revision. Art. 133 EC allows the council, acting on a proposal of the commission, to extend the scope of commercial policy to services and intellectual policy. Art. 67 EC transfers to the council, acting unanimously after consulting parliament, the power to further 'communitarize' the decision-making and judicial procedure in the new title IV of the EC treaty (visa, asylum, immigration) after a period of five years (the so-called 'mini-passerelle' clause).

28 See Art. 22 EC which empowers the council to add rights of Union citizens; Art. 269 EC which empowers the council to amend the system of its own resources; Art. 190 (4) EC empowers the council to establish a common electoral procedure for the elections to parliament. The Amsterdam-born Art. 42 EU provides for the so-called 'grande passerelle', namely the possibility that the council decides that action in areas covered by title VI of the EU treaty (provisions on police and judicial cooperation in criminal matters, the so-called third pillar) falls under title IV of the EC treaty (provisions on visa, asylum, immigration) and determines at the same time the relevant voting rules. This goes also for the Amsterdam-born Art. 17 EU which empowers the European council to convert the common defence policy into a true common defence and to integrate the WEU into the Union.

29 On the convention method see e.g. G. de Burca, 'The drafting of the EU Charter of Fundamental Rights', *European Law Review*, 26 (2001), 214; F. Deloche-Gaudez, 'The

convention on a charter of fundamental rights: a method for the future', *Research and Policy*, paper 15 (2001), Notre Europe; C. Deubner and A. Maurer, 'Ein konstitutioneller Moment für die EU: Der Konvent zur Zukunft Europas' (Stiftung Wissenschaft und Politik Berlin, discussion paper, 2002); L. Hoffmann, 'The Convention on the Future of Europe – thoughts on the convention-model', *Jean Working Monnet Paper*, 11 (2002); G. N. Toggenburg, 'Vertragsänderung im Tandem: Regierungskonferenz und Europäischer Konvent', *European Law Reporter*, 11 (2002), 398–402; C. Closa, 'Improving EU constitutional politics? A preliminary assessment of the convention constitutionalism web-papers', *ConWEB Papers* (http://les1.man.ac.uk/conweb/), 1 (2003).

30 One might though doubt whether the celebrated transparency of the convention does internally really guarantee equal access to deliberation and decision-making. Who really takes decisions under the pressure of a considerable paper-overload remains open only to insiders. One can assume that the presidency played a crucial role in a process which produced in 17 months and nearly 30 plenaries more than 50 contributions by the presidency, and nearly 2000 oral and nearly 400 written contributions by the convention members; not to mention the hundreds of contributions submitted to the 11 working groups. Moreover, the convention was confronted with well over 1000 contributions by NGOs. See for the work of the convention its website which remains for consultation (http://european-convention.eu.int/). NGO contributions can be tracked on the futurum website (http://europa.eu.int/futurum/index_en.htm).

31 See European University Institute, 'Reforming the Treaties' amendment procedures'. The issue became topical especially after the Von Weizsäcker, Dehaene/Simon report of 1999. Note however that even the European council itself raised the question in its Laeken declaration, whether the treaty revision procedure should differentiate between 'the basic treaty and … the other treaty provisions'.

32 When the council, after the Maastricht treaty, was increasingly deciding by qualified majority in crucial areas (esp. the common market), the court was more and more confronted with overruled member states doubting the legality of certain measures of secondary law and asking for their annulment. The introduction of qualified majority in certain competence provisions pushed therefore the court to fulfil a long-neglected role, namely that of a competence court. One could expect that the introduction of treaty splitting regarding the treaty-reforming procedure would also raise new questions of legality and give practical relevance to the academic debate on the above mentioned 'hyper-constitutional' values. See note 24.

33 See in detail European University Institute, 'Reforming the Treaties' amendment procedures'.

34 Not even to speak about mechanisms which would involve the European peoples, such as a popular constitutional initiative or a duty to approve (certain) constitutional changes by a Europe-wide referendum.

35 Note that the feasibility study on a draft constitution which was circulated at the end of 2002 as a 'non-paper' by the Commission (the so-called 'Penelope' study, see http://europa.eu.int/futurum/documents/offtext/const051202_en.pdf, 17 December 2003) proposed in its Art. I-101 to introduce a new sort of autonomous procedure as a general revision procedure by making the European council (i.e. an EU institution) responsible for the adoption (by a qualified majority) of the changes proposed by a convention. This usage of an EU institution rather than the member states themselves has been criticized as undermining the treaty nature of the constitutional treaty. See B. de Witte, 'Entry into force and revision', in B. de Witte (ed.), *Ten reflections on the Constitutional Treaty for Europe* (Florence: Robert Schuman Centre for Advanced Studies, 2003), pp. 207–23, at p. 220.

36 The parliament welcomes this provision as the parliament's future '*de facto* control over the use of this new instrument of constitutional revision'. See parliament report on the

draft treaty establishing a constitution for Europe and the European parliament's opinion on the convening of the intergovernmental conference, A5–0299/2003, 10 September 2003, par. 31.

37 The German version is more 'honest' in this respect as it evidences the resulting insecurity: '*sind ... Schwierigkeiten bei der Ratifikation aufgetreten, so befasst sich der Europäische Rat mit der Frage*'.

38 'The new treaty will be signed after accession', Presidency Conclusions, Copenhagen 12 and 13 December 2002, par. 8. The accession treaty says in its second article that it shall enter into force on 1 May 2004 'provided that all the instruments of ratification have been deposited before that date'. If an accession state fails to ratify, enlargement takes place without it (that is spelled out in Art. 2 par. 2 of the accession treaty which foresees that in this case the council has to provide for the necessary changes in the accession treaty, the act of accession and the annexes), whereas if a member states fails to ratify the accession treaty, enlargement (at least on the basis of the current accession treaty) fails as a whole. The accession treaty itself contains only 3 articles whereas the act of accession amounts to nearly 5000 pages.

39 See de Witte, 'Entry into force and revision', p. 213.

40 Compare Art. 41 of the Vienna convention on the law of treaties ('Agreements to modify multilateral treaties between certain of the parties only'). See de Witte, 'Entry into force and revision', p. 216.

41 The feasibility study (non-paper Penelope) 'does not necessarily represent the views of the European Commission'.

42 Penelope, pages A to D.

43 The Penelope paper 'resolves' this problem by providing for entry into force after at least five-sixths of the states have ratified the agreement (therefore, in the case of twenty-five states signing the agreement, only five states could block the entry into force). The 'overruled' states would then have the possibility to deliver the declaration mentioned above until the entry into force of the constitutional treaty, unless 'it shall be deemed to have decided to leave the Union at that date' (Penelope, Art. 6 par. 2 of the agreement). The Penelope paper admits that this is contrary to Art. 48 EU but upholds that this clause is 'consistent with international law' as the proposed solution requires unanimous agreement 'at the time of signature' (Penelope, p. 12). However, Penelope does not explain why this exchange of revision procedures should not be in need of proper ratification.

44 Quoted in the *Financial Times* (11 November 2002), p. 4.

45 Carl Schmitt says that ruptures ('*Durchbrechungen*') show '*die Überlegenheit des existentiellen über die bloße Normativität*'. See C. Schmitt, *Verfassungslehre and dritte, unveränderte Auflage* (Berlin: Duncker & Humblot, 1928 and 1957), p.107.

46 According to Carl Schmitt the *Verfassungsdurchbrechung* is an expression of highest sovereignty ('*Wer zu solchen Handlungen befugt und imstande ist, handelt souverän*') and goes back to the absolutistic monarchs which were '*legibus solutus*'. See Schmitt, *Verfassungslehre,* p. 107.

47 See in detail de Witte, 'Entry into force and revision', pp. 210–17.

48 Art. 51 EU. Compare, however, Art. 62 of the Vienna convention on the law of the treaties, United Nations, *Treaty Series,* vol. 1155, p. 331 ('fundamental changes of circumstances').

49 See e.g. M. Röttinger, in C. Otto Lenz (ed.), *EG-Vertrag Kommentar,* 2nd edn (Basel: *Helbing & Lichtenhahn,* 1999), p. 2017, who considers even the 'mere volition' to seccede unilaterally as a violation of the EC treaty ('*Willensäußerung wäre selbst schone eine Vertragsverletzung*'). Compare e.g. also T. Stein, 'Der Kreuzzug der Vierzehn gegen Österreich', in K. Adenauer Stiftung (ed.), *Die Europäische Union und Österreich* (working paper 2000), who accepts the recourse to Art. 60 par. 2 lit. a) of the Vienna convention (termination of a multilateral treaty after a material breach by one of the parties)

in the context of expulsion, but rejects a recourse to the *clausula rebus sic stantibus* (Art. 62 of the Vienna convention) in the context of unilateral withdrawal (pp. 24, 25).

50 The sanctions may consist of the suspension of certain of the rights deriving from the treaty, including voting rights in the council (Art. 7 par. 3 EU).

51 J. Bergmann and C. Lenz, *Der Amsterdamer Vertrag* (Köln: Omnia Verlag, 1998), p. 32.

52 See S. Griller, D. Droutsas, G. Falkner, K. Forgó and M. Nentwich, *The Treaty of Amsterdam* (Vienna: Springer Verlag, 2000), p. 183.

53 See particularly Art. 8 of the Statute of the council of Europe. See the survey by M Hofstötter, 'Suspension of rights by international organizations: the European Union, the European Communities and other international organizations', in V. Kronenberger (ed.), *The European Union and the International Legal Order: Discord or Harmony?* (The Hague: Asser Press, 2001), p. 23.

54 However, because of several deficiencies of the mechanism, it was difficult to make an overall positive assessment of the latter. First, the possibility of imposing severe sanctions is not counterbalanced by strict respect for the principle of *audiatur altera pars* and by judicial protection for the member state in question. Secondly, it is evident that the procedural and substantive thresholds within the mechanism are so high that it is difficult to envisage its actual use. It can be seen as an instrument that is better suited for the prevention of human rights breaches than for redressing such breaches. See in detail F. Schorkopf, *Homogenität in der Europäischen Union – Ausgestaltung und Gewährleistung durch Article 6 Abs. 1 und Article 7 EU* (Berlin: Duncker & Humblot, 2000); H. Schmitt von Sydow, 'Liberté, démocratie, droits fondamentaux et Etat de droit: analyse de l'article 7 du traité UE', *Revue du Droit de l'Union Européenne* (2001), p. 285 or A. Hau, *Sanktionen und Vorfeldmaßnahmen zur Absicherung der europäischen Grundwerte* (Baden-Baden: Nomos, 2002).

55 In the Austrian elections of October 1999 the far right Freiheitliche Partei Österreichs (FPÖ), then headed by Jörg Haider, obtained 26.9 per cent of the vote and entered the federal government. The other fourteen EU member states tried to avoid this by imposing sanctions in the name of the presidency of the European Union. Art. 7 EU was not applied but the event raised considerable interest in this new mechanism. See B. de Witte and G. N. Toggenburg, 'Human rights and Membership of the Union', in S. Peers and A. Ward (eds), *The EU Charter of Fundamental Rights. Politics, Law and Policy* (Hart, 2004), pp. 59–82; M. Happold, 'Fourteen against one: the EU Member States' response to Freedom Party participation in the Austrian government', *International and Comparative Law Quarterly*, 49 (2000), 953–63; G. N. Toggenburg, 'La crisi austriaca: delicati equilibrismi sospesi tra molte dimension', *Diritto publico comparato ed europeo* (2001), 732–56; W. Hummer and W. Obwexer, 'Die Wahrung der Verfassungsgrundsätze der EU', *Europäische Zeitschrift für Wirtschaftsrecht* (2000), 485–9 or P. Cramér and P. Wrange, 'The Haider affair, law and European integration', *Europarättslig tidskrift* (2000), 28–59.

56 Instead of the unanimity-minus-one that continues to be required in the later stages of the procedure.

57 See Art. 7 (1) EU as amended by the treaty of Nice, OJ 2001 C 80, 1, at 6. The far-reaching Belgian proposal to permit 'appropriate measures' already in the course of a monitoring procedure was not accepted.

58 Art. 2 of the constitutional treaty contains the value 'equality' (not contained in Art. 6 EU) but not the 'fundamental freedoms' (contained in Art. 6 EU).

59 Otherwise one would have, first, to submit that the Union's perception of 'cultural diversity' is an inclusive one referring not only to diversity between the member states but also to diversity *within* the states and, secondly, to ask what the EU's prescription for a pluralistic society looks like. Compare in this context G. N. Toggenburg, 'Diversity at the background of the European debate on values: an introduction', in F. Palermo and G. N. Toggenburg, *European Constitutional Values and Cultural Diversity* (European Academy,

Bolzano/Bozen: Quaderni/Arbeithefte, 2003), pp. 9–23. Compare on the EU's notion of 'diversity' also B. de Witte, 'The constitutional resources for an EU minority protection policy', in G. N. Toggenburg (ed.), *The Protection of Minorities and the Enlarged European Union* (Budapest/New York: Local Government Institute, forthcoming 2004). ftp://ftp. eurac.edu/publications/european_constitutional_values.pdf, accessed 17 December 2003.

60 See Art. I-59 CONV 850/03.

61 The representative of the withdrawing member state shall not participate in council of ministers or European council discussions or decisions concerning it.

62 It has even been argued that this new provision on withdrawal might open the door to cases of political blackmail. See J. A. Emmanouilidis and C. Giering, 'Licht und Schatten – eine Bilanz der Konventsergebnisse', *Konvent-Spotlight*, 2003 (August), 7.

63 Such as happened in Austria long before it applied for EU membership. This phenomenon has been labelled with the slightly contradictory but very telling term of '*autonomer Nachvollzug*' ('autonomous adherence').

64 Compare e.g. the European Economic Area agreement establishing the EEA which was signed in 1992. It soon lost political importance as Sweden, Finland and Austria became in 1995 full members of the European Union, leaving only Iceland, Norway and Liechtenstein as non-EU members of the EEA.

65 Switzerland e.g. rejected in a referendum in 1992 to become a member of the EEA and developed in sequence a sophisticated *sui generis* relationship with the Union on a bilateral basis. Seven agreements concluded between Switzerland and the EC and its member states entered into force in June 2002. They will further integrate Switzerland into the European market but also further limit the legislative autonomy of Switzerland.

66 See the European Council conclusion, 1994 meeting in Essen on 9 and 10 December, Annex IV. See in this respect e.g. E. Evtimov, *Rechtsprobleme der Assozierung der Mittel- und osteuropäischen Länder und der Voraussetzungen für ihren Beitritt zur Europäischen Union* (Bern: Peter Lang, 1999), pp. 103–13. Note also that the applicant states were taking part on an equal footing with the member states in the European convention as well as in the IGC 2004 (Bulgaria, Romania and Turkey were invited as 'observers').

67 The so-called 'Europe agreements' concluded between the European communities and its member states on the one hand and the respective applicant country on the other gradually established free trade areas between the contracting parties. See in detail A. Ott and K. Inglis (eds), *Handbook on European Enlargement* (The Hague: TMC Asser Press, 2002). After (successful) enlargement in 2004 Bulgaria, Romania and Turkey continue to hold this special status. The Turkish association agreement even provided for the establishment of a customs union with the EC (in existence since 1995).

68 Compare e.g. Charles Grant, who argues that countries leaving the Union should be allowed to remain in the eurozone, being fully represented in the European central bank. C. Grant, 'Designing an exit door for the EU', in K. Barysch et al., *New Designs for Europe* (London: Centre for European Reform, 2002), p. 32.

69 Countless catchwords describe the phenomenon of flexibility. However, notions such as 'two-speed Europe', 'Europe à la Carte', 'Pick-and choose approach', 'hard-core Europe', '*Europe à plusieurs vitesses*', '*Politik der konzentrischen Kreise*', 'strengthened cooperation', enhanced cooperation all point to different approaches. For an assessment see e.g. K. Forgó, 'Zwischen "Europe à la carte" und Einheit: Modelle differenzierter Integration', in F. Breuss and S. Griller (eds), *Flexible Integration in Europa* (Vienna/New York: Springer Verlag, 1998), pp. 41–78.

70 See the general provisions in title VII (provisions on enhanced cooperation) of the EU treaty (Arts 43–5). See for enhanced cooperation in the first pillar Art. 11 of the EC treaty. The provisions for enhanced cooperation in the third pillar (police and judicial cooperation in criminal matters) are found in Art. 40 of the EU treaty. The treaty of Nice

extended the scope of enhanced cooperation even to the second pillar (common foreign and security policy – the area of defence policy was excluded, Arts 27a–27e EU). Before Nice, the second pillar knew only the method of 'constructive abstaining' as an element of 'flexibility' (Art. 23 TEU).

71 The member states which want to cooperate have to address this request to the commission (Art. II-327). Only in the area of common foreign and security policy has this request to be addressed to the council.

72 The treaty of Nice established the requirement that a minimum of eight member states are involved (whereas before Nice a 'majority of member states' was required).

73 For a comparative survey see E. Fossas Espadaler, 'Autonomía y asimetría', *Informe Pi y Sunyer sobre Comunidades Autónomas* (Barcelona: Funació Carles Pi i Sunyer d'Estudis Autonòmics i Locals, 1995), p. 890.

74 First of all the parliament is relatively strengthened as all the members of the parliament remain involved in the decision-making process of the subgroups (i.e. also the members of parliament who represent member states not cooperating within that specific group), whereas the council decides in a reduced composition (depending on the composition of the respective subgroup). Furthermore, authorization for the establishment of a new enhanced cooperation (save for those in the area of common foreign and security policy) needs the consent of the parliament (Art. III-325 par. 1). Outside the area of the former second pillar the European commission (representing the 'federal' community interest) plays an essential role as it proposes to the council whether a cooperation should be authorized and confirms later participation of further member states. Moreover, Art. III-328 contains two *passerelle* clauses which allow the subgroup to move issues from unanimity to qualified majority voting and allow the council to decide to act under the ordinary legislative procedure instead of under a special procedure. Compare F. Goudappel, 'The influence of flexibility on the institutional balance of the European Community and the European Union', in A. Schrauwen (ed.), *Flexibility in Constitutions* (Groningen: Europa Law Publishing, 2002), pp. 77–83.

75 Which is the reason why the flexibility provisions were initially a corset allowing only for a very rigid form of flexibility.

76 Art. III-329 of the constitutional treaty obliges the council and the commission to 'ensure consistency of activities undertaken in the context of enhanced cooperation and the consistency of such activities with the policies of the Union'.

77 See Art. 10 of the constitutional treaty ('Member States shall take all appropriate measures, general or particular, to ensure fulfilment of the obligations flowing from the constitution or resulting from the Union Institution's acts'). According to the case law of the European Court of Justice this principle binds also the community vis-á-vis the member states. On flexibility as challenge to the principle of loyalty see also A. Hatje, *Loyalität als Rechtsprinzip der Europäischen Union* (Baden Baden: Nomos, 2001), pp. 93–100.

78 Ludwig Wittgenstein, *Tractatus Logico-Philosophicus*, point 5.6. See e.g. the English translation L. Wittgenstein, *Tractatus Logico-Philosophicus* (London: Routledge Classics, 2001).

79 See, among others, M. Pechstein and C. Koenig, *Die Europäische Union*, 2nd edn (Tübingen: Mohr Siebeck, 1998), chapter 10; C. Franck, 'Traité et constitution: les limites de l'analogie', in P. Magnette (ed.), *La Constitution de l'Europe* (Brussels: Editions de l'Université de Bruxelles, 2000), p. 31. The whole story is taken up again in an impressive analysis by S. Oeter, 'Föderalismus', in A. von Bogdandy (ed.), *Europäisches Verfassungsrecht* (Berlin: Springer Verlag, 2003), pp. 59–119. Oeter shows how much the German debate was and is influenced by the historical debate in the scientific community which tried to assess the nature of the German Empire of 1870. Even then, the scholars confronted with a not so dissimilar entity had major difficulties in accepting the idea of shared sovereignty.

80 This being the formula that Werner Heisenberg first outlined in 1927 in his uncertainty paper. See W. Heisenberg, *The Physical Principles of the Quantum Theories* (New York: Dover Publications, 1949).

81 For the distinction between state and non-state see Stefan Griller who concludes that 'the existing relationship between the Union (and the Communities) and its Member States does not decide the statehood of the Union conclusively'. Griller continues: 'Why, then, is the Union not perceived as a state, if the existing powers might actually be sufficiently comprehensive, if a European territory and a European population can be identified, meeting the requirements of international law as well as those of the general theory of law and state, that is to say, if the structural state of affairs is sufficient? The contention is that the reason is simply the absence of will, on the part of the Member States and the institutions of the Union, to found a European State, and the absence of corresponding acts recognizing the Union's statehood on the part of the international community.' S. Griller, 'Le Grand Debate', *Europe* (2004), http://europa.eu.int/comm/governance/ whats_new/europe2004_en.pdf, 17 December 2003.

82 Note that it is the treaty establishing the European community and rarely the treaty establishing the European Union which is referred to as 'constitution'. The reason behind this distinction is that the European court of justice only referred to the former as being a 'constitutional charter'. This seems consequent as the highly complex TEU shows considerable 'black holes' under the perspective of the principle of the rule of law (the lack of judicial review in the second pillar featuring here as the most prominent example).

83 'Report on the draft treaty establishing a constitution for Europe and the European Parliament's opinion on the convening of the Intergovernmental Conference', A5–0299/2003 final, 10 September 2003, p. 13.

84 The declaration of Laeken was still undecided whether or not to introduce the notion of 'constitution'; however, the European convention applied from the beginning a 'constitutional speak'.

85 See Title III of Part I of the treaty.

86 Note that certain provisions deriving originally from the second or third pillars are still subject to special procedure (see e.g. Art III-165 which states that acts in the area of judicial cooperation in criminal matters and police cooperation can be adopted on the initiative of a quarter of the member states).

87 A term used in the context of the Maastricht treaty by Curtin. See D. Curtin, 'The constitutional structure of the Union: a Europe of bits and pieces', *Common Market Law Review*, 30:1 (1993), 17–69, at p. 67.

88 See e.g. G. de Búrca, 'Fundamental rights and citizenship', in de Witte (ed.), *Ten Reflections on the Constitutional Treaty for Europe*, pp. 11–44.

89 See e.g. Art. III-135.

90 Of course, many of the linguistic and mistakes in logic will be erased. Compare in this context the document 'Editorial and legal comments on the draft treaty establishing a constitution for Europe – Basic document', submitted to the intergovernmental conference, CIG 4/1/03 REV 1.

91 As postulated by the Laeken declaration.

92 The parliament became *pro toto* a co-legislator which shall 'jointly with the Council of Ministers enact legislation' (Art. I-19 par. 1), co-decision became the ordinary legislative procedure (Art. III-302) and the distinction between obligatory and non-obligatory expenditure in the budget has been abolished.

93 Note that a whole title is dedicated to the 'democratic life of the Union' (Title VI of Part I). Art. I-46 par. 4 reads: 'No less than one million citizens coming from a significant number of Member States may invite the Commission to submit any appropriate proposal on matters where citizens consider that a legal act of the Union is required for the

purpose of implementing the Constitution'.

94 Such as e.g. Art II-8 (combatting discrimination), II-10 (the right to vote in European and municipal elections) and III-227 (signing up to the European convention on human rights). Moreover, the commission proposes to introduce at least clauses which would foresee a move from unanimous to qualified majority voting from a specific date onwards in fields such as family law and police cooperation. See the commission's communication 'A constitution for Europe', *COM 548* (17 September 2003), p. 7.

95 For an overall view on the different positions of the member states see 'Convention Watch', second issue, October 2003, edited by the Istituto Affari Internazionali, Rome. See also B. Scholl, 'Wie tragfähig ist die neue institutionelle Architektur der EU? Der Verfassungsentwurf des Konvents im Spiegel der nationalstaatlichen Präferenzen', *Integration*, 3 (2003), 204–17.

96 Compare E. A. Young, 'Protecting Member State autonomy in the European Union: some cautionary tales from American federalism', *New York University Law review*, 77 (2002), 1612–737, who says at p. 1726 that 'To the extent that Europe wants to preserve a strong form of Member State autonomy, the American experience is relevant as a cautionary tale.'

97 Art. IV-1.

SERGIO ORTINO

13

Functional federalism between geopolitics and geo-economics

In today's political analysis of the international system, and more specifically of Europe, the usual starting point is the disintegration of the Soviet Empire and the subsequent end of worldwide bipolarism. The first reaction to the collapse of almost all communist regimes aroused widespread optimism in Western democracies. The expansion of the European Union to include ex-communist countries – according to this conception – should also be included in the historical process set out by the victory of the liberal–democratic ideology of the West over the marxist–leninist ideology of the East. This interpretation of the political situation in the international arena exhibited shortcomings as soon as the excitement of being on the 'winning side' of the Cold War dissipated. Assessments became not only measured in their content, but even unmistakably pessimistic regarding the future of liberal democracies. The belief created by the collapse of the Soviet system that Western democracies were free from the same destiny started to waver. It is no more rare to find people who fear that Western democracies could well face the same fate as that of communist regimes, although this is likely to occur by different processes. If the new world order could have simply been based on the extension of the institutional principles and forms of the liberal democracies, as expressed in the legal systems of the Western states, to the former members of the Soviet bloc, we may well have witnessed the 'end of history'.[1] The truth is that the fall of the Berlin Wall in 1989 not only marked the end of Soviet-style communism, but was also the external manifestation of a silent earthquake shaking the foundations of world power.

According to popular opinion, it seems that a new watershed of contemporary history has been created by the terror attacks of 11 September 2001 in New York and Washington DC, which have completely transformed the world prior to that event. The Note published in the *Harvard Law Review* in February 2002 offers an example of the new perspectives from which we will interpret the events of our public and private lives in the future. The Note highlights the substantial changes in American attitudes and strategies towards terrorism, rightfully point-ing out that the number of deaths and the extent of damage caused by the terror attacks on the Twin Towers and the Pentagon do not render the crime different in kind from the crime committed by earlier episodes of terrorism (Pan American Flight 103 of 1988, 1993 the World Trade Center bombing, the embassy bomb-ings in Africa of 1998). 'The point is not that the 11 September attacks were no different from past terrorist attacks, but rather that they were not so different that the criminal law had not contemplated them.'[2] Notwithstanding this fact, the American response to September 11 has taken place largely outside the criminal justice system. Labelling September 11 as an act of war, the US government has justified an extensive American military response. In doing that the US govern-ment has transferred the terror attacks of September 11 from the province of ordinary crime into the realm of war. Furthermore, in terms of foreign policy September 11 has changed the American approach to terrorism from one of multilateral negotiation, recourse to international institutions and recognition of equality among sister states to one of unilateral development and enunciation of policy to be executed jointly – by military force if necessary – by the United States and its allies. In particular the so-called 'Bush doctrine', which treats states that harbour terrorists on a par with the terrorists themselves – is a momentous rejection of the classic liberal model of sovereign equality in international law.

I do not contest this way of interpreting contemporary human history, but I consider it more fruitful to explore whether there is a common cause that explains these two epochal events of our recent history. The fall of communism was not merely the repudiation of one ideology and the triumph of another ideology, just as the terror attacks of 11 September were not merely a clash of civ-ilizations or the inclusion of non-state actors in the war arena, but something more. The two epochal occurrences represent an outward sign of one of the most important revolutions in the history of human organization: a space revolution.

Towards a new ordering of space

During the last decades of the twentieth century and the beginning of the twenty-first century we have witnessed the birth of a new ordering of space; that is, of a new set of rules, standards, and limits depending on the different space modes in which relationships among activities, things and concepts, and by extension among people, are perceived. The ordering of space which we are leaving behind was born five centuries ago following the technological innova-tions that led to the discovery of new continents and to the circumnavigation of the Earth. That ordering of space consisted of a new ordering of the land mass, up until that point the only one which existed, continuing with the ordering of the sea, thanks to the geographical discoveries of the sixteenth century, and of the air, thanks to the new technologies of our epoch.[3]

The revolution in the concept of space that occurred during the last decades of the twentieth and beginning of the twenty-first centuries has already been the subject of considerable analysis. In short, the world is now tied together by a giant electronic network that transmits, at increasingly low costs, a massive amount of news and data with the speed of light to anywhere on the globe. Instant global communication brings together the individuals of the planet in one converging, interdependent world. It connects every single place on Earth, no matter how remote, with the rest of the world. Thus, we can speak about both 'a global world' and 'a global village'; the two terms describe the same reality from opposing viewpoints.[4]

In the global world, everyone has access to everything.[5] This fact tends to decentralize power, as the fact of being so interconnected decentralizes knowledge. Modern electronic technology fosters radical individualism,[6] and mass culture controls political leaders much more than political leaders control mass culture. Because of instant global communication, a monopoly of force can no longer sustain a monopoly of communication, either internally or with the rest of the world. Territorial borders do not define information boundaries.

The huge increase of interdependency among peoples throughout the world is rapidly constructing a new functional reality for most people, a new order based upon its own dynamics and not confined to traditional social understandings. We are, therefore, witnessing structural modifications in our basic beliefs and in our behaviour, including changing relationships among governments, between the government and the citizen, between corporations and regulators, among individuals, and the rearrangement and reunification of the diverse societies of the world in new and complex ways.

Perhaps the most relevant consequence of the present revolution in the concept of space is the crisis of the nation-state, the fundamental structure of the present world order. These tectonic changes reveal an inability of the traditional state to master such events, and undermine the idea on which our political culture has been founded for centuries, according to which the nation-state is the only natural means of aggregating people and of finding solutions to economic and social issues. The waning of the nation-state is a direct consequence of the globalization processes occurring in economics and society due to new communication and computer technologies. The globalization of economic and cultural relations has placed many economic and social functions beyond the control of states, even rich and powerful ones like the United States or Japan, challenging the existing notions of territory, sovereignty and nation.[7]

The clearest evidence in support of this scenario is the manner in which the Soviet Empire collapsed. According to the common parameters of history, the confrontation between two antithetical superpowers finds its end when the fatal stroke of one leads to the fall of the other. On the contrary, the international bipolarism of the late twentieth century ended because one of the two poles collapsed on itself like a huge building, completely corroded and irremediably cracked inside. The corollary of this truth is that the intensity of the crisis which affects all states depends on the degree of bureaucratic centralism.

Given this background, it is not inconceivable that China should start to crack apart in the manner of the former Soviet Union, albeit the political leaders of China are doing their best to maintain the communist organization of power compatible with capitalism. The key factor in the potential disintegration of China is not that the major non-Chinese national areas (Tibet, Xinjiang, Inner Mongolia, Guangxi, Ningxia) have separate histories and strong traditions of independence (although these five areas have special status as autonomous regions, they do not have substantial relevance in face of the central government). The decisive factor is rather that China's rapid economic development since 1978, and the different levels of the consequent regional economic growth, have the potential to lead, if not to political disintegration, to a high degree of regional autonomy. How national non-Han entities might find support for independence or more autonomy in economic matters is clearly demonstrated by the situation in the province of Xinjiang.[8] A solution which might accommodate increased regionalism would be a great Chinese confederation, including the new autonomous, quasi-independent provinces of mainland China, plus Hong Kong, Singapore and Taiwan, along the lines of the Commonwealth of independent states established by units of the former Soviet Union.

No matter what the form of individual states (authoritarian, democratic), the future belongs to the post-territorial sovereign state. Obviously, nation-states will not immediately vanish, but their tasks, power and purpose will be eroded. They will provide certain services, but will no longer pretend to solve all the problems of a people in a particular territory, as has been the case in previous centuries.

As is the case with any revolution, a revolution in the concept of space brings about a shift in the balance of power. Generally speaking, multinational corporations are considered the winners of the new era. As Rifkin points out, they have taken the place of the old rulers.[9] They are capable of designing successful networks of new relationships around the world, based on an organization with a multiplicity of dispersed nodes and without a real centre. This organization is capable of reducing costs and improving rates of return, thanks to the freedom of choosing from the global marketplace the cheapest labour and taxation regulations, as well as the most lucrative areas to sell their products.

There are certainly other winners in this revolution. Perhaps the winner in absolute terms of the information revolution is finance capital. Like companies, financial investors are able to maximize the return on capital without regard to national interests or social consequences. They are also able, however, to punish both corporations, if their returns weaken, and governments, if their economies appear to be creating impediments to profitable enterprises or unpleasant surprises for capital. The citizen may also be considered a winner of the information revolution, both as a consumer, thanks to the wider choices offered by the world markets, and as a free-thinking human being, since the spread of information about alternative lifestyles and value orientations in other countries threatens the validity of official doctrines, the credibility of certain leaders, and the permanence of social and cultural traditions.

The effect of globalization on corporations, finance capital and some aspects of the citizen's life has weakened labour characterized today by mass unemployment or declining real wages, as well as national governments that are no longer able to steer the economy, to maintain the welfare state or to safeguard the uniformity of social and cultural values at a national level. The weakening of the state structure by global market forces is aggravated when bitter historical memories of social and cultural divisions erupt with a vengeance and challenge the territorial integrity of existing nation-states. All these changes foreshadow the coming world. Generally speaking, in specialized literature the pessimistic scenarios prevail. According to these scenarios, the world of the future ranges from one of regional nuclear wars and holy wars among civilizations, to a world dominated by the wide and pervasive violence of gangs, drugs and drug cartels.[10]

On a more positive note, people have a previously unimaginable opportunity to increase their prosperity if they are capable of effectively participating in the advantages of the world economic market and of the various cultural patterns.[11] The revolution in the concept of space may be a stimulus to opening new dimensions of democracy and citizenship, enhanced forms of community, reconciliation between individual and group needs, and more flexible and focused types of government which offer more choices to citizens than simply which elite will govern them.[12]

The revolution in the concept of space has created scenarios of possible future societies which are very different from earlier scenarios. The critical point, however, is that the globalization processes have their own rules, or better, their own logic.[13] As Thurow has written: 'what technology permits, our ideology will require'.[14] Indeed, no one formally runs the revolution in the concept of space, since this revolution runs itself, following patterns of behaviour brought about by human inventions. Whoever masters the rules of this 'logic' can try to direct it along a scientific path. In the near future, we will discover that the winners of this planetary game were those who first understood and dominated the globalization 'logic'.

Micro-regionalism

Reinforcement and enlargement of the market economy suggest that, in general terms, many powers are moving away from the centre towards the localities. Foreign trade and capital provide those localities with alternative means for their economic development. These emerging economic areas cannot afford to be victims of tight, centralized control.

However, if it is true that economic activities in today's borderless world follow information-driven efforts to participate in the global economy, such efforts tend not to happen randomly. According to the new perspective suggested by Kenichi Ohmae,[15] the trajectory along which priorities shift as economic areas move through successive phases of development is fairly predictable. Movement up the ladder of development depends on the ability to put the right policies, institutions and infrastructure in place at the right time.

The tectonic changes brought about by information technology reveal that the affluent economic zones throughout the world – often cross-border zones developed around a regional economic centre – are the units that are bringing real, concrete improvements in the quality of life. What contributes to form these business units is, first of all, the presence of a geographical clustering of broad similarities in tastes and preferences. The borders of these economic regions are not imposed by political decisions, but drawn by the global market for goods and services. These lines do not precede, but accompany, the concrete relations of human activity, confirming daily the configurations created by countless individual decisions.

These natural regions are powerful engines of development because their primary orientation is towards – and their primary connection is with – the global economy. They are, in fact, among its most reliable 'ports of entry'. They have closer links to other natural regions in the global economy than to the other parts of the country to which they belong politically. They must be small enough for their citizens to share interests as consumers, but still of sufficient size to justify economies not of scale (that can be leveraged from a base of any size), but of service (i.e. the infrastructure of communications, transportation and professional services essential to participation in the global economy). According to Ohmae, these business units generally have a population ranging from a few million to 10–20 million. When a geo-economic area prospers, its good fortune spills over to adjacent territories inside and outside the political order of which it is part. Today, the catalyst effect of geo-economic regions is visible in many instances.[16]

Ohmae calls these economic areas 'region states'. This term does not adequately describe the phenomenon, however. The literal meaning of the two words is that they are states with smaller dimensions than ordinary states (similar to the more common expression 'city state' of the ancient and medieval ages), implying that the only institutional change necessary in order to cope with the new realities of our epoch is to reduce the size of the larger and middle states. Because Ohmae himself recognizes that these new emerging zones do not need to be politically independent sovereign communities, but only need to have considerable freedom of action in economic matters, it would be better to call these phenomena 'geo-economic regions' or, perhaps more accurately, 'geo-economic micro-regions'. This label would distinguish this fundamental intrastate or transborder state phenomenon from the continental or intercontinental macro-regions phenomenon. This latter phenomenon is dealt with below. In institutional terms, the consequences of the formation of these zones are evident. Because economically homogeneous regions are necessary in order to take advantage of the global economy, the central government must not only remove barriers between the global economy and local residents, but also abandon the idea that the whole country has to be treated economically and socially as a uniform and compact unity.

In sum, the revolution in the concept of space has caused a deep rift between politics and economics, between state and market, between legitimacy and wealth. While the small and mid-size areas that are united by common prosperity and that acquire autonomy in economic international relations increase rapidly, the traditional nation-state often survives as an almost empty suprastructure.[17] Every human phenomenon has a space dimension. In today's world, this truth has assumed particular significance, since the geo-economics of our time must consider more carefully than before the diversity and multiplicity of actors in the economic world market.

I need hardly say that the impulses towards devolution in Russia and in many member states of the European Union (Belgium, Spain, Italy, the United Kingdom, Germany, France and Austria), the separatist movements in Eastern Europe (the former Soviet Union, former Czechoslovakia, former Yugoslavia) and the aggregation impulse in many international and cross-border zones of the globe, highlight this world trend. Of course, not all of these micro-regionalism processes have geo-economic origins, but some of them (such as north-eastern Italy, Catalonia, southern Scotland and the richer *Länder* of Germany) could in the future demonstrate geo-economic characteristics.

Macro-regionalism

If it is true that technological innovations and the consequent globalization of the markets will be the forces of non-territorial aggregation, we must not underestimate the value that coordinated common governments can still provide, such as military security, a sound currency, infrastructure standards, and the like.

The federative model is one of the most appropriate forms of aggregation capable of providing an overarching 'cover', a political organization within which multiple regions can independently flourish in the context of a global economy and still be linked with the broader national and federative interests. The federative model offers the possibility of resolving certain public tasks within the old territorial mechanisms of the traditional nation-state.

A federative state is a political order founded on a permanent, indissoluble agreement, freely entered into by the contracting parties, created for the purpose of pursuing common ends. This political order is composed of a community body which came into being ex novo in consequence of agreement, and of political entities with their own governments and equal judicial status with respect to each other. In giving rise to the federative agreement, these political entities modified their original constitutions to a substantial degree.[18] This form of state does not differ from confederal, federal or regional states in the degree of devolution and autonomy in legislative, administrative and judicial affairs, but in the specific principles that define its structure and establish its operation. Essential elements of the federative state are the homogeneity of the participating members and the federative legitimacy of the joint bodies.

Federative systems presuppose the 'homogeneity' of the participating members, particularly their basic affinity. This homogeneity may include various factors, such as geographical location, cultural or legal identity, or a community of economic or political interests. In every federative order, participants must regard themselves as homogeneous in at least one fundamental aspect of their associative life, such as the threat posed by a common danger, shared experiences and common ideals, or having been founded upon an essentially similar morality. The features of this homogeneity cannot be set categorically. In any event, they do not necessarily coincide with the features that have typically defined a nation (a language, culture, common traditions, etc.).

The primary feature of the federative state is the preservation of each member's sovereignty (political identity) through the decision-making process of the common bodies. The federative state is a sovereign political order not solely because the member states decided to surrender partial sovereignty to common institutions, but also because the states jointly assert their right of sovereignty in matters reserved for the overall common institutions. Both the decision leading to the joint exercise of the special rights of sovereignty and the actual joint exercise of the above mentioned rights of sovereignty must be founded on the fact that in the decision-making community institutions, there should be: a) equality of votes among the member states' representatives, and b) unanimous consensus of all member states of the common sovereign body. Beside homogeneity and federative legitimacy there are many other principles that characterize the federative state.[19] One in particular frequently omitted by scholars is that of the perpetuity of the pact. According to the constitutions of past federative states, member states were not free to enter or to exit. Here it suffices to remember the very name of the first US constitution: articles of confederation and perpetual union.

This analysis of the fundamental elements of federatively based states suggests that the experiences of all confederal and quasi-federal orders, both past and present, belong in this category. Examples here include the seven united provinces of the Netherlands (1579–1795), the United States of America at the time of the articles of confederation and perpetual union and perhaps until the civil war, the Swiss Confederation (1815–48) and the German Bund (1815–67, and, to some extent, until 1918). In more recent times, the European supranational institutions since 1951 and, to some extent, the 1974 constitution of the socialist federative Republic of Yugoslavia[20] and Canada after 1982 can be classified as confederal regimes.

According to this definition, all states that cannot be classified as federative states must be considered unitary states, regardless of the degree of decentralization or autonomy enjoyed by the peripheral entities. Therefore, not only do the classical highly centralized states such as France belong to the category of 'unitary state', but also present federalist states such as Austria, Germany,[21] Switzerland and the United States of America (even though in these latter two cases the less statist and centralistic concept of political power[22] mitigates their unitary features). Since each classification is relative and fluid, individual cases, especially if they are considered in light of larger historical developments, demonstrate certain characteristics of both federative and unitary states. Legally, the boundary between the federative state and the highly decentralized unitary state (the so-called 'federal state') is defined by the right of the member state to change its constitution without the consent of the larger state in which it is a member. Indeed, because every modification of the federative constitution (the original pact) implies the modification of the constitutions of the member states, the federative constitution may be modified, at least in its fundamental aspects, only with the consent of all member states.

In conclusion, the associational criterion in unitary states which legitimizes the sovereign power (dynastic, democratic, personal and charismatic, etc.) must be based on procedures that guarantee a definitive decision; in democratic regimes the procedure of decision-making is primarily majority rule. In federatively based states, on the contrary, decisions can in principle never be of such importance that they are imposed against the will of even one of the federation units, since the associational criterion which legitimizes the sovereign power is the unanimous consent of all members of the common sovereign body.

Of course the federative model is not the only way of having macro-regionalism. Following the path laid out by European integration, but without having reached the same degree of integration, many other continental associations have been set up or expanded according to several international agreements, including NAFTA (Canada, Mexico, United States of America); MERCOSUR (Argentina, Brazil, Paraguay, Uruguay); APEC (Australia, Brunei, Canada, Chile, Hong Kong, Indonesia, Korea, Japan, Malaysia, Mexico, New Zealand, Philippines, Papua New Guinea, Singapore, Thailand, United States of America, China Taipei); and ASEAN (Brunei, Cambodia, Indonesia, Laos, Malaysia, Myanmar, Philippines, Singapore, Thailand, Vietnam). All these treaties and agreements represent macro-regional vehicles for promoting open trade and practical economic cooperation and to help the economies of the participant nation-states to be consistent with the new realities of our time. Even though all these continental integration processes are different, in particular in their organizational frameworks, they are an indisputable sign of the tectonic modifications concerning the nation-states of our epoch.

In the birth or evolution of these macro geo-economic regions, the principle of 'geographical sequencing' also deserves particular attention. As Inotai and Sass note, international experience demonstrates that at least in the first period of successful modernization, developing economies have generally relied on their traditional, and geographically close, more economically developed partners. In a more general sense, and without stressing the difference between developed and less developed countries, the geographical scope of external economic relations can only be expanded gradually.[23] Indeed, present day economic blocs (with or without an institutional framework) must be considered in this light.[24]

What is important to stress is that all economic blocs and other forms of geo-economic associations at continental or intercontinental level have evolved from the state system established by European governments in the world since the middle of the seventeenth century. From this point of view, they will only replace national governments in certain specific functions. These associations

constitute an intermediate phase of economic consolidation, prior to fully entering the world's inter-linked economy (so-called 'geographical sequencing'). As
we have seen, varying degrees of development demand specific means and
instruments in the field of institutional mechanisms and of political economy.
In order to solve these difficult problems, policy-makers and scholars must look
beyond national borders, to open bargaining and partnership.

Global–localization

The term 'global–localization' (or 'glocalization')[25] provides an emphasis in the
emerging order of space in that local autonomy and decentralization must be
considered not merely as internal affairs, severed from external ones, but as parts
of macro-developmental processes. Indeed, the theoretical approach apt to
build new structural and functional systems capable of coping with today's new
realities proceeds from the observation that, because of new technologies, the
global–local interplay in the fields of economic, cultural and political relations
has to be thought of as a single, complex totality including two opposite realities
in everlasting movement. One of the outcomes of this interplay is a process of
recomposing the territorial articulation of all public bodies and powers, as well
as a process of reshaping individual behaviour.

In this global–local institutional process, it is important to note that
while geo-economic micro-regions are the direct consequence of the interactions of many different participants (downwards), macro-regions are creations
of nation-states (upwards).

The clash of institutions and the new world order

If present trends continue, the ideological conflict that has dominated the twentieth century will soon be supplanted not by conflict between civilizations or
social groups, nor by other forms of traditional conflicts,[26] but rather by confrontation among the new emerging aggregating units and the old ones. These
institutional units are, on the one hand, the inclusive, flexible, open, prosperous,
globally connected, geo-economic micro-regions and, on the other hand, the
single most identifiable determinant of events in the international arena, the
exclusive, territorially inviolable, sovereign, impermeable, geopolitical nation-
states. This confrontation will be characterized not quantitatively by different
extents of fundamental elements of the same structure, but qualitatively by the
completely different nature of the two competing structures.

The winner of this race will be the institution capable of giving the best
answers to the different social, ethnic, cultural and environmental problems of
our time. Needless to say, the way the two structures operate in almost opposite
ways. While the nation-state first occupies a territory (internally dominating
and externally excluding), and then divides and exploits it, the geo-economic
region first exploits the networks of information all over the world (enriching

internally and including the neighbouring areas) and then divides the wealth internally among its citizens. Obviously, the fundamental principles of the two structures are completely different. While the nation-state defends itself as a transcendent and eternal entity, and presumes to solve directly most of the problems of the ruled people, the economic region considers itself a passing, ever changing body and does not want to be a 'nanny state',[27] but simply the instrument through which the people can finance directly their own necessities.

One of the decisive arenas in which the confrontation between these two institutions will take place is probably the supranational aggregations of our age. Which form will prevail mostly depends on the evolution of these supranational entities. If they become just a level of the future reticular governance of the world, they will be favourable instruments to the geo-economic micro-regions. In fact, in order to facilitate the rise of geo-economic micro-regions, on the one hand, and to permit existent nation-states to cope with the new realities created by information technology, on the other hand, federalism becomes inevitable, not only internally within the existent states[28] – as we have seen – but also externally through these supranational associations. For these reasons, continental integration processes should find in future inspiration from this geo-economic perspective. More precisely, they should proceed not only relying on market forces, the influence of ideas, the flow of goods and services, and voluntary participation, but also by considering the internal imbalances in society and economy as opportunities for the creation of new wealth, not as disadvantages that can be overcome only through traditional government activity.

In particular the European Union should preserve the original principles of the federative model, relying less on the strengthening of its own political institutions and thereby avoiding rebuilding at the supranational level the old structures of the bygone nation-state. On this matter it is noteworthy to refer to the discussion which has recently arisen on the role of the European central bank in the Union. Since its birth this body, foreseen by the Maastricht treaty of 1992 as the central bank for governing the new monetary unit in Europe, has shown some particular features that could give it a rather unexpected role.[29] According to the treaty the European central bank possesses a unique status in comparison to all the other central banks in the world. Its special position depends on its independence from the European authorities, as well as from the single national governments of the member states (Art. 108 TEC), and on the circumstance that its goals are predetermined by the treaty (Art. 105 TEC). Furthermore, it is not included in the list of the European institutions (Art. 7 TEC) but it is mentioned separately (Art. 8 TEC).[30] From this special legal framework it could be possible to infer that from this authority there is the possibility of developing an autonomous activity not exclusively directed to the stabilization of the common currency within the European community (the so called 'Eurozone'), but also of participating in the regulation of the entire international monetary system. In other words, its federative elements led the European Union to build a very special model of central bank, capable of developing into a monetary junction of the reticule global government.

Thus, if these international or supranational entities transform themselves into territorial, boundary, sovereign super-nations, they will represent the last historical phase of the five-century-old nation-state. The possibility of this second evolution is not low at all. If it does occur, an institutional clash could develop between the most ambitious regions of Europe and Brussels.[31]

Geopolitical considerations

Because geopolitics will continue to manifest itself whenever substantial modifications to intercontinental relations appear possible, fearful or desirable,[32] the enlargement of the European Union towards the Eastern countries could offer the opportunity to turn the attention of policy-makers and scholars to well-known geopolitical theories of the past. Thus, for instance, the mono-centric vision of international relations postulated by Halford J. Mackinder, and summarized in the famous words: 'Who rules East Europe, commands the Heartland [the Eurasian lowland]: Who rules the Heartland commands the world-island [Asia, Europe, Africa]: Who rules the world-island commands the world',[33] could be of vital importance in understanding the consequences of the enlargement of the European Union. Although there are many features that distinguish the global framework of 1919, when Mackinder's conception was set out, from the present, not least of which is the role played by NATO, a military alliance with its epicentre in the Atlantic Ocean and not in the Eurasian continent, many scholars and politicians would find truth in Mackinder's thesis.

The fear that a larger and larger 'super-nation' would arise after the collapse of the communist bloc in Europe led Pierre Béhar to suggest the reconstruction of the European continent according to models of vanished empires. This approach would mean the development in Eastern Europe of a sub-system of confederations within a larger reticular system of governance, capable of creating the conditions for stability and balance in the Eurasian continent.[34] Béhar admits that the heritage of the past (especially the despotism of the twentieth century), may have created in these countries psychological, intellectual and moral obstacles to the spirit of cooperation in favour of sectarianism and nationalism. However, he thinks that the following geopolitical factors, which have been persistent throughout history, will be sufficiently strong to influence developments: the presence of a common culture from the middle ages to 1919, from 1945 a similar status of serfdom and from 1990 a similar status of regained freedom; of the same neighbours (Germans and Russians); and of the same space (Central as to geography, Western as to culture). It is not necessary here to discuss in detail whether these common features of the East Central European countries are as clear as Béhar indicates. Vojtech Mastny, in chapter 2 of this book, suggests that the commonality is not so clear, while Kristian Gerner's and András Bozóki's considerations on this subject in chapters 4 and 5 are more cautious. Historical evaluations aside, the already decided participation of ten new countries in the European Union has rendered Béhar's proposed confederations a moot point.

It is worth stressing that these kinds of confederations, to which Béhar refers, could have represented in general terms an extraordinary tool for avoiding the dangerous nationalistic revivals of the interwar years and the totalitarian legacy of the Soviet experience and, therefore, for leaving behind an obscure political landscape.[35] As we know, a federative order helps to reduce economic, ethnic, religious and other internal divisions among the member states, and to offer greater opportunities for negotiated cooperation. In particular, the relationship between national minorities in the newly nationalized states, and the external national homelands to which those minorities belong by ethno-cultural affinity but not by legal citizenship, could be better managed within a federative order. These kinds of confederations could have assisted in the common goal of rebuilding political and economic systems along the lines of those found in pluralistic democracies and market systems, without necessarily being incorporated in a unique federal-unitary state.

It is probably a mistake to treat the countries of East Central Europe as a homogeneous regional group. Previous chapters of this book have shown[36] that the peoples of this region have different histories, profess three major religions (Western Christianity, Byzantine orthodoxy and Islam) and have different levels of economic development. However, for the establishment of federative organizations, we must focus not on what divides but on what unites. The Visegrád cooperation between Poland, Czechoslovakia and Hungary in 1991 serves as a recent example of such unity. The idea of East Central Europe as 'Europe in-between', described in chapter 5, provides perhaps the best perspective for grasping the commonality of these countries. From this viewpoint, it would have made little difference if a single European federative state, two federative states (the West and the East European confederation) or even more had been established in the area between the Atlantic and the borders of Byelorussia and Ukraine.

The danger in geopolitical terms must not be seen in the enlargement of Europe as such, nor in the number of powers assigned to the joint bodies of the European Union, but rather in the way such powers are wielded. In my view, only the federative state is an indisputable guarantor of a limited and balanced exercise of power, because of the need for unanimous consent in the joint supreme bodies on basic issues, and because of the vertical separation of normative power from the so-called 'executive federalism' (normative joint bodies at a superior level, executive state organs at a subordinate level).

Ahead of the enlargement of the European Union to include ten new sovereign states, it would seem that the arguments of those who support the transformation of the European Union into an authentic federal state, within which the member states dissolve their sovereignty while maintaining strong autonomous residual powers, will be more and more convincing.[37] This course, implicitly dealt with in the preambles of certain related European treaties,[38] is highly probable, due to the near impossibility of applying the present European system to a geographical area consisting of at least twenty-five countries. If it is true, however, that the prospective impact of Eastern enlargement may well be the moment in the process of European integration when quantitative changes turn into qualitative challenges, then the evolution of the European Union cannot be understood merely in numeric terms, but rather should be understood in terms of the principles that regulate existing European institutions.

The argument that the present European Union cannot work if the number of member states keeps increasing is straightforward. First, it is difficult to maintain sustainable coherence in the decision-making process when there are more than a dozen participant members. There are, of course, means of simplifying the process, such as according one vote to every three or four smaller states,[39] or creating more confederations within the larger and looser one.[40] This is often referred to as 'multiple speed' or 'variable geometry' or 'à la carte'.[41] Past experience demonstrates that this latter option would eventually undermine the confederation.[42] Secondly, almost all former communist countries in Europe meet the criteria for homogeneity set out in the European treaties. All belong to Europe and all (at least formally) have declared their willingness to abide by the principles of Western pluralistic democracies.[43] During the Cold War, this second requirement was of utmost importance. The Maastricht treaty of 1992 has added a third requirement to the other two requirements of the original pact; in order to permit the introduction of a European monetary unit: 'the economy of each member state must be characterized by stable prices, sound public finances and monetary conditions, and a sustainable balance of payments' (Art. 4 [ex 3A] EC treaty). These are difficult criteria to meet, even for the founding states of the European community.

As a result of the evolution of the last years in the construction of the European Union (especially after 1997), the creation of one or more confederations in East Central Europe is no longer feasible. Therefore, the integration of the former communist countries of Europe into the European Union can occur, in a more or less long period of time, by one method only: through the transformation of the federative-egalitarian European Union into a traditional federal-unitary state, where majority rule will replace unanimous rule in the decision-making process. Such a scenario would be similar to that of German reunification in 1990 when the Federal Republic of Germany incorporated the German Democratic Republic, a former communist country.

The only transitional alternative to this classical institutional framework may be the development of the European Union towards an intermediate solution lying somewhere between the existent federatively based state and a completely new decentralized unitary state. In this scenario, the centre would be represented by a core of states, connected with several sub-systems of other states through links of different kinds and intensity. The result would be a hierarchic–pyramidal European Union which would provide core states the opportunity of controlling the rest of the area. It is not difficult to imagine that Germany would occupy a dominant position in such an institutional framework.

The draft constitution elaborated by the European convention seems to follow this transitional alternative. Clear signs of this choice can be found in many places of the document. A few examples will suffice.

First, the very definition of the new amending act as a 'constitutional treaty' gives the general thrust of transition by mixing together two intrinsically different revision procedures, that of a constitution by the will of the people and that of a treaty by the will of the member states. This formal procedural contamination is also reflected under more substantial aspects, when the draft constitution establishes at the very beginning the double legitimation of Union power: democracy and federative principle ('Reflecting the will of the citizens and states of Europe to build a common future'; Art. I-1 (1)). As we know, the idea of this double legitimation of power was an invention of the founding fathers of the US constitution, built on a senate made of an equal number of senators for each state and in a house of representatives elected on the basis of the population. However, this double legitimation of power does not find correspondence in the institutional framework created by the draft constitution, because of a still too weak European parliament compared with the council of ministers.

Secondly, the draft constitution tries to escape from the fundamental principle of collegiality typical of the federatively based state, introducing in some way or other more visible leaders of the Union through a new president of the European council (Art. I-21), a stronger president of the commission (Art. I-26) and a new union minister for foreign affairs (Art. I-27). This attempt has only partially succeeded because the draft constitution deprives the three organs of their vote, when they participate in the European council (Art. I-24).

Thirdly, the draft constitution recognizes the right of voluntary withdrawal from the Union by any member state (Art. I-59). According to a well-distinguished doctrine the fundamental pact on the bases of which these sorts of institutions are created is permanent (perpetual, *ewig, von nun an, beständig, ewyghen, illimitato*). The idea derives from the consideration that the pact is a contract of *status*, that obliges the parts for life and not simply for a limited period of time, because of the impossibility of foreseeing the exact moment of the achievement of the new community goals, defined in the pact.[44] The right of voluntary withdrawal proposed by the European convention can be explained as another instrument – together with the enhanced cooperation (Title VII [ex VI bis T]EU, Title VI chapter III draft constitution) or the possibility to stay out of the Eurozone conferred to the single member states (the so-called 'opting out' clause) – introduced in order to increase the possibilities of creating a Europe at multiple levels of aggregation with a core group of states that will assume a stronger and stronger position. This interpretation could be suggested by the fact that the draft constitution contemplates the possibility to 'negotiate an agreement with that state [that has decided to withdraw from the Union], setting out the arrangements for its withdrawal, taking account of the framework for its future relationship with the Union' (Art. 59 (2)).[45]

Two final conclusions at international level. First, the effects of European integration on the rest of the world in general cannot be underestimated. The anxieties of those who consider the evolution towards continental regionalism as a threat to the balance of the international order because of the division of world power into separate blocs (European, American, Asian-Pacific) are well known. Many observers see this phenomenon in the recent establishment or expansion of several international agreements (NAFTA, MERCOSUR, APEC, ASEAN). All these treaties and agreements could be considered not only as regional vehicles for promoting open trade and practical economic cooperation, but also as a response to the European Union. From this perspective, an over-integrated Europe could be interpreted as a threat to other areas, and consequently as a model that should be imitated. This belief could start dangerous geopolitical competition among continental mega-blocs.[46] Once again, it is important to stress that the preservation of fundamental features of a federative structure in the European Union would represent a reassuring sign of geopolitical balance, offsetting the perceived threat of enlargement.[47]

Secondly, no matter who is the winner of this confrontation – the new micro geo-economic region operating within the framework of a reticular global governance or the old nation-state in the form of the mega continental unit – the traditional dualistic world order, built by the Westphalian peace in 1648 on the basis of the two pillars of the international organization as just the meeting place of almost two hundred conflicting national states, on the one hand, and of the all-purpose national states,[48] on the other will soon come to an end.

The new institutional principles

No one can predict the future. But I am firmly convinced that the new world order cannot simply be a transposition to an intercontinental level of the experience of nation-states, designed as a meeting point of a few continental units or even as a global central government. On the contrary, the horizontal globalization of economic and social life must be cut across by complex vertical organizations, capable of interacting with the forces of the global market and global culture, sometimes supporting, sometimes restricting, sometimes opposing them. The important thing is that institutional interaction with global forces should not be carried out by a rudimentary and inadequate all-purpose traditional state at national, regional–continental or even world level, but by various flexible governments that will have to be picked according to a well-constructed and complex federalist process downwards, upwards and outwards.

Generally, in the most traditional and deeply rooted forms of federal state such as the United States, Switzerland, Germany, Canada and Australia, by federalism one meant just the political order through which were shared out the sovereign rights among central and peripheral entities placed within its territory: thus, a federalism which still had as its basic political structure the idea of the state born in Europe in the sixteenth century. From such a perspective, as we have seen above, the distinction made between unitary states and federal states is a distinction that does not undermine the principles of the traditional national state, both a territorial and a boundary-state. This kind of federalism can be called 'structural federalism'. The step towards this kind of classic federalism is necessary in almost all centric states of our epoch, because without the preliminary subdivision of the traditional nation-state into federal member states one cannot produce those institutional premises apt to outline adequate forms of functional federalism; that is, a federalism in which the territorial extension as well as the jurisdictions of the supranational, national and local authorities are subjected to change according to the situation. The legal–institutional outcome is an intermediate solution, combining elements of structure (classical federalism) and the logic of action (functionalism) apt to organize the government both along the line of specific ends and needs, and on the basis of a set constitutional division of rights and powers.[49] I believe nobody has grasped the nucleus of functional federalism better than president Yeltsin. As O'Brien reports in chapter 3, Yeltsin vividly affirmed, using one of his campaign promises: Tatarstan 'may take as much sovereignty as [it] can swallow'.

In this sense the principle of subsidiarity will substitute the principle of sovereignty as a fundamental element of the new legal orders.[50] In this new world order, sovereignty will be subject to a general deconstruction through processes of downsizing, devolution and specialization. Old and new entities will emerge exercising some but not all of the characteristics we have come to associate with the traditional nation-state. Autonomy instead of sovereignty will be the fundamental principle of organizing political communities.[51] In this multidimensional world no organization can monopolize all the dimensions of sovereignty.

Similarly, all the different Western experiences of decentralization, devolution or regionalization of our epoch have shown that the principle of asymmetry will supplant the homogeneity principle among territorial entities within a same governmental level. Needless to say that asymmetry can have an important role in reconfiguring the new principles of government only in a reticular dimension, not within a concentric framework of power built to affirm the supremacy of some states over other states, as shown above in relation to the new tendencies of European integration.

Chapter 6 of this volume has thoroughly shown how useful the principle of asymmetry could have been in avoiding the tragic consequences of disintegration and war in the former Yugoslav federation. Nowadays the pursuit of efficiency has become much more relevant than the maintenance of absolute sovereignty or of legal equality.[52]

According to this analysis, the world order will be formed by a plurality of territorial and non-territorial multi-levels of governance, deeply interconnected among themselves. Under this viewpoint, the choice between total independence because of self-determination and strong autonomy because of devolution is no more a true, dramatic dilemma as it was in the past, because every entity must have its own autonomy and be connected with the rest of the world.[53]

Thus, functional federalism, on the basis of subsidiarity and asymmetric principles, will be capable of redesigning and reshaping, in a fairly short time and in a lasting way, the present global order in connection with the great tectonic changes of this era. One must by no means think that, in the global process of constitutional changes, such changes take place once and for all. But, again, it is important to stress the fact that the starting point of this institutional revolution towards a new space order will be the geo-economic micro-region, the new emerging fundamental structure of our epoch.

On a global level a widespread process will soon develop of federalization of the political structures by means of transferring powers of the national state both upwards (confederal organizations such as the European Union, and quasi-confederal organizations such as the United Nations), downwards (minor territorial entities as regions, cantons, provinces and municipalities) and outwards (autonomous bodies of supranational, national and sub-national control, as well as private economic and no economic subjects). The all-purpose national state will be replaced by a plurality of public and private entities potentially competent in performing only specific duties, in order that efficiency and efficacy, as well as responsibility and transparency, will prevail in any common action.

In the future functional federalism will allow each individual to decide not only how much power to reserve to the public or to the private sphere, but also the most proper territorial level of government, from the smallest entity (municipality) to the largest (international organization). The new world order will be a pluralistic order in which each individual can choose the most suitable, old or new level of territorial government for the solution of his or her problems (municipalities, provinces, regions, states, confederations of homogeneous states, international organizations), as well as the unit, independent and autonomous from all territorial public power, suitable for safeguarding specific interests (in this last case the patterns vary in independence and autonomy; that is, from the IATA to OPEC, to the World Bank, to the World Trade Organization, to the Bank for International Settlements, from the International Organization of Securities Commissions, to any woman world association, or to entrepreneurial bodies striving for the reduction of laws in the state where they work). Each of these decision-making bodies has to be chosen when it is shown to be the most reliable and feasible centre for giving to the individuals channels through which they can participate in deliberations over the shape of the related regulations.[54]

It is only thanks to this pluralistic vertical and horizontal organization of new political entities and autonomous and independent bodies, capable of real-locating many of the duties of the present states, that the mass society caused by the globalization of economy and of social life will become much more diversified, enriched and articulated. In this new federalist order, while each individual is connected to groups, communities and various bodies from the simplest to most complex – both public and private, the national state will become only one of the systems, even if for just a few more decades the most important politically, inside which individuals act.

In this way it will be possible to prevent consumers' sovereignty replacing, and not enriching, the sovereignty of the people. And this will also make it possible to avoid the increasing identities and loyalties of individuals to a multiplicity of local and international communities and groups, that lead them to fight one another or to become 'small, fragile pieces of driftwood caught up in the general flux'. And finally, it will make it possible to avoid the decision-making centres losing their liberty to the 'tyranny of little decisions' because of lack of accountability of the decision-making processes.[55]

The legal science of our epoch is hence bound to abandon the restful, relaxing scheme of the sovereign, independent state worked out over the course of the last five centuries, in order to explore developments of political communities that can no longer be understood from that exclusive viewpoint. Under this aspect the model of the European Union, as it has evolved until now, ought not to be regarded merely as a transitional moment within the long process of political aggregation under way since the end of World War II in Europe, but as a supranational order with up-to-date institutional appurtenances, at times in need more of strengthening than of transformation.[56]

Of course, introducing the functional aspect in the debate on federalism makes inevitable the raising of issues regarding the demarcation of the regions. As a matter of fact, in structural federalism the distribution of powers between centre and periphery, as a constituent part of this kind of state, presumes an even stronger protection of the historically given territorial foundations of the single member states.[57] This historical aspect of the identity and the uniqueness of the constituent parts, on the one hand, and the demand for efficiency and efficacy of the territorial organizations in a functional sense, on the other, create a clash of institutions that must be resolved through rational constitutional rules capable of evaluating the perils and the benefits of the proposed solutions of maintaining old territorial units or creating new ones. Chapter 5 of this volume clarifies very well the conflicting institutional vision in East Central Europe between the innovative transborder Euro-regions and the former communist states searching for national identity.

This is especially true if we consider the new above-discussed phenomenon of geo-economic micro-regionalism. As far as these new transborder economic areas are concerned, it will probably be necessary to set up new administrative public organizations, both in terms of autonomous competences and in terms of new territorial boundaries. The issue becomes even more delicate when the economically interesting area belongs to more than one state. From comparative legal experience it seems that we have to make stronger efforts and further improvements on these matters.[58]

An example of functional federalism
There are many constitutional ways of facing the new challenges of our epoch. We could think on the following criteria.[59]

Each of the existing levels of government (state, regions, provinces, counties, cities) has legislative power in a few matters established by the constitution and exercised through two chambers (except the lowest level, all the other levels of government have a second chamber where the entities of the lower level of government are represented). The competences on these matters, that can be defined as 'fixed competences', are those which justify the very existence of each of the respective levels of government. These competences are exercised according to the Westminster model: electorate, two-party system, chamber of representatives, head of the executive, vote of confidence, dissolution.

Each of the four levels of government may exercise 'mobile or optional competences' as well; that is, any competence that is not already attributed as 'fixed competence' to one of the levels of government by the constitution.[60] In order to pursue that goal, two conditions have to be complied with. First, in order to have a mobile or optional competence, each level of government must express its will with a vote in favour by the majority of the chamber of representatives (under the form of a right to present the draft) and a vote in favour by the quasi-unanimity of the second chamber (under the form of a right to discuss and, if necessary, modify the draft, and definitively approve the law).

Secondly, the consent of the two above mentioned bodies has to be expressed not only in regard to the attribution of the new competence, but also to the modalities through which that competence must be exercised. That means that the two bodies on the same occasion have to approve the full text of a law in which the questions related to the issues must be specified; first of all the cost of the service, the levy of taxes, the administrative structure, and so on. This law is not a simple ordinary law, but rather a law with the same force as a constitutional law. That means that the other laws necessary for implementing this basic law shall be approved respectively by the first chamber with a simple majority of votes.

The are two main ideas to this project. First, the application of the Westminster model and the application of the fundamental principles of the federative state. Secondly, the modification of the constitution relating the mobile competences must be easier than the modification of the constitution regarding the fixed competences (and all the other matters). Of course, in the same legal framework it would be possible to create new territorial levels of government according to diverse matters, for example cultural and ethnic identities, economic and social relationships and environmental issues. Many similarities with this model of functional federalism can be found in the experiences considered in the previous chapters, especially when the constitutional norms regulate hypotheses of asymmetry among the sub-national units.[61]

If we apply this model of functional federalism at the European Union level, we could transform the prevalent federative structure today into a more integrated system of multi-levels of governance,[62] without the danger of setting up in the near future a very strong state-centric body and without the risk of seeing continually 'the growing dissociation between authoritative allocations, territorial constituencies and functional competences'[63] of the present European Union. According to this plan, the European parliament should have the right to approve the draft proposing a new competence for the EU, and the council of ministers (a sort of second chamber) would maintain the right to discuss and, if necessary, modify the draft, and definitively approve the law. The draft constitution set up by the European convention has created a sort of functional federalism in embryo, by adding to the simple proclamation of the subsidiarity principle (Art. 5 [ex 3A] TEU, Art. I-9 draft constitution) a complex procedure apt to verify the legal conditions for the exercise of legislative power by the Union, which do not fall within its exclusive competences. At point 6.3 of the protocol on the application of the principles of subsidiarity and proportionality, annexed to the draft constitution, we can read that 'where reasoned opinions on a commission proposal's non-compliance with the principle of subsidiarity represent at least one third of all the votes allocated to the member states' national parliaments and their chambers, the commission shall review its proposal'.

Notes

1 F. Fukuyama, *The End of History and the Last Man* (New York, NY: Free Press, 1992).
2 Responding to terrorism: 'crime, punishment, and war (note)', *Harvard Law Review*, 115 (February 2002), 1217–26.
3 C. Schmitt, *Der Nomos der Erde im Völkerrecht des Jus Publicum Europaeum* (Berlin: Ducker & Humblot, 1950); S. Ortino, *The Nomos of the Earth* (Baden-Baden: Nomos, 2002), 1st edition *Il nuovo Nomos della terra* (Bologna: Il Mulino, 1999).
4 M. McLuhan, *Understanding Media*, 1964 (reprinted 1997 by Routledge, London), was the first author to provide a detailed analysis of the subject.
5 Of course, possibilities of undermining consumer choice always exist because of monopoly practices; see M. Krantz, 'Will Reno brake windows?', *Time* (3 November 1997), p. 40 ff. and, from a more general point of view, J. Rifkin, *The Age of Access. The New Culture of Hypercapitalism Where All of Life is a Paid-For Experience* (New York: Jeremy P. Tarcher/Putnam, 2000).
6 Z. Bauman, *Liquid Modernity* (Oxford: Polity Press Cambridge and Blackwell Publishers Ltd, 2000).
7 Also M. Hardt and A. Negri, *Empire* (Boston: Harvard University Press, 2000), consider our era characterized by a deep discontinuity with the recent past. Notwithstanding this premise, these authors still see in the present United States of America the centre of a new form of global polity capable of dominating the world as it did in the twentieth century. The linear interpretation of human history of these authors, according to their marxist ideology, is incompatible with the discontinuity approach thesis. Anyway, after the studies of J. Diamond, *Guns, Germs, and Steel* (New York/London: Norton, 1997) and M. De Landa, *A Thousand Years of Nonlinear History* (New York: Zone Books, 1997), also a revised, post-modern materialist dialectic is much harder to be reasonably accepted.
8 D. S. G. Goodman, *The Political Economy of Regionalism in China: Economic Development and the Prospects for Political Disintegration* (Western Australia, Murdoch University: Asia Research Centre, 1993), working papers 26.
9 R. Reich, *The Work of Nations* (New York: Simon & Schuster, 1993); J. Rifkin, *The End of Work: The Decline of the Global Labor Force and the Dawn of the Post-Market Era* (New York: G. P. Putnam's Sons, 1995).
10 For further details on these scenarios, see D. J. Elkins, *Beyond Sovereignty: Territory and*

Political Economy in the Twenty First Century (Toronto/Buffalo/London: University of Toronto Press, 1995), pp. 4–6.

11 J. D. Davidson and W. Rees-Mogg, *The Sovereign Individual. The Coming Economic Revolution. How to Survive and Prosper In It* (London: Macmillan, 1997).

12 L. A. Kahn, *The Extinction of Nation-States* (The Hague: Kluwer Law International, 1996).

13 M. Castells, *The Rise of the Network Society* (Oxford: Blackwell, 1996, 2000), clearly defines the paradigm of information technology (Ch. I).

14 L. C. Thurow, *The Future of Capitalism: How Today's Economic Forces Shape Tomorrow's World* (New York: William Morrow and Company, Inc., 1996), p. 87.

15 K. Ohmae, *The End of the Nation State. The Rise of Regional Economies. How New Engines of Prosperity are Reshaping Global Markets* (New York: Free Press, 1995).

16 According to Ohmae, *End of the Nation State*, such units include: Lombardia; north-eastern Italy; Baden Würtemberg; Wales; San Diego/Tijuana; Hong Kong/Southern China; the Silicon Valley/Bay Area in California; Pusan (at the southern tip of the Korean Peninsula); the cities of Fukuoka and Kitakyushu in the north of the Japanese island of Kyushu; the Growth Triangle of Singapore, Johore (the southernmost member state of Malaysia) and the neighbouring Riau Islands of Indonesia (including Batam, a large tax-free zone); Research Triangle Park in North Carolina; the Rhône-Alps region, centred on Lyons, with its tight business and cultural ties to Italy; the Languedoc-Roussillon region, centred on Toulouse, with its close connection with Catalogna; Tokyo and its outlying areas; Osaka and the Kansai region; the Malaysian island of Penang; and the newly emerging Greater Growth Triangle, unveiled in 1992 across the Strait of Malacca, connecting Penang, Medan and Phuket in Thailand.

17 P. Moreau Defargues, *Introduction à la géopolitique* (Paris: Éditions du Seuil, 1994).

18 For further details of the questions dealt with in this section, see S. Ortino, *Diritto costituzionale comparato* (Bologna: Il Mulino, 1994).

19 See Ortino, *Introduzione al diritto costituzionale federativo*.

20 See chapter 6 of this volume.

21 See chapters 7 and 8 of this volume.

22 On the differences between the Bodinian (static) and the Althusius (federalist) model of the ideal polity, see D. Elazar, 'The United States and the European Union: models for their epochs', *The Federal Vision. Legitimacy and Levels of Governance in the United States and the European Union*, in K. Nicoloaidis and R. Howse (eds) (Oxford: Oxford University Press, 2001), p. 31 ff.

23 A. Inotai and M. Sass, *Economic Integration of the Visegrád Countries: Facts and Scenarios* (Budapest: Hungarian Academy of Sciences: Institute for World Economics, May 1994), working papers 33.

24 A. Gamble and A. Payne, *Regionalism and World Order* (Houndmills: Macmillan Press Ltd, 1996).

25 A. Aykaç, *Transborder Regionalisation* (Sindelfingen: Libertas Verlag, 1994). D. Blumenwitz, 'Der Grenzüberschreitende Regionalismus als mögliches Instrument der Konfliktenschärfung', *INTEREG* (Symposium Marienbad, 23–26 October 1997). P. Pernthaler and S. Ortino (eds), *Europaregion Tirol/Egregio Tirolo, Autonome Region Trentino-Südtirol* (Bolzano/Bozen: EURAC, 1997).

26 See for example: S. Huntington, *The Clash of Civilization and the Remaking of World Order* (New York: Simon & Schuster, 1996) (civilization clashes); A. Hoogvelt, *Globalization and the Postcolonial World. The New Political Economy of Development* (Baltimore: The Johns Hopkins University Press, 1997) (social clashes); and Thurow, *The Future of Capitalism* (political clashes).

27 In Peter Druker's sense, *Post-Capitalist Society* (New York: Harper & Business, 1993), p. 122 ff.

28 The reluctance of France to introduce more decentralized institutions could explain the deep crisis that troubles this country according to many observers and scholars (see recently N. Baverez, *La France qui tombe* (Paris: Perrin, 2003)). As Poggeschi shows in chapter 11, there are many traditional conceptions and institutions that delay the federalizing process in France.

29 See the controversy developed in some issues of *Common Market Law Review* between 1999 and 2002: C. Zilioli and M. Selmayr, 'The external relations of the Euro area: legal aspects', 36:2 (1999), 273–349; R. Torrent, 'Whom is the European Central Bank the central bank of? Reaction to Zilioli and Selmayr', 36:6 (1999), 1229–41; C. Zilioli and M. Selmayr, 'The European Central Bank: an independent specialized organization of Community law', 37:3 (2000), 591–644; F. Amtenbrink and J. De Haan, 'The European Central Bank: an independent specialized organization of Community Law', 39:1 (2002), 65–76.

30 While the version of the draft constitution of 26 May 2003 includes in Art. I-18 the European central bank within the institutions of the Union (CON 724/03), the second version of 13 June and 10 July 2003 (CON 850/03) excludes the European central bank from this list, confirming not only the present legal situation, but opening the role of this body to the future evolution.

31 See 'Europe's rebellious regions', *The Economist* (15 November 2003), p. 32.

32 P. P. Portinaro, 'Nel tramonto dell'occidente: la geopolitica', *Comunità*, 36 (1982), 42.

33 H. J. Mackinder, *Democratic Ideals and Reality: A Study in the Politics of Reconstruction* (Holt/New York, Henry Holt and Co., 1919), p. 150.

34 P. Béhar, *Une géopolitique pour l'Europe. Vers une nouvelle Eurasie?* (Paris: Editions Desjonqueres, 1992), considers indispensable for the balance of the entire Eurasian continent the presence of these three confederations: a) Central Europe: set up by Poland, the Czech Republic, Slovakia, Hungary, Slovenia, Croatia (and Austria); b) Baltic: set up by Estonia, Latvia and Lithuania (and Finland, and perhaps a northern federation together with the three Scandinavian states); and c) Balcanic: set up by Serbia and its associates, Romania, Bulgaria, Albania, Greece and Turkey.

35 See chapter 2 for historical developments in East Central Europe.

36 See chapters 2, 4 and 5 of this book.

37 A large majority of scholars support this course for the EU. See R. Dehousse, *Europe: The Impossible Status Quo* (London: Macmillan Press Ltd, 1997 for the Club of Florence).

38 The first sentence of the preamble of the EEC treaty of 1957, for example, states that the EEC is 'determined to lay the foundations of an ever closer union among the peoples of Europe'.

39 See, for instance, Art. 4 of the German confederation of 1815.

40 We can interpret the TEU dispositions regarding the enhanced cooperation (Title VII [ex VI BIS]) in this perspective.

41 H. MacRae, *The World in 2020. Power, Culture and Prosperity: A Vision of the Future* (London: HarperCollins, 1994), p. 229 ff., paperback edition 1995, presumes the EU will become a wider association with several different classes of membership.

42 It suffices here to mention the German customs union of 1819 and the agreement among the Swiss Catholic cantons of 1847, which brought to an end the German confederation of 1815 and the Swiss confederation of 1815 respectively.

43 The authoritarian tendencies of some countries of the region are well known. For details see chapter 4 of this book.

44 C. Schmitt, *Verfassungslehre* (1928), 3rd edn (Berlin: Duncker & Humblot, 1957), p. 367. The German Bund of 1815 (Art. 5 WSchlA) and the federation of the Seven United Provinces of 1579 (Art. I) prohibited the withdrawal of member states expressly.

45 See on these issues 'Membership of the Union' in chapter 12 of this book (p. 258 ff.).

46 Among the possible mega-conflict scenarios in the twenty-first century, is that between

Europe and the United States (see, for example, J. Redwood, *Stars and Strife: The Coming Conflicts between the USA and the European Union* (Basingstoke: Palgrave Macmillan, 2001)).

47 On this issue, see M. Beeson, 'The clash of institutions: APEC and institutional theory' (Toronto: paper prepared for the International Studies Association Conference, 18–22 March 1997).

48 N. MacCormick, 'Beyond the sovereign state', *The Modern Law Review*, 56:1 (1993), 1–18.

49 For the meaning of functionalism, see D. Mitrany, *A Working Peace System* (Chicago: Quadrangle, 1966).

50 See in particular chapter 9 of this volume.

51 Paradigmatic on this point is Art. 114 of the reformed Italian constitution which reads as follows: 'The Republic comprises the municipalities, the provinces, the regions and the State'. 'The municipalities, the provinces and the regions are autonomous entities with their own powers'; see chapter 9 of this volume.

52 On the subject, see chapters 7, 9 and 10 of this volume.

53 A. Buchanan, *Secession* (Boulder: Westview Press, 1991); C. Margiotta-Broglio, *Il 'diritto' di secessione: presupposti teorici e profili internazionalistici* (Firenze: European University Institute, 2002).

54 On the role of the international agencies and bodies as mechanisms for the democracy of the people see diffusely J. Braithwaite and P. Drahos (eds), *Global Business Regulation* (Cambridge: Cambridge University Press, 2000), p. 606: 'In a world of increasingly internationalized regulation, focusing weak glimmers of scrutiny from a hundred national consumer groups onto one international forum of decision-making may increase popular sovereignty from nothing to something.' On the subject see also Federico Ortino, *Basic Legal Instruments for the Liberalisation of Trade. A Comparative Analysis of EC and WTO Law* (Oxford and Portland, Oregon: Hart Publishing, 2003).

55 J.-M. Guéhenno, *The End of Nation-State* (Minneapolis: University of Minnesota Press, 1995), pp. 74, 84.

56 The debate on the new 'constitution' drafted by the convention set up by the Laeken declaration of December 2001 is still characterized by the confrontation of the two radically opposite points of view. See chapter 12 of this volume.

57 See, for instance, the US constitution, Art. IV, sec. 3: 'but no new State shall be formed or erected within the jurisdiction of any other State'.

58 See in general U. Leonardy, 'Demarcation of regions: international perspectives', in B. de Villiers and J. Sindane (eds), *Regionalism: Problems and Prospects* (Pretoria: Human Sciences Research Council, 1993).

59 S. Ortino, *Per un federalismo funzionale* (Torino: Giappichelli, 1994).

60 In the same sense see M. Forsyth, 'The modern concept of confederation', *CSCE ODIHR (Commission on Security and Cooperation in Europe Office for Democratic Institutions and Human Rights) Bulletin*, 2:3, 11–15.

61 The institutional legal model described in the text finds many economic applications; among the latest books see Alberto Alesina and Enrico Spolaore, *The Size of Nations* (Cambrdige, MA and London: The MIT Press, 2003).

62 G. Marks, L. Hooghe and K. Blank, 'European integration from the 1980s: state-centric v. multilevel governance', *Journal of Common Market Studies* (1996), p. 341 ff.

63 P. C. Schmitter and J. I. Torreblanca, 'Eastern enlargement and the transformation of the European Union', in W. Loth and W. Wessels (eds), *Theorien europäischer Integration* (Oplader: Leske and Budrich, 2001), p. 219 ff.

self-government 36–7, 75, 183, 185–6,
193–4, 197n.3, 226–7, 234–7, 241
self-management 113–17, 119
self-rule 5, 6, 101
Serbia 88, 92, 94, 96, 100, 110, 115–20,
123, 127, 131nn.32, 35 and 41,
296n.34
autonomous provinces of Kosovo and
Metohia 121
constitution 121, 129n.15, 131n.36
see also Milošević, S.
SFRY *see* Socialist Federative Republic of
Yugoslavia
Shakhrai, S. 47, 55–6, 62nn.30 and 31
shared rule 5, 6, 101
Shaymiyev, M. 58, 60, 62n.41
Siiman, M. 69, 71
Single European Act (1987) 101, 178n.41,
206, 247
Slovak–Hungarian treaty *see*
Hungarian–Slovak treaty
Slovakia 65, 73–4, 77–81, 83nn.1, 21 and
22, 84nn.36, 37, 38 and 41, 85, 88,
94–8, 100, 103, 296n.34
language law 78
Matica Slovenká cultural organization,
*The History of Slovakia and
Slovaks* 74
new constitution (1992) 73
Slovak National Party (SNS) 74
see also Dzurinda, M.; Mečiar, V.;
minorities; Schuster, R.;
sovereignty, of Slovakia;
Slovenia 76, 80, 88, 92, 93, 97, 99, 103,
116, 119–20, 122–5, 128n.6,
131nn.33 and 40, 132n.50, 296n.34
constitution 121–2, 131n.39
independence (1992) 122, 130n.29
Sociological Association in Ljubljana
124
Writers' Association 124
socialist autonomous provinces (SAPs)
116–17, 130n.28, 131n.34
socialist commonwealth 38
Socialist Federative Republic of Yugoslavia
(SFRY) 114, 121–2, 127
constitution (1963) 114, 130nn.21, 23,
24 and 27

constitution (1974) 116–17, 119, 121,
130nn.26, 27, 28 and 29, 131n.31,
281
disintegration 127, 131n.40
Socialist Republic of Serbia
Constitution (1974) 119
'social state' 158
South Africa 169, 229
constitution (1996) 201n.48
South Tyrol 88, 152n.31, 154n.45, 184,
194, 197n.4, 200n.36, 241
Bolzano 140, 196n.1, 197nn.5 and 9
Degasperi–Gruber agreement 184
German-speaking minority 184,
196n.1, 197n.5
sovereignty 10, 11, 21, 25, 30, 38, 41,
48–50, 61n.8, 66, 89–91, 98, 101,
113, 117, 127, 156, 159, 164, 166,
168, 175n.1, 195, 240, 258, 263,
275–7, 282, 286, 290, 292,
294n.10
of Baltic states 68, 70
of Chechnya 57–8
division of sovereignty 229
dual sovereignty 13
member state sovereignty 216, 252,
260, 281
national sovereignty 65, 104, 236
nominal sovereignty 215
parade of sovereignty 50, 52
parliamentary sovereignty 229
partial sovereignty 281
of Poland 88
popular sovereignty 297n.54
republic sovereignty 61n.21
of Russian Federation 55–6
shared sovereignty 118, 271n.79, 289
of Slovakia 73
of Tatarstan 51–6 *passim*, 60, 61n.14,
62n.29
*see also under individual
denominations*
of Westminster 231
sovietization 36
Soviet Union 26, 31–2, 34, **36–9**, 44n.41,
45n.72, 46n.74, 49–50, 52, 56–7,
62n.39, 65–6, 68, 75, 86–7, 93–4,
277, 280